T0305725

New Drugs, Fair Prices

New Drugs, Fair Prices addresses the important question of how we might get the innovative new medicines we need at prices we can afford. Today, this debate is impassioned but sterile. One side calls for price controls, discounting their impact on investment in innovation. The other points to miraculous new therapies, disregarding their affordability and social inequity. This polarized argument creates more heat than light, threatening the social contract between the industry and society on which pharmaceutical innovation depends.

This ground-breaking book takes a wholly new perspective on the issue and raises the debate to a more informed and productive level. Drawing on interviews with more than 70 experts across the pharmaceutical innovation world and combining a diverse literature from scientific, political, economic and business domains, it describes how a sustainable and affordable supply of new medicines is possible only by balancing pharmaceutical innovation's complex, adaptive ecosystem. By considering how each of the ecosystem's seven habitats work and interact with the others, it makes a comprehensive set of recommendations for achieving that ecosystem balance.

The core message of *New Drugs, Fair Prices* is important to anyone who ever has needed or will ever need a medicine: we can have a sustainable supply of new medicines that are both innovative and affordable if we manage the pharmaceutical innovation ecosystem intelligently.

Brian D. Smith is an academic, author and advisor who has worked in and studied the life sciences sector for over 40 years. He has published over 300 books, papers and articles and worked with most of the world's leading pharmaceutical companies.

New Drugs, Fair Prices

Managing the Pharmaceutical Innovation Ecosystem for Sustainable and Affordable New Medicines

Brian D. Smith

Edited by
Lindsay Bruce Smith

LONDON AND NEW YORK

Cover image: TRAFIK.studio.

First published 2023
by Routledge
4 Park Square, Milton Park, Abingdon, Oxon OX14 4RN

and by Routledge
605 Third Avenue, New York, NY 10158

Routledge is an imprint of the Taylor & Francis Group, an informa business

British Library Cataloguing-in-Publication Data
A catalogue record for this book is available from the British Library

Library of Congress Cataloging-in-Publication Data
Names: Smith, Brian D. (Author of new drugs, fair prices), author.
Title: New drugs, fair prices : managing the pharmaceutical
innovation ecosystem for sustainable and affordable new
medicines / Brian D. Smith.
Description: Milton Park, Abingdon, Oxon ; New York, NY :
Routledge, 2023. | Includes bibliographical references and index. |
Identifiers: LCCN 2022023203 | ISBN 9781032352237 (hardback) |
ISBN 9781032361055 (paperback) | ISBN 9781003330271 (ebook)
Subjects: LCSH: Drugs—Prices—United States. | Prescription
pricing—United States. | Pharmaceutical industry—United
States. | Drugs—United States—Cost control.
Classification: LCC HD9666.5 .S59 2023 |
DDC 338.4/361510973—dc23/eng/20220527
LC record available at https://lccn.loc.gov/2022023203

ISBN: 9781032352237 (hbk)
ISBN: 9781032361055 (pbk)
ISBN: 9781003330271 (ebk)

DOI: 10.4324/9781003330271

Typeset in Gill Sans
by codeMantra

To Lindsay, Eleanor, Catherine and Rosalind

Contents

Preface: writing with intent   x
Acknowledgments   xii

1 Balancing tomorrow with today   1
   Precis 1
   How important a question is this? 5
   How American a question is this? 6
   First, do no harm. What might change put at risk? 8
   Does pharmaceutical innovation have a problem? 10
   Where does this leave us? 14

2 A new paradigm for a wicked problem   24
   Precis 24
   Why did the drug pricing debate become so sterile? 29
   Are we looking at drug pricing the wrong way? 32
   What is the case for the ecosystem paradigm? 34
   What is the pharmaceutical innovation ecosystem? 36
   What does the ecosystem perspective imply for the
      affordability debate? 39
   Pharmaceutical innovation emerges from the pharmaceutical
      innovation ecosystem 39
   The pharmaceutical innovation ecosystem is fragile 40
   The pharmaceutical innovation ecosystem can only be managed
      systemically 40
   How can we resolve our dilemma? 41

3 The discovery habitat   53
   Precis 53
   What is the discovery habitat and who inhabits it? 60
   What does a healthy PIE require of the discovery habitat? 62

Is the discovery habitat capable of supporting a healthy PIE? 65
How can we improve the discovery habitat? 77
Will this be enough? 82

4   The innovation habitat   95
Precis 95
What happens in the innovation habitat and who inhabits it? 97
What does a healthy PIE require of the innovation habitat? 99
Is the innovation habitat capable of supporting a healthy PIE? 101
How can we improve the innovation habitat? 108
Will this be enough? 114

5   The coalition habitat   123
Precis 123
What happens in the coalition habitat and who inhabits it? 127
What does a healthy PIE require of the coalition habitat? 129
Is the coalition habitat capable of supporting a healthy PIE? 131
How can we improve the coalition habitat? 139
Will this be enough? 144

6   The value habitat   149
Precis 149
What happens in the value habitat and who inhabits it? 152
What does a healthy PIE require of the value habitat? 155
Is the value habitat capable of supporting a healthy PIE? 158
How can we improve the value habitat? 166
Will this be enough? 170

7   The pricing habitat   179
Precis 179
What happens in the pricing habitat and who inhabits it? 181
What does a healthy PIE require of the pricing habitat? 186
Is the pricing habitat capable of supporting a healthy PIE? 187
How can we improve the pricing habitat? 200
Will this be enough? 204

8   The competition habitat   213
Precis 213
What happens in the competition habitat and who inhabits it? 217
What does a healthy PIE require of the competition habitat? 219

Is the competition habitat capable of supporting a healthy PIE? 221
How can we improve the competition habitat? 236
Will this be enough? 244

9   The patient habitat   255
    Precis 255
    What happens in the patient habitat and who inhabits it? 258
    What does a healthy PIE require of the patient habitat? 260
    Is the patient habitat capable of supporting a healthy PIE? 262
    How can we improve the health of the patient habitat? 272
    Will this be enough? 278

10 Breaking ground, raising the debate   283
    Precis 283
    Where are we now? 284
    Breaking ground on a PIE for the future 286
    The valuable innovation project 290
    The valid value pricing project 292
    The managed competition project 293
    Raising the debate 295

Index   299

Preface

Writing with intent

I have written "*New Drugs, Fair Prices*" with a single-minded intent, to raise the level of debate around the pricing of innovative medicines.

The current debate is heated, polarized, politicized, and largely sterile. It is, as the French say, "un dialogue de sourds." This is important and dangerous. Important because pharmaceutical innovation is both socially and economically valuable. Dangerous because it weakens the social contract on which pharmaceutical innovation depends. If society decides it's getting a bad deal from its research funding and the laws and regulations it passes to limit competition among innovators, it may decide to reduce the support and incentives it gives pharmaceutical innovation, and we will all be the poorer for that. We all need the debate over the cost of innovative medicines to be well informed, balanced and constructive.

The aim of "*New Drugs, Fair Prices*" is not to take sides in this debate, but to change how it is framed. Arguing over whether we should improve affordability through price controls or incentivize innovation through free pricing is the wrong question. The right question is, how can we get an economically sustainable supply of innovative medicines at prices that make them accessible to everyone? This is a very, very difficult question. To make it a little easier, I've tried to answer it only in the exceptional context of the US, although that includes much that is relevant outside of the US. I've also focused on new drugs, although generics and biosimilars play their roles in the story. Even simplified like that, it's still too difficult a question to answer without some kind of thinking tool.

For scientists like me, our thinking tools are our theories, our explanations of how the world works. For this job, I picked up the complexity science thinking tool, which explains pharmaceutical innovation as a complex, adaptive ecosystem. From this perspective, the new drugs we get and what they cost are emergent properties of the pharmaceutical innovation ecosystem, which I abbreviate as the PIE. And because, like any ecosystem, everything is connected to everything else, it is naively simplistic to think that you can pull one policy lever and get what you want, without any unintended consequences. Ecologists work by understanding the habitats within the ecosystem and holistically managing the complex interactions between them.

As I worked with this ecological perspective, I found it useful to view the pharmaceutical innovation ecosystem as seven distinct but connected habitats. For each of these, I considered who its inhabitants were. I then considered what that habitat must provide if the PIE is to provide innovative, affordable medicines, sustainably. I then explored what was preventing each habitat from giving the PIE what it needed. That diagnosis led to 27 complementary therapies that, because of their synergies, coalesce into three big-but-doable projects. Executed well, these would allow the PIE to give us affordable, innovative medicines. This would increase the social and economic benefits of pharmaceutical innovation and strengthen the social contract.

Whilst knowing my work's limitations and weaknesses, I offer it as a sincere contribution to the debate. I hope it will be criticized by those at either pole of the debate, in which case I will have achieved my goal of balance. I hope some will criticize it for not making detailed policy recommendations, in which case I will know they've accepted the big, ecological picture I've painted. In addition to that criticism, I hope most of all that "New Drugs, Fair Prices" will stimulate debate about how we can manage the pharmaceutical innovation ecosystem to give us not new drugs or fair prices but both. That, at least, is the right debate to have.

Brian D Smith
May 2022

Acknowledgments

All authors owe a debt to the many people who helped them create their book. This is especially so when, as in this case, the book's scope makes the author reliant on dozens of people with diverse backgrounds and knowledge.

Whilst stressing that the findings and conclusions in this book are my own, I would like to thank the following for their help.

The 80 expert informants who shared their expertise with me. Those who gave me permission to identify them are listed below.

Those industry friends who read and criticized my drafts, especially Dr Austin Doyle, Dr Peter De Veene and Dr William Mattern.

The National Pharmaceutical Council (NPC) who provided research funding for this book. All findings and conclusions are my own and do not reflect NPC's or its members' views.

I would also like to thank:

Rebecca Marsh, Lauren Whelan and their colleagues at Taylor and Francis, for their support in developing and publishing this book.

Gyuri Ruisz and his talented team at Trafik Productions, for designing the original illustrations.

My three wonderful daughters, Eleanor, Catherine, and Rosalind, for reminding me that there is much more to life than research and writing.

And, finally, Lindsay Bruce Smith, the remarkable woman who is both my wife and my editor. I am the luckiest of men.

List of interviewees

Lawrence W Abrams
Cyrus Arman, PhD MBA, Biotechnology Executive and Investor
Daniel Brennan, CEO/Founder, Alentia Therapeutics
Kim A. Caldwell, RPh, Principal, Texas Star Healthcare Consulting, LLC

Pedro J Cejas PhD, Discovery Research Leader, Spark Therapeutics

Amitabh Chandra, Ethel Zimmerman Wiener Professor, Harvard Kennedy School of Government; McCance Family Professor of Business Administration, Harvard Business School

Daniel M Cohen, PhD, Vector Optimization Research Leader, Spark Therapeutics

Joshua P Cohen, Independent Healthcare Analyst

Rena Conti, Dean's Research Fellow, Associate Professor, Markets, Public Policy and Law, Questrom School of Business, Boston University

Dan Copeland, CEO, Renovion

Thomas D'Orazio, CEO, SpayVac

Graham Dutfield, Professor of International Governance, University of Leeds

Sarah K Emond, EVP and COO, Institute for Clinical and Economic Review

Phyllis Barkman Ferrell, Global Head External Engagement, Alzheimer's Disease, Eli Lilly & Company

John Glasspool, CEO, Anthos Therapeutics

Alberto Grignolo, PhD, Fellow of DIA; Corporate Vice President, Corporate Strategy and Thought Leadership, Parexel International; Editor-in-Chief, DIA Global Forum

Neil Grubert, independent market access consultant

Ian Henshaw, professional in the biopharmaceutical industry for 25 years

Michael W Hodin, PhD, CEO, Global Coalition on Aging

Prof RG Hill FBPharmacolS FMedSci, Honorary Professor of Pharmacology, Faculty of Medicine, Imperial College London

Joerg Holenz, PhD, Senior Vice President, Head Boston Innovation Hub, Grünenthal Group

Michael R Jackson, Senior VP Drug Discovery and Development, Sanford Burnham Prebys Medical Discovery Institute

James Kenney, RPh MBA, President, J T Kenney LLC

Peter Kolchinsky, PhD, Managing Partner of RA Capital Management LP; author of "The Great American Drug Deal"

Dr John L LaMattina, Senior Partner, PureTech Health

Scott M Lassman, Principal, Lassman Law+Policy

Fred D Ledley, MD, Professor, Departments of Natural & Applied Science and Management; Director, Center for Integration of Science and Industry, Bentley University

Dr Ben Locwin, healthcare and pharmaceutical expert

Lawrence Liberti, PhD RAC RPh, Adjunct Research Professor, Regulatory Affairs and Quality Assurance Graduate Program, Temple University School of Pharmacy

William Looney, Executive Editor, Informa Pharma Intelligence PLC

Z John Lu, PhD, Associate Professor of Economics, California State University, Channel Islands; Director, UCLA Seminar on Pharmaceutical Economics and Policy

Anders Lundstrom, COO, Banner Life Sciences

Matthew Magestro

Killian J McCarthy, Associate Professor of Innovation Management and Strategy, University of Groningen Faculty of Economics and Business

Sean McGowan

Matthew McMahon, Director SEED Office, National Institutes of Health

Lisa Stockwell Morris, PhD RPh, VP & GM, Real World Solutions, IQVIA

Michael R Myers, PhD, Associate Vice-President, LRL – Due Diligence, Eli Lilly & Company

Peter J Neumann, Center for the Evaluation of Value and Risk in Health, Tufts Medical Center

Anders Lærke Nielsen, Vice President, Novo Nordisk

Len M Nichols, PhD, Non-Resident Fellow, Health Policy Center, Urban Institute; Professor Emeritus, George Mason University

Sonia Tadjalli Oskouei, PharmD, Vice President, Biosimilars at Cardinal Health

Sue Peschin, MHS, President and CEO, Alliance for Aging Research

Edmund Pezalla, MD MPH, CEO, Enlightenment Bioconsult LLC

Wendell Potter, former health insurance company executive; President, Center for Health and Democracy

Mark Ralph, Executive Director, Boehringer Ingelheim Venture Fund

Juliana M Reed, Executive Director, The Biosimilars Forum

Michael J Rothrock, President, Allegheny Strategic Partners LLC

Ed Schoonveld, Author of "The Price of Global Health"

Melanie Senior, Biopharma Journalist and Science Writer

David Setboun, PharmD MBA, Pharmaceutical C Executive

Aubrey Stoch, Head of Translational Medicine, Merck

Harald F Stock

Mark Trusheim, Visiting Scientist, MIT Sloan; President, Co-Bio Consulting

Wayne Winegarden, Senior Fellow, Pacific Research Institute

Gillian R Woollett, MA DPhil, interviewed while Principal Scientist and FDA Team Lead at Avalere, and then as VP, Regulatory Strategy and Policy at Samsung Bioepis

1 Balancing tomorrow with today

Precis

- The US spends over $500 billion on over 6 billion prescriptions each year.
- Almost 90% of those prescriptions are imitative medicines, but they cost only about 20% of the money spent because they are relatively inexpensive.
- A little more than 10% of those prescriptions are for branded, innovative medicines, and they take about 80% of the money spent because they are relatively expensive.
- Those higher prices incentivize investors to fund research into new innovative medicines.
- The challenge is to make innovative medicines more affordable without discouraging investment.
- This question is asked all over the world, but it's especially relevant in the US.
- About 50 new medicines are approved each year.
- The pharmaceutical industry is a jewel in the economy of the US.
- Some new medicines are not innovative, are expensive, and not societally important.
- The current debate about the pricing of innovative medicines is a dialogue of the deaf.
- The social contract between society and innovators is under threat.
- This book aims to raise the level of that debate.
- It asks how we might have affordable prices today AND innovative medicines tomorrow.

This book is about how we get the new medicines we want; those that save, extend, and improve our lives better than the medicines available to us today. Or, more simply, it's about pharmaceutical innovation.

DOI: 10.4324/9781003330271-1

This is an important subject because pharmaceutical innovation will inevitably affect you and those you love, probably at the most vulnerable times of your lives. This is not a detached, abstract topic. It matters in the real world and deserves serious attention.

Box 1.1 What is pharmaceutical innovation?

Although semantic purists can always quibble, in this book, I'm going to define pharmaceutical innovation as the bringing to market of a medicinal therapy that was not previously available. I'm going to include only those medicines that require regulatory approval and whose use must be authorized via qualified healthcare professionals. I'm going to exclude those medicines that are generally bought over the counter and so-called alternative therapies. I'm going to focus on medicines that make claims to be different from other drugs and exclude "me-too" products, although I will look at the important, cyclic relationship between innovative medicines and imitative drugs called generics and biosimilars. I'm also going to exclude medical devices and other "hardware," except those that are sold in combination with medicines. I appreciate that this is an imperfect definition, but I think it's a "good enough" working definition for the purposes of this book.

It's important to remember that not all pharmaceutical innovations are the same. Individual pharmaceutical innovations can and do differ greatly from each other with respect to many characteristics, including:

- The targeted conditions and patients.
- The mode of action and technology employed.
- The required complementary technologies or systems.
- The costs and risks associated with bringing the innovation to market.
- The size of the population that may be affected by the innovation.
- The economic accessibility of the innovation to that population.
- The degree of impact on the lives of those who gain access to the innovation.

- The value of the innovation to those using it, prescribing it, and paying for it.
- The value the innovation creates for the wider healthcare ecosystem and society.

Pharmaceutical innovation then is both a singular term for a particular new medicine and a collective term for all those new medicines that reach the market. And, because each new medicine is different, pharmaceutical innovation in the collective sense is a very diverse phenomenon. For the most part, when I use the term pharmaceutical innovation, I will be referring to that collective, diverse phenomenon.

Pharmaceutical innovation is one of those terms that can mean different things to different people, so I want to begin by following Voltaire's advice: "Define your terms ... or we shall never understand one another."[1] In Box 1.1, I give the working definition of pharmaceutical innovation that I'll use throughout this book (see Box 1.1).

As you might see, this working definition is straightforward enough. It's not above criticism and there are cases that are borderline and debatable, but there is a deeper point to be made here. While almost all pharmaceutical innovation meets this definition, not all pharmaceutical innovation is the same. The innovative medicines (or, increasingly, combinations of medicines, devices, and services) that reach the market vary continuously along all those characteristics listed in Box 1.1, so that every individual pharmaceutical innovation is unique and, when we group pharmaceutical innovations together, it is a very diverse category. This diversity is important because, as I'll discuss later in this chapter, we care not only about how many pharmaceutical innovations reach the market but also what kind. The sort of pharmaceutical innovation we get is as important as how much, which means that simple metrics, such as how many new drugs are approved or how many patents are granted, is a pretty poor measure of what we're really interested in. So, in this book, I'm concerned with both the quantity and quality of the pharmaceutical innovation we get.

In centuries past, we obtained our medicines from an apothecary, who often kept their own garden, called a "Physic Garden," of plants with medicinal properties. These ancestors of today's pharmacists worried about how to get the most medicines from their garden, for the least cost, without exhausting their plants and soil. In this book, I'm going to explore the 21st-century version of the apothecary's question: how can we get the medicines we need today, for the least cost, while ensuring that we continue to get innovative medicines tomorrow? Like the apothecary's problem, this is a question about balancing today and tomorrow. It would be easy to ensure the flow of pharmaceutical innovations by allowing (or continuing to allow) the high prices that attract more investment in innovation. It would be just as easy to limit the prices of medicines today, deter investors, and in the long run, reduce the quantity and quality of pharmaceutical innovations. Either of these approaches, and any others we can think of, will influence both the amount and the type of new medicines we get in the future. The much more difficult question is how to have the affordable medicines we want today *and* the innovative, life-changing new medicines we want tomorrow. On first look, this is a case of wanting to have your cake and to eat it, as the saying goes.[2]

How to balance today's affordability with tomorrow's innovation is a big and difficult question. To explore it in one, reasonably sized book means deciding not to answer some relevant but adjacent questions. So, this book will restrict itself largely to the US market, except to draw parallels with other countries when it is useful to do so. Nor will this book explore, at least not in detail, how we might change the way healthcare is delivered in the US or how it is paid for. I'm also going to assume that the US's exceptional healthcare market reflects the exceptionality of American society and, consequently, will remain largely unchanged. To do otherwise would be to write an entirely different book. So, to set your expectations, I'm going to explore how we can get the medicines we need today, for the least cost, while ensuring that we continue to get innovative medicines tomorrow, more or less within the context of the current US healthcare system.[3] To many people, there are simple answers to this difficult question. When I hear them, I'm reminded of the philosopher H. L. Mencken when he said, "There is always a well-known solution to every human problem—neat, plausible, and wrong." In this book, I'm interested in finding the right answer, however messy it is and however much it contradicts the obvious, simple answers. Even within the constraints I've set myself, this is a big and difficult question. It's also an important one.

How important a question is this?

As I begin this exploration of pharmaceutical innovation, it is worth taking a moment to consider the scale and scope of what we're looking at.[4] In the US in 2020, 6.3 billion prescriptions were dispensed, a figure that is growing at around 2% a year. About 80% of these prescriptions were for chronic (that is, ongoing) diseases and, generally speaking, the growth in prescriptions is largely the result of an aging population. People under 25 average about five prescriptions per year while their elders over 65 average around 50, a figure that reflects both their failing health and, very often, their burden of several conditions (co-morbidities, in the jargon). Altogether, Americans, through their various payment channels, spent about $540 billion on medicines in 2020, a figure that is growing at about 3.5% per year. So, by any definition, the US pharmaceutical market is enormous economically and, because each one of these prescriptions is about someone's life, in human terms.

Within this big picture, there is some detail that is important to our exploration of how we get our new, innovative medicines. About 88% of all the prescriptions dispensed in the US are for generic medicines and only the remaining 12% are what we might loosely call innovative medicines. I say loosely because they might not be particularly innovative, but they are covered by patents or regulatory protection of their intellectual property rights. Sometimes, you will read of medicines being branded, in contrast to generics, but this is a little misleading too, since there are branded generic medicines. For example, Trimox is the branded form of the generic amoxicillin. However, you look at it, about nine out of ten prescriptions are products that don't have patent protection and, in this part of the market, competition is usually intense and prices low. But look at the market in dollars, rather than prescriptions, and the picture more or less reverses. Only about 19% of the money Americans spend on medicines goes on generics, either branded or unbranded, and the remainder is spent on innovative medicines. On the one hand, you can read these numbers as a reflection of the much higher prices of innovative medicines, compared to generics. On the other, you can see them as evidence of the secondary, longer-term benefit of pharmaceutical innovation. All of those generic medicines were expensive, patent-protected medicines once and the patent expiration process has created a large number of relatively inexpensive generic medicines.[5] But in any case, these proportions tell

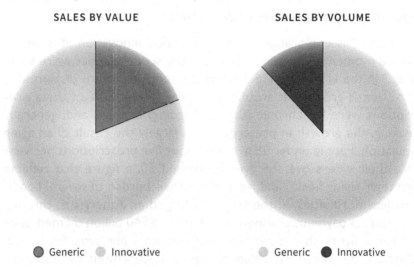

SALES BY VALUE   SALES BY VOLUME

    ● Generic ● Innovative   ● Generic ● Innovative

Figure 1.1 The US pharmaceutical market by volume and value

us that the issue of drug pricing is largely one of pricing patent-protected, innovative medicines (see Figure 1.1).

These starkly inverted proportions help us to focus our question about how we get the medicines we need today while ensuring that we continue to get innovative medicines tomorrow. First, we need to understand how the cost of innovative medicines is related to the continuity of innovation. Second, we need to understand how that costly innovation feeds through to our supply of much less costly generic medicines. In any case, with billions of prescriptions and hundreds of billions of dollars involved, with life-changing consequences for many of us, there's no doubt that the question of how we get, and continue to get, our innovative medicines is an important one.

How American a question is this?

As I've already said, I'm going to restrict my exploration of this question to the US market. Is it a uniquely American issue? No, our question is not uniquely American but the answer probably is because the US market is quite different from any other. All developed countries and, increasingly, emerging markets are trying to ensure that they can balance the cost of medicines today and the availability of innovative medicines in the long term.[6] But very early on in this exploration, I decided that I should restrict myself to the US market because both the demand and supply sides of the US pharmaceutical market are so very different from other nations. On the demand side, the US is the world's largest pharmaceutical market, accounting for more than a third of global pharmaceutical expenditure, and the highest per capita spend in the world.[7] This is partly because the US is a large, rich country but also because the prices of innovative pharmaceuticals in the US are significantly higher than in comparable, developed countries.[8] This in turn is related to the fact that, while most other countries control the price of medicines in some way, the US is exceptional in its free-market approach to setting the prices of innovative medicines.[9] The aggregate of these demand side factors means that the US is an outlier and, in terms of answering our question, a case apart.

The supply side of US pharmaceutical innovation is also an international exception. The pharmaceutical industry is a jewel in the US economy, contributing over 3% of the nation's gross domestic product.[10] US-headquartered companies are the majority in most lists of the industry's biggest companies. They account for almost half of global pharmaceutical sales; and pharmaceuticals represent one of the country's most valuable classes of exports. The industry employs around 800,000 people, a high proportion of them in high-value, knowledge-intensive roles. And behind these headlines is a huge economic hinterland of academic research, support services, and financial infrastructure that is much larger and more globally important than that of any other country. Just as the demand side of its pharmaceutical market makes the US exceptional, so too does its supply side. As with the demand side factors, these facts set the US apart from the rest of the world.

Together, the two sides of the US pharmaceutical market are so unusual that any exploration of our question relevant to the US is unlikely to be relevant to other countries and vice versa. The US is just too different to be considered as part of a larger, international study of pharmaceutical innovation. That's not to say that other countries don't share some of the US's features and issues. It's also true that what happens in the US does influence the global pharmaceutical market and vice versa. But this is a difficult enough question to address in a purely US context. To attempt it on a more global basis would be to try to boil the ocean. That at least is the choice I made as I planned this work.

First, do no harm. What might change put at risk?

It's implicit in our exploration of pharmaceutical innovation that we might find things that we wish were different. This brings to mind the Hippocratic exhortation to "first, do no harm."[11] Defenders of the current pharmaceutical innovation system do, quite reasonably, point to the economic success of the industry and the US's global primacy as an argument against major change to the current pharmaceutical innovation system. But, in addition to this economic point, there are at least three other reasons to be cautious about the unintended consequences of any changes to the pharmaceutical innovation system.

The first is the argument most strongly made by the pharmaceutical innovators themselves, that the current system is good at encouraging investment into innovative medicines. This is certainly borne out by the data. In 2020, about $14 billion of investment from venture investors flowed into pharmaceutical innovation, about 75% of it into US companies.[12] Separately, US pharmaceutical companies also invested heavily in research and development. For example, the $83 billion invested in 2019 was about 25% of net revenues and is part of a long-term increasing trend. All of this investment is correlated with a significant increase in both new drug applications for approval and in new drugs approved for sale.[13] Obviously, the risk is that any change in the current system might reduce this rate of pharmaceutical innovation. We'll return to this argument, especially with respect to price controls, later in the book. But for now, it's reasonable to observe that pharmaceutical innovation attracts a lot of investment and that leads to lots of new medicines. That alone gives us cause for caution when we think about changing the system.

A second reason to be cautious comes to us from the history of the pharmaceutical industry.[14] It is hard to believe now but the US hasn't always held the global leadership in pharmaceuticals it does today. In my father's youth, between the world wars, Germany (and to some extent Switzerland) was the scientific and commercial leader in the field. The US was a relative laggard with a fragmented industry concentrating on extracting natural products rather than synthesizing novel drugs. It was only in the 1940s that the US pharmaceutical industry transformed itself and that transformation created the basis for today's globally dominant industry. This remarkable change had many causes, some of which were, without detracting from the efforts and skills of those involved, not attributable to the industry itself. For example, wartime exigencies allowed free access to British discoveries around penicillin and the US government intervened in various ways to enable a number of selected companies to meet demand for this breakthrough. The profits and experience gained from the huge demand for penicillin helped these privileged US companies to participate in a post-war revolution in pharmaceutical innovation and eclipse German dominance. That same war obviously set back the German pharmaceutical industry. This historical picture is, like all history, complicated, and I don't want to oversimplify it. But it is reasonable to conclude that the evolution of an entire industry can be dramatically changed, positively and negatively, by external developments such as scientific discovery, government intervention, and international competition. This is a second reason to be cautious about changing the current system.

A third reason to have concerns about changing the current system of pharmaceutical innovation is the geopolitical. Most countries identify particular industries as strategically important to the security of the country. This status often allows preferential treatment in government procurement and investment, trade policy, and protection from foreign control.[15] Many countries, including the US, consider pharmaceuticals to be one of those strategic industries. Even before COVID, there were concerns that, for economic reasons, the majority of generic pharmaceutical production had relocated to India and China, putting supply chains at risk.[16] This concern about security of supply in the generic part of the market has always been tempered by its relatively low economic importance, but that isn't the case for the increasing concern about the rise of Chinese pharmaceutical innovation. As in some other industries, China's state-enabled advance from low-cost player to innovator has been remarkable.[17] In this, it has been helped by many Western companies relocating their manufacturing and research and development to China as well as by Chinese companies developing a presence in Western pharmaceutical innovation hubs.[18] The broader context of this is the "Made in China 2025" policy, an essentially mercantilist approach that includes pharmaceuticals as one of its strategic industries.[19] China is not alone in its ambition to compete with US dominance in pharmaceutical innovation. Most advanced economies have a place for pharmaceuticals in their industrial policy and China is just the largest of these rivals. Considering these competitive threats is not, of course, to deny any country its right to compete. But it is a reasonable observation that US dominance of pharmaceutical innovation is under growing international challenge and a loss of dominance would have significant economic and strategic consequences for the US. This is a third reason to be cautious about changing the current system.

So, if our exploration of pharmaceutical innovation reveals some things we might wish were different, are we at risk of doing more harm than good? Looking at only this side of the equation suggests that we ought to be cautious about messing with the current way of bringing innovative medicines to market. The US is singularly blessed with a globally dominant industry that makes a lot of money and brings lots of innovative medicines to market. History tells us that industries are shaped by all kinds of external forces and we'd be naïve to think that influence can only be for the good. And, as if these concerns weren't enough, to interfere at a time when the US's advantageous position faces serious Chinese competition seems a potentially dangerous thing to do. But there are two sides to every story and there are reasonable arguments for suggesting that how we get our innovative medicines, and how we can continue to do so, may need to change.

Does pharmaceutical innovation have a problem?

In the context of an enormous, thriving industry that contributes impressively to the US economy but is under challenge from international rivals, the "first do no harm" principle seems sound. But there are other principles that are relevant here too. Not least, the principle of the common good, which thinkers from Aristotle to Rousseau have understood to be the basis of a good society and the highest aim of government. At the birth of the US, James Madison's contribution to The Federalist Papers tied the principle of the common good to justice and the aims of civil society.[20] It was also the basis of the most famous line in John F Kennedy's inaugural address.[21] The pervasiveness of the common good in American culture makes it reasonable to ask if the way we get our innovative medicines is consistent with this principle. To be clear, this isn't to imply that pharmaceuticals should not be a commercial market but that, in this market more than most, societal and commercial concerns go hand in hand.

There's also another, more pragmatic, principle at play here – the idea that it's better to change before it's too late. You might know this principle as the boiling frog story[22] or the idea that complacency is the enemy of progress. In other words, if we wait until we have un-disputed evidence that the pharmaceutical innovation system needs to be improved, then we will already have endured significant harm and, perhaps, left it too late. With both the common good and the boiling frog in mind, there are three reasons to think there might be a significant problem with the way we get our innovative medicines.

The first of these is affordability. Any thinking about this point has to be in the context, described above, that the large majority of prescriptions are for generic drugs and the large majority of spending is on that small fraction of medicines that are protected from competition by some kind of exclusivity (see Figure 1.1). It is the smaller volume, higher value part of the market where affordability is in question. Critics of the current system point to US prices far above those of other countries and to the health and social implications when patients can't afford the medicines they need.[23] Affordability is perhaps the hottest topic in the whole pharmaceutical innovation discussion. Every piece of evidence is challenged and qualified, but neither side of the debate disagrees that innovative medicines should be more economically accessible. The debate is around why they are not and how to make them so. To some critics of the current situation, the cost of innovative medicines is mostly the fault of avaricious pharmaceutical companies.[24] As evidence of this, they point to price increases above inflation[25] and to the relationship between prescription cost and non-treatment.[26] To defenders of the current system, high prices are a requirement for innovation but are exacerbated by "middlemen" such as insurers and pharmacy benefit managers (PBMs).[27] In defense of higher prices than other developed nations, the industry simply argues that other countries are "free riding on American innovation."[28] An important point here is that arguments about drug pricing are obscured and complicated by which price is being considered,[29] and there is some evidence that the net price received by pharmaceutical companies after discounts and rebates is declining.[30] It is also important to remember that this debate around the cost of innovative medicines is decades old but it has been amplified by technological advances. As relatively inexpensive small molecules have given way to advanced but more costly biologics and cell and gene therapies, the very high prices of these newer products add to the affordability issue.[31]

In summary, the debate around affordability of innovative medicines is a complex, hotly debated one but there is common ground. Everyone in the debate would like to maximize accessibility today and also for the new, miraculous but expensive medicines that we anticipate tomorrow. That consensus alone would justify investigating the way that pharmaceutical innovation works but there are other issues to address.

After affordability, the second indicator that the pharmaceutical innovation system may not be all that we wish for is how much it innovates. This may seem to contradict the points I made above, that the system churns out a lot of new drug applications for approval and a lot of new, approved medicines. But here we run into the whole issue of "What is innovation?" that I began this chapter with. As Box 1.1 shows, pharmaceutical innovation is a diverse phenomenon, but one important dimension of that diversity is whether the medicine is truly innovative, as opposed to being an incremental advance. To be clear, this isn't necessarily a question of how novel or clever the science is; that would be a very tricky, subjective judgment.[32] One alternative approach to assessing pharmaceutical innovation is to ask how much good it does in comparison to what's already available. This is the basis of the differentiation between incremental, substantial, and radical pharmaceutical innovation made by some researchers.[33] This distinction raises the question of how much of pharmaceutical innovation is radical versus substantial or incremental. No one seems to have measured this important aspect of pharmaceutical innovation. One indicative measure of it is how many new drugs are approved using the FDA's "breakthrough" category – and in 2020, this was about 40% of new approvals[34] – but this is only a rough proxy for what we're trying to measure. A British study, which is likely to be similar to the US, suggested that only about a quarter of new drugs were highly innovative.[35] Again, there are different ways of interpreting the data, but it seems uncontroversial to say that not all pharmaceutical innovation is radically innovative and of high societal value. Of course, innovative and valuable are not synonymous, and incremental innovations can provide both therapeutic and economic advantages. For example, incremental innovations that are similar to and follow on from "first in class" therapies may provide treatment alternatives, improve security of supply and, by increasing competition, reduce prices.[36] Similarly, the repurposing of existing drugs as new treatments would often not be classed as radically innovative but is sometimes a way to bring useful therapies to market faster and cheaper.[37] And the small changes in formulation and posology (how much and how often a drug is taken) that pharmaceutical companies employ as part of what they call "life cycle management" are seen as valuable by at least some of those who use the drugs.

Again, through the contested debate over how innovative pharmaceutical innovation is, some common ground emerges. Some pharmaceutical innovation is radical and some of it is indisputably valuable and some of it is incremental and of limited value to society. That conclusion alone supports the idea that we should at least ask if our current approach to pharmaceutical innovation might be adapted to improve the mix of innovation that our system delivers.

The third reason that justifies an examination of pharmaceutical innovation is related to both the idea of public good and the "bang for bucks" of the current system. It's hard to quantify the total amount of money that is spent each year to deliver the 50 or so new drugs, of varying innovativeness and value, that reach the market. But a rough guide is to add the amount spent by the pharmaceutical industry, the amount invested by venture capitalists into embryonic companies and the amount spent on funding the National Institutes of Health (NIH). In round numbers, this total is about $140 billion. That's about the same as the federal government spends on military procurement or twice as much as it spends on the administration of justice.[38] If we accept the public good argument, it is a reasonable question to ask if that spend is giving value for money. The argument that this money is well spent is mostly based on the success stories of pharmaceutical innovation. And it is true that our current system has produced many life-saving and life-changing medicines. One poster child often cited is Sovaldi and its successor Harvoni, which transformed Hepatitis C from a serious, life-threatening condition into a mostly curable disease.[39] A similar story can be told about the protease inhibitors, which can keep HIV levels so low that patients never develop AIDS.[40] Another inspiring story can be told about how various kinds of immunotherapy have revolutionized cancer treatment.[41] It wouldn't be difficult to write a long chapter on the recent contributions of pharmaceutical innovation to medical science. When we consider historical breakthroughs, from antibiotics to beta-blockers to immunosuppressants, that contribution is even stronger. And, when we look at pharmaceutical innovations on the horizon, from RNA silencing to targeted protein degradation therapies, the promise of the pharmaceutical innovation system seems obvious.[42]

Nobody argues that the current system does not produce "bangs." The question is, might we get more of them for our bucks. Criticism of the current system is based on a view of what needs to be done rather than what has been done, a glass-half-empty perspective.[43] For example, almost 80 years after the post-war birth of the modern pharmaceutical industry, we still only have approved treatments for less than 10% of the 8,000 diseases that affect humans. The cost of bringing a new drug to market is increasingly expensive at around $2 billion, in part because the success rate, from discovery to market, is tiny. A complementary argument is that even the pharmaceutical innovation that has reached the market doesn't fully reflect society's needs and so is not good use of society's resources. There are, for example, now several treatments for "frown lines" and other aesthetic issues. More seriously, recent trends in FDA approvals show a relative neglect of neurological disorders, such as depression and psychosis, and of lifestyle diseases, such as obesity and diabetes.[44] Other researchers have suggested that the current focus on oncology is disproportionate.[45] More remarkably, the shift of pharmaceutical innovation toward diseases that affect very small numbers of people has been striking.[46] Finally, and perhaps most disturbingly, is the widely accepted observation that the current pharmaceutical innovation system, in which innovation is largely influenced by market forces, is failing to develop new antibiotics.[47]

Together, these issues make the question of whether we get "bang for bucks" from the many billions spent on pharmaceutical innovation open to debate. Glass-half-full defenders of the status quo, or something close to it, are right when they point to the wonders of immunotherapy and other miraculous developments. Glass-half-empty critics are right to wonder if we could get more for our money both in the amount and type of pharmaceutical innovation. While recognizing what has been achieved, it is reasonable to ask what could yet be.

Where does this leave us?

In this chapter, I've introduced the idea that pharmaceutical innovation, which improves, extends, and saves our lives and those of our loved ones, is a wonderful and diverse thing. We want its benefits today and we also want them, amplified by scientific progress, for our descendants tomorrow. These twin desires leave us with the same question that apothecaries faced in the past as they tended their Physic Gardens. How can we get the medicines we need today, for the least cost, while ensuring that we continue to get innovative medicines tomorrow? This is a hugely important question, both economically and socially. And, although it's far from a purely American question, American exceptionalism means that the answer in the US will not be the same as that in any other country.

We should be very careful about tinkering with a system that has, for decades, delivered both miraculous treatments and enormous wealth. We know that industries are shaped in unpredictable ways by external factors, including legislation. But we shouldn't be complacent or wait, like that frog, until the water becomes intolerable. It is reasonable to ask now if our system can deliver more and better innovation at better value for money. And the need to answer that question is made more urgent by trends in science, economics, and demographics. We need an answer that works at a time when huge numbers of aging Americans want the very best that pharmaceutical innovation can provide in an economic context where we can't simply spend more and more of our personal and public wealth on medicines.

Of course, this isn't a new question. A similar question arose in the middle and late 20th century, when pharmaceutical innovation became truly scientific and the potential for pharmaceutical therapies expanded rapidly. At that time, the answer was an implicit but quite clear social contract between American society and the pharmaceutical industry – we the people will enable you to make an appropriate return on investment from our illness by funding basic research, building regulatory barriers against charlatans, creating temporary monopolies, encouraging health insurance, and subsidizing the medicines of the old and poor. In return, you the industry will provide us with safe, effective, and innovative medicines that we can afford and that, in time, become inexpensive generic medicines. That social contract has endured for many decades now. Not without tension but not without some degree of success. Many of us are alive today only because of this social contract. And it seems very likely that some revised version of the social contract will be the answer to the same question in the very different conditions of the mid-21st century. But that social contract will need discussion and renegotiation until, like all sustainable contracts, both sides feel like they are getting a good deal.

Our present problem is that the discussion about the social contract isn't really working as it should. Like a heated argument between old friends, it has in large part descended into insults, name-calling, and straw man arguments where the energy is focused on defending positions rather than building bridges or finding solutions. And, just like an argument where both sides feel misunderstood and misrepresented, the danger is that it might get out of hand. Society might decide to unilaterally rewrite the rules, for example about pricing or patent law. Pharmaceutical companies and investors might walk away from the table and invest their money in another market, like information technology or clean energy. If either of those things were to happen, the result would be a broken relationship that both would probably come to regret.

And that's why I chose to write this book. My aim isn't to make detailed quantitative analyses and build elaborate policy proposals. Others have done that already. My plan is to explore this messy area in an investigative, reflective way, avoiding partisanship or polemics. I hope to "see the forest for the trees" and to find where the common ground is. My hope is to enable a more informed discussion that helps American society decide how to renew its social contract with the pharmaceutical innovators.

Notes

1 Although it is most often quoted as "If you wish to converse with me, first define your terms," I'm choosing to use this translation of Voltaire's original "Définissez les termes, vous dis-je, ou jamais nous ne nous entendrons," taken from *Dictionaire Philosophique* (1764).
2 Many cultures have an equivalent idiom. The Poles say, "The wolf is full and the lamb whole," the Germans that "You can't dance at two weddings at the same time" and, when I teach my Italian students, they tell me "You can't have the barrel full and the wife drunk." In every culture, refusing to accept the tradeoff is seen as being unrealistic. In the UK, during the heated arguments over Brexit, the pro-Brexit position that the UK could have the benefits of EU membership but none of the costs or constraints (an example of wanting to have your cake and to eat it) became known as "cakeism."
3 This book makes no attempt at judging the US healthcare system but I do have sympathy with the view that the US doesn't have a healthcare "system" in the sense of an orchestrated set of institutions. It is more true perhaps to say the US has a healthcare market. For a discussion of this, See ref 1. For an interesting take on how the US healthcare system reflects its societal values, See ref 2.
4 The figures in this section are taken mostly from the IQVIA Institute's May 2021 report. See ref 3.
5 Generic medicines, which are small-molecule drugs, and biosimilars, which are large, biological molecule drugs, are made possible by innovative medicines losing the exclusivity granted by patents or other forms of temporary monopoly.
6 In a term appropriated from international trade negotiations, issues around pricing and payment for pharmaceuticals are called "Market Access" by the industry. A good summary of how widespread and varied pharmaceutical market access issues are is given by a Datamonitor report, whose introduction sums up the situation very well:

> *Rising drug spending and increased desire for expenditure controls are consistent themes across the US, Europe, and emerging markets. With governments and*

private healthcare systems under increasing pressure to fund high-cost, innovative therapies, which often launch with limited clinical trial evidence, payers are looking towards new and enhanced reimbursement processes which align drug funding with patient value.

See ref 4.

7 The figures here are taken from: 5. IQVIA. Global Medicine Spending and Usage Trends: Outlook to 2025. 2021.

8 The US pays more for its innovative medicines but less for its generics than most countries. To quote the report:

U.S. prices for most subsets of drugs, and particularly brand-name originator drugs, were higher than those in comparison countries. The one exception was unbranded generic drugs, for which U.S. prices were on average 84 percent of those in other countries.

See ref 6.

9 For a discussion of pharmaceutical price control policies around the world, See ref 7.

10 Figures here taken from https://www.phrma.org/-/media/Project/PhRMA/PhRMA-Org/PhRMA-Org/PDF/D-F/Economic-Impact-US-Biopharmaceutical-Industry-December-2019.pdf. For a more global perspective on the importance of the industry, see also https://www.ifpma.org/wp-content/uploads/2021/04/WifOR_Global_Economic_Footprint_Study_September_2020.pdf.

11 Although this phrase is often said to be part of the Hippocratic oath that many doctors take, it is not part of that oath. The phrase from which it is translated *"primum non nocere"* comes from another of Hippocrates' works, "Of the Epidemics." See https://www.health.harvard.edu/blog/first-do-no-harm-2015 10138421.

12 These most recent figures are a little distorted by the influence of COVID, but the general picture of the attractiveness of the sector to investors is clear. Interestingly, this data also shows a focusing of investment, with more money going to fewer recipients. See ref 8.

13 These headline figures mask a lot of detail about what kinds of new drugs are reaching the market but the general picture is of a thriving research and development environment for pharmaceuticals. These numbers are taken from a CBO report of April 2021; See ref 9.

14 This point draws on two rich sources. See refs 10, 11.

Both works show how the evolution of the industry was not, as some might tell the story, an example of enterprise and scientific prowess but rather a complex mix of factors, not least the political. To quote Younkin:

Between 1940 and 1950 the American pharmaceutical industry transformed itself from a collection of several hundred, small, barely profitable firms to a small group of large, highly profitable firms.... I find that while the previous economic explanations may explain subsequent successes, they do not explain the initial change in the industry. Instead, the transformation of the industry into an oligopoly was largely the unintentional result of direct intervention by the US government.

15 In June 2021, the director of the National Economic Council, Brian Deese, gave a speech to the Atlantic Council that succinctly summarized the Biden administration's proactive attitude toward strategic industries. See ref 12. This echoed an emergent view in foreign policy circles that industrial strategy should be considered a component of the US's grand strategy. See, for example, ref 13. Bernstein J. "The Time for America to Embrace Industrial Policy Has Arrived." Foreign Policy 2020.

16 This information is taken from a testimony by Dr Janet Woodcock, Director of the Center for Drug Evaluation and Research, to the House Committee on Energy and Commerce, Subcommittee on Health. To quote Dr Woodcock:

> *Historically, the production of medicines for the U.S. population has been domestically based. However, in recent decades, drug manufacturing has gradually moved out of the United States. This is particularly true for manufacturers of active pharmaceutical ingredients (APIs), the actual drugs that are then formulated into tablets, capsules, injections, etc. As of August 2019, only 28 percent of the manufacturing facilities making APIs to supply the U.S. market were in our country. By contrast, the remaining 72 percent of the API manufacturers supplying the U.S. market were overseas, and 13 percent are in China.*

See ref 14.

17 See, for example, McKinsey's take on this. To quote:

> *Innovation in Chinese biopharma is fast becoming a notable story, underscored by significant value creation on global capital markets. The market value of publicly listed biopharma innovation players from China across the Nasdaq, Hong Kong Stock Exchange (HKEX), and Shanghai Stock Exchange Science and Technology Innovation Board (STAR) has surged from $3 billion in 2016 to more than $380 billion in July 2021. Biotechnology companies originating in China accounted for $180 billion of that total (Exhibit 1). Public debuts for Chinese players have also accelerated, with 23 IPOs in 2020 alone. Indeed, Chinese biotechs are leading on IPO fundraising—seven out of the world's top ten largest biopharma IPOs from 2018 to 2020 originated from China.*

See ref 15.

18 China has taken a two-strand approach to acquiring expertise in pharmaceutical innovation. It has encouraged the location of Western pharmaceutical companies into China, while at the same time Chinese companies have expanded into innovation hubs in the US and elsewhere. See refs 16, 17.

19 China's ambitions to become a global pharmaceutical innovator are quite explicit. Its tactics to do so, in addition to building and acquiring expertise, include encouraging industry consolidation, increasing regulation and accelerating the approval process. See refs 18, 19.

20 The idea of the common good is a pervasive theme from Aristotle and Plato through Thomas Aquinas and John Locke to John Stuart Mill and John Maynard Keynes. Madison wrote of it in Number 10 of the Federalist Papers. See ref 20.

21 "Ask not what your country can do for you – ask what you can do for your country." According to Kennedy's biographer Chris Matthews, Kennedy appropriated the line from his former headmaster. See ref 21.

22 The boiling frog story is that if you place a frog in a pan of boiling water it will jump out immediately, but if you place it in a pan of cold water and raise the temperature gradually, it will allow itself to be boiled to death. The story, which biologists refute, is an apologue. That is, it's a short story that is meant to convey a lesson. In this case, the lesson that there may be things wrong with how we get our innovative medicines and we ought to correct that before too much harm is done.

23 The topic of affordability is discussed throughout this book but for a good summary of some of the basic information I suggest you read two sources: See ref 22. and, for balance: See ref 23.

24 There are a great many books that take this position. They make for troubling reading but some readers might think that their lack of balance weakens their argument. See, for example, refs 24–27.

25 For example, one study found that half of all Part D covered drugs (50% of 3,343 drugs) and nearly half of all Part B covered drugs (48% of 568 drugs) had price increases greater than inflation between July 2019 and July 2020, which was 1.0%. See ref 28.

26 There is clear evidence that the more it costs to fulfil a prescription and the poorer the patient, the more likely it is that the prescription will be abandoned and the patient left untreated. See ref 29.

27 To quote from one paper typical of such criticism:

> The persistence of controversial PBM practices suggests that business model changes were mostly cosmetic, without altering key marketplace dysfunctions. Examples include "spread" pricing, in which PBMs pay pharmacies less than employer-paid amounts; rebate-influenced formulary development; and shifting of prescription volume to PBM-owned pharmacies.

See ref 30.

28 Although these points in defense of the pharmaceutical industry have been made by many industry spokespersons, a good example of the argument is provided by Pfizer CEO Albert Bourla's statements at an October 2021 conference. To quote from reports of that meeting: "The issue of drug pricing is a real issue in the U.S.," Bourla said. "But it is not the issue that some people think and present." See ref 31. For the "free riding" quote, See ref 32.

29 As will be discussed later in the book, pharmaceuticals do not have a single price. In particular, there is a big difference between what price the manufacturer lists and what they receive. See ref 32.

30 The issue of drug pricing is confounded by a complex system of rebates by pharmaceutical innovators to their immediate customers such as PBMs. As we'll discuss later in the book, there is evidence of a "bubble" as list prices and discounts increase and, in some cases, net prices decrease. To quote:

> When rebates and discounts were factored in, brand-name drug prices declined—or grew slowly—in 2020. Consistent with our previous analyses, rebates and discounts reduced the selling prices of brand-name drugs to less than half of their list prices. What's more, net drug prices have declined for the past four years.

See ref 33.

31 The price differences between small molecules and biologics are part of the reason that a relatively small proportion of prescriptions make up a large percentage of drug spending. See 34. But even biologics can look inexpensive when one looks at the prices of cell and gene therapies. For example, Novartis' Zolgensma, a one-time gene therapy for spinal muscular atrophy, has a list price of $2.125 million. But again, note that this is list price and the net price may differ. See ref 35.

32 The difficulty of assessing radical drug innovation in particular is nicely described in "Do current radical innovation measures actually measure radical drug innovation?" To quote from one piece of research in this area: *"Findings indicate that current measures of radical drug innovation are associated with very inconsistent outcomes and do not appear to measure what they purport to measure."* See ref 36.

33 Morgan and his colleagues suggested that pharmacological innovation was a function of two things: comparative effectiveness and the gravity of the unmet need. A drug that was only a little more effective for a condition that was not very serious was, in their terms, an incremental innovation. By contrast, a drug that was very much more effective than existing medicines in treating a serious disease was a radical innovation. Morgan called innovations between these two extremes "substantial." See ref 37.

34 The FDA has four routes to expedite drug approval and, in 2020, 36 out of 53 new drug approvals went through one of these four pathways. See 38. But the various categories don't necessarily map well onto Morgan's (above) definitions, so this figure isn't necessarily correlate to almost 70% of the new drugs being radical or even substantial innovations.

35 To quote this work:

> Highly innovative new drugs comprise only around a quarter of all new drug launches in the UK. In contrast, drugs categorized as only slightly innovative comprised well over half of all new drugs and annual numbers in this category are increasing.

See ref 39.

36 A good simple summary of these arguments is given here: See ref 40.

37 Drug repurposing isn't quite as easy as it sounds. A good review, with interesting examples, is given here: See ref 41.

38 This is not, of course, an argument about how much the federal government spends. I'm simply making the point that when we spend taxpayer dollars directly, as for military procurement or the justice system, we quite rightly expect good value for money. I'm further suggesting that, when American society chooses to spend a similar amount money via a combination of NIH, tax breaks for R&D spending or putting at risk some of its savings by investing in pharmaceuticals, then it is also reasonable to ask that those dollars are used efficiently. The source for federal spending numbers is https://www.cbo.gov/publication/57172.

39 The story of how Michael Sofia and his colleagues transformed Hepatitis C treatment makes fascinating reading. See ref 42.

40 This too is an inspirational story. Anthony Fauci describes it as "transformational" that a once-daily pill can now allow people with HIV to live a "relatively healthy, normal life" and make it "essentially impossible" to transmit HIV to a sexual partner. See ref 43.

41 Immunotherapy is one of a set of advances in cancer treatment that has made a difference to many lives but also has a long way to go. See 44.

42 It's useful to appreciate that current trends in pharmaceutical innovation don't only include variations on existing mechanisms of action. A whole series of new technologies is emerging with huge therapeutic promise. A good summary is given here: See ref 45.

43 Many of the points made here are based on Christopher Austin's paper "Opportunities and challenges in translational science." See ref 46.

44 This relative neglect of very high needs is partly because of a focus on other areas, such as oncology. As we'll discuss later in the book, pharmaceutical innovation is largely led by what the market will pay for and it is not clear that market signals accurately reflect societal needs or priorities. See refs 9, 47.

45 There are two separate but related arguments here. There is widespread agreement that the current system does not meet the needs of developing countries. There is less agreement, but still evidence for, the argument that the current market-led system does not reflect the needs of developed countries. See ref 48.

46 One measure of this is "Orphan Drug Designation," an outcome of the 1983 act that was intended to incentivize development of drugs for patient populations of less than 200,000 people. The number of orphan drug designations has quadrupled since the passing of that act. See ref 49.

47 The threat that a pathogen resistant to current antibiotics might emerge is truly terrifying. See ref 50. The failure of the current, market-led, system to address this threat is summarized well here: See ref 51.

References

1 Rich J. America doesn't have a health care system. *The Outline* [Internet]. 1st April 2020. Available from: https://theoutline.com/post/8899/us-healthcare-system-coronavirus-icu-beds.

2 Khazan O. How can the US health care system be more like the UK? *The Atlantic* [Internet]. 21st June 2019. Available from: https://www.theatlantic.com/health/archive/2019/06/how-can-us-health-care-system-be-more-like-uk/592321/.

3 IQVIA. The use of medicines in the United States; 2020.

4 Datamonitor. Market access trends in the US, Europe, and emerging markets; 2019.

5 IQVIA. Global medicine spending and usage trends: Outlook to 2025; 2021.

6 Mulcahy AW, Whaley CM, Gizaw M, Schwam D, Edenfield N, Becerra-Ornelas AU. *International Prescription Drug Price Comparisons: Current Empirical Estimates and Comparisons with Previous Studies.* Santa Monica, CA: RAND Corporation; 2021.

7 Ginsburg PBL, Steven M. Government regulated or negotiated drug prices: Key design considerations; 2021. USC Schaeffer/Brookings

8 Brown AE, Edwin. Biopharma and venture capital: A deep dive; 2021. Evaluate.

9 Batta A, Kalra B, Khirasaria R. Trends in FDA drug approvals over last 2 decades: An observational study. *Journal of Family Medicine and Primary Care.* 2020;9(1):105–14.

10 Dutfield G. *That Highest Design of Pure Gold.* World Scientific Publishing Co; 2020. London.

11 Younkin P. Making the market: How the American pharmaceutical industry transformed itself during the 1940s 2008. Available from: https://escholarship.org/uc/item/2g67r185.

12 Deese B. The Biden White House plan for a new US industrial policy 2021. Available from: https://www.atlanticcouncil.org/commentary/transcript/the-biden-white-house-plan-for-a-new-us-industrial-policy/.

13 Bernstein J. The time for America to embrace industrial policy has arrived. *Foreign Policy.* 2020.

14 Woodcock J. Safeguarding pharmaceutical supply chains in a global economy 2019. Available from: https://www.fda.gov/news-events/congressional-testimony/safeguarding-pharmaceutical-supply-chains-global-economy-10302019.

15 Han KLD, Zhang F, Zhou J. The dawn of China biopharma innovation 2021. Available from: https://www.mckinsey.com/industries/life-sciences/our-insights/the-dawn-of-china-biopharma-innovation.

16 WHO. China policies to promote local production of pharmaceutical products and protect public health. *World Health Organisation*; 2017.

17 Kazmierczak M. *China's Biotechnology Development: The Role of US and Other Foreign Engagement*; 2019. US-China Economic and Security Review Commission.

18 Made in China 2025: Global ambitions built on local protections 2017. Available from: https://www.uschamber.com/assets/archived/images/final_made_in_china_2025_report_full.pdf.

19 Torrey Z. China prepares for big pharma. *The Diplomat* [Internet]. 2018. Available from: https://thediplomat.com/2018/03/china-prepares-for-big-pharma/.

20 Madison J. Federalist Papers No. 10 1787. Available from: https://billofrightsinstitute.org/primary-sources/federalist-no-10.

21 Matthews C. *Jack Kennedy: Elusive Hero.* New York: Simon and Schuster; 2011.

22 Cicchiello AG, Lovisa. Brand-name drug prices: The key driver of high pharmaceutical spending in the U.S. 2021. Available from: https://www.commonwealthfund.org/publications/2021/nov/brand-name-drug-prices-key-driver-high-pharmaceutical-spending-in-us?utm_source=alert&utm_medium=email&utm_campaign=Controlling+Health+Care+Costs.

23 Cost & value of medicines: PhRMA; 2021. Available from: https://www.phrma.org/policy-issues/cost-and-value.

24 Angell M. *The Truth about the Drug Companies: How They Deceive Us and What to Do About It.* New York: Random House; 2005.

25 Posner G. *Pharma: Greed, Lies, and the Poisoning of America.* Simon and Schuster; 2020. New York.

26 Kenber B. *Sick Money: The Truth about the Global Pharmaceutical Industry.* Canongate Books; 2021. Edinburgh.

27 Kinch MW, Lori. *The Price of Health: The Modern Pharmaceutical Enterprise and the Betrayal of a History of Care.* Pegasus Books; 2021. New York.

28 Cubanski JN, Tricia. Prices increased faster than inflation for half of all drugs covered by medicare in 2020; 2022. Available from: https://www.kff.org/medicare/issue-brief/prices-increased-faster-than-inflation-for-half-of-all-drugs-covered-by-medicare-in-2020/.

29 Medicine Spending and Affordability in the U.S.: IQVIA; 2020.

30 Motheral BRF, Kathleen A. Changes in PBM business practices in 2019: True innovation or more of the same? *Journal of Managed Care & Specialty Pharmacy.* 2020;26(10):1325.

31 Bourla A. Pfizer's Bourla on drug pricing: "We have a problem here." *Biospace* [Internet]. 2021. Available from: https://www.biospace.com/article/pfizer-s-bourla-on-drug-pricing-in-us-we-have-a-problem-here-/.

32 Pfizer: Countries free-riding on US innovation 2019. Available from: https://www.bbc.co.uk/news/business-47377427.

33 Fein AJ. Gross-to-Net Bubble Update: Net Prices Drop (Again) at Six Top Drugmakers 2021. Available from: https://www.drugchannels.net/2021/04/gross-to-net-bubble-update-net-prices.html.

34 Makurvet FD. Biologics vs. small molecules: Drug costs and patient access. *Medicine in Drug Discovery.* 2021;9:100075.

35 Nuijten M. Pricing Zolgensma - the world's most expensive drug. *Journal of Market Access & Health Policy.* 2021;10(1):2022353-.

36 Stiller I, van Witteloostuijn A, Cambré B. Do current radical innovation measures actually measure radical drug innovation? *Scientometrics.* 2021;126(2):1049–78.

37 Morgan S, Lopert R, Greyson D. Toward a definition of pharmaceutical innovation. *Open Medicine.* 2008;2(1):E4–E7.

38 Pal S. Recent trends in approvals of novel drugs. US Pharmacist October 15th 2021.

39 Ward DJ, Slade A, Genus T, Martino OI, Stevens AJ. How innovative are new drugs launched in the UK? A retrospective study of new drugs listed in the British National Formulary (BNF) 2001–2012. *BMJ Open.* 2014;4(10):e006235–e.

40 Petkantchin V. The advantages of incremental pharmaceutical innovation. *Institut Economique Molari*; 2012.

41 Jourdan JP, Bureau R, Rochais C, Dallemagne P. Drug repositioning: A brief overview. *Journal of Pharmacy and Pharmacology.* 2020;72(9):1145–51.

42 Maron DF. Inventor of Hepatitis C Cure wins a major prize—and turns to the next battle. *Scientific American* [Internet]. 2016. Available from: https://www.scientificamerican.com/article/inventor-of-hepatitis-c-cure-wins-a-major-prize-and-turns-to-the-next-battle/.

43 Nania R. 'Exciting' discoveries could finally mean the end of AIDS 2019. Available from: https://www.aarp.org/health/conditions-treatments/info-2019/hiv-now-chronic-condition.html.

44 Zhang Y, Zhang Z. The history and advances in cancer immunotherapy: Understanding the characteristics of tumor-infiltrating immune cells and their therapeutic implications. *Cellular & Molecular Immunology.* 2020;17(8):807–21.

45 Buvailo A. The explosion of therapeutic modalities: Small molecules, biologics, and everything in between. *biopharmatrendcom* [Internet]. 2022. Available from: https://www.biopharmatrend.com/post/402-the-explosion-of-therapeutic-modalities-small-molecules-biologics-and-everything-in-between/.

46 Austin CP. Opportunities and challenges in translational science. *Clinical and Translational Science.* 2021;14(5):1629–47.

47 Brown DG, Wobst HJ. A decade of FDA-approved drugs (2010–2019): Trends and future directions. *Journal of Medicinal Chemistry.* 2021;64(5):2312–38.

48 Milne C-P, Kaitin KI. Are regulation and innovation priorities serving public health needs? *Frontiers in Pharmacology.* 2019;10:144-.

49 Miller KL, Fermaglich LJ, Maynard J. Using four decades of FDA orphan drug designations to describe trends in rare disease drug development: Substantial growth seen in development of drugs for rare oncologic, neurologic, and pediatric-onset diseases. *Orphanet Journal of Rare Diseases.* 2021;16(1):265-.

50 Graham CJ. The global threat of antibiotic resistance: What can be done? *Journal of Global Health*; Vol. 1. 2017.

51 Fisher L. Antibiotics: Poster child for market failure. *Miliken Institute Review* [Internet]. 2016. Available from: https://www.milkenreview.org/articles/antibiotics-poster-child-for-market-failure.

2   A new paradigm for a wicked problem

Precis

- Affordable medicines today or innovative medicines tomorrow is a dilemma.
- Radical, publicly funded resolutions seem impractical in a US context.
- The public debate is sterile because this is a "wicked" social problem.
- Viewing pharmaceutical innovation as mechanistic is unhelpful.
- We need a new way to look at the issue.
- Ecology, as a paradigm not a metaphor, provides that new perspective.
- This sees pharmaceutical innovation as a complex, adaptive ecosystem.
- Innovation and prices emerge from that pharmaceutical innovation ecosystem (PIE).
- The PIE is fragile and susceptible to unintended consequences.
- The PIE cannot be directed, only holistically and systematically managed.
- The PIE has seven interconnected habitats.
- In a healthy PIE, each habitat provides the PIE with essential inputs.
- Only a healthy PIE can provide both innovative and affordable medicines.

In Chapter 1, I described the dialogue of the deaf in American society around the affordability of innovative medicines. Even the most casual observer is struck by how each side has dug in its position and made its mind up. This deep-rooted disagreement matters because, through its public institutions and private organizations, society's feelings influence its behavior. And how society behaves about drug pricing matters because, whether it chooses to control prices,

DOI: 10.4324/9781003330271-2

allow the market free rein or anything else, it influences the new medicines we get and what they cost. This is important to Americans, especially when they are at their most vulnerable, and the US's dominant position in the global pharmaceutical market makes it a global issue too.[1]

This societal discord is most visible in the heat and fury surrounding the most immediate issues, such as "out of pocket" costs for those living with ongoing conditions, or access to costly therapies for those dying of rare diseases. These proximate issues are very important, especially to those facing them, but they are not the ultimate cause of our societal division. Underpinning these entrenched positions and closed minds is an unresolved dilemma. On the one hand, we want and need the fruits of pharmaceutical innovation. We take for granted past discoveries like anticoagulants to prevent blood clotting and analgesics to reduce pain. And we look forward expectantly to cures for the thousands of diseases, from cancers to dementia, for which our doctors can currently offer little hope. On the other hand, while we fully accept that pharmaceutical innovation is expensive, we're not comfortable with the corollaries of that fact. We want those new therapies to be affordable to all. And, in US society, this unresolved dilemma is magnified by a culture that prioritizes personal responsibility and eschews socialized medicine. HL Mencken was, as usual, insightful when he said that life is a constant oscillation between the sharp horns of a dilemma. In the case of the affordability of innovative medicines, this oscillation has produced a sterile debate which generates more heat than light. That sterility is now a growing problem for our society, as ever more expensive medicines, for ever more conditions, come to market.

Box 2.1 Self-imposed or world-imposed: what kind of dilemma do we face?

Some moral philosophers would class the affordability of innovative medicines as a self-imposed dilemma, created by our own choices. From that perspective, we could choose to devote much more public spending to providing expensive, innovative drugs to everyone who needs them. That would at least partly resolve the dilemma. So, too, would making different choices about who funds drug development. Currently, we ask venture capitalists and shareholders to put their own capital at risk. Because that risk is large and other, less risky, investments are available, private investors require high returns on their investment. But we could, if we chose, fund drug development from taxpayers' funds, borrowed at much lower, bond market rates, and so reduce costs. Because we could make different choices that might solve the dilemma, those philosophers would say we face a self-imposed dilemma.

But moral philosophers rarely agree about anything. Others would class our situation as a world-imposed dilemma. Their position would be that pharmaceutical innovation is always going to be expensive and risky, while demand for innovative medicines is, for all practical purposes, unlimited and insatiable. From that perspective, we're always going to face a problem with the affordability of innovative medicines, whatever choices we make. Those philosophers would see us as facing a world-imposed dilemma, created by unalterable scientific and social realities.

Both the self-imposed and world-imposed views are reasonable interpretations of the dilemma we face, and you might see elements of truth in each of them. As you consider which one you agree with most, it is worth reflecting on the words on Karl Marx's tomb in Highgate Cemetery, London. "The philosophers have only interpreted the world, in various ways. The point, however, is to change it." You don't have to be a Marxist to conclude that, however we interpret the dilemma around the affordability of innovative medicines, we need to resolve it.

There are, of course, radical views on how we might resolve this dilemma. The globally respected, and famously left-leaning, economist Mariana Mazzucato argues that the pharmaceutical industry's "entrenched short-termism and misalignment with the public interest" justifies something approaching nationalization of the pharmaceutical industry. Although she suggests that the complete transfer of ownership to the state is not necessarily required, she argues for an "entrepreneurial state" that creates and shapes markets.[2] Mazzucato's ideas for the supply side of the dilemma are matched on the demand side by those who propose universal, state-funded healthcare in the US, akin to what exists in some other developed economies. For example, Gabriel Zieff and his co-authors believe that shifting from the current, market-based system to a free-at-point-of-access system would be better, in the long term, for both the health and the economy of the country.[34] Neither of these radical positions is without merit. But I haven't considered either of them seriously in this book because both are unrealistic in the foreseeable political and social context of the US.[5] The nation's current and persistent level of political polarization means that the political coalition required for their enactment is unimaginable.[6] Even without the politics, such fundamental change seems to be incongruent to the individualist values that differentiate Americans from their western European peers, and which have been characteristic of the nation since Alex de Tocqueville described them in the 1830s.[7] In my exploration of this topic, I decided that a radical transformation of the US healthcare system was so unlikely that it was not worth exploring.

If I put aside solutions that seem improbable in a US context, like nationalizing the industry or a US version of the UK's National Health Service, I'm left with the polarized and unproductive national debate about the affordability of innovative medicines in something similar to the current context. On the one side of this debate, impassioned advocates of drug pricing controls, typified by organizations like "Patients for Affordable Drugs," claim that "drug corporations have literally rigged the system" [against patients].[8] On the other side of the debate sit defenders of the research-based part of the industry, such as PhRMA, who claim declining net prices, point to the costs incurred in the supply chain and, of course, the association between drug prices and innovation.[9] Both sides of this debate make valid points and, in private discussions, many on both sides hold private views that are more nuanced than they espouse in the public domain. But the most obvious feature of this debate is, as I've already characterized, that it is "a dialogue of the deaf," to translate the French idiom. Those advocating pricing controls ignore any wider implications of removing many billions of dollars from the profits of pharmaceutical innovators and the concomitant reduction in the sector's attractiveness to investors. At the same time, most innovators downplay the societal concern about the affordability of medicines and the perceptions created by their pricing strategies, simply calling for more spending on drugs and hoping their large lobbying efforts will be enough to prevent price controls. To read the published announcements of both sides is to receive an education in the selective use of information and the "straw man" method of argument.[10]

This low level of debate is not only unproductive, but also dangerous. It threatens the social contract between society and pharmaceutical innovators. That informal contract, which has held for almost as long as the industry has existed, allows pharmaceutical innovators to profit from human illness in return for providing a stream of new, effective medicines. Like all informal contracts, this social contract evolved over time and has survived because it brought benefits to both sides. But, like all contracts, it is weakened if the parties adopt the entrenched, disregarding positions we see in this debate.[11]

The particular circumstances that currently exist in the US make it easy to see how this erosion of the social contract could play out. Demographics and lifestyle factors will create greater demand for many kinds of pharmaceutical innovation.[12] Some innovation will increase demand by making previously untreatable conditions treatable.[13] Economic growth rates, which will be slow relative to these growing demands, will constrain health spending, both public and private. Increases in wealth inequality, even if slower than recent trends, will increase health inequality.[14] This gradual widening of the gap between what pharmaceutical innovation is available and what is affordable is politically sensitive, so it will be amplified through social media and partisan politics. Together, these factors will create the environment in which simple solutions, which play well to the media, become politically popular. This is already evident in, for example, strong popular support for measures such as enforced genericization and public disclosure of research and development costs.[15] But the affordability of innovative medicines is nothing if not a complex problem and, to quote HL Mencken again, to every complex problem there is a simple solution, and it is usually wrong. So, it is very easy to imagine a resolution to the innovative medicines dilemma that is simple and politically popular, but which has unintended and negative consequences. Whether that populist resolution favors one side of the current debate or none, it is quite easy to imagine policies and practices that hinder innovation or affordability or both at the same time. To avoid that simple but wrong solution, we need first to understand why such an important debate has descended into sterility and then find another, more productive way to look at the problem.

Why did the drug pricing debate become so sterile?

It's not surprising that the debate around the pricing of innovative medicines has become sterile. It has exactly the right four ingredients needed to make it that way.

Firstly, it is a "wicked problem" which means, in the social policy sense, it is difficult or impossible to solve (see Box 2.2). Rittel and Webber's characterization of wicked problems certainly sounds very familiar to anyone who has thought about the affordability of medicines. Thinking about our issue as a wicked problem helps explain why the debate around it has turned sterile. Policy makers, the media, and the public are comfortable with thinking about "tame" problems that can be solved by science, such as the development of a COVID vaccine or putting a man on the moon. Given the many past successes of that approach to tame problems, it is not surprising that our instinct is to address all problems the same way. But drug pricing is a wicked problem, and any debate that frames it otherwise will inevitably become sterile.

Box 2.2 What are wicked problems?

In their influential 1973 paper, Rittel and Webber contrasted the difficult but "tame" problems that could be solved by conventional science with the "wicked" problems faced by social planners.[16] In their view, wicked problems have a number of distinctive characteristics, which include:

- There is no definitive formulation of a wicked problem.
- Solutions to wicked problems are not true-or-false, but better or worse.
- There is no immediate and no ultimate test of a solution to a wicked problem.
- Every wicked problem is essentially unique.
- Every wicked problem can be considered to be a symptom of another problem.
- Those trying to solve wicked problems are liable for the consequences of their actions.

Although Rittel and Webber wrote about social policy in general, all these characteristics can be seen in the specific issue of affordability of innovative medicines. It is essentially unique, unlike any other. It is a symptom of wider healthcare system problems. Whatever solutions we might propose, we can't immediately know if they are right or wrong. In particular, those trying to solve the problem have a moral responsibility for the consequences of their actions. The affordability of innovative medicines is a wicked problem and treating it as a difficult but tame problem contributes to the sterility debate.

Secondly, drug affordability has what political scientists call "Issue Salience."[17] By this, they mean it is an issue with which voters engage and, consequently, politicians pay attention to. For example, in the run up to the 2020 presidential election, the economy, healthcare, and supreme court appointments were the three most salient issues; and economic inequality, climate change, and abortion the least salient.[18] This is significant because saliency influences the way we behave. Opinions about salient issues become more entrenched and less amenable to facts and argument. We can see this by contrasting how American society engages with issues it regards as highly salient, such as the economy, and those they don't, such as income inequality. In that research prior to the 2020 election, Pew found that healthcare, of which drug pricing is a component issue, was second only to the economy in political salience. The consequent salience-driven entrenchment of views around drug pricing is one of the factors that makes this such a sterile debate. Political salience gives topics an ironic quality: because the affordability of innovative medicines is important to us, we're less willing to enter into constructive debate about it.

The third factor inducing sterility in this debate is that it is strongly aligned to partisan divisions in society. Those who identify as Democrats and Republican have grown further apart on policy preferences for some decades. The division on healthcare matters, such as insurance reform and Medicare spending, which relate to the affordability of medicines, is especially stark.[19] This polarization has been attributed to many causes, from President Obama's concern about an "epistemological crisis" – who we trust, what we believe, what we think is real – to the rise of identity group politics and other factors.[20] Whatever the reasons, Americans' political allegiances rarely change and, increasingly, they align to their mostly static educational and racial demographics.[21] Whatever the causes of this polarization, its consequences are what concern us here. The anchoring of already entrenched views on drug pricing to largely unchanging political allegiances reduces still further the chances of a genuine marketplace for ideas and sterilizes the debate.

The final factor that hampers discussion of our issue flows from the unique characteristics of the pharmaceutical market. There are few, if any, markets that touch so many Americans so significantly. Everyone is a participant, sooner or later. And, unlike equally ubiquitous markets like electronics or groceries, our experience with pharmaceuticals is always a distress purchase, often made out of dire necessity. That distress purchase is frequently compounded by feelings of uncertainty over what the price might be and lack of control over the purchase decision. It's hard to imagine another market in which individuals are obliged to participate, and in which they have so little influence over their expenditure. The aggregate consequence of these factors is that almost everyone has, or knows someone who has, a disconcerting tale to tell about the price of drugs. And if they don't, they hear those tales via social media or sites like "TruthinRX."[22] This is important because, even if those stories are untrue or inaccurate, many of us are prone to believe anecdote and alternative facts.[23] As hard as it is for scientists and trained critical thinkers to understand, not everyone regards peer-reviewed data as the gold standard of evidence. For many, a Facebook post may carry more weight.[24]

And there's the rub. We've been fretting about the price of innovative medicines for a very long time. On May 8th 1961, a Senate committee report said that the industry charged unreasonably high prices, placed monopolistic restrictions on the market, abused patents, and wasted resources in its selling practices.[25] That committee sat because there was already a public debate about drug pricing and that debate has continued, without resolution, for the last six decades. That so much hot air is expended to such little avail is because of the four reasons above. They are reasons why our public debate about the affordability of innovative medicines is unproductive. It's a wicked problem: hard to define, hard to solve, and hard to know if you've solved it. The wickedness of the problem is amplified by its salience, which makes people embed their positions and close their minds. That intransigence is reinforced by its attachment to political allegiances, which rarely change and are often aligned to racial and educational demographics. And, if we hope to solve the problem by weight of rational evidence, we are frustrated by the credibility given to personal experience and anecdote. Unless we want to be having the same discussion in another 60 years, we need to look at the issue a different way.

Are we looking at drug pricing the wrong way?

It's an old maxim, often attributed to the pioneering inventor Charles Kettering that, if you can't solve a problem, you should look at it from a different angle. And of course many of the great advances in human knowledge have been made possible by a new way of thinking about old questions. When astrology was still a powerful belief system, predicting the movements of the planets was important but problematic. As observational evidence increased, the Ptolemaic idea of the Earth at the center of a number of concentric crystal spheres became increasingly inadequate. It took Copernicus's new perspective, placing the sun at the center of our system, to solve that problem and eventually help us understand our place in the cosmos. Similarly, creation stories were, by the 19th century, increasingly at odds with the accumulating observations of geologists and biologists. Famously, Charles Darwin, along with Alfred Wallace, reframed those observations with his theory of natural selection. Evolutionary science subsequently transformed our understanding of biology and several other fields. In medicine, the centuries-old idea that disease was spread by evil smelling miasmas held back public health until Pasteur, Koch, and others began to explain infection in terms of germ theory. Thomas Kuhn, the hugely influential American philosopher of science, called these fundamental changes in the way we look at the world "paradigm shifts" and, despite its subsequent dilution by abuse, this is still a useful concept. Kuhn saw paradigm shifts as occurring when the old way of looking at the world no longer seems to work, for example in explaining or managing some observed phenomena.[26] As American society struggles to explain and manage the wicked problem of the affordability of innovative medicines, the need for a paradigm shift of the kind Kuhn describes becomes clear.

Listen to both critics and defenders of drug pricing and you will find that, despite their opposing views, their public statements suggest the same underlying way of looking at the issue. It's quite clear that the paradigm shaping both camps' thinking is the mechanistic paradigm, a view of the pharmaceutical market as a machine. Some writers even refer explicitly to the pharmaceutical innovation machine.[27] In one camp, those who think innovative medicines are too expensive propose pulling levers that, for example, weaken patents or tie US prices to those in other countries.[28] Their mechanistic thinking sees those levers as being directly connected to the affordability of medicines, with relatively little connection to, for example, the attractiveness of markets to investors. On the other side, those who defend the status quo of mostly free market pricing apply the same mechanistic paradigm but to different effect. They propose leaving the free-pricing valve in its open position to allow capital to flow copiously into the market and, specifically, towards R&D investment.[29] They see the free-pricing mechanism as working directly on innovation with little influence on, for example, the social contract that underpins the market. Of course, not everybody involved in the debate thinks in such binary terms. Some on each side are more nuanced in their view and some who espouse strongly mechanistic views in public are more discriminating in private conversation. But the loudest, most influential voices in this debate use the mechanistic paradigm to caricature their opponents and influence policymakers. The mechanistic paradigm works well as a rhetorical device but, because it doesn't reflect the complexity of pharmaceutical innovation, it can't help us to understand or to solve the issue of affordability of innovative medicines.[30]

Paradoxically, the mechanistic paradigm that is used by both sides of the debate co-exists alongside a completely different and competing paradigm, that of the biological ecosystem. When think tanks discuss how to maintain the US's pre-eminence in the sector, they talk about the importance of its ecosystem.[31] When consultants talk about the rise of China's biopharma industry, they worry most about the development of that country's ecosystem.[32] And, when regions within the US want to promote themselves as homes for the industry, they do so in terms of their local ecosystem.[33] This borrowing from biology works rhetorically by communicating the heterogeneity, interconnectedness, and adaptability of the sector. It works well as a metaphor because, when the industry talks about its many different entities interacting in a complex way and adapting to each other and to the external environment, their language could almost be taken from an ecology primer.

The paradox lies in using two markedly different, indeed competing, paradigms at once. Ecosystems don't behave like machines and machines don't behave like ecosystems.[34] They are fundamentally different ways of thinking about how pharmaceutical innovation works and they can only co-exist because they are not being used literally but only metaphorically. As philosophers from Plato to Nietzsche have argued, the fact that the metaphor doesn't correlate closely to reality doesn't matter if it's rhetorically effective.[35] So, people talking about pharmaceutical innovation can use the mechanistic metaphor when they want a rhetorical device for implying simplicity and obviousness. If they choose to ignore the non-sequiturs of the machine metaphor, such as predictability of outcome, then that's using the machine as a metaphor and not in its literal sense. At the same time, they can use the ecosystem metaphor when they want to imply that pharmaceutical innovation has many of the positive characteristics of life itself, like richness, variety, and adaptability. If they choose not to follow through to other implications of the ecosystem metaphor, such as sustainability, balance, or ecosystem fragility, then that's a choice to use the metaphorical value of the ecosystem and ignore its more literal value.

In the debate about the affordability of innovative medicines, the dominant paradigm is a mechanistic one, even though it's a poor one for understanding the complex reality of pharmaceutical innovation. It is used because of its rhetorical value, not for its realism or validity. At the same time, the notion of pharmaceutical innovation as an ecosystem is commonly used, but again only as metaphor and not in any literal sense. However, as I'm about to argue, that's a mistake. The ecosystem paradigm, when it is used literally rather than metaphorically, is the key to raising the debate about the affordability of innovative drugs from its current, sterile state to a more productive level. And, as I've said above, that's something we need to do.

What is the case for the ecosystem paradigm?

In their defense, metaphors are very useful. They help us to reduce complex phenomena, such as the relationship between the price of drugs and pharmaceutical innovation, into something we can communicate easily. They also carry emotional implications well, whether that's the mechanical "obviousness" that controlling prices improves affordability or the ecological "profundity" that every part of the system is connected to the others. For these reasons, the language of science is largely metaphorical.[36] But metaphors have their weaknesses. When they are taken too literally, they hinder our understanding and progress. For centuries, the bird metaphor hindered the development of human flight by channeling inventors toward flapping. The household expenses metaphor used by many politicians has long constrained macro-economic policy. So, I want to make the point that, as I make the case for the application of the ecosystem paradigm to the affordability of innovative medicines, I'm *not* using it as a metaphor. I'm not saying that how we get innovative medicines is *like* an ecosystem, I'm saying it *is* an ecosystem. In this, I'm taking my cue from two of my intellectual influences, Hodgson and Knudsen, whose work is about applying Darwinian evolution to social systems.[37] They argue that a Darwinian perspective on social institutions is not a metaphor but an "ontological communality," a shared way of understanding different things. Similarly, I'm saying that it's useful to think about the way we get innovative medicines using the same sort of thinking that an ecologist uses to look at the way we get, for example, fruit from an orchard.

In the next section, I'll describe how the ecological perspective applies directly to innovative medicines. But the term "ecosystem" has been and continues to be used so loosely that it's worth taking a few lines to summarize the history of the perspective and why it is a good candidate for our much-needed new paradigm. The term "ecosystem" was first coined in 1935,[38] in relation to vegetation, but its use only grew after about 1960, when the idea of the ecosystem as a biological unit became well established in the life sciences. After that, various writers drew parallels between biological and economic systems, but that idea really germinated with James F. Moore's article "Predators and Prey: A New Ecology of Competition."[39] Moore's work was anchored in the information technology sector, and he referred explicitly to the ecosystem as a metaphor. He gave further impetus to the metaphorical perspective with his later book and, today, there are innumerable books that use the word ecosystem in relation to industries or other economic systems. But a critical reading of these works reveals that the limitations of Moore's perspectives persist. They are still heavily slanted towards the technology sector; and they still tend towards ecology as a metaphor rather than as an ontological communality with biologists' thinking.[40] So let me stress again, because it's important, that when I use the ecosystem paradigm I'm not using it as a loose, rhetorical metaphor in the way that almost all other business authors do. I'm using it in a much more literal sense.

That others throw around the term ecosystem loosely doesn't lessen the case for using this perspective to understand pharmaceutical innovation. After all, the reality is that innovative medicines do emerge from the adaptive interaction of many different types of entity, from universities to biotechs to regulators. It is also clear that those many entities are influenced by a wider environment, such as politics, the economy, and demography. The aim of this inter-activity is to make best use of societal resources to deliver innovative medicines as efficiently and effectively as possible. And we want that outcome on a long term, sustainable basis. All of these are characteristics that, to a biological ecologist, would scream out "this is an ecosystem." There is then a case for adopting the ecosystem perspective to look at pharmaceutical innovation. It's that case that I'll develop in the next section, all the time stressing that I'm not following the ecosystem as metaphor path taken by many others.

What is the pharmaceutical innovation ecosystem?

When we use the word ecosystem, we can use it in one of two meanings. We can use it in the biological sense of many organisms interacting both with each other (which biologists call the *biotic* environment) and with their wider environment of climate and geology (the *abiotic* environment). This is the prototypical use of the word. But we can also use it in its borrowed sense of the term, that of a complex, interconnected network. This is closer to Moore's definition of "an economic community supported by a foundation of interacting organizations and individuals." In whatever sense we use the term, it's important to realize that an ecosystem (strictly speaking a biological term) is simply a particular example of a wider phenomenon – the complex adaptive system – that can be biological or social. This semantic refinement helps us to move from "ecosystem as a metaphor" to "complex adaptive system as a scientific concept" that we can apply to the reality of pharmaceutical innovation.[41]

Definitions of complex adaptive systems tend to be either very technical or somewhat circular, so the best way to understand them is by thinking about their characteristic features. These are variously

---

Box 2.3 The characteristics of complex adaptive systems

The characteristics of a complex adaptive system[42] are easily recognizable in pharmaceutical innovation. In a complex adaptive system:

- Individual agents are very numerous and heterogeneous.
- Those agents interact dynamically, guided by simple rules.
- Those interactions are rich, affected by and affecting many other agents.
- Those interactions are non-linear, so small changes can cause large effects.
- Those interactions are primarily but not exclusively with immediate neighbors.
- Those interactions can operate in feedback loops.
- The systems may be open, so it may be impossible to clearly define its boundaries.
- Complex systems require interactions to maintain their organization.
- The present state of a complex system is influenced by its past.
- Individual agents may not be fully aware of the system's behavior.
- The behavior of the system is not predicted by the behavior of the individual agents.

---

described by different authors, but Paul Cilliers' list of these is the perhaps the clearest and most useful characterization (see Box 2.3).

Please take a moment to look at these characteristics of a complex, adaptive ecosystem and compare them to the reality of pharmaceutical innovation. I hope it's obvious that pharmaceutical innovation has all the characteristics of a complex adaptive system. The numerous and heterogeneous agents involved in pharmaceutical innovation include pharmaceutical companies, biotechs, and their various sub-contractors but also universities, venture capitalists, regulators, insurers and PBMs, healthcare providers, pharmacies, state and federal government and, of course, patients and patient organizations. Together, these organizations form the equivalent of the biotic environment, and they operate in the equivalent of an abiotic environment that has both so-ciological and technological components. The former includes demo-graphics, disease patterns and social attitudes, and political policies. The latter includes the state of basic and applied scientific knowledge and technological capabilities. The interactions between organizations and with sociological and technological environments are dynamic and rich, as is characteristic of a complex adaptive system. They include – but are not limited to – formal and informal interactions, exchange of information, movement of personnel, mergers and acquisitions and, of course, commercial exchange of goods and services. Each agent in-teracts with many other agents, although primarily through its closer, immediate relationships. This web of interactions has non-linear ef-fects, such as the impact on company valuation of a single trial result, and these effects can work in feedback loops, such as when success or failure in a given therapy area influences organizational reputation.

Although complex, these interactions are guided by simple rules. In biological ecosystems, these rules are about maximizing reproductive success while avoiding death. In pharmaceutical innovation, interaction is guided by simple rules about maximizing risk adjusted return on in-vestment, while avoiding legal and compliance issues that would com-promise future operations. The system of pharmaceutical innovation that is constituted by these agents and their rule-guided interactions is impossible to define precisely, blurring as it does into the wider sys-tems of healthcare, social care, capital flows, and scientific research. It is also clear that pharmaceutical innovation is "path dependent," shaped by its past. Thalidomide for example, helped shape the current regulatory environment[43] and the current generic/innovative market structure was heavily shaped by the Hatch-Waxman act of 1984.[44] It is also apparent that pharmaceutical innovation depends on a constant flow of interaction between agents to maintain the system.[45] Finally, it is inconceivable that every agent involved in pharmaceutical innovation has a perfect understanding of the system or that they would not in-teract most strongly with their immediate neighbors in that system.[46]

As I hope the above paragraphs make clear, the case that pharma-ceutical innovation is best understood as a complex adaptive system is compelling. From that perspective, innovative medicines are what results from the working of that system that, from now on, I'll refer to as the pharmaceutical innovation ecosystem (PIE). To be clear, the PIE is much broader than the pharmaceutical industry and includes all the entities involved in making innovative medicines available to the patient. As we'll see in the rest of this chapter and book, the PIE is an effective, insightful way to look at the affordability of innovative medicines. It helps us to understand and manage that issue in the same way that the biological ecosystem paradigm, with which it has ontological communality, helps us understand and manage our natural and agricultural environments.

What does the ecosystem perspective imply for the affordability debate?

When we take the ecosystem idea and apply it to pharmaceutical innovation, we're practicing what the learning theorist Donald Schön termed the displacement of concepts.[47] As Schön observed, by taking well-understood ideas from one situation we can, with caution, use them to understand more quickly another, different situation. The displacement of concepts idea is relevant to us, because ecologists have learned a lot about how their ecosystems work and, when we displace ecologists' concepts into the context of pharmaceutical innovation, we can draw three significant implications that inform the debate about the affordability of innovative medicines.

Pharmaceutical innovation emerges from the pharmaceutical innovation ecosystem

To ecologists, ecosystems are characterized by properties that their individual parts don't have but which emerge from the system as a whole. Intelligence emerges from the brain, flocking behavior emerges in birds, and hill-building emerges from ant colonies. None of these things are directed by a leader or organizing entity, they emerge from the system. Emergent properties are the consequence of the rich interaction between the system's many parts and can't be attributed to particular agents in the system.[48]

Displacing this concept to our context, pharmaceutical innovation emerges from the rich interaction between researchers, investors, developers, regulators, physicians, insurers, patients, and others. No single agent or part of the system determines what medicines will emerge, how effective they will be or how affordable they will be. The medicines we get are an emergent property of the pharmaceutical innovation ecosystem.

The pharmaceutical innovation ecosystem is fragile

To ecologists, the sustainability of an ecosystem depends primarily on three things: making efficient use of the natural resources available to them to sustain the system, adapting to environmental change, and mutualistic balance between the different parts of the system. Stable ecosystems, such as the ancient temperate rain forests of the north-western US, achieve these conditions. When these conditions are violated, often by human intervention, ecological instability and sometimes collapse follows. The most famous examples of this are the 1930s Southern Plains dust bowl and the Grand Banks fisheries.[49]

Displaced to pharmaceutical innovation, sustainability depends on the same three things: making efficient use of the economic, human knowledge, and other resources to meet our health needs, adapting to technological and societal change, and achieving balance between the parts of the PIE. If pharmaceutical innovation comes to consume too much of our national resources, if it fails to adapt to society's changing needs, or if parts of the system extract more value than they contribute,[50] the PIE is in danger of failure or collapse.

The pharmaceutical innovation ecosystem can only be managed systemically

To ecologists, ecosystems are densely interconnected webs in which any intervention may have consequences elsewhere in the system. Good practice in ecosystem management is systemic, allowing for both that dense connectivity and society's needs of the system. There are many examples of this in sustainable agriculture and in managing natural environments for sustainable tourism. When ecosystem management is not systemic it has unintended consequences. We see this in degradation of the natural environment and, in time, its failure to meet society's needs.[51]

Displaced to pharmaceutical innovation, connectivity between parts of the PIE also implies that it can only be managed systemically and with the needs of society in mind. Single actions or inactions, that do not consider systemic effects are likely to have unintended consequences for how well the PIE meets society's needs of the system. The damage to the social contract and patient health that this might cause is equivalent to the degradation of the natural environment.[52]

These three lessons are important to raising the debate about the sustainable affordability of innovative medicines. They flow from shifting from a mechanistic paradigm to an ecological one and moving on from using ecosystems as a metaphor. That new paradigm sees all those involved in pharmaceutical innovation as part of a complex adaptive system, the PIE. This allows us to displace concepts from biological ecosystems, which then allow us to understand that pharmaceutical innovation is an emergent property, that the PIE is fragile and that it should be managed systemically, never simplistically. The ecosystem perspective and its lessons are not the resolution to our dilemma about the affordability of innovative medicines. But these are the tools to help us find that resolution.

How can we resolve our dilemma?

In this chapter, I've argued that the discord we see in American society about drug pricing exists because we are on the horns of an unresolved dilemma. Americans want the benefits of innovative medicines, including the ever more advanced and expensive therapies that are in the foreseeable future. At the same time, we want those life-saving, life-prolonging, and life-enhancing benefits to be generally affordable and therefore accessible. The failure to resolve that dilemma leaves us with sterile, polarized debate that doesn't take us forward and risks taking us backwards. That deadlock is hard to break, because making innovative medicines widely affordable is a wicked problem, one that is politically salient, often partisan and, for most of us, a very personal experience.

To move forward, we need a new way of thinking about the issue, a paradigm shift in the true meaning of Thomas Khun's often debased term. And the intricate, multipart nature of pharmaceutical innovation makes it obvious that an ecosystem perspective, which frames the issue as a complex adaptive system, is the appropriate new paradigm. By displacing concepts from biology, the ecosystem perspective tells us that the affordability of innovative medicines is an emergent property that requires systemic, not mechanistic, management. That perspective also tells us that the pharmaceutical innovation ecosystem is a fragile one and that simple actions or inaction might cause it to collapse, in the manner of the Southern Plains dust bowl or the Grand Banks fisheries, to everyone's detriment.

So, how do we resolve this dilemma? We begin by agreeing what we might reasonably aim for and, in contrast, what is unattainable. Our goal is a healthy PIE: a pharmaceutical innovation ecosystem that makes efficient use of society's resources to provide us with medicines that are both innovative and affordable and adapts to our rapidly changing technological and social environments in order to do so sustainably.[53]

By contrast, it is naïve to expect the ecosystem to provide all the medicines we want at the very low prices we've come to expect from generics. If you reflect back on Box 2.1, you will see that, whatever constraints we've placed on ourselves, world-imposed factors make this practically unachievable. Instead, it means asking the ecosystem to deliver us the medicines we want, including those for currently untreatable conditions, at prices that ensure continuity of innovation – but no more than that; because every penny over that amount is money that could be used for other valuable purposes, from social care to education, or left in patients' pockets. Even this moderated goal, which ought to be acceptable to everyone involved in the debate, is big, hairy, and audacious.[54] The premise of this book is that this sustainable state can only be achieved by deliberate and systemic management of the pharmaceutical innovation ecosystem. The aim of that management would be to ensure that all of the various parts of the system are working efficiently and are in balance with each other.

The following chapters will consider how that might be done. The chapter topics, their common structure, and their content all emerged from the research for the book (see Box 2.4). Chapters 3–9 each deal with one part of the PIE, a habitat within the overall ecosystem, and consider who inhabits it, how it works, and what a healthy PIE requires of that habitat. Then, each chapter draws out the critical issues that affect, or will affect, the functioning of that habitat and its relationship with the PIE as a whole. The final sections of each chapter will consider some of the possible approaches to managing that habitat for the overall health of the PIE. This will include elucidating some of the difficult choices and political and practical difficulties inherent in those choices. But, as is appropriate for a complex adaptive system, I will leave those choices and the details of how to execute them with those who should make the decisions. My aim with this book is to inform the debate around the affordability of innovative medicines, not instruct it.

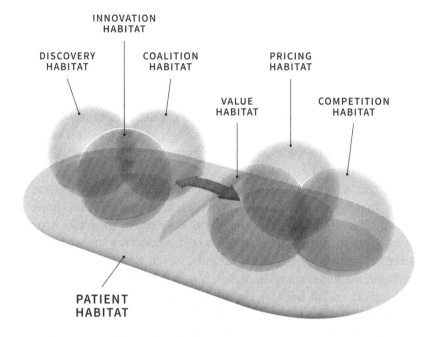

INNOVATION
HABITAT

DISCOVERY
HABITAT

COALITION
HABITAT

PRICING
HABITAT

VALUE
HABITAT

COMPETITION
HABITAT

PATIENT
HABITAT

Figure 2.1 The component habitats of the pharmaceutical innovation ecosystem

Box 2.4 How do you research a wicked problem?

I was trained as a research chemist and began my career at the laboratory bench. Although I didn't learn the words until much later, I was steeped in a logical positivist epistemology and drilled in quantitative scientific methods. More than 40 years later, those views and practices are still central to how I work. I may share that background and those habits with many of the readers of this book. But when, after 20 or so years in industry, I became an academic researcher in a business school, this old dog had to learn new tricks.[55] The research questions I was facing, which concerned how pharmaceutical companies compete and evolve, were simply not amenable to my one-tool toolbox. I had to learn qualitative methods that I'd previously looked down upon and develop a pragmatist epistemology.[56] This unusually two-sided background informed the research for the book.

I began the research with unstructured discussions with eight people, each of whom have deep knowledge of different aspects of how innovative medicines reach patients. I supplemented these interviews with a wide-ranging, catholic literature search, as is always necessary at the early stages of such work. This allowed me to understand the huge breadth of the PIE and its component habitats. Although I recognize the oversimplification, the working model that came out of this early work is shown in Figure 2.1.

But this scoping research also taught me that no one person could make sense of each of these parts of the PIE, let alone the whole system. The hideous complexity of, for example, drug development or the systems of market exclusivity and patents, makes it necessary to be immersed in each field for years just to begin to understand it. Inevitably, that immersion develops subjectivity too. It became obvious that I would need to tap into the wisdom of many experts who differed not only in their expertise but also in their opinions. I'd then need to find a way of synthesizing their individual, differing perspectives.[57]

To achieve this, I sought 6 or more people in each of the PIE's habitats, a total of 70 expert informants. In each group, I tried to achieve a blend of complementary perspectives so that, while they all shared a high level of experience and expertise, they did not share the same views. Each of these experts gave generously of their time, with interviews and written answers. Each focused on their part of the PIE, but willingly shared their views on contiguous parts of the system with which they had experience. Alongside this primary research phase I continued to develop the literature review, which was greatly helped by experts pointing to what I had missed.

I then synthesized their views and the extended literature review into ten long documents, which I called "first iteration syntheses." These tried to capture everything I had learned about each area, and especially tried to "see the forest for the trees." I shared these with my expert informants which, as intended, released an avalanche of further input, that I captured via more interviews and correspondence. This expert input and literature background provided the raw material for the book. However, while these inputs were the beginning of my expert informants' contribution, they were not the end. As I developed drafts of each chapter, I shared these with the relevant experts, who again offered constructive criticism. The findings of the following chapters therefore owe their relevance and originality to those expert informants, while any errors of fact or thought belong exclusively to me.

The research method underpinning this book, based on critically synthesizing the views of expert informants and the extant literature, is not the only method I could have adopted. But it was the only method I thought capable of addressing such a wicked question.

Kelly LM, Cordeiro M.

Notes

1 Although I am considering this from a US perspective, what happens in the US has global importance because around 48% of global pharmaceutical sales are in the US. See: https://www.statista.com/statistics/266547/total-value-of-world-pharmaceutical-market-by-submarket-since-2006/.
2 Mazzucato, with her colleague Henry Lishi Li, made this point in a "head to head" debate article in the British Medical Journal. Although she has particular views on the pharmaceutical industry, she expresses similar views on state involvement in industry generally and innovative industries in particular. See 1.
3 Zieff and his co-authors do acknowledge the "significant upfront costs and logistical challenges" associated with their recommendations, but they pay rather less attention to the cultural political barriers of transplanting essentially European ideas into a US context. See ref 2.
4 For a balanced, insightful discussion of how universal healthcare, or "Medicare for All" might work in the US, listen to the discussion between Wharton's Mark Pauly and Drexel's Robert Field at https://knowledge.wharton.upenn.edu/article/could-universal-health-care-work-in-the-u-s/.
5 During the writing of this chapter, the Commonwealth Fund announced a commission that seeks to articulate a vision for how U.S. federal authority, resources, and leadership can join to create a national public health infrastructure, one that improves health and equity every day and enhances the nation's preparedness for future crises. See https://www.commonwealthfund.org/about-us/public-health-commission?utm_source=alert&utm_medium=email&utm_campaign=Improving+Health+Care+Quality.

6 Research into this polarization reveals both an increasing trend but also that opinions are strongly correlated to age and party affiliation. See ref 3.

7 After almost 200 years, De Tocqueville's observations on American exceptionalism remain useful. See ref 4.

8 This quote is taken from the website of Patients for Affordable Drugs (https://patientsforaffordabledrugs.org/). In using it, I neither support nor criticize it. But the strength of the language, from a major pressure group and not from an outlying individual, illustrates the polarization of the debate.

9 The PhRMA, which represents pharmaceutical innovators, is generally more restrained in its comments, as one would expect of an experienced and professional pressure group. But, on November 2nd 2021, speaking of then-current policy proposals to enable Medicare negotiation, the PhRMA president said, "Under the guise of 'negotiation,' it gives the government the power to dictate how much a medicine is worth and leaves many patients facing a future with less access to medicines and fewer new treatments." (See https://phrma.org/resource-center/Topics/Cost-and-Value/PhRMA-Statement-on-Democrats-Drug-Pricing-Deal-in-Reconciliation-Package.) Again, I am neither supporting nor criticizing this statement. I am merely using it to exemplify the polarization of the debate on drug affordability.

10 Although both sides indulge in hyperbole, one striking example of this the PhRMA campaign in the Fall of 2021, which was judged to be an inaccurate portrayal of recent legislation. (See https://www.factcheck.org/2021/10/phrma-ad-misleads-on-medicare-drug-negotiation-legislation/.)

11 A good discussion of the strain the pharmaceutical social contract is under can be found at: https://www.statnews.com/2020/03/13/mending-broken-social-contract-pharmaceutical-pricing-innovation/. Although not specifically about the social contract between society and the pharmaceutical industry, a 2020 report by the McKinsey Global Institute paints a thought-provoking picture of how the relationship between individuals and institutions is evolving. To quote that report: *"While many have benefited from this evolution, for a significant number of individuals the changes are spurring uncertainty, pessimism, and a general loss of trust in institutions."* (See https://www.mckinsey.com/industries/public-and-social-sector/our-insights/the-social-contract-in-the-21st-century.)

12 A good summary of the impact of demographic can be found in a report by the American Hospital Association. Its headlines include that the over-65 population will triple by 2030 and that six out of every ten of these will be managing more than one chronic condition (See https://www.healthdesign.org/sites/default/files/news/How%20Boomers%20Will%20Change%20Health%20Care.pdf).

13 A 2021 projection of US prescription spending, led by Boston University, predicted that "Total drug spending will grow from 13.7% to 13.9% of National Health Expenditure, from about $500 billion in 2018 to $863 billion in 2028" and "Two factors contribute substantively to drug spending growth: new drugs and expanded use of existing, high-price drugs." See ref 5.

14 The relationship between wealth inequality and health inequality is well-accepted. In 2021, Ana V. Diez Roux summarized this as:

> We have enough evidence from multiple sources to know that inequality (including wealth inequality) is a key driver of population health and of the stark disparities in health by race and class present in our society. The question now is, can we act on this knowledge?

See ref 6.

15 These views were expressed in a poll whose findings may have been distorted by its method (See https://www.filesforprogress.org/memos/pharma-reforms.

pdf) but more recent and rigorous research by the Kaiser Foundation points in the same direction. (See https://www.kff.org/health-costs/poll-finding/public-opinion-on-prescription-drugs-and-their-prices/.)

16 To quote from this work: *"The search for scientific bases for confronting problems of social policy is bound to fail, because of the nature of these problems. They are 'wicked' problems, whereas science has developed to deal with 'tame' problems."* See ref 7. A more recent review of the "wicked problem" concept can be found here: See ref 8.

17 The salience of an issue is important not just in quantitative terms but also in qualitative terms. When an issue is salient, we don't just react more to it compared to a less salient issue, we react differently. This is a well understood phenomenon in social policy. To quote from one especially insightful article of this topic: *"Long lines of research have taught us that both citizens and political elites may respond differently to issues that are salient to them than to those that are not."* See ref 7.

18 More than 60% of registered voters thought these salient issues were "very important" and the economy consistently tops such polls. (See https://www.pewresearch.org/politics/2020/08/13/important-issues-in-the-2020-election/.) Hence the 1992 quip by President Clinton's strategist James Carville: "It's the economy, stupid."

19 The issue of partisan polarization is well described. To quote:

> *In 2019, average Democrats differed from average Republicans in their views across 30 policy-related issues about what government should do in the future by 39 percentage points, more than double the gap in 1994. What is not often recognized is how profoundly divided those who identify as Democrats and Republicans are on key issues of health care policy today, such as Medicaid spending and abortion.*

See refs 8, 9.

20 President Obama's comments are taken from his interview in "The Atlantic." See ref 10. The view that identity politics exacerbates political division is well described by Amy Chua. See ref 11.

21 The observation that party affiliation changes little is taken from comparisons between 2018 and 2019 but fits with longer term studies. (See https://www.pewresearch.org/politics/2020/08/04/voters-rarely-switch-parties-but-recent-shifts-further-educational-racial-divergence/.) This work also noted that the politically consistent are more politically engaged than party switchers, which seems to amplify the effect of party allegiances.

22 The TruthinRX website is another example of the polarization and sterility of the debate around the affordability of medicines. Even if one accepts the moving anecdotes that the site collects (and I have no reason to doubt them), it offers little constructive by way of resolving the issue. (See truthinrx.org).

23 In an interesting 2020 meta-analysis, researchers from the University of Texas found that, while overall statistical evidence exerts a greater impact on persuasion than anecdotal evidence, anecdotal evidence is more persuasive than statistical evidence when emotional engagement is high, as when issues involve a severe threat, health, or oneself. See ref 12.

24 The impact of social media as a news source is arguably one of the most underestimated factors in the drug pricing debate. About a third of Americans get their news from Facebook, for example. (See https://www.pewresearch.org/fact-tank/2021/06/01/facts-about-americans-and-facebook/.)

25 See ref 13.

26 There is a particular phrase in Kuhn's work that strikes me as exceptionally apposite to our need to look at the issue of the affordability of innovative medicines in a different way.

> ...*Scientific revolutions are inaugurated by a growing sense, again often restricted to a narrow subdivision of the scientific community, that an existing paradigm has ceased to function adequately in the exploration of an aspect of nature to which that paradigm itself had previously led the way. .... the sense of malfunction that can lead to crisis is prerequisite to revolution.*

To my mind, the phrase a "sense of malfunction" is good description of how I feel when listen to the current sterile debate. See Kuhn, TS, 1962. Page 104. See ref 14.

27 In these cases, you can sense that the term is being used to imply efficiency or productivity of the innovation process. See for example 15.

28 This was the reasoning behind the Elijah E. Cummings Lower Drug Costs Now Act, a.k.a. H.R.3, introduced to the House of Representatives in September 2019 and passed the following December. In an illustration of the partisan divide on the subject, the Republican controlled senate did not bring up the bill for a vote.

29 To quote from one paper typical of this perspective: "...*volatility in the expected firm's profitability will negatively impact its market capitalization, and hence limit its capacity to fund R&D activities in detriment of future innovations.*" See ref 16.

30 The flawed use of the mechanistic paradigm is not restricted to pharmaceutical innovation. For a good review of why economic systems are better described by analogy to biology, few express it better than Hodgson:

> *Unfortunately, the metaphor of a machine excludes knowledge, qualitative change and irreversibility through time, and entraps economics in an equilibrium schema. The value of the alternative metaphor from biology consists in part in its remedy to these deficiencies and in part as an allied science of complexity.*

See ref 17.

31 This is particularly seen in work that looks at the wider industry sector, including its links to academia. See refs 18 and 19.

32 McKinsey's emphasis here is that the growth in China's life sciences ecosystem is, despite the current lack of globally important pharmaceutical companies, the antecedent to the growth of a research-based industry. See ref 20.

33 The implicit assumption of these aspirant hubs is that their local pharmaceutical industry ecosystem supports the growth of immigrant companies. This has become a fashionable way to talk about the sector. See https://mcamericas. org/news-events/news/what-is-a-life-sciences-ecosystem, https://www.gensler. com/blog/considerations-for-life-sciences-ecosystems-developers.

34 The philosophy of science has a long history of oscillation between reductionist, mechanistic paradigms and more holistic, ecological paradigms. An interesting review of this captures the differences between them nicely:

> *The basic tension is one between the parts and the whole. The emphasis on the parts has been called mechanistic, reductionist, or atomistic, the emphasis on the whole, holistic, organismic, or ecological. In twentieth-century science, the holistic perspective has become known as 'systemic' and the way of thinking it implies 'systems thinking,' as we have mentioned.*

See ref 21.

35 This point is well discussed in George Lakoff's classic text. See ref 22.

36 The promise and problems of metaphor in science communication is well discussed by Taylor and Dewsbury. See ref 23.

37 The idea of ontological communality, as distinct from analogy or metaphor, is at the center of Hodgson and Knudsen's book "Darwin's Conjecture." Although it

sounds intimidating, it translates, simply and accurately, as "thinking in the same way." See ref 24.

38 A succinct, interesting, and beautifully understated history of the term ecosystem is provided by Willis:

> The now widely used term 'ecosystem' has had quite a long history and at various times interest has been focused on different aspects of its meaning. Not infrequently the term has been imprecisely or even incorrectly employed. This account aims to outline the changing emphasis of the term and seeks to promote its more exact use.

See ref 25.

39 Moore's colorfully titled article and following book can probably be said to have initiated the fashion for using the term ecosystem in business circles: To quote him directly: *"In fact, it's largely competition among business ecosystems, not individual companies, that's fueling today's industrial transformation."* While Moore deserves some credit for that, the main premise of the article is not particularly compelling and fails to differentiate clearly from other related concepts, such as networks or even supply chains. See ref 26.

40 Moore's book illustrates this well. It takes quite a narrow view of the ecosystem, mostly referring to it being built around specific firms. See ref 27.

41 In the discussion of complex adaptive systems, you may recognize features from other domains such as systems thinking, non-linear dynamical systems or agent-based modelling. That is because they are all overlapping aspects of the same broad domain of complexity science. The Santa Fe Institute provides a good introduction to complexity science. See https://www.santafe.edu/what-is-complex-systems-science.

42 This is list is based mostly on Paul Cilliers' excellent "Complexity and Post Modernism: Understanding Complex Systems," although the wording has been simplified for clarity. Other characterizations of complex adaptive systems say much the same thing. See ref 28.

43 The story of how the Thalidomide tragedy, which resulted in more than 10,000 birth defects, shaped the US regulatory environment is a perfect example of the path-dependency of the current pharmaceutical environment. (See https://embryo.asu.edu/pages/us-regulatory-response-thalidomide-1950-2000.)

44 Hatch-Waxman, and its later amendments, were aimed at balancing the ecosystem so that it both encouraged pharmaceutical innovation and realized the benefits of generic competition. It had mixed results, both encouraging generics, but also producing some unintended consequences of "gaming" of the patent system. A good review of the act and its implications, written 25 years after its passing, was provided by Rumore. See ref 29.

45 An interesting example of what happens when interaction is hindered was provided by the COVID pandemic, which provided a small natural experimental demonstration of how stopping interactions hindered the working of the clinical development part of the system. However, it also seems to have demonstrated that the clinical trials process is more flexible than many thought. See ref 30.

46 One of the most strikingly paradoxical things I observed during the research for this book was that the impressively deep knowledge of the experts I interviewed was often accompanied by surprising ignorance of industry topics with which they were not involved. This is an indication of how complex pharmaceutical innovation is.

47 Donald Schön was an exceptionally interesting and versatile thinker. A philosopher and professor of urban planning, his own difficulties in understanding

how planning systems work led him to develop the displacement of concepts idea. This led to him becoming one of the most influential people in the field of organizational learning. See ref 31.

48 This is a necessarily simplified description of emergence and emergent properties. A fuller, broader explanation of emergence in the context of social structures, as opposed to physical or biological systems, can be found in Cilliers (ibid).

49 Two factors make the Grand Banks and the Dust Bowl interesting examples of unsustainable ecosystems that are relevant in the context of pharmaceutical innovation. First, in both cases their collapse was preceded by a period of very high yield, such that predictions of ecosystem collapse could be and were dismissed. Second, although in both cases there was an apparent single cause (drought, over-fishing), the reality of each collapse was a much more complex story. See ref 32 and 33.

50 The concept of balance in ecosystems should not be misunderstood as some form of selflessness or altruism. In all ecosystems, agents attempt to get more out and put less in. Balance is achieved by a constant, dynamic tension between parts of the system. Only when some part of the ecosystem has the power to extract more than it contributes does the system lose its balance. I suggest you hold on to this idea as it becomes especially relevant in the pricing and competition habitats later in this book. A good description of this from an ecology perspective is given by Begon and Townsend. See ref 34.

51 In a strange coincidence, as I wrote these words about the unintended, often negative, consequences of simplistic interventions into ecosystem, my streaming service chose to play me the Joni Mitchell song "Big Yellow Taxi." The line "give me spots on my apples but leave me the birds on the trees" seemed especially resonant.

52 Peter Kolchinsky rightly focuses on the importance of maintaining the social contract although he focuses particularly on ways that society might damage the contract, for example by price controls, with somewhat less emphasis on how the pharmaceutical innovators might weaken the relationship. See ref 35.

53 If you have followed my argument, you will see immediately that this goal is somewhat tautological because innovative, affordable, efficient and adaptable are the requirements for a sustainable pharmaceutical innovation ecosystem. To aspire to a long-term resolution is to aim for all four of those characteristics.

54 The term "big, hairy, audacious goal" ("BHAG") is borrowed from Collins' and Porras' 1994 book "Built to Last." Their idea is that great achievements are facilitated by goals that are very difficult to achieve but within the realms of possibility. Although the phrase has become a superficial meme in many business circles, a wider reading of their work shows that BHAGs depend on being able to see the line between desirable and possible and having some idea about how to get to the goal. The concept is apposite for what we need to achieve in pharmaceutical innovation.

55 I am and always will be indebted to my brilliant and very understanding PhD supervisor, Professor Malcolm McDonald. I vividly remember sitting in his office at Cranfield University, feeling perplexed and frustrated. His advice that day has stayed with me forever. "Before you try to *prove* anything, try to *understand* it first."

56 As an epistemological position, pragmatism has a meaning that is related to but deeper than the everyday usage of the word. I like the way Kelly and Cordeiro express it: "*...pragmatism is premised on the idea that research can steer clear of metaphysical debates about the nature of truth and reality and focus instead on 'practical understandings' of concrete, real-world issues.*" See 1. If this interests you,

I can strongly recommend the historical description of its origins in "The Metaphysical Club" (Louis Menand, 2001).

57 Readers familiar with qualitative research will recognize that I eventually chose a modified form of the Delphi methodology. The principal difference between this and traditional Delphi approaches was that I didn't seek to build a consensus view, but rather to differentiate between what was generally understood in each area and what was not. You can find considerations of the Delphi method in any good qualitative methods textbook.

References

1. Mazzucato M, Li HL, Darzi A. Is it time to nationalise the pharmaceutical industry? *British Medical Journal.* 2020;368:m769–m.

2 Zieff G, Kerr ZY, Moore JB, Stoner L. Universal healthcare in the United States of America: A healthy debate. *Medicina (Kaunas, Lithuania).* 2020;56(11):580.

3 Yuan Y, Lee KS, Lu Y. Public support for government intervention in health care in the United States from 1984 to 2016. *Socius: Sociological Research for a Dynamic World.* 2022;8.

4 Eisenberg DA. Tocqueville on liberty, inequality, and American exceptionalism. *Public Discourse: The Journal of the Witherspoon Institute* [Internet]. 2019. Available from: https://www.thepublicdiscourse.com/2019/05/51178/.

5 Conti RM, Turner A, Hughes-Cromwick, P. Projections of US prescription drug spending and key policy implications. *JAMA Health Forum.* 2021;2(1):2.

6 Diez Roux AV. The pervasive influence of wealth inequality on health. *JAMA Health Forum.* 2021;2(7):e211647–e.

7 Epstein L, Segal JA. Measuring issue salience. *American Journal of Political Science.* 2000;44(1):66–83.

8 Blendon RJ, Benson JM. Implications of the 2020 election for U.S. health policy. *The New England Journal of Medicine.* 2020;383(18):E105–e.

9 Blendon RJ, Benson JM, Schneider EC. The future of health policy in a partisan United States: Insights from public opinion polls. *JAMA: The Journal of the American Medical Association.* 2021;325(13):1253–4.

10 Goldberg J. Why Obama fears for our democracy. *The Atlantic* [Internet]. 2020. Available from: https://www.theatlantic.com/ideas/archive/2020/11/why-obama-fears-for-our-democracy/617087/.

11 Chua A. *Political Tribes.* London: Bloomsbury; 2018.

12 Freling TH, Yang Z, Saini R, Itani OS, Rashad Abualsamh R. When poignant stories outweigh cold hard facts: A meta-analysis of the anecdotal bias. *Organizational Behavior and Human Decision Processes.* 2020;160:51–67.

13 Steele H. Patent restrictions and price competition in the ethical drugs industry. *The Journal of Industrial Economics.* 1964;12(3):198–223.

14 Kuhn T. *The Structure of Scientific Revolutions.* 50th Anniversary Edition ed. University of Chicago Press; 1962.

15 Evens RP, Kaitin KI. The biotechnology innovation machine: A source of intelligent biopharmaceuticals for the pharma industry-mapping biotechnology's success. *Clinical Pharmacology and Therapeutics.* 2014;95(5):528–32.

16 Moreno SG, Epstein D. The price of innovation - the role of drug pricing in financing pharmaceutical innovation. A conceptual framework. *Journal of Market Access & Health Policy.* 2019;7(1):1583536-.

17 Hodgson GM. The economy as an organism - not a machine. *Futures: The Journal of Policy, Planning and Futures Studies*. 1993;25(4):12.
18 Kennedy J. How to ensure that America's life-sciences sector remains globally competitive; 2020. Information Technology and Innovation Foundation.
19 Melese T, Heather F, Marshall, A. The evolution of life science ecosystems. IBM 2015.
20 Han KLD, Franck; Zhang, Fangning; Zhou, Josie. The dawn of China biopharma innovation 2021. Available from: https://www.mckinsey.com/industries/life-sciences/our-insights/the-dawn-of-china-biopharma-innovation.
21 Capra F. *The Systems View of Life: A Unifying Vision.* Cambridge: Cambridge University Press; 2016.
22 Lakoff G. *The Metaphors We Live By.* Chicago, IL: University of Chicago Press; 1980.
23 Taylor C, Dewsbury BM. On the problem and promise of metaphor use in science and science communication. *Journal Microbiology Biology Education.* 2018;19(1):19.1.46.
24 Hodgson GM, Knudsen T. *Darwin's Conjecture: The Search for General Principles of Social and Economic Evolution.* Chicago, IL: Chicago University Press; 2010.
25 Willis AJ. The ecosystem: An evolving concept viewed historically. *Functional Ecology.* 1997;11(2):268–71.
26 Moore JF. Predators and prey: A new ecology of competition. 1993;71(3):75–86. Available from: https://go.exlibris.link/WYrVBNRH.
27 Moore JF. *The Death of Competition: Leadership and Strategy in the Age of Business Ecosystems.* New York: HarperBusiness; 1996.
28 Cilliers P, Spurrett D. *Complexity and post-modernism: understanding complex systems.* South African Journal of Philosophy. 1999;18(2):258–74.
29 Rumore MM. The Hatch-Waxman Act--25 years later: Keeping the pharmaceutical scales balanced. *Pharmacy Times* [Internet]. 2009. Available from: https://www.pharmacytimes.com/view/generic-hatchwaxman-0809.
30 Ledford H. The COVID pandemic's lingering impact on clinical trials. *Nature (London).* 2021;595(7867):341–2.
31 Schon DA. *The Displacement of Concepts.* London: Tavistock; 1963.
32 Harris M. *Lament for an Ocean: The Collapse of the Atlantic Cod Fishery: A True Crime Story.* Toronto: McClelland & Stewart Ltd; 1998.
33 Worster D. *Dust Bowl: The Southern Plains in the 1930s.* Oxford: Oxford University Press; 1992.
34 Begon MT, Colin R. *Ecology: From Individuals to Ecosystems.* 5th ed. Oxford: Wiley; 2021.
35 Kolchinsky P. *The Great American Drug Deal.* Boston, MA: Evelexa Press; 2020.
36 Kelly LM, Cordeiro M. Three principles of pragmatism for research on organizational processes. *Methodological Innovations.* 2020;13(2):2059799120937242.

3 The discovery habitat

Precis

- Research relevant to pharmaceutical innovation varies from basic, curiosity-driven research to applied, solution-driven research.
- The discovery habitat is the part of the pharmaceutical innovation ecosystem (PIE) where basic research happens.
- The discovery habitat is inhabited largely by academic research institutions, with the publicly funded National Institutes of Health (NIH) taking a central role in funding and direction of research.
- The discovery habitat connects to the innovation and coalition habitats.
- A healthy PIE requires that the discovery habitat provide access to a substantial flow of relevant new knowledge that is likely to translate into pharmaceutical innovation.
- The discovery habitat's ability to support a healthy PIE is constrained by:
  - Uneven public funding that has hindered the discovery habitat's ability to adapt to its rapidly changing technological and sociological environments
  - Embedded cultures that have hindered the co-evolution of the discovery, innovation, and coalition habitats
  - The conflation of translational science with translational research, leading to a "tragedy of the commons" effect that reduces the predictivity of the discovery habitat's outputs
- The discovery habitat would be better able to support a healthy PIE if:
  - Its funding were increased and made more predictable
  - Its activities were more aligned toward society's health and economic needs

DOI: 10.4324/9781003330271-3

- Academic and commercial cultures and practices were better aligned
- Translational science, rather than translational research, was transformed

An apothecary's garden is a particularly apposite metaphor for the part of the pharmaceutical innovation ecosystem (PIE) where the basic scientific research is done. As in any other garden, the apothecary's soil was the ultimate source of a plentiful and sustainable harvest. By providing the essential nutrients for medicinal plants, the soil was the basis of the entire ecosystem. In the PIE, basic research plays the same role,[1] providing the fundamental knowledge that, eventually and laboriously, grows into innovative medicines. As I'll discuss more in this chapter and in Chapter 4, The Innovation Habitat, basic research doesn't really invent new, usable drugs.[2] Rather, it discovers the new knowledge that is the essential starting point in their journey to market. For that reason, and because it is a sub-environment within the overall PIE, I've called this part of the ecosystem the discovery habitat.

But what is basic research? As I explored this topic, by reading the published literature and talking to my expert informants, two salient points emerged.

First, the definition of basic research is fuzzy.[3] Its borders with applied research are indistinct and, to some extent, basic research fits into the category of "I know it when I see it."[4] In my exploration, I'm going to avoid this semantic quicksand and use the working definition that basic research is research motivated mostly by curiosity and is not directed at product development. This is an imperfect but good-enough definition.

The second salient point to emerge is that, to a very large degree, basic research is taken to be synonymous with scientific and technological research, while other domains of knowledge, such as social sciences and organizational research, are relatively neglected.[5] In an area like pharmaceutical innovation, which is carried out by many different interacting organizations to meet both the clinical and non-clinical needs of patients, in the context of society's healthcare system, this is a narrow way to frame what basic research is. Many of the expert informants made this point and expert informant Eleanor Perfetto expressed this view eloquently:

If basic research was about patients' experience and lives as much as it is currently about products' features and presumed benefits it would completely change the way we define pharmaceutical innovation and the way we create it.

Eleanor Perfetto

So, understanding the discovery habitat and how it provides the fundamental knowledge that drives pharmaceutical innovation can't just be an issue of science and technology alone. We need a wider, fuller definition than that. See Box 3.1.

Box 3.1 What do we mean by basic research in pharmaceutical innovation?

At one level, basic research is easily recognized and distinct from applied research. Vannevar Bush said it is "performed without thought to practical ends" and "results in general knowledge of and understanding of nature and its laws." Other authors often refer to it being "curiosity driven" as opposed to "solution oriented." These seem good-enough working definitions, allowing us to both differentiate between basic and applied research and to appreciate that there's a fuzzy overlap between the two.

But definition is not just about differentiation; we need to be clear not only about what is outside of basic research but also about what is included in that category. When I explored that question, something important emerged. Firstly, the curiosity-driven work carried out in the name of pharmaceutical innovation is dominated by scientific and technological research, such as how the body works and what happens when it doesn't work well. Only a much smaller part of it is focused on organizational and sociological research, such as how complementary bodies of knowledge are brought together to create innovative medicines and how human behavior shapes the requirements for them and their use in the real world. Secondly, even that limited amount of organizational and sociological research is performed in a way that imitates the scientific and technological research, approaching a very different set of problems with much the same set of mental attitudes and research tools.[6]

To someone like me, who has been fortunate to train as both a physical scientist and a social scientist, this seems problematic. It is reminiscent of CP Snow's famous lectures about societal progress being hindered by the divisions between two, mutually ignorant cultures.[7] The nature of basic research in pharmaceutical innovation also seems to be a clear example of something organizational researchers call "institutional isomorphism," a sort of organizational groupthink that occurs when organizations in the same field behave similarly not because that's the right thing to do but because of various sociological forces.[8] Whatever the explanation, framing basic research in pharmaceutical innovation as mostly about biological science and performing it using the tools of the natural sciences seems a narrow, limiting way of creating essential fundamental knowledge.

So, in this exploration of how we might manage and enrich the basic research "soil" of the pharmaceutical innovation ecosystem, I am of course going to include the basic scientific and technological research we automatically think of. But I'm also going to consider the organizational and sociological research that is its necessary but rather less considered complement.

Although the "curiosity driven vs solution oriented" distinction is a useful one, it's important to recognize that basic and applied research differ not only in their goals but also in their practices and in their underlying culture. This can be hard for a non-scientist to grasp but the differences in their practices are well illustrated by Figures 3.1 and 3.2.[9]

It's not necessary to fully understand every part of these diagrams but note how little of each figure is in the basic research area. What struck me most as I looked at these figures was that basic and applied research, for all their connectivity, involve very different activities. Applied research to develop innovative medicines is not simply the "scaling up" of work that has already been done in basic research; it includes many additional sets of activities that are not part of basic research. The capabilities required by individuals and by organizations in the two fields are quite different. Many of the expert informants had experience in basic research, and this difference between basic and applied was often mentioned. Daniel Cohen captured their shared view well:

*Having worked as a scientist in both basic research and in a commercial busi-
ness, the differences in practice are extensive and significant. They include the
scale of the work done, obviously, but also critical factors such as the models
chosen and the characterization of outcomes. It is essential that the criteria for
in vivo model selection and study design principles be transparent in product
development. Academic studies may accept trade-offs for expediency (model
availability) or cost (cohort size) that may be viewed differently in industry, and
this gap limits the ability to build directly upon such studies without investing
in extensive validation/reproducibility studies.*

Daniel Cohen

But there is more that divides basic and applied researchers than just
the work they do. Academic researchers who study organizational
culture think of the everyday practices and behaviors in an organization as the explicit artifacts of an organization's mostly implicit culture.
This means that the differences in practice between basic and applied
research, mentioned by the expert informants, are also the visible
indicators of fundamental differences between their organizational
cultures.[10] Although, to an outsider, basic and applied researchers are
both scientists working on new medicines, they are quite different
creatures. The behaviors that are appropriate, the values they hold
and the beliefs that underly behaviors and values differ significantly
between basic and applied researchers. This is not to say one is better
or worse than the other, only that each is differently adapted to its
own context. Again, this was a common theme in the observations of
the expert informants and Michael Jackson expressed it clearly:

*Compared to a product-development setting, the culture that operates in an
academic, basic research setting is quite different. Research is often arranged
around key individuals who have a large degree of personal freedom, although
paradoxically they have a heavy administrative load related to research grants.
They are driven very strongly by the need to publish, which in turn pushes
them towards narrow, single theory research and discourages sharing of data.
It's not that this is a good or bad thing, it is simply what works, or has worked,
in that academic environment and it's different from what works in other,
non-academic, environments.*

Michael Jackson

So, a first look at the discovery habitat, the "soil" of the PIE, tells us
two important things. First, it's richer than we might first think. It
contains the sociological and organizational, as well as scientific and
technological, knowledge, that is needed to bring pharmaceutical innovations to market. Second, the discovery habitat is as distinct from

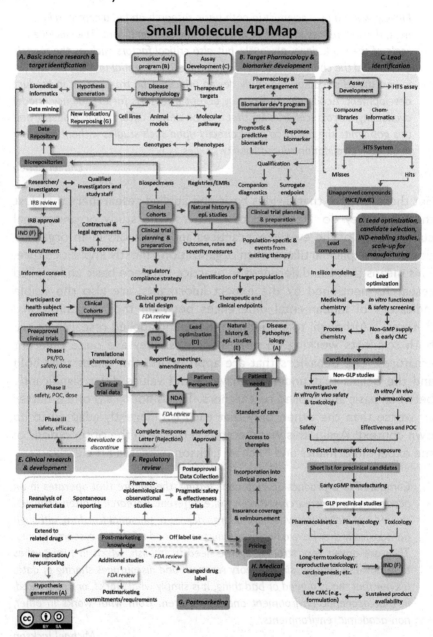

Figure 3.1 The small molecule development pathway

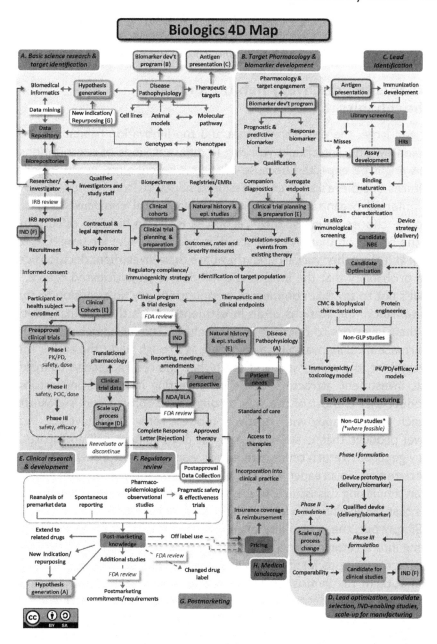

Figure 3.2 The biologics development pathway

the innovation habitat as a plant is from its soil. It is different in its aims. It is different in the scale and scope of its practices. It is different in the beliefs, values, and behaviors of its culture. As I'll describe in the following sections, these characteristics of the discovery habitat shape how it contributes to the functioning of the wider PIE.

What is the discovery habitat and who inhabits it?

By and large, the discovery habitat and the innovation habitat are occupied by different people working in different kinds of organizations. This might be expected because of their different aims, practices, and cultures but there's an even more fundamental reason: money. Where commercial organizations, such as pharmaceutical companies and biotechs, choose to invest their resources is driven by their calculation of the return on that investment, adjusted for risk and for time. Or, to look at it the other way around, they base their investment decisions on the probability that the investment will deliver an anticipated return.[11] That's not to say that commercial organizations pay no attention to the non-financial implications of an investment but it's their primary duty to their investors to optimize their wealth.[12] The investments made in pharmaceutical innovation are risky and, as a rough guide, the earlier the investment, the riskier it is and the higher the return needed to make that investment attractive. Someone investing in a well-understood product that is most of the way through development and is close to launch will be happy with relatively modest returns. An investor in a novel product that is still very early in development will anticipate a very generous return on investment or else will invest elsewhere. I appreciate that, to a reader well versed in investment finance, I am greatly over-simplifying this issue. But it is these investment finance fundamentals that determine who inhabit the discovery habitat.

Simply put, the probability of an investment in basic research translating into a return on investment is so small and so far away that the return required to justify it would be incredible, in the original sense of that term. So, in most countries and in most markets, including and especially pharmaceuticals, purely commercial entities can't survive in the discovery habitat.[13] In the natural world, when harsh habitats exclude most life forms, the gap is filled by species who survive in unusual ways.[14] In the same way, the absence of commercial entities means that the discovery habitat has instead become populated by non-commercial entities and, in particular, by publicly and philanthropically funded academic research.[15]

In the discovery habitat, the dominant public entity is the NIH, which currently spends about $42 billion a year.[16] The NIH is analogous to what biologists term a "keystone species," meaning an entity that holds the rest of the ecosystem together.[17] The NIH plays a unique and fundamental role in the discovery habitat and, to understand that role, it's important to grasp some important points of detail about this hugely important entity. First, NIH funding has a history of fluctuation and has not attained its 2003 real-terms peak of funding, even after several recent years of growth.[18] Second, not all NIH spending is on basic research; much of it is spent on applied research. From 2003 to 2020, between 40 and 50% of its budget distribution was designated as applied.[19] Third, the large majority of NIH spending and activity is "extra-mural," meaning it is allocated in the form of competitive research grants to bodies outside the NIH, such as universities. Finally, the NIH is less of a single entity and more of a conglomeration of bodies. It has a very complex structure, with 27 sub-units, such as the National Cancer Institute and the National Center for Translational Science, and an even more sub-divided organizational structure beneath that.[20] When thinking about the NIH's role in the discovery habitat, it's important not to think of it as a single-minded body that is purely focused on basic research. As expert informant Matthew McMahon described it succinctly:

> *Each of the Institutes and Centers fund a mix of basic, translational,[21] clinical, and implementation science. Each of them is constantly working on getting that mix right.*
>
> Matthew McMahon

Important as it is, the NIH is not the only funder of the discovery habitat. There is also a lesser but significant role for philanthropy. Data is hard to come by in this area and transparency is one of the issues in understanding its role.[22] In general, it's true to say that philanthropic organizations play a much smaller role in the discovery habitat than does public funding. Not only are the amounts involved much smaller, but it is also diffused across different areas of healthcare, such as health needs in the developing world. Some interesting trends are visible here, however. Generally speaking, charitable giving to medical research is shifting toward larger donations from fewer, richer people. And, while philanthropy has historically complemented public spending by supporting research that did not attract government funding, the trend seems to be shifting toward mirroring public spending patterns. Finally, there is a trend, especially amongst the larger philanthropic institutions, toward spending on late-stage research and early development via investment rather than research grants, a trend known as venture philanthropy.[23] As with the NIH, when thinking about the philanthropic funding of pharmaceutical innovation, it's inaccurate to think of a monolithic entity giving money generously to basic researchers. Medical philanthropy is much more complex than that.[24]

So, the discovery habitat is largely populated by academic institutions funded mostly by the NIH but with some lesser role for philanthropy. Beneath this superficially simple picture lie two observable features that are important to how this habitat contributes to the PIE. First, the variable, politicized nature of NIH funding, at a time when scientific possibilities are expanding, suggests that the US might be neglecting the soil of pharmaceutical innovation. Second, the complexity and politicization of NIH resource allocation, echoed by that in the philanthropic sector, suggests that the soil might not be providing the right nutrients (that is, new knowledge) to support a healthy PIE. It was with these concerns in mind that I continued to explore the discovery habitat and I began by asking what the PIE requires of it.

What does a healthy PIE require of the discovery habitat?

The discovery habitat takes inputs from the patient habitat, in the form of funding, legislation, and direction, and uses them to create fundamental knowledge. That knowledge feeds into the innovation habitat, which works with the coalition habitat, to create innovative medicines. Importantly, the knowledge needed to create affordable and innovative medicines isn't just about biology and medicine. Although it's less obvious, creating affordable and innovative medicines also needs an understanding of related sociological and organizational subjects, such as how patients behave and how companies work together. It is this rich, varied mixture of knowledge that the innovation and coalition habitats translate into products for the market. At the same time, the discovery habitat creates a substrate of scientifically educated workers.[25] To extend Christopher P Austin's soil metaphor, in the same way that chemical nutrients such as nitrogen, phosphorus, and potassium are taken up from the soil by plants, the nutrients of knowledge and qualified people from NIH and philanthropically funded basic research institutions are taken up into the innovation and coalition habitats, which are made up of mostly commercial entities such as biotech and pharmaceutical companies. But, as any pedologist will tell you, there is a great deal more to good soil than its chemical composition.[26] As I explored the discovery habitat, it became clear that, for the PIE to sustainably provide innovative and affordable medicines, it requires more than just good basic science. What emerged was that, for the PIE to be healthy, it needs three things from the discovery habitat.

The discovery habitat must provide sufficient, relevant, and complementary new knowledge

A constant flow of new knowledge and understanding is essential to the functioning of the PIE. This includes the obvious scientific and technological scientific domains, such as human biology and disease mechanisms. But it also includes new knowledge in the sociological and organizational domains. This social science knowledge is a necessary complement to the more obvious biomedical science. It includes understanding of patients' non-clinical needs, how cross-disciplinary teams work, and how organizations interact to deliver therapeutic innovations affordably to the market. And, while recognizing that basic research is not product-related, these streams of new knowledge should be relevant to society's needs and priorities, both medical and economic. By contrast, a discovery system that fails to create new knowledge in sufficient quantity, or only in some but not all relevant knowledge domains, or creates knowledge that isn't aligned to society's priorities, would not sustain a healthy PIE.

The discovery habitat must provide predictive new knowledge

It's not enough for the discovery habitat to deliver relevant and complementary new knowledge. A healthy PIE also requires that this new knowledge has the quality of predictivity,[27] meaning that its findings are likely to be reproducible in human beings in real-world settings and therefore useful to the innovation habitat. Predictivity is, at least in part, a function of how that knowledge is created. To be useful in the development of innovative medicines, new scientific and technological knowledge has to flow from well-designed research, using validated methods and using models of biological activity that closely resemble human biology. Similarly, new organizational and sociological knowledge must be based on valid and well-executed research that reflects real-world contexts. By contrast, if basic research is designed and executed to meet only the requirements of scientific peer-review, which has very different requirements from the innovation habitat, and has low predictivity once it is applied to the development of innovative medicines, then the discovery habitat is unlikely to sustain a healthy PIE.

The discovery habitat must provide accessible new knowledge

It is not enough that the discovery habitat generates sufficient, relevant, and highly predictive new knowledge. That knowledge must be accessible to the innovation and coalition habitats. This means that the processes of accessing new knowledge – finding it, gaining access to it, and making use of it – must be efficient and effective. This has to be so, despite the volume and variety of new knowledge, its fragmented and dispersed nature, and the varied, situation-specific needs of the knowledge creators and knowledge users.[28] By contrast, a discovery habitat that makes it difficult or costly to find, to access or to make use of its new knowledge outputs is unlikely to sustain a healthy PIE.

I've summarized these requirements in Figure 3.3. In short, the soil metaphor is useful for understanding the discovery habitat and its relationship with the rest of the PIE. Good soil provides plants with easy access to the right nutrients in the right amounts. In the same way, a well-functioning discovery habitat needs to provide the PIE (particularly the innovation habitat) with a plentiful supply of a wide range of new knowledge, in a form that's easy to use and at an acceptable cost of access. The parallels between the PIE and the natural ecosystem of the apothecary's garden are clear.

So, having explored who occupies the discovery habitat, why they do so and what the PIE requires of their basic research activity, I now felt in a position to examine how well it worked. In particular, I wanted to understand if the discovery habitat was capable of meeting the three requirements, described above, well enough for the PIE to be a sustainable source of innovative and affordable medicines.

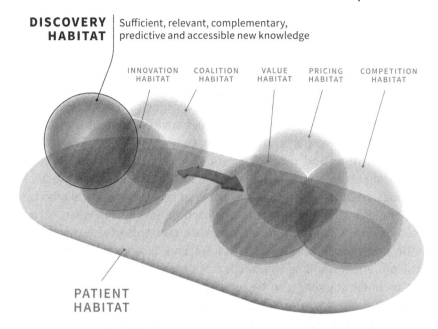

DISCOVERY | Sufficient, relevant, complementary,
HABITAT | predictive and accessible new knowledge

INNOVATION   COALITION   VALUE   PRICING   COMPETITION
HABITAT   HABITAT   HABITAT   HABITAT   HABITAT

PATIENT
HABITAT

Figure 3.3 The discovery habitat's contribution to a healthy PIE

Is the discovery habitat capable of supporting a healthy PIE?

It might seem presumptuous to question the working of the discovery habitat. It's populated by the brightest people who, by and large, are motivated by a desire to improve human health. Their track record of discoveries is, without hyperbole, quite amazing. But of course, I'm not questioning those people, their motivations or the quality of their science. I'm trying to understand whether the whole habitat does or can provide the PIE with what it needs to sustainably deliver affordable, innovative medicines. That's a much wider question and, both from my conversations with the expert informants and my reading of the others' research, I found four indications of the discovery habitat's possible weaknesses.

The discovery habitat is lagging behind its technological environment

In Chapter 2, when I displaced concepts from biological ecosystems to the PIE, I drew parallels between the climatic and geological abiotic environment of natural ecosystems and the sociological and technological abiotic environment of the PIE. Simply put, any healthy ecosystem makes good use of what its abiotic environment provides and adapts to do so, even as that environment changes. This is as true for the PIE and its habitats as it is for a natural ecosystem. The only difference is that it is not climatic and geological conditions that the discovery habitat must adapt to and exploit, but technological and sociological.

As Figure 3.4 shows, the technological environment of the discovery habitat has two parts, the proximate and the distal. The former includes scientific and technological factors directly related to pharmaceutical research, the latter those that are important but indirect influences on basic research. Both parts of this technological environment are changing at rates that are hard to follow and even harder to summarize. Changes in the proximate technological environment can be imperfectly abridged as the systems biology revolution, the shift from understanding the biology of organs and other parts of the body to understanding the bigger picture of how biological systems function.[29] Even if you've never heard of the systems biology revolution, you've heard about it. When you read of "the 'omics," such as genomics and proteomics, you are reading about different aspects of systems biology.[30] Systems biology is a fundamental transformation in how we understand the science that informs pharmaceutical innovation. This transformation is part of a wider change of biology from an often qualitative, observational science into an information science.[31]

Closely related and overlapping with the systems biology revolution is the rapid change in the distal technological environment, the

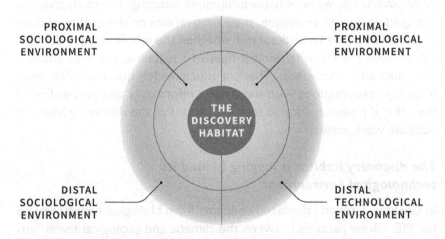

PROXIMAL
SOCIOLOGICAL
ENVIRONMENT

PROXIMAL
TECHNOLOGICAL
ENVIRONMENT

THE
DISCOVERY
HABITAT

DISTAL
SOCIOLOGICAL
ENVIRONMENT

DISTAL
TECHNOLOGICAL
ENVIRONMENT

Figure 3.4 The discovery habitat's abiotic environment

technologies that influence basic research. These include the cheap, powerful computing that has affected all our lives but, in particular, has enabled bioinformatics, the analysis of biological data.[32] Significant advances in the distal technological environment of the discovery habitat also include many biology-specific technologies such as DNA and RNA sequencing technology[33] and novel forms of microscopy.[34] Together with many other changes in the proximate and distal technological environment, these few examples represent a rapid and fundamental change in the discovery habitat's abiotic environment. It is hard to overstate how different that environment is from that which I entered as a young research scientist and how quickly it is changing.[35]

The question, then, is whether the discovery habitat is adapting well enough and fast enough to take full advantage of these rapid and important changes in the technological part of its abiotic environment. That the new science and technology is being used is evident. Expert informant Pedro Cejas expressed it well:

> *In my field, but also in most others in biological science, if you were to leave the field for just a couple of years you would return to find that the science and technology had left you behind. Our understanding of the biology and the technology available to understand it is moving at an incredible speed.*
>
> Pedro Cejas

But is the discovery habitat making good enough use of its new environment to enable the PIE to sustainably provide affordable, innovative medicines? Absorbing new knowledge and buying new technology is expensive and is only possible if funding keeps pace with technological change. Continuing with our garden metaphor, plants need water to use sunlight and research institutions need money to make use of new science and technology.[36] Yet the funding of the NIH has, for decades, varied with the political and economic climate.[37] As a result, its funding has been uneven and variable.[38] This variability has implications beyond just the absolute level of year-on-year funding. One of the ways the discovery habitat feeds new knowledge into the PIE is by training new knowledge workers, experts who take decades to reach their peak of productivity. Cycles of "boom and bust" have side effects on this human resource output,[39] hindering career development and limiting the knowledge pool, and there is also evidence that changes in funding levels have a non-linear, disproportionate impact on research activity.[40]

NIH funding for basic research is not the whole picture of course. Philanthropic funding and, to some extent, industry investment in basic research also matters, but most of those investments go toward late-stage research. The influence of the NIH as the "keystone species" in the discovery habitat means that NIH funding is a reasonable proxy for how well the habitat is able to take advantage of its changing scientific and technological environment. To return to the garden metaphor, the declining, erratic pattern of the NIH's budget "rainfall" doesn't match well with the bright, continuing sunlight of the scientific and technological environment. Of course, it's impossible to directly correlate the former, measured in dollars, with the latter, which is multidimensional. But it is reasonable to infer that erratic and, over the long term, declining funding means that the discovery habitat may not be extracting all it could from its rich and changing technological habitat. That inference is supported by the very high number of potential new drugs that emerge from basic research but fail to reach the market, suggesting that the discovery habit is failing to meet the predictivity requirement described above. Even a well and consistently funded discovery habitat might struggle to keep up with the scientific and technological revolution currently going on around it. It would be surprising if a less well and erratically funded discovery habitat did not lag behind its technological environment.

The discovery habitat is lagging behind its sociological environment

Science and technology are only half of the discovery habitat's abiotic environment. The other half is its sociological environment, which also has proximal and distal elements. The former includes directly relevant health-related social issues, while the latter includes indirectly relevant social, economic, and political factors, as shown in Figure 3.4. This sociological environment of the discovery habitat is, like its technological counterpart, also undergoing fundamental change although, as is the nature of sociological change, that change is both more gradual and less obvious.

The elements of the sociological environment that are directly relevant to the discovery habitat are those related to illness and disease. These include demographic shifts, such as an aging population, and shifts in disease patterns, which are related to demographics but also to lifestyle, wealth, and other social factors. Collectively, these are known as the social determinants of health.[41] As with scientific and technological change, the pattern of change here is so complex that any summary risks oversimplification but there are broad, general truths that are evident in the research literature. Salient among these is the growing burden of chronic disease, and increasingly patients with multiple chronic diseases, that is the primary driver of ill-health in the US.[42] In addition to those chronic diseases, mental health, rare diseases, and preventative medicine are also health priorities today that would have surprised earlier generations. These shifting demands are part of a larger, longer set of trends known as epidemiological transitions, the shifting of society's healthcare requirements over time.[43]

Running alongside directly relevant factors such as social determinants of health are other sociological factors that are indirectly relevant to the discovery habitat, including politics, economics, and other social issues.[44] These factors are undergoing changes analogous to, and just as important as, epidemiological transitions. Again, this is a complex picture and clarification risks oversimplification but in other writing I've summarized this phenomenon as the Great Value Shift.[45] This phenomenon emerges when economic growth is slow, relative to the growth of healthcare costs, and is amplified when there is political reluctance to increase public funding for healthcare. The result is increased demand, from all parts of society, for value for money in healthcare. Of course, healthcare systems have always wanted value for money, but this combination of increased demand and reduced relative resources has now shifted the balance of societal priorities strongly toward affordability. The charged debate about pharmaceutical pricing is, along with the debate about healthcare costs and insurance, one symptom of the Great Value Shift. Combined with epidemiological transitions, the Great Value Shift represents a change in the discovery habitat's abiotic environment as important as those scientific and technological changes already described. One expert informant, who chose to remain anonymous, summed up the views of many of the expert informants on this topic.

> *I think the whole industry recognizes that we need to change and that value has become as important as clinical outcome. The challenge lies in how to achieve that value and demonstrate it to payers and patients.*
>
> *Anonymous*

So, although the inhabitants of the discovery habitat might naturally think first about the scientific and technological elements of their abiotic environment, the sociological elements exist and are important to its functioning. What society wants from the PIE is gradually but inexorably shifting, both clinically and economically. Is the discovery habitat adapting to these changes well enough and fast enough to allow the PIE to sustainably provide affordable, innovative medicines? There's little evidence that it is and some evidence that it isn't. Strategic direction of the NIH comes from its parent body, the Department of Health and Human Services (HHS), whose strategic goals are very broad.[46] In their generality, they seem to pass over the issues of adapting to the Great Value Shift. As these goals cascade down into the NIH, that important body also seems to neglect, relatively at least, the affordability issue.[47] Nor does the allocation of resources by NIH seem to fully recognize the epidemiological transitions that are shaping the abiotic environment.

This part of my exploration left me concerned that the discovery habitat was lagging behind its sociological environment but for different reasons from its technological lag described above. Increased funding might allow the discovery habitat to take advantage of scientific and technological advances more effectively. But lagging behind changes in the sociological environment looks to be an organizational behavior issue and so much harder to change.

Co-evolution of the discovery habitat is hindered by embedded cultures

In my first two concerns about how well the discovery habitat supports the PIE, I have focused on its adaptation to its abiotic environments, both technological and sociological. Adaptation to and exploitation of these environments is necessary if the discovery habitat is to support a healthy PIE. But it isn't sufficient, because it must also adapt to and exploit its biotic environment, those organizations in and around the discovery habitat. In other words, how well the discovery habitat meets the three demands that the PIE makes of it depends in large part on how well these organizations adapt to each other. Just as with species in a natural environment, this mutual adaptation is a co-evolutionary process (see Box 3.2) and, as I explored it, I observed two ways in which it appeared to be hindered by cultural differences within the habitat.

Box 3.2 What is co-evolution in the context of the discovery habitat?

You might be familiar with the idea of co-evolution in nature when species evolve complementary traits to their mutual benefit. The honeybee and flowering plants are the prototypical example. As with other aspects of evolutionary science, the concept of co-evolution has been usefully displaced into other areas, including systems of organizations.

Co-evolution is more complex than the honeybee/flower example suggests. As well as pairwise co-evolution involving a tight relationship between two interacting species, there is also multispecies or "guild" evolution involving suites of species.[48] The latter more accurately reflects what is happening in the discovery habitat as multiple "species" of organization, from university labs to NIH bodies, are all interacting at once.

Modern theories of co-evolution reveal even more complexity in its mechanisms. At its simplest, co-evolution requires organizations to adapt in ways that are mutually beneficial and interactions that allows those mutual benefits to be realized. But those adaptations and interactions are influenced by local conditions, resulting in co-evolutionary hotspots and coldspots, in which the co-evolutionary process works well, not at all or can even create negative outcomes.[49]

In the context of the discovery habitat, successful co-evolution is when organizations interact and adapt efficiently to each other's needs to better meet the needs of the PIE described above. Anything that hinders that interaction and adaptation hinders the functioning of the habitat and the PIE.

The first observation is that changes in the discovery habitat have amplified some existing cultural differences between research institutions, biotechs, venture capitalists, and pharmaceutical companies. Universities have adapted to changes in federal law[50] by creating technology transfer offices to capitalize on their discoveries via commercial arrangements with companies.[51] At the same time, pharmaceutical companies have adapted toward "external innovation," in which early-stage development, which historically happened within big companies, now happens mostly in small biotechs.[52] This means that academic researchers are now less likely to be dealing with a large company and more likely to be dealing with a specialized biotech, financed by ambitious venture capital and judged on risk-adjusted rate of return. Similarly, pharmaceutical companies now find themselves dealing less with scientists and more with technology transfer professionals who are judged by how much money they can make for the university. In quantitative terms, this commercialization of the relationship between academic research and the industry has increased both patenting and university revenue, but it has also had unintended consequences for how the discovery habitat functions.[53] In many cases, universities have struggled with reconciling "entrepreneurial" activity with their teaching and research roles.[54] On the other side of the relationship, venture capitalists sometimes see universities as unrealistic in their expectations. This was a common opinion amongst expert informants used to dealing with university technology transfer offices and it was eloquently summarized by Doug Stover.

> *The capabilities and experience of technology transfer offices vary greatly. Whilst a few are very experienced and capable, many are naïve about risk and unrealistic about issues such as dilution and voting rights. And, in addition to these capability issues, trust and personal relationships can do a surprising amount to help or hinder the transfer of IP and technology.*
>
> Doug Stover

The second observation concerned co-evolution between academic researchers, rather than between them and others in the discovery habitat. As scientific knowledge grows, it fragments and researchers find themselves working in an ever-narrower knowledge silos.[55] At the same time, scientific research, which formerly might have been concentrated in a small number of familiar centers, becomes dispersed across many, less familiar centers.[56] Together, this fragmentation and dispersion make it harder to gather and synthesize different academic findings, as is usually necessary to translate basic research into applied development.[57] From a co-evolutionary perspective, this means that researchers need to develop stronger knowledge management and sharing capabilities than were previously necessary. The evidence suggests that this co-evolution is being hindered by culturally embedded behaviors. For example, some studies record what they call "knowledge hiding behavior" by academic researchers.[58] Knowledge sharing can also be hindered by collaborations with industry, when commercial confidentiality may be an issue[59] and also by fear of competition in academic publishing.[60] These culturally embedded behaviors are amplified by real-world difficulties in sharing data, which can vary greatly in type, source, and format but have to be standardized in some ways to be usable.[61] This combination of cultural and practical difficulties in knowledge sharing came up in various forms during the expert informant discussions and it was summarized well by Michael Jackson:

> *We need better ways of sharing data but it's not a simple problem. Because much basic research is narrow and reductionist, but translational research tends to be broader and multi-theoretic, we need to combine many kinds of data from many researchers. That data may be quantitative and qualitative, tacit and explicit and there are issues of competition and secrecy. To share knowledge effectively, and for example to apply AI to making sense of it, you would need to overcome all these issues first. In that sense, the current system is "semi-broken."*
>
> *Michael Jackson*

Taken together, then, there's an issue that the inhabitants of the discovery habitat are not co-evolving well enough to meet the requirements of the PIE. As their environment places a "selection pressure" on them to share knowledge better, their both cultural and technological issues are hindering their mutual adaptation. And, at the borders between discovery, coalition and innovation habitats, where legal changes make it necessary for basic researchers to co-evolve with commercial entities, embedded cultural differences between academic and commercial also hinder co-evolution. Both factors mean that the discovery habitat can't support a healthy PIE as well as we would like it to.

The discovery habitat is hindered by neglect of the translational science commons

The ability of the discovery habitat to fully adapt to and exploit its technological environment (point 1) and its sociological environment (point 2) are both important to its ability to generate the new knowledge the PIE requires. So too is the mutual, co-evolutionary adaptation of the various entities in the discovery, innovation, and coalition habitats (point 3). But, even if these things were addressed and the knowledge output of the discovery habitat greatly increased, it might have little impact on the health of the PIE because of the last of my four concerns. This centers around the subject of translation.

In the context of the PIE, translation means carrying over the results of basic research into the innovation habitat, where they might be developed into innovative medicines. For two reasons, translation is fundamentally important to our question about how we can best manage the PIE for sustained, affordable innovation. Firstly, and quite obviously, innovative medicines are the results of translation and, without translation, we are left with only incremental advances or serendipitous discoveries.[62] Secondly, and less obviously, the cost of developing innovative medicines is directly proportional to the efficiency of translation (see Box 3.3). For both these reasons, translation – especially the efficiency of translation – is important to the PIE. The second of the three requirements the PIE has of the discovery habitat, that for predictivity, could be rephrased as "a healthy PIE requires high translatability."

Box 3.3 How does translation efficiency influence the affordability of innovative medicines?

The cost of developing innovative medicines and their price is directly related to the efficiency of translation in two ways.[63]
The first is that the costs of developing innovative medicines includes both the development costs of those medicines that reach the market and those of medicines that fail to. If only 1/100 of scientific discoveries that are picked up by a pharmaceutical company eventually reach the market, the price of that one product must cover its own development cost *and* that of the 99 that failed to reach the market.

So, the costs of developing an innovative medicine are related to the efficiency of translation of basic discoveries into marketable products. Fewer failures lower the product development costs and vice versa. To the degree that the prices of innovative medicines are related to their costs, a lower failure rate offers the potential for lower prices.

The second is that the cost of the capital required to develop an innovative medicine is proportional to the risk that the medicine might fail in development or, inversely, the probability that it might reach the market. This is simply the result of the way capital markets work. If I ask you to invest your pension fund in something that is reasonably certain to pay back (government bonds, for example), you will probably be willing to accept a low rate of return. If I ask you to invest in something that has a very low probability of paying back (the intellectual property rights of a basic scientific discovery, for example), you will expect a much higher rate of return. But if that latter probability can be increased, and your risks reduced, by a significant increase in translational efficiency then you would be willing to moderate your expectations. The costs of capital are part of the cost of bringing a scientific discovery to market. So, this is a second way in which the costs of developing an innovative medicine are related to the efficiency of translation of basic discoveries into marketable products. Few failures, lower cost of capital, and vice versa. Again, to the degree that the price of innovative medicines is related to their costs, a lower failure rate offers the potential for lower prices.

This is not to imply that translation efficiency is the only factor influencing development costs, or that development costs are the only factor influencing price, or even that price is the only factor in affordability, but translational efficiency is an important mechanism through which the discovery habitat influences affordability.

As I explored the issue of translation, it became clear that there was widespread lack of clarity and precision in the terms used. In particular, there is often conflation of the terms translational *research* and translational *science*. These are two different things and their conflation is more than a matter of semantics; it hinders the functioning of the discovery habitat. Christopher P Austin cuts through this confusion with a useful distinction that I paraphrase here.[64]

Translational research is the work carried out with the intent to translate one or more basic research discoveries into an innovative medicine, usually for a particular disease or condition.

Translational science is the work carried out with the intent to understand the general scientific principles that explain how basic scientific discoveries translate into medicinal use.

So, importantly, translational research and translational science are not the same thing, even though the terms are often used as if they were.[65]

As Austin put it, the target of translational research is a disease, the target for translational science is translation itself. This semantic distinction is important because it reveals a characteristic of the discovery habitat that limits its ability to meet the requirements of the PIE, particularly the requirement for predictivity.

Compared to translational science, translational research is pervasive. It takes place right across the discovery habitat and crosses over into the innovation habitat, where biotechs and pharmaceutical companies do most of the translational research that is done. Most of the NIH's agencies allocate significant resources to translational research and many academic research institutions do both basic and translational research. Some researchers argue that, because its outputs can become patentable intellectual property, applied research, including translational research, is displacing genuinely basic academic research.[66]

By comparison, translational science is much less widespread. By definition, it is not product or disease specific and its outputs are more akin to a public good. As a result, it is much less well-resourced and at risk of a "tragedy of the commons"[67] in which commercial organizations are happy to benefit from it but are not prepared to contribute to it. That there is a "tragedy of the translational commons" is a plausible and significant explanation for the persistently high attrition rates as basic research discoveries moves from the discovery habitat to the innovation habitat.[68]

The need to avoid this tragedy and to advance translational science is not a novel observation. The NCATS agency of NIH was founded ten years ago with this in mind. But, even after ten years of progress, there remains a huge translational science agenda to address.[69] Until that agenda is addressed, the predictivity of new knowledge emerging from the discovery habitat will remain poor. Until that predictivity is significantly improved, the efficiency of the translation process will remain low. Until that efficiency improves substantially, the risks and costs of bringing innovative medicines to market will remain high. Reducing those costs and risks is one of the things that needs to happen to make innovative medicines sustainably affordable. This reality was one of the most striking things to emerge from the expert informant discussions, so striking that I doubted it until I was able to triangulate it with previously published research. Although several expert informants made this point, I was struck by the conviction of Aubrey Stoch's words.

> The predictive validity of much basic research is weak when translated into humans. We see this in safety, tolerability, response curves and other factors.

This leads to high failure rates and the need to expensively repeat work. There are fundamental biological reasons for this, which make it impossible to mitigate fully, but we should and we must find the technical answers to this issue.

Aubrey Stoch

So, my exploration of the discovery habitat led me to conclude that it is not, in its current state, able to support a healthy PIE. It seems, partly because of erratic and uneven funding, to be lagging behind its rapidly changing scientific and technological environment. It seems, for various organizational behavior reasons, to be lagging behind the changing demands of its sociological environment. Its inhabitants seem, because of their deeply embedded cultures, to be failing to co-evolve as they need to. These three ailments seem to contribute to a fourth, a tragedy of the translational commons in which the neglect of translational science is disguised by the semantic conflation with translational research. Taken together, these weaknesses make it seem unlikely that, without change, the soil of the PIE can support the sustainable, affordable innovation we need. Having reached this point in my exploration, I pushed on to the question of how the discovery habitat, the soil of the PIE, might be improved.

How can we improve the discovery habitat?

As described in Chapter 2, the health of the PIE depends on the health of all its habitats (see Figure 2.1), so an improvement of the discovery habitat alone might not make an immediate and significant difference to the overall health of the PIE. That said, the role of this habitat as the soil of the ecosystem means that improvements to basic research would probably have the most fundamental, long-term effect of any change of the PIE's component habitats. And so, like gardeners conditioning their soil with manure and compost, we must aim to make the discovery habitat better able to meet the three requirements laid out earlier in this chapter. In this section, I describe four remedial steps in the direction of an improved discovery habitat, guided by the four observations of the preceding section.

Increase and stabilize basic research funding

It seems uncontroversial that there is a mismatch between the erratic, uneven funding for basic research and the rapid transformation in the scientific and technological environment. From this, I have inferred that, without better and more consistent funding, basic researchers cannot hope to fully adapt to and exploit the opportunities available to them. In this case, better funding means more than simply increased funding. It also means funding that is more sustained and predictable to avoid the disproportionate issues created by boom-and-bust cycles. This point was made by several expert informants and I vividly remember Amitabh Chandra, while kindly giving up some of his paternity leave to help me, leading off with exactly this point.

> *The first thing I'd do is substantially increase and then sustain NIH funding.*
> *I have no doubt that the tangible and intangible returns on that would justify*
> *the relatively small amounts required.*
>
> *Amitabh Chandra*

Exactly by how much funding should increase, and by what mechanisms, are matters of detailed policy that I won't touch on here.[70] That said, my exploration of the discovery habitat suggests three things that policy makers should bear in mind when improving basic research funding. The first is that increased funding is unlikely to improve the health of the discovery habitat without three complementary changes. These changes are discussed below. The second is that cosmetic changes to the organization of basic research may, by substituting for substantial change, reduce the impact of funding increases. For example, the intention to set up a new agency within NIH, ARPA-H, has the potential to both accelerate progress or to be a cosmetic exercise of giving new names to an extension of existing activity, depending on how it is executed.[71] The third is that the dominant position of public funding ought not to blind us to the possibilities of improving charitable and philanthropic funding. The concentration of donations into fewer, larger donors suggests there is potential to restore the US's historical trait of charitable giving by the middle classes. The effective altruism movement may have lessons to offer in how philanthropy is encouraged and directed[72] and novel mechanisms for funding basic biomedical research have great potential.[73]

It would be naïve, of course, to ignore that public funding for pharmaceutical innovation competes with other, equally laudable, ways to spend taxpayer dollars. This means that any substantial and sustained increase in funding for basic research implies certain tradeoffs and political choices. For example, it requires a choice to invest in basic research today to improve the affordability of innovative medicines tomorrow. It also means choosing to trade off some political account-ability of NIH so that the discovery habitat is insulated to some extent from the vicissitudes of politicized budget allocation. Finally, legislative amendments to Bayh-Dole might be needed to rebalance academic researchers' interest in patents and commercially oriented activity.[74] All of these things would run counter to the recent history of manag-ing the discovery habitat.

Align basic research to societal needs

It seems uncontentious that a discovery habitat that is predominantly publicly funded should be aligned to society's evolving needs. The cur-rent mechanism of alignment operates through the goals and strategic objectives of HHS and NIH. These seem to encompass everything, exclude little and, as described above, look to be unresponsive to shifts in the abiotic environment, especially the Great Value Shift. The discovery habitat would serve the needs of the PIE better if it were aligned to the changing health and economic needs of American soci-ety as well as to scientific possibilities.

To be clear, I am not proposing that basic research should be closely directed toward specific goals in some form of Soviet-style centralized planning. In such a complex system, any attempt at precise direction would be most unlikely to work. A better approach would be what behavioral economists call "nudges," influences on behavior that are indirect and rely mostly on positive reinforcement.[75] The NIH's cur-rent systems for awarding grants already strongly nudge researchers toward specific scientific objectives, so a nudge approach that added societally aligned awarding criteria would only be an adaptation of ac-cepted practice and so more likely to work.[76]

Again, it is beyond the scope of this book to make specific recom-mendations for what those nudges should be, but there are three considerations that should be foremost in the minds of those who direct funding for basic research. The first is that resource allocation should be responsive to the shifts in society's health needs, such as widely prevalent chronic diseases. The second is that basic research should also be nudged in the direction of society's economic needs, such as toward prevention and cure rather than management and to-ward therapies that are less costly to administer. The third is that basic research should encourage knowledge creation in the social sciences that might inform pharmaceutical innovation, countering the institutional isomorphism that pushes it toward the topics and methods of the biomedical sciences. My exploration of the discovery habitat found that, while there was evidence of all three of these things being considered in basic research funding, none of them were fully reflected in the current discovery habitat.

In recommending how the discovery habitat might be better aligned to society's needs, I recognize that there are reasons it is currently out of alignment. Research tends to build on research, so there is a natural tendency for past funding allocations to shape future allocations, even when that doesn't reflect current needs. Basic research is far removed from the market, and that distance reduces the consideration that is given to the Great Value Shift, even when it is a salient societal need. And because the discovery habitat has far more biologists than it has social scientists, they have more influence over what is researched and how it is researched. In practice, these three inertial factors mean that those with the power to nudge the discovery habitat will have to nudge very hard. They will need to be willing to kill some sacred cows, to define interdisciplinary research as not just cross-sciences but cross-domains and cross-epistemologies. They will need to widen the definition of research that addresses unmet needs to include economic and well as clinical needs. All these things run counter to current practice, from which I infer that a change in thinking may need to precede any change in practice.

Align commercial and academic cultures

It seems self-evident that, as their wider technological and sociological environment changes, the entities in and around the discovery habitat must adapt. In particular, they need to develop improved traits of knowledge management and sharing, and of working across the translational boundary between the discovery, coalition, and innovation habitats, even as Bayh-Dole has commercialized the nature of that boundary. There are tangible issues involved here, such as the heterogenous nature of biological data, but the necessary co-evolution seems to be hindered mostly by the differing and deeply entrenched cultures of academia and the pharmaceutical business.

Any change that involves cultural or behavioral change is difficult and it is again outside the remit of this book to make specific proposals. Even so, my exploration of the topic does suggest three factors that should be borne in mind by those who inhabit these connected habitats. First, the cultural differences between academia and commercial organizations run deep and arise from fundamental differences in how success is achieved in each area. This means that superficial and limited programs will not reduce these cultural differences or the problems they cause. Bridging between the two will require multiple extensive and complementary actions, such as exchange programs between business and academia, changes to how academic career development is managed and capability development on both sides of the interaction. Second, sharing knowledge between academic researchers and commercial entities is always going to be hindered by both commercial confidentiality and academic competition. Overcoming this will need the development of new ways of pooling knowledge that mitigate the conflicts between knowledge sharing and competition. Finally, since our understanding of how these important organizations co-evolve is relatively primitive, the co-evolution of the entities in these habitats is hindered by the lack of social science research in this area. Directing research into this area would enable co-evolution within these habitats.

In suggesting ways that this co-evolutionary process might be accelerated, I fully recognize that my suggestions are premised on three ideas that are not currently well-accepted amongst its inhabitants. The first is that this is less of a technological matter than it is an organizational culture matter, which affects how the problem is addressed. The second is that, in evolutionary terms, the environment selects for the fitness of knowledge-sharing groups, not individual entities. The third is that knowledge about how organizations co-evolve is, in this context, as important as biological or medical knowledge. None of these three ideas is salient or well-accepted at present. Gaining acceptance for them is a necessary precursor to enabling co-evolution in this habitat.

Transform translational science

Once the distinction between translational research and translational science is made, the tragedy of the translational commons seems a significant issue. Although not a panacea for improving either translational efficiency or affordability, the predictivity of basic research is a bottleneck in our attempts to manage the discovery habitat and the PIE. What is needed is an orders-of-magnitude improvement in our understanding of translational science across the very wide range of sub-fields within the subject.

As already discussed, Christopher P Austin has proposed an extensive research agenda in this field and, at least to a first approximation, his agenda gives an idea of the work needed to achieve the necessary improvements in translational efficiency. I will leave it to those more qualified than me to improve on his ideas and translate them into a specific action plan. That said, my exploration of this area does give three broad pointers to those who might lead this improvement in translational science. First is that the scale and scope of this work implies a level of resourcing that is far beyond that of NCATS current allocation.[77] Although the term is often misused, achieving the required goals in translational science is likely to require a "moonshot" in terms of ambition and funding. Second, that the aims of that moonshot must not be distracted by conflation of translational science with translational research. It must, in Austin's words, be focused on the "disease" of translational inefficiency and leave disease-area translational research to other programs. Finally, the scope of a translational science moonshot must not be constrained by the institutional isomorphism that translational science must be biological science. A translational science moonshot must also include the social science needed to understand and improve translational efficiency.

When I recommend a translational science moonshot, I recognize that those who lead it will need to take positions that won't sit comfortably with some in the discovery habitat. Those leaders will need to raise the status of translation science, which favors the common good, relative to translational research, which will always be able to claim more specific utility. At the same time, they will need to raise the status and rigor of social science research to the same level as that of biomedical research, a promotion that will represent a cultural change within the biology-focused discovery habitat. Third, those who lead the translational science moonshot will need to ensure that that its findings and outcomes are made available to the discovery and innovation habitats, avoiding the limitations of intellectual property rights. All three of these leadership tasks will jar with much current practice.

Will this be enough?

These four broad recommendations are based on the four main issues that seem to constrain the discovery habitat and its capacity to meet the requirements of a healthy PIE. They would, if all four were fully and well implemented, go most of the way to allowing the habitat to meet those requirements. It's possible, likely even, that I've missed some other remedies that the habitat would benefit from but, with the help of the expert informants and researchers who have preceded me, I don't think I've missed anything of similar magnitude to these four recommendations.

But that is not the same as saying that these four recommendations, however well implemented, are sufficient to make the PIE healthy and capable of sustainably delivering affordable, innovative medicines. To do that, we need to consider and address the other habitats.

Notes

1 I took this soil metaphor from Christopher P Austin who used it in a "Vital Health" podcast in July 2021, soon after he had stepped down as Director of the NIH's National Center for Advancing Translational Sciences. In that podcast, he attributed the success of American pharmaceutical innovation to the symbiotic relationship between basic research and applied development. See https://podbay.fm/p/vital-health-podcast/e/1626769783.

2 Government funding of basic science has been a staple of US industrial policy since at least 1945. Credit for this is usually given to Vannevar Bush, who was a little-known hero of American history. As Director of the Office of Scientific Research and Development, his combination of scientific and leadership skills helped bring penicillin, radar, proximity fuses and nuclear weapons to fruition. In 1945, in response to a request from President Roosevelt, he wrote a report "Science -The Endless Frontier" that marked the beginning of science policy as we now understand it and popularized the phrase "Basic Research." See ref 1.

3 The OECD defines basic research as "Experimental or theoretical work undertaken primarily to acquire new knowledge of the underlying foundations of phenomena and observable facts, without any particular application or use in view" but in practice this is open to interpretation. As will become evident in this chapter, being clear about what basic research is and how it contributes to the PIE is important. For background on the discussion about what basic research is. See refs 2 and 3.

4 The reader may recognize that this term was made famous by the US Supreme Court Justice Potter Stewart who, in 1964, used it in reference to pornography. Apparently, the phrase was given to him by his law clerk Alan Novak. See https://www.wsj.com/articles/BL-LB-4558. Like pornography, basic research is very hard to distinguish from other, similar activities and is often subjective. This becomes more than semantic when we have to decide what to fund and how to do it.

5 This is not to say that it is ignored completely. In particular, there is a strong recent trend toward including "the voice of the patient" in clinical research. See, for example, ref 4. Despite this trend, it remains true that, in the minds of many and in practice, basic research in pharmaceutical innovation is predominantly in the scientific and technological, rather than organizational and sociological, domains of knowledge.

6 Without getting into the long grass of epistemology, it's broadly true that those who work in biology and other natural sciences look at the world through what is called a "logical positivist" lens and use the methods that this lens implies. It's a good approach that works very well when you are trying to understand

molecules, cells and other things in a reductionist approach to a problem. But there are other lenses, and many social scientists, who study organizational and individual behavior, tend to eschew such reductionist, logical positivist approaches. Social scientists often favor a more holistic approach, looking at the world through a "pragmatist" or other lens and using a wider variety of methods. What is interesting about the pharmaceutical innovation basic research literature is that, as well as being dominated by scientific and technological subjects, even the smaller amount of organizational and sociological research is mostly carried out in the logical-positivistic way natural scientists do research, and chooses its methods accordingly. This raises the question of whether such a natural sciences approach is appropriate to social science problems, or whether the approach has been thoughtlessly and inappropriately transferred from one academic domain to another, without too much thought for its effectiveness.

7 In 1959, the British scientist and novelist CP Snow gave two influential lectures that were later published as "The Two Cultures and the Scientific Revolution" in which he argued that the intellectual divisions between the sciences and humanities hindered the resolution of the various problems facing the world. See ref 5.

8 The idea of institutional isomorphism is well accepted among organizational researchers. It was developed by DiMaggio and Powell in their influential 1983 paper. See ref 6.

9 I'm grateful to the helpful people at NIH for sourcing these figures for me. As well as illustrating that basic and applied research are connected but different activities, these two diagrams also show how much more there is to bringing an innovative medicine to market than the basic scientific discovery. These two images are licensed to the public under the Creative Commons Attribution-Share Alike 4.0 license. The figure should be attributed to: Wagner JA, Dahlem AM, Hudson LD, Terry SF, Altman RB, Gilliland CT, DeFeo C, and Austin CP. Drug Discovery, Development and Deployment Map (4DM): Small Molecules. Available at https://ncats.nih.gov/translation/maps.

10 Organizational culture is one of those phrases that is used loosely and, consequently, has lost some of its value. In this case, I'm strongly influenced by Edgar Schein's work on the subject, which sees culture as visible artefacts, such as behaviors, that are shaped by shared, often unspoken, values that in turn are determined by deeply held, often implicit, assumptions about how the world works. See ref 5.

11 Another important point here is that expected investment returns are discounted not only against risk or probability but also for "the time value of money," which allows for the fact that a dollar today is worth more than a dollar in the future. Pharmaceutical investment is often decided using a calculation called risk-adjusted net present value, or rNPV. A good primer on this can be found at. See ref 6.

12 When talking to the leadership of pharmaceutical and biotech companies, one will often hear them talk of their "fiduciary duty" to optimize the wealth of shareholders. In order to align the interests of leadership to this fiduciary duty, companies often award stock options as a major part of executive remuneration. Biopharmaceutical companies use this device more than most sectors. In one study, options were found to make up 46% of long-term incentives for biopharma executives, much more than for the other sectors in the study. See https://www.willistowerswatson.com/en-US/Insights/2021/01/biopharma-industry-still-relies-on-stock-options.

13 To put this in a wider context, there is an increasing trend for firms to spend less on the earlier, riskier end of research and development. This is not a purely

pharmaceutical market phenomenon but seems to be associated with the financialization of business. See refs 7–9.

14 My biologist colleagues refer to such creatures as "extremophiles." Polar bears and emperor penguins are examples of extremophiles. It's an interesting term that, in this context, reminds me that commercial organizations and grant-funded research organizations are quite different creatures.

15 Ever since 1945's "Science – The Endless Frontier," the US government (and those of other developed countries) have broadly accepted the need to fund basic research not only in pharmaceuticals but also in other areas. They do so, it seems, because they believe it to have an economic and social value that can't be recognized and rewarded by free market. This is supported by academic analysis. For example, Jones and Summers argue that "Overall, our estimates suggest that the social returns (on basic research) are very large. Even under conservative assumptions, innovation efforts produce social benefits that are many multiples of the investment costs." See ref 10.

16 It's relevant to note that NIH's mission statement includes fundamental discovery and their application. Although associated mostly with basic research, its goals are broader than that. See https://www.nih.gov/about-nih/what-we-do/mission-goals.

17 In biological ecosystems examples of keystone species include sharks, sea otters, starfish and African elephants. Being a keystone species is less about numbers and size and more about connectivity with the ecosystem.

18 To quote from the Congressional Research Office (see https://sgp.fas.org/crs/misc/R43341.pdf),

> When looking at NIH funding adjusted for inflation (in projected constant FY2022 dollars using the Biomedical Research and Development Price Index; BRDPI), the purchasing power of NIH funding peaked in FY2003—the last year of the five-year doubling period—and then declined fairly steadily for more than a decade until back-to-back funding increases were provided in each of FY2016 through FY2021. The FY2021 program level is 3.3% below the peak FY2003 program level. The FY2022 budget request would provide a program level that is 14.4% above the peak FY2003 program level.

This variability of funding is not a solely NIH issue. There is a long-term trend of decline in federal funding for research and development. See ref 11.

19 See https://officeofbudget.od.nih.gov/pdfs/FY21/spending-hist/Basic%20and%20Applied%20FY%202003%20-%20FY%202020%20(V).pdf.

20 The evolution of the NIH's structure is a study in itself. There is a long history of political concern, some might say interference, in its workings. See refs 12 and 13.

21 Translational research is that which attempts to "translate" basic research discoveries into useful pharmaceutical innovations. However, as I'll come to, not all translational research is the same and the term is often used loosely in pharmaceutical innovation.

22 To quote one study in this area,

> There is a need for increased transparency about who the main funders of health research are globally, what they fund and how they decide on what gets funded, and for improving the evidence base for various funding models. Data on organizations' funding patterns and funding distribution mechanisms are often not available, and when they are, they are reported using different classification systems.

See ref 14.

23 This picture of what is happening in philanthropy for medically related research is pieced together from many sources. See in particular 15 and 16.

24 The philanthropic funding of medical research has always been complicated and intertwined with public funding. It is also influenced by the emotional impact of certain disease classes. In Siddhartha Mukherjee's "Emperor of All Maladies," his description of cancer-related philanthropy is as interesting as his description of the science. See ref 17.

25 To avoid oversimplification here, the discovery habitat also contributes strongly to the human resource capital of the PIE by training scientists and others. Many of these people don't stay in basic research but contribute to the capabilities of the other habitats in the PIE. For example, many of those who work in the PIE received some of their education in NIH-funded basic research. I'm not neglecting this role of the discovery habitat, but I am viewing those human resources as one of the ways that new knowledge is packaged.

26 Pedologists are scientists who study the origin, composition and distribution of soils. This part of my research reminded me of an episode in my early career in which I was usefully reminded that I wasn't as clever as I thought I was. For a short period, I worked in the agrochemical division of a major pharmaceutical company and consequently worked with some quite brilliant scientists who didn't share my pharmaceutical background. I confess to the youthful arrogance of thinking that medicines were much more scientifically interesting than the dirt in which crops grow. I was quickly to learn that soil science, like any other, has depths and intricacies that are invisible to the layperson. One of my patient, tolerant mentors told me "Anyone can dump bags of fertilizer onto a field. Good soil management is about making the right sort of nutrients easily available to the crop in the right proportions, year after year after year, at an affordable cost." Decades later, these words struck me as a reasonably good description of what the PIE requires of the discovery habitat.

27 This term is gratefully borrowed from Christopher Austin (Ibid).

28 Some readers will see that this issue relates to the topic of Transaction Cost Economics, an important field that is about the costs of running an economic system. In the discovery habitat context, transaction cost economics is concerned with the costs and efficiencies of finding the new knowledge needed, of arranging the transaction between the interested parties and of managing the transactional relationship afterwards. It is quite possible for markets not to work, even when there is supply and demand, when the costs and difficulties of transaction hinder the working of the market. For an introduction to this topic. See ref 18.

29 A good introduction to systems biology and its implications for medicine is given here. See ref 19. This systems approach to medicine is often contrasted with the Oslerian tradition, named after William Osler a Canadian physician who pioneered medical education in the later 19th and early 20th centuries. The Oslerian tradition included not only an organ-based view of medicine but also many cultural traditions that shaped medicine in the 20th century. See https://profiles.nlm.nih.gov/spotlight/gf/feature/biographical-overview.

30 Part of the systems biology revolution is the combination of genomics, proteomic, metabolomics into a "multi-omics" view of disease. See ref 20.

31 The roots of this transformation are deep, interesting and go back to the 1960s. See https://web.stanford.edu/dept/HPS/TimLenoir/shapingbiomedicine.html.

32 For a fascinating brief history of bioinformatics. See ref 21.

33 The evolution of gene sequencing technology is a remarkable example of how learning and experience curves can drive progress. We are now in the "third generation" of DNA sequencing. For a good summary of the history of this topic, see https://www.pacb.com/blog/the-evolution-of-dna-sequencing-tools/.

34 The evolution of imaging technologies attracts less attention than other areas but is nonetheless remarkable. See ref 22.
35 To quote an interesting review of the speed of change of technologies influencing the life sciences: "There is immense diversity and rapid evolution of technologies with relevance to (or impact on) the life sciences enterprises." See: National Academies of Sciences, Engineering, and Medicine. 2006. *Globalization, Biosecurity, and the Future of the Life Sciences.* Washington, DC: The National Academies Press.
36 Harold Varmus, the Nobel prize winning former director of the NIH put it well: "Appropriations are the lifeblood of an agency." In his fascinating account of his time there, he makes clear the connection between the NIH's funding and politics. See ref 23.
37 Varmus' successor, Francis Collins, expanded on the political issues when he wrote on his retirement that "I won't miss the nasty politics." See ref 24.
38 At the time of writing, current budget proposals from the Biden administration include a 20% increase in NIH funding. This emphasizes, rather than refutes, the idea that NIH funding is variable and subject to the political weather. See https://sgp.fas.org/crs/misc/R43341.pdf.
39 Michael Lauer, the NIH's deputy director of extra-mural research, described the effect of the early-2000s budget increase as inducing a state of "euphoria." "The community responded exactly as you'd think it would ... There was an assumption that the growth would continue forever — and that assumption turned out to be incorrect." See ref 25.
40 This non-linearity, again a feature of complex adaptive systems, seems to be due to the way research grants are structured over time. To quote from this research: "...an apparently modest increase or decrease in funding levels can have dramatic effects on researchers, graduate students, postdocs, and the overall research enterprise." See ref 26.
41 The social determinants of health are an enormous topic on their own. See ref 27.
42 The importance of chronic diseases, defined broadly as conditions that last more than a year, has attracted a lot of research. The summary of this is that chronic diseases, driven in part by age and in part by lifestyle, are the leading driver of ill-health and healthcare costs. The Centers for Disease Control and Prevention estimates that chronic diseases, such as heart disease, diabetes and cancers, affect 60% of adults in the US and that 40% of adults have more than one such condition. See https://www.cdc.gov/chronicdisease/about/index.htm and See 28. It is also worth quoting at length from this study of chronic disease in the US:

> More than two thirds of all deaths are caused by one or more of these five chronic diseases: heart disease, cancer, stroke, chronic obstructive pulmonary disease, and diabetes. Additional statistics are quite stark: chronic diseases are responsible for seven out of 10 deaths in the U.S., killing more than 1.7 million Americans each year; and more than 75% of the $2 trillion spent on public and private healthcare in 2005 went toward chronic diseases. What makes treating chronic conditions (and efforts to manage population health) particularly challenging is that chronic conditions often do not exist in isolation. In fact, today one in four U.S. adults have two or more chronic conditions, while more than half of older adults have three or more chronic conditions. And the likelihood of these types of comorbidities occurring goes up as we age. Given America's current demographics, wherein 10,000 Americans will turn 65 each day from now through the end of 2029, it is reasonable to expect that the overall number of patients with comorbidities will increase greatly.

43 Epidemiological transition theory was proposed by Omran. See ref 29. Epidemiologists now talk of the fourth stage of epidemiological transition. See ref 30. Note that, in this part of the discussion, I'm restricting myself to how American society's demands on the PIE are shifting. Much of this is true in other parts of the developed world but I'm choosing not to address the large and important issue of global health needs, which is a much bigger, more difficult topic. See ref 31.

44 A good example of changing sociological factors is the expectations we now have of healthcare, which are somewhat different from those of earlier generations. See ref 32.

45 In my earlier work, I've identified six great shifts in the abiotic environment of the pharmaceutical industry, of which the Great Value Shift is one. See ref 33.

46 The HHS sets out five strategic goals, including to "Foster Sound, Sustained Advances in the Sciences," which breaks down to four strategic objectives, which include to "Advance basic science knowledge and conduct applied prevention and treatment research to improve health and development." This then breaks down into four strategies, led by "Discern risk factors and mechanisms underlying the leading causes of death to accelerate applied and preventive research solutions." What is notable is that this cascade of objectives doesn't seem to have changed much from plan to plan and makes little reference to the need for the discovery habitat to contribute to the affordability of medicines. See https://www.hhs.gov/about/strategic-plan/index.html.

47 The NIH-wide strategic plan for 2021–25 has a cascade of objectives that reflect those of the HHS. In these, there is again a strong bias toward adapting to the scientific and technological part of the abiotic environment and rather less to sociological change. Again, it would be hard, on reading the NIH strategy, to see any salience given to affordability. That said, some attention is paid to translational science and, as I'll come to, this is relevant to affordability.

48 Again, I'm simplifying the concepts. For a fuller explanation. See ref 34.

49 These ideas are displaced from the geographical mosaic theory of coevolution. See ref 35.

50 I'm referring here to the consequences of the Bayh-Dole act of 1980 which gave universities the rights to the intellectual property generated from federal funding and resulted in the rise of university technology transfer offices. Note however that entrepreneurial academics often complement these formal technology transfer processes with informal processes. See ref 34.

51 The growth of technology transfer in response to Bayh-Dole, is not a purely pharmaceutical phenomenon. An investigation into it by the National Academy of Sciences, Engineering and Medicine found it to be a generally positive adaptation but not without its problems. See ref 35.

52 The pronounced shift of early development to outside of large company research and development, known as external innovation, is more complicated than simply outsourcing to biotech. It includes the restructuring of large company R&D to be more like small biotech. These shifts are driven by multiple factors. See refs 36 and 37.

53 Note that the effects of this increased commercialization are not wholly positive. To quote from a retrospective review of Bayh-Dole's consequences:

> ...countries looking to boost commercialization should be wary of the myth that the act transformed US universities into entrepreneurial institutions capable of generating successful spin-off firms, high-tech jobs and self-sustaining research funds — and all at no cost to the taxpayer. Instead, they should note the problems that have arisen with the act, such as the overly restrictive patenting and licensing mentality it has generated among many technology-transfer offices, and craft their own legislation to avoid these pitfalls.

See ref 38.

54 Advocates of entrepreneurial universities refer to the "Triple Helix" model of education, research and innovation, a model developed by Etzkowitz. See 39. But the literature in this area also suggests that making this model work is far from straightforward and heavily influenced by the persistent academic culture of universities. See ref 40.

55 This is a phenomenon common in all scientific disciplines and fragmentation is associated with slower progress. This issue seems to be less in fields like biology, which have unifying bodies of accepted theory, than in fields such as psychology, which more often have conflicting schools of thought. See ref 41.

56 The globalization of scientific research is a remarkable feature of how the discovery habitat's biotic environment has changed. There are a number of competing explanations for why this has happened, and it is likely that all of these explanations are partly correct. See ref 42. The point remains, however, that the fragmentation and globalization of science increases the difficulty researchers face in managing and share knowledge in their field.

57 One of the characteristics of modern research is that it is a team game. The popular vision of a lone scientist working away to achieve a Eureka moment is, if it were ever true, a thing of the past. See ref 43.

58 To quote from some of this research:

> ...*in realistic management situations, the knowledge sharing of scientific research teams always appears to be unsustainable ... (knowledge hiding behavior) is capable of affecting sustainable knowledge sharing by reducing the supply of knowledge, creating a poor knowledge sharing atmosphere, and forming an interpersonal distrust relationship.*

See ref 44.

59 This observation was strikingly visible in a study of over 200 academic researchers in the life sciences. To quote from that work:

> *Researchers in academia who actively collaborate with industry are more likely to omit relevant content from publications in co-authorship with other academic researchers; delay their co-authored publications, exclude relevant content during public presentations; and deny requests for access to their unpublished and published knowledge.*

See ref 45.

60 To quote from some of the work in this area: "The results suggested that reciprocal benefit and fear of being scooped were significant in affecting implicit and explicit knowledge sharing behavior in health and life sciences research communities." See ref 46.

61 The benefits and practical issues around sharing research data are a long-standing point of concern for researchers. Various efforts are underway to enable data sharing via technological platforms and, in February 2022, the NIH issued a mandate to encourage data sharing amongst the researchers it funds. See refs 47 and 48. Much of the difficulty lies in common standards, as aspired to in the FAIR guidelines, which identify that data should be Findable, Accessible, Interoperable and Reusable. See ref 49. However, this seems to be more than a merely technological problem. In the words of one study of the subject: "The impediments (to data pooling) are diverse, nuanced and not reducible to collective action problems that are already understood by legal scholars and economists." See ref 50.

62 Again, the picture is more complex than this. The importance of translation is premised on the assumption that it is the main source of innovation. The history of medicine contains many empirical discoveries and even today many new medicines are incremental innovations made without an understanding of

the basic science. Despite this, as a first approximation, the translation of basic science, that emerges from the discovery habitat, is what drives pharmaceutical innovation.

63 Note that the cost of an innovative medicine and its price are two different things and are only loosely related to each other. This discussion does not imply that an improvement in translation and consequent reduction in development costs would necessarily be reflected in the pricing of innovative medicines. As discussed later in this book, innovative medicines are priced to optimise risk adjusted rate of return and are more heavily influenced by value and competition than by costs. The cost of an innovative medicine, of which development costs are a component, only sets a lower limit for its price.

64 These ideas draw heavily on the work of Christopher P Austin, who founded the NIH's National Center for the Advancement of Translational Science (NCATS) and led it for its first ten years. See ref 51.

65 This distinction might seem a little abstract to non-scientists and perhaps a metaphor will help. As I write this, to my left sits my saxophone and some tasks given to me by my saxophone tutor. The first task is to learn to play a particular piece well, at the right speed, with appropriate expression, the correct dynamics and a good technique. The second is to sight read a study with the aim of improving my understanding of timing and rhythm. The first task will lead to a better, specific performance and is akin to translational research, since it leads toward a particular finished piece of music. The second task will improve my ability to play any piece and is equivalent to translational science, since it will not lead to any particular finished piece of music but will improve my ability to create any piece of music. So, although the two pieces of work are both music practice, they are not the same thing. In the same way, although translational research and translational science are both about translation, they are not the same thing. The latter has a specific aim, the former is more foundational and has wider value.

66 To put this in context, as long ago as 1994 Gibbons argued that basic research (which he called mode 1) had was no longer the core mode of knowledge production and had been displaced by applied research (which he called mode 2). Although Gibbons was not referring specifically to life sciences research, later researchers have also suggested that Bayh-Dole and the commercialization of basic research had caused a shift within academic research away from basic research and toward translational research. See ref 53–55.

67 In an 1833 essay, the British economist William Foster Lloyd wrote about how unregulated grazing of commonly held land, known in Britain as the commons, to illustrate how self-interest unhampered by rules could lead to the degradation of shared assets. Since a 1968 article by Garrett Hardin, the term "tragedy of the commons" has become a metaphor for any situation in shared resources, such as the environment can be degraded by individual users acting selfishly. The 2009 Nobel Prize for Economic Science was award to Elinor Ostrom for demonstrating how the tragedy of the commons could be avoided.

68 Attila A Seyhan summarized this well:

> A rift that has opened up between basic research (bench) and clinical research and patients (bed) who need their new treatments, diagnostics and prevention, and this rift is widening and getting deeper. The crisis involving the 'translation' of basic scientific findings in a laboratory setting into human applications and potential treatments or biomarkers for a disease is widely recognized both in academia and industry. Despite the attempts that have been made both in academic and industry settings to mitigate this problem, the high attrition rates of drug development and

the problem with reproducibility and translatability of preclinical findings to human applications remain a fact and the return on the investment has been limited in terms of clinical impact.
See ref 56.

69 Austin identifies an exhaustive list of research priorities. Austin 2021.
70 At the time of writing, the Biden administration was proposing a $9 billion increase in NIH funding. This is in line with suggestions by think tanks to bring NIH funding in line with its previous 2003 peak. See ref 57.
71 In June 2021, the outgoing leader of the NIH, Francis Collins welcome ARPA-H but stressed that its success depended on understanding the strengths and weaknesses of current biomedical research and to learn from ARPA-H's model DARPA. See ref 58. At the same time, some commentators expressed concern that locating ARPA-H in the NIH might miss an opportunity to escape the NIH's culture and habits. See ref 59.
72 The effective altruism movement attempts to use evidence to increase the value created by charitable donations. See https://www.effectivealtruism.org/.
73 For an interesting topic on novel mechanisms for funding biomedical research, see this panel discussion https://www.youtube.com/watch?v=eiasnWPVcbY.
74 For an enthralling case study of how commercial considerations can colour basic research, Walter Isaacson's description of CRISPR in "The Code Breaker" is recommended.
75 The reader may recognize here the thinking of Richard Thaler, the Nobel Prize winning behavioral economist. See ref 60.
76 I'm aware that many in the NIH would argue that the current system is already designed this way. From my exploration of the topic, I inferred that NIH tries very hard to allocate resources to the best science but is relatively less influenced by society's medical and economic needs. This seems to be an artefact of the expert panels used, which are dominated by scientists. See refs 61 and 62.
77 NCATS FY2022 budget request for 2022 is $879 million (see https://ncats.nih.gov/about/center/budget). In 2021, it is $778 (see https://ncats.nih.gov/about/center/budget/past#fy2021).

References

1 Pielke R. In retrospect: Science — the endless frontier. *Nature.* 2010;466(7309): 922–3.
2 Kidd CV. Basic research--description versus definition. *Science.* 1959;129(3346): 368–71.
3 Schauz D. What is basic research? Insights from historical semantics. *Minerva.* 2014;52(3):273–328.
4 Elmer M, Florek C, Gabryelski L, Greene A, Inglis AM, Johnson KL et al. Amplifying the voice of the patient in clinical research: Development of toolkits for use in designing and conducting patient-centered clinical studies. *Therapeutic Innovation & Regulatory Science.* 2020;54(6):1489–500.
5 Schein EH. What is culture? In Frost PJ, Moore LF, Louis MR, Lundberg CC, editors. *Reframing Organizational Culture.* First ed. Newbury Park, CA: Sage; 1991. p. 243–53.
6 Peire AF, Patrik. What is the value of a deal? Nature Biopharma Dealmakers; June 2016. pp. B27–B28.
7 Foroohar R. *Makers and Takers: The Rise of Banking and the Fall of American Business.* New York: Crown Business; 2016.

8 Wu J. Why US business R&D is not as strong as it appears. *Information Technology and Innovation Foundation*; 2018.

9 O'Connor G. Real innovation requires more than an R&D budget. *Harvard Business Review*; 2019.

10 Jones BFS, Lawrence H. A calculation of the social returns to innovation. In Glosbee AJ, Benjamin, editor. *Innovation and Public Policy*. Chicago, IL: University of Chicago Press; 2022.

11 Mandt RS, Kushal CH, Michael C. Federal R&D funding: The bedrock of national innovation. MIT Science Policy Review. 2020;1:44–54.

12 Abelson PH. Biomedical science and its administration. *Science*. 1965;148(3667):171-.

13 The Evolution of NIH's Organizational Structure. Enhancing the Vitality of the National Institutes of Health: Organizational Change to Meet New Challenges: National Research Council (US) and Institute of Medicine (US) Committee on the Organizational Structure of the National Institutes of Health.; 2003.

14 Viergever RF, Hendriks TCC. The 10 largest public and philanthropic funders of health research in the world: What they fund and how they distribute their funds. *Health Research Policy and Systems*. 2016;14(1):12.

15 Maclean M, Harvey C, Yang R, Mueller F. Elite philanthropy in the United States and United Kingdom in the new age of inequalities. *International Journal of Management Reviews*. 2021;23(3):330–52.

16 Murray F. Evaluating the role of science philanthropy in American research universities. *Innovation Policy and the Economy*. 2013;13(1):23–60.

17 Mukherjee S. *The Emperor of All Maladies*. New York: Scribner; 2010.

18 Greve HR, Argote L. Behavioral theories of organization. In Wright JD, editor. *International Encyclopedia of the Social & Behavioral Sciences (Second Edition)*. Oxford: Elsevier; 2015. p. 481–6.

19 Apweiler R, Beissbarth T, Berthold MR, Blüthgen N, Burmeister Y, Dammann O et al. Whither systems medicine? *Experimental & Molecular Medicine*. 2018;50(3):e453–e.

20 Hasin Y, Seldin M, Lusis A. Multi-omics approaches to disease. *Genome Biology*. 2017;18(1):83.

21 Gauthier J, Vincent AT, Charette SJ, Derome N. A brief history of bioinformatics. *Briefings in Bioinformatics*. 2019;20(6):1981–96.

22 Fleming N. The microscopic advances that are opening big opportunities in cell biology. *Nature (London)*. 2019;575(7784):S91–S4.

23 Varmus H. *The Art and Politics of Science*. New York: W.W. Norton & Company; 2009.

24 Kaiser J. NIH's Collins steps down: 'I won't miss the nasty politics'. *Science (American Association for the Advancement of Science)*. 2021;374(6575):1547-.

25 Woolston C. Proposed NIH windfall raises hopes — and fears. *Nature (London)*. July 27 2021.

26 Larson RC, Ghaffarzadegan N, Diaz MG. Magnified effects of changes in NIH research funding levels. *Service Science*. 2012;4(4):382–95.

27 Braveman P, Gottlieb L. The social determinants of health: It's time to consider the causes of the causes. *Public Health Rep*. 2014;129(Suppl 2):19–31.

28 Raghupathi W, Raghupathi V. An empirical study of chronic diseases in the United States: A visual analytics approach. *International Journal of Environmental Research and Public Health*. 2018;15(3):431.

29 Omran AR. The epidemiologic transition: A theory of the epidemiology of population change. *The Milbank Quarterly.* 2005;83(4):731–57.
30 Hazra NC, Gulliford M. Evolution of the "fourth stage" of epidemiologic transition in people aged 80 years and over: Population-based cohort study using electronic health records. *Population Health Metrics.* 2017;15(1):18.
31 Yegros-Yegros A, van de Klippe W, Abad-Garcia MF, Rafols I. Exploring why global health needs are unmet by research efforts: The potential influences of geography, industry and publication incentives. *Health Research Policy and Systems.* 2020;18(1):47.
32 Lakin K, Kane S. Peoples' expectations of healthcare: A conceptual review and proposed analytical framework. *Social Science & Medicine.* 2022;292:114636.
33 Smith BD. *Darwin's Medicine: How Business Models in the Life Science Industry are Evolving.* Abingdon: Routledge; 2016.
34 Schaeffer V, Öcalan-Özel S, Pénin J. The complementarities between formal and informal channels of university–industry knowledge transfer: A longitudinal approach. *The Journal of Technology Transfer.* 2020;45(1):31–55.
35 Council NR. *Managing University Intellectual Property in the Public Interest.* Merrill SA, Mazza A-M, editors. Washington, DC: The National Academies Press; 2011. 118 p.
36 Schuhmacher A, Gassmann O, McCracken N, Hinder M. Open innovation and external sources of innovation. An opportunity to fuel the R&D pipeline and enhance decision making? *Journal of Translational Medicine.* 2018;16(1):119.
37 Yeung AWK, Atanasov AG, Sheridan H, Klager E, Eibensteiner F, Völkl-Kernsock S, et al. Open innovation in medical and pharmaceutical research: A literature landscape analysis. *Frontiers in Pharmacology.* 2021;11.
38 Sampat BN. Lessons from Bayh–Dole. *Nature.* 2010;468(7325):755–6.
39 Etzkowitz H. The second academic revolution: The role of the research university in economic development. In Cozzens SE, Healey P, Rip A, Ziman J, editors. *The Research System in Transition.* Dordrecht: Springer Netherlands; 1990. p. 109–24.
40 Czerniachowicz B, Wieczorek-Szymańska A. Selected problems of an entrepreneurial university - a theoretical perspective. *Balkan Region Conference on Engineering and Business Education.* 2019;1:426–37.
41 Balietti S, Mäs M, Helbing D. On disciplinary fragmentation and scientific progress. *PloS One.* 2015;10(3):e0118747–e.
42 Marginson S. What drives global science? The four competing narratives. *Studies in Higher Education.* 2021:1–19.
43 Bennett LM, Gadlin H. Collaboration and team science: From theory to practice. *Journal Investigate Medicine.* 2012;60(5):768–75.
44 Liu F, Lu Y, Wang P. Why knowledge sharing in scientific research teams is difficult to sustain: An interpretation from the interactive perspective of knowledge hiding behavior. *Frontier Psychology.* 2020;11:537833-.
45 Gerbin A, Drnovsek M. Knowledge-sharing restrictions in the life sciences: Personal and context-specific factors in academia–industry knowledge transfer. *Journal of Knowledge Management.* 2020;24(7):1533–57.
46 Park J, Gabbard JL. Factors that affect scientists' knowledge sharing behavior in health and life sciences research communities. *Computer Human Behaviour.* 2018;78(C):326–35.
47 Kozlov M. NIH issues a seismic mandate: Share data publicly. *Nature (London).* 2022;602(7898):558–9.

48 Navale V, von Kaeppler D, McAuliffe M. An overview of biomedical platforms for managing research data. *Journal of Data, Information and Management*. 2021;3(1):21–7.

49 Wilkinson MD, Dumontier M, Aalbersberg IJ, Appleton G, Axton M, Baak A et al. The FAIR guiding principles for scientific data management and steward-ship. *Nature (London)*. 2016;3(1):160018-.

50 Mattioli M. The data-pooling problem. *Berkeley Technology Law Journal*. 2017;32(1):179–236.

51 Austin CP. Opportunities and challenges in translational science. *Clinical and Translational Science*. 2021;14(5):1629–47.

52 Austin CP. Translational misconceptions. *Nature Reviews Drug Discovery*. 2021;20(7):489–90.

53 Loewenberg S. The Bayh–Dole act: A model for promoting research transla-tion? *Molecular Oncology*. 2009;3(2):91–3.

54 Link AN, Danziger RS, Scott JT. Is the Bayh-Dole act stifling biomedical innova-tion? *Issues in Science and Technology*. 2018;34(2):33–5.

55 Boettiger S, Bennett AB. Bayh-Dole: If we knew then what we know now. *Na-ture Biotechnology*. 2006;24(3):320–3.

56 Seyhan AA. Lost in translation: The valley of death across preclinical and clinical divide – identification of problems and overcoming obstacles. *Translational Med-icine Communications*. 2019;4(1):18.

57 Atkinson RD. Healthy funding: The critical role of investing in NIH to boost health and lower costs. *Information Technology and Innovation Foundation*; 2019.

58 Collins FS, Schwetz TA, Tabak LA, Lander ES. ARPA-H: Accelerating biomedical breakthroughs. *Science*. 2021;373(6551):165–7.

59 Kaiser J. Biden wants $6.5 billion for new health agency to speed treatments. *Science*; April 9 2021.

60 Sunstein C, Richard T. *Nudge: Improving Decisions about Health, Wealth and Hap-piness*. London: Penguin; 2009.

61 Fang FC, Bowen A, Casadevall A. NIH peer review percentile scores are poorly predictive of grant productivity. *eLife*. 2016;5:e13323.

62 Pier EL, Brauer M, Filut A, Kaatz A, Raclaw J, Nathan MJ et al. Low agreement among reviewers evaluating the same NIH grant applications. *Proceedings of the National Academy of Sciences - PNAS*. 2018;115(12):2952–7.

4 The innovation habitat

Precis

- The innovation habitat is the part of the pharmaceutical innovation ecosystem (PIE) where scientific discoveries are turned into innovative, prescribable medicines.
- Pharmaceutical innovation requires an extensive and diverse set of knowledge, assets, and resources and the capabilities to aggregate and coordinate them.
- Increasingly, this is done not by individual firms but by networked "holobionts" of biotechs, venture capitalists, specialized contractors, larger pharmaceutical companies, and regulatory agencies.
- The innovation habitat connects to the discovery and coalition habitats.
- A healthy PIE requires that the innovation habitat efficiently and effectively provides innovative medicines that meet society's needs.
- The innovation habitat's ability to support a healthy PIE is constrained by
  - The low predictivity of the discovery habitat's outputs
  - Lagging adaptation of the regulatory system to the increasingly heterogeneous nature of pharmaceutical innovation
  - Lagging adoption of technological and organizational improvements in pharmaceutical innovation
  - Wasteful duplication of effort and failure to share knowledge
  - Sensitivity to market uncertainty
- The innovation habitat would be better able to support a healthy PIE if:
  - Its basic research inputs were made more predictive
  - Its regulatory environment speciated into different forms

DOI: 10.4324/9781003330271-4

- It adopted new technologies and methods more quickly
- Knowledge were shared more fully between competing firms
- Market risks were reduced for societally valuable products

In Chapter 1, I defined pharmaceutical innovation as the bringing to market of a medicinal therapy that was not previously available. By that definition, what emerges from the discovery habitat is far from pharmaceutical innovation. Even the most brilliant scientific discoveries, those that have a high probability of translation into medicines that society needs and values, are not pharmaceutical innovation in this sense because they are not yet medicinal therapies. At this stage, we don't yet know what to administer, to whom, how to do so, or, if we did administer, what would be the balance of benefits and risks. Even if we did know these things, we don't yet have regulatory permission to do so or even the right kind of information needed to apply for that permission. What the discovery habitat delivers, even at its best, is one or more of the ingredients of pharmaceutical innovation but not an innovative medicine.[1] This is an important point because it strongly qualifies claims that new medicines are invented by publicly funded university researchers. There's a grain of truth in that, but it's not usually an accurate representation of reality.

The discovery habitat doesn't provide innovative medicines because it can't. To turn the discoveries of basic research into a prescribable innovative medicine is an enormously complex undertaking. It requires the aggregation of a large and diverse set of knowledge, assets, and resources that don't exist in the discovery habitat. It also requires the capabilities to combine and align them in a sophisticated way that leads to an approved medicinal therapy. Some indication of the scale and scope of what is needed is given in Figures 3.1 and 3.2, particularly in the parts of those figures that show the drug development process beyond basic research. The difficulty of this development process is a defining characteristic of the research-based pharmaceutical industry that sets it apart from other industries. The innovation habitat is where this difficult aggregation occurs and where basic research discoveries are translated into innovative medicines. Who is involved, what they do, and how well they do that is central to our question of how we might manage the pharmaceutical innovation ecosystem (PIE) to sustainably deliver affordable innovative medicines.

What happens in the innovation habitat and who inhabits it?

As Figures 3.1 and 3.2 reveal, the answer to the question "what happens in the innovation habitat?" is "many very different and difficult things." It's easy to get lost in this maze of activity, so it's useful to take a step backward and see the innovation habitat as involving three principal activities:[2]

- Deciding which innovative medicines to invest resources into
- Applying those resources in such a way as to develop an innovative medicine
- Gaining regulatory approval to market that innovative medicine

To understand how the innovation habitat works, it is important to appreciate that each of these three activities is burdened with high degrees of uncertainty and risk. This issue shapes what happens in the innovation habitat, whose actors and processes are driven by the need to mitigate that risk and to improve the probability of success. As part of that risk management, these activities are organized not to be sequential, like a chain, but interwoven, like a fabric. For example, resources are allocated not in one big decision but at stage gates, when new information is considered and risk is re-evaluated. The risk profile of these decisions is highly context specific, varying between types of therapy, between therapies, and with the investors' experience, knowledge, and wider strategy. As a result, although the innovation process works roughly similarly in different cases, the decisions made and the outcomes might differ greatly between cases.[3]

So, developing an innovative medicine requires the aggregation of knowledge, resources, and capabilities in a way that mitigates risk and maximizes the probability of success. These considerations shape who inhabits the innovation habitat and how they behave, both of which have changed over the last two decades or so. Historically, this aggregation mostly took place inside medium and large pharmaceutical companies who integrated all the necessary activities under one roof, sometimes literally. In the last decade or two, however, this has changed in two (connected) ways. The first is outsourcing to and the growth of large contract research organizations.[4] The second is loosely labeled open innovation or the trend for the early stages of pharmaceutical innovation to be done by small, focused biotechs. If successful, these biotechs are then usually either acquired or they may license their partly developed innovative medicines to larger companies to finish development, gain registration, and market.[5] Importantly, open innovation has led venture capitalists (VCs) to enter the innovation habitat, often financing start-up companies that are part-owned by the universities and scientists who made the discoveries on which they are built.[6]

Together, the need for lots of different assets, resources, and capabilities to be aggregated and the trends toward outsourcing and open innovation have made the answer to the question "who inhabits the innovation habitat?" much more complicated than it used to be. With the involvement of universities and scientists, it blurs into the discovery habitat more than the historical, integrated model did. With the entry of VCs and the outsourcing of many research and development activities, the picture comes to contain more and different elements. One useful way to think of the innovation habitat is that it is populated by many overlapping networks, each containing some combination of VCs, universities, biotechs, larger pharmaceutical companies, and their contractors. In my other writing, I've called these networks "holobionts."[7] Importantly, such holobionts are not fixed, permanent arrangements. They form, dissolve, and reform as needed according to the requirements of each pharmaceutical innovation. And because these holobionts need to deliver innovative medicines that are approved for use, they also incorporate regulatory bodies such as the Food and Drug Administration (FDA)'s Center for Drug Evaluation and Research (CDER), albeit as a kind of symbiont attached to the commercial activity.[8]

So, the innovation habitat is even more messy and difficult to understand than Figures 3.1 and 3.2 imply. It has three interwoven sub-processes and requires the aggregation of usually more than one area of new knowledge with existing knowledge and a host of human, financial, and other resources and assets. To make an innovative medicine requires the capabilities to assemble and use this aggregation. No one organization has all these things, so any given innovation usually requires a holobiont of complementary organizations of different kinds. And since each innovation might involve a separate holobiont, the innovation habitat comes to resemble a tangle of overlapping, interlocking companies. With this less-than-straightforward picture in my mind, I continued my exploration by asking what the PIE requires of the innovation habitat.

What does a healthy PIE require of the innovation habitat?

The innovation habitat takes its inputs from multiple sources. The most obvious is the flow of new knowledge from the discovery habitat, which largely determines what innovation can be done. But what can be done is only half the picture. The other half is the choice of what, of all the scientific possibilities, *will* be done. This is determined by estimations of the likely risk-adjusted return on investment. Consequently, the innovation habitat is intimately connected to those parts of the PIE that influence market size, pricing, and other factors that determine risk-adjusted rate of return. These are discussed in the patient, value, pricing, and competition habitats in later chapters. The innovation habitat is also connected to the coalition habitat, in which the aggregates of resources and capabilities are formed. A well-functioning innovation habitat takes signals and inputs from all these parts of the PIE and feeds back what the PIE needs to be healthy. From this perspective, the health of the PIE requires three things of the innovation habitat.

The innovation habitat must provide innovative medicines efficiently

The innovation habitat consumes societal resources to create innovative medicines, and a healthy PIE requires that it does so efficiently. The output of the innovative medicines should be proportional to the resources consumed, and the efficiency of the innovative habitat should increase over time, commensurate with experience curves. By contrast, an innovation habitat that fails to provide innovative medicines or is wasteful of available resources or that does not increase its efficiency over time is unlikely to sustain a healthy PIE.

The innovation habitat must provide innovative medicines effectively

Efficient provision of innovative medicines is a necessary but not sufficient requirement of the innovation habitat. A healthy PIE also requires that those innovative medicines closely reflect society's needs – medical, economic, and other. The innovation habitat must be effective at understanding those needs, reflecting them in its allocation of resources, and using those resources to optimize the probability that those needs will be met. By contrast, an innovation habitat that fails to understand societal needs or does not allocate resources toward them or makes poor use of those resources or substantially fails to meet those needs is unlikely to sustain a healthy PIE.

The innovation habitat must provide economic sustainability

A healthy PIE requires that pharmaceutical innovation is not only efficient and effective but also economically sustainable, balancing the economic needs of both innovators and society. An innovation habitat that did not allow sufficient returns would not attract sustained investment. Equally, returns that exceed that level would misallocate societal resources and undermine the social contract. An innovation habitat that allowed either condition is unlikely to sustain a healthy PIE.

I've summarized these conclusions in Figure 4.1. Again, the apothecary's garden metaphor is apposite. Our gardeners need to see lots of growth, but it must be the growth they want, not weeds. And what they harvest must be worth what they invested in the garden but not

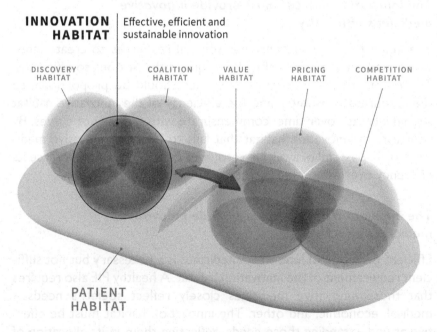

Figure 4.1 The innovation habitat's contribution to a healthy PIE

so much that it is unsustainable. In the same way, a well-functioning innovation habitat needs to provide the PIE with a sustainable supply of innovative medicines that are what society needs, economically and medically. Again, the parallels between the PIE and the natural ecosystem of the apothecary's garden are clear.

So, having explored what happens in the innovative habitat, who occupies it, and what the PIE requires of it, I moved on to explore how well it is working. As in the other habitats, I wanted to understand whether the innovation habitat could deliver the three requirements described above well enough for the PIE to be a sustainable source of innovative and affordable medicines.

Is the innovation habitat capable of supporting a healthy PIE?

It's not unreasonable to question how well the innovation habitat meets the needs of a healthy PIE. The public concerns described in Chapter 1 make it reasonable to examine all the habitats of the PIE and, since the innovation habitat is central to the health of the PIE, it deserves at least as much examination as the other habitats. But there are three reasons for considering the working of the innovation habitat in particular. First, in any discussion of pharmaceutical pricing, the cost of innovation is the main justification for high prices. If the innovation habitat is a cause of high prices then, given our question about sustainable, affordable innovative medicines, it's only sensible to look at that habitat. Second, both the surge of venture capital into the innovation habitat and the notable financial success of many research-based pharmaceutical companies are indicative of an attractive market. This makes it reasonable to ask if it is too attractive and if its occupants are achieving a return above what is needed to sustain innovation. Finally, pharmaceutical innovation has long been characterized by lengthy development times and a careful regulatory assessment process. Yet COVID-19 has shown that, in certain circumstances, both development and regulatory assessment can be compressed, with benefits for society and pharmaceutical innovators. It's not unreasonable to ask if any lessons learned from that experience can be generalized to other parts of the innovation habitat. Based on these justifications, I began my exploration of the working of the innovation habitat and uncovered five causes for concern.

The innovation habitat depends on weak inputs from the discovery habitat

As my exploration of the discovery habitat revealed (see Chapter 3), the innovation habitat is not receiving the flow of highly translatable basic research output it needs. This results in most of those discoveries failing to be translated into prescribable medicines. Most fail to cross the colorfully named "valley of death between the bench and the bed."[9] I won't reiterate the causes and consequences described in Chapter 3, but it was most succinctly captured in a video by Christopher P. Austin, whose work I discussed earlier.

> *I've seen a revolution, in my professional lifetime, in basic research. How we understand how humans function, and health and disease. But there hasn't been a commensurate increase in our ability to diagnose, treat and cure disease. And that is the translational problem. How do we get better at doing that?*
>
> Christopher P. Austin[10]

The impact of the discovery habitat on the innovation habitat is fundamental. The effect of any changes to the latter will be limited in their effect unless accompanied by effective changes in the former. But as the following points describe, this is not the only factor that seems to constrain the ability of the innovation habitat to support a healthy PIE.

The innovation habitat is constrained by an evolutionary lag in regulation

At the climax of pharmaceutical development lies the unavoidable tension that all medicines balance risks and benefits.[11] Only when that ratio is demonstrably acceptable to the regulatory authorities has the innovation process delivered what the PIE asks of it. At the same time, the innovation habitat must minimize the time and financial costs of achieving regulatory approval. This tension pervades the innovation habitat and shapes how it works. Pharmaceutical innovators design their development programs, especially their clinical trials, around the regulators' requirements, while complaining of the time and cost involved.[12] In response, regulators adapt their processes to make approval as fast and inexpensive as they can, while worrying about the possibility of putting patients at risk.[13] Despite attempts by both innovators and regulators to manage this risk/benefit tension, there remains a significant issue of the regulatory system not being well adapted to the needs of the innovation habitat. One expert informant put it this way:

> There's a pressing need to optimize the regulatory and oversight process for safety, affordability and patient outcomes. I say "optimize" because there are of course tradeoffs between these things and they have to be balanced with all of society's needs in mind.
>
> Gillian Woollett

From an ecological perspective, this long-standing tension has been amplified by recent changes in the wider sociological and technological environments. The regulatory system we have today has been shaped by its historical goal of achieving a reasonable risk/benefit ratio for relatively simple therapies, with the time and cost of regulation being secondary concerns. But society is changing the balance of what it asks of the regulators. We now ask for much more advanced therapies[14] to be brought to market as quickly and cheaply as possible, while being no less sensitive to the risk/benefit balance. Unsurprisingly given these changes, what we seem to be experiencing is an evolutionary lag between the rapid change in the environment and, notwithstanding the FDA's adaptations, the slower change of regulatory processes. This is not simply a matter of FDA tardiness, since the speed of approvals has improved[15] and the FDA has, since 2004, had a program dedicated to improving the regulatory process.[16] But the flexibility of the regulatory process is inevitably limited by the risks to patients and by the implications of regulatory change for international agreements. The regulatory system is not just the FDA; it is a global network of regulatory bodies, pharmaceutical companies, and others.[17]

So, my exploration of the innovation habitat found that a lag in the evolution of the regulatory system, relative to what is now being asked of it, that was hindering the innovation habitat's ability to meet the requirements of the PIE. This doesn't seem to be attributable to any "bad actors" and is true despite the efforts of both regulators and pharmaceutical innovators to adapt to a rapidly changing environment. But given the centrality of regulatory approval in the innovation habitat, closing this lag seems important to the working of the habitat and the health of the PIE.

The innovation habitat has unrealized potential for technological and organizational improvement

In points 1 and 2 above, I've described how the supply of scientific discoveries and the regulatory process bookend the development of innovative medicines. Both are critically important to the innovation habitat, but they are not all that matters. Between them sits the long, laborious, multistage process of turning basic science into a useable medicine. Reducing the cost and increasing the speed of this process has been a focus of the pharmaceutical industry for a long time with only debatable success.[18] In particular, pharmaceutical innovators focus on the need to "fail early," since the later the failure, the larger the wasted investment.[19] Despite this focus, attrition rates have remained stubbornly high; the duration of the development process frustratingly resistant to compression; and, consequently, the efficiency of drug development has remained static or may even have decreased.[20] Although there is much debate about methodologies and numbers, there is a consensus that the costs of drug development are one of the more significant factors in the cost of innovative medicines and, to the extent that costs are related to price, influence their price.

My exploration of this topic was guided by several expert informants who understood the drug development process very well, and what they told me, substantiated in the published literature, surprised me. The development process has significant potential, by applying new technologies and process reorganization, to be both faster and cheaper. To quote Raymond Hill, an expert informant who literally "wrote the book" on drug development:

> Significant developments in the drug development process are within reach through the application of enabling technology and changes in practice, although some of these require corresponding changes in the regulatory environment.
>
> Raymond Hill

As Raymond Hill suggests, the opportunities to improve the drug development process are both technological and organizational.[21] The former includes the application of artificial intelligence (AI), genomics, and computer-aided drug design. Organizationally, the design and execution of clinical trials seems especially ripe for improvement. Opportunities here include so-called adaptive trial design, the greater use of "real world data,"[22] and redesigning clinical trials to reflect the trends in biomarkers and personalized medicine.[23] Among the expert informants and in the wider literature, there is a consensus that drug development can be done faster and cheaper.[24] The possibilities here made me wonder what it was that has prevented or slowed these opportunities from being fully realized, and whether this lagging effect hindered the innovation habitat's ability to support a healthy PIE.

The innovation habitat has unrealized potential for sharing knowledge

Like other complex systems, pharmaceutical innovation can be understood as a process of Darwinian evolution. Just as in biological systems, variations in approaches emerge and are selected for or against by the market environment. The "fittest" survive and these are copied by others.[25] This is relevant because, for all its effectiveness, evolution is a very inefficient process, and this can be seen in pharmaceutical innovation. As expert informant Anders Neilsen pointed out, "pharmaceutical research and development is in large part a data generating exercise." As he and other expert informants explained to me, the essence of pharmaceutical innovation is the creation of data, information, knowledge, and insight[26] about what works, when, for whom, and why. Each individual innovator (or, more accurately, each innovative holobiont) generates large amounts of these four things, and particularly when working in the same scientific or disease area, much of it is either duplicated or potentially complementary but mostly not shared. This obvious inefficiency, an unintended consequence of commercial competition, occurs at every stage of the development process. As expert informant Larry Liberti put it:

> *A large amount of costly research effort is duplicated and sometimes wasted by competitive research efforts. At the same time, these competitive efforts often create knowledge that, if shared, would save time and money. This is true throughout the development process but often the biggest cost and time impacts are in clinical trials. The potential for collaboration is enormous.*
> *Larry Liberti*

This inefficiency matters because the costs of such duplicated effort are reflected in the costs of innovative medicines and, to the extent that they are connected, their price. As with other efficiency factors in the development process, the wastefulness of competitive research and development has long been understood by academic researchers and the industry.[27] That cooperation in research and development has benefits and the innovative habitat has already evolved several approaches to what is broadly termed pre-competitive collaboration.[28] Current approaches vary greatly in their goals, the scope of their cooperation, and their membership.[29]

As I explored how various models of collaborative research worked, it became clear that they were still at an early stage of evolution and that much potential for collaboration was still unrealized. We are a long way away from the optimum of everything possible being shared by everybody who could collaborate with everybody who could benefit. There are several good reasons for this. The fragmentation of collaborative research efforts, the lack of research about what collaboration works and what doesn't, and the still unresolved issues of intellectual property and value capture all limit the degree of pre-competitive collaboration.[30] There are those who think these issues are so hard to resolve that pre-competitive collaboration in pharmaceutical innovation is a myth.[31] Whatever the truth, it's clear that the innovation habitat doesn't share all its knowledge, that this is wasteful, and that there's potential to reduce that waste. So, perhaps a more sanguine, balanced view is that there is significant, valuable potential for pre-competitive cooperation in drug development, but realizing that potential will be difficult. The realization of that potential would, obviously, allow the innovation habitat to better support a healthy PIE.

The innovation habitat is sensitive to market uncertainty

As I've discussed, pharmaceutical innovation is a costly business that requires investors to place large amounts of their capital at risk. This makes it inevitable that the behavior of innovators is shaped by the need to manage the two main components of that risk. First, the risk that the innovation may not reach the market (pre-market risk or probability of technical and regulatory success). Second, even if it does reach the market, that it may not make the expected returns (in-market risk). These risks influence the cost of capital, investment choices, and pricing strategies, which together make them highly relevant to our question of how we might manage the PIE for a sustainable yield of affordable, innovative medicines. If these twin risks could somehow be reduced significantly, the investment economics would mean more drugs would be developed and the returns expected by investors would be less.

In points 1–4 above, I've already described factors that influence pre-market risk. The predictivity of basic research, the regulatory process, the technological and organizational improvement of the development process, and pre-competitive collaboration are all factors in the costs and risks of reaching the market. In my exploration of the innovation habitat, I found that VCs and pharmaceutical companies were attentive to and relatively sophisticated at assessing and managing pre-market risks.[32] But I did not find the same to be true for in-market risk, which is made up of several interconnected component risks.[33] That is not to say that innovators do not consider in-market risk, but the "state of the art" is much less than for pre-market risk and managing in-market risk is somewhat more subjective. Compared to pre-market risk, there is much less published on in-market risk, and what there is tends to be quite simplistic and narrowly focused.[34] Interestingly, the dominant in-market risk theme in the pharmaceutical literature concerns the impact of price controls which are common outside of the US.[35]

In-market risk is multifactorial and difficult to manage, but the less-developed ability to predict and mitigate it shapes investment decisions in the innovative habitat in particular ways. It makes markets with low or predictable in-market risk especially attractive,[36] and it makes returns in the early years after launch more attractive than returns many years after launch.[37] Conversely, it makes some markets considerably less attractive or at least harder to assess. Those with intense competition or unpredictable markets, such as some anti-infective markets, struggle to attract investment even if there is a significant social need.[38] The in-market risk calculation also perversely influences innovations that create value beyond the immediate use of the product – for example, innovations that cure rather than manage a disease – because it is harder to capture such value in a revenue stream. This is because curative therapies effectively erode their own market and so change the nature of the return-on-investment calculation.[39] A similar argument holds true for innovations that prevent illness, rather than manage or cure it.[40] To quote expert informant Anders Neilsen:

> There is an issue with current economic models of drug development particularly related to curative or disease modifying therapies. From a classical business model perspective, such innovations would essentially eat tomorrow's revenue. This is hard to reconcile with shareholders and equity owners and thus, such innovations are likely to come from privately owned companies, from public investments or new hybrid models.
>
> *Anders Neilsen*

In my exploration of the innovation habitat, risk was the pervasive issue that shaped almost everything. The most salient and talked-about issue was pre-market risk, at least among those involved in the US market. Outside the US, in-market risk and especially market access risk was raised more often. But that shouldn't imply that pre-market risk is more important than in-market risk as a shaper of the innovation habitat. I inferred that both were important, but that in-market risk was simply less well addressed. This has downsides, nudging innovation away from some socially desirable goals, such as preventative therapies, but also an upside. If the habitat is sensitive to in-market risk, then managing that risk might be a powerful tool for encouraging the innovation habitat to deliver what the PIE requires.

So, my exploration of the innovation habitat led me to conclude that it is not functioning well, if we define good function as being able to give the PIE what it needs. This is due in part to the inputs it receives from the discovery habitat, but the innovation habitat has its own, internal issues too. The regulatory system, while working hard to overcome its history and adapt to a changing world, is struggling to balance safety and innovation in an environment that is ever more scientifically and economically heterogeneous. There is considerable potential for organizational and technological improvements to how drug development is done. The wastefulness inherent in competitiveness is not fully addressed by what seems to be embryonic and limited pre-competitive collaboration. The entire habitat is pervaded by the need to manage risk, yet managing in-market risk is neglected as a means of nudging the market, leaving imperfect market forces to do what they are not fully capable of doing. Collectively, these factors make it unlikely that the innovation habitat can give the PIE what it needs to provide what we ask of it, a sustainable flow of affordable innovative medicines. I reached these conclusions with no less admiration of how the innovation habitat translates scientific discovery into innovative medicines that are important to society. And having reached this point in my exploration, I pushed on to the question of how the working of the innovation habitat might be improved.

How can we improve the innovation habitat?

The innovation habitat is a frenzied, hectic place. It is populated by academics trying to translate their discoveries, VCs and biotechs engaged in early development, contract researchers playing their roles, larger pharmaceutical companies trying to pick and exploit winners, and regulators trying to balance patient safety against encouraging innovation. Although it is sometimes described as a pipeline, its many diverse interactions make it more like the web of a drunken spider. This web is not the whole of the PIE, but it is probably what comes to mind first for most people when they think of pharmaceutical innovation. It seems obvious that, if the innovation habitat isn't working well, the PIE can't deliver the affordable innovation needed to maintain the social contract. And yet, as the preceding section describes, an exploration of the habitat finds several ways in which the habitat's working is constrained. Based on those constraints, in this section, I'll describe some possible steps toward an innovation habitat that better supports a healthy PIE.

Improve the predictivity of basic research

I have already discussed the reliance of the innovation habitat on the outputs of the discovery habitat in Chapter 3 and again earlier in this chapter. I won't repeat myself, except to say that it won't be enough just to throw more money at the National Institutes of Health (NIH) and other basic researchers. The innovation habitat needs more exciting scientific discoveries, but they need to be more translatable discoveries too. That means basic research, done in a way that enables translation, and it means the transformation of translational science, rather than just more translational research.[41] If the PIE is to deliver what we ask of it, it can no longer be based on taking lots of low probability "shots on goal," it must work toward fewer but better shots. At the same time, those discoveries, while driven by curiosity, must be colored by what society needs and nudged toward socially valuable goals. Even then, the whole process depends on co-evolving the abilities of the organizations involved in discovery to share information and work together across the "valley of death" between discovery and innovation.

I'm sure that readers who know the industry will find little that is novel in this conclusion. The basic ideas, if not the implementation details, are well accepted in the industry. The question is why the innovation habitat still accepts these "weak passes" from the discovery habitat and does not do more to take fewer, better shots on goal. From the ecosystem perspective, this suggests that adaptation (that is, improving the innovation habitat's basic research inputs) must be harder than not adapting (that is, accepting high R&D costs and passing them on to the market).[42] It is at least arguable that, historically, this has been true. As the industry's sociological and technological abiotic environment changes, the adapt/don't adapt calculation must change too.

In particular, the shift toward value-based pricing discussed in Chapter 6 would change this calculus by making it harder to pass inefficiencies onto the payers and patients.

Improving the innovation habitat's inputs is more than a technological exercise. It also involves societal choices that will jar with some. For example, those who think that basic research is a case of "socializing risk, privatizing profit"[43] may need to accept that other models of incentivizing pharmaceutical innovation also have their problems and that the current "pull" model, while it may be augmented by "push" models in some situations, is not likely to be replaced completely.[44] At the same time, pharmaceutical companies may need to accept that the flow of returns to society, whether through the Bayh–Dole rights of inventing institutions, more accessible pricing, or via less aggressive tax avoidance, is connected via the social contract to the public funding of basic research.[45] Equally, nudging basic research toward certain aims will raise concerns about protecting "curiosity driven" research and the so-called Haldane principle that researchers should direct their own research.[46] Using public funding to direct academic research is, of course, a sensitive political issue, but it is one that needs to be considered as part of improving the inputs into the innovation habitat. Absent of that, the innovation habitat will not support the health of the PIE as well as it could.

Speciate the regulatory environment

The regulatory system plays an unenviable, invidious role in the innovation habitat. Not only must it balance the risk/benefit assessment against the need to facilitate innovation, but it also must maintain that balance as both science and social expectations change quickly. When I suggest that pharmaceutical regulation should adapt, I don't mean to imply any criticism or lack of sympathy for the FDA and other regulatory authorities. Quite the opposite.

Again, I should and will leave the details of how regulation should adapt to experts in that field, but I will offer three factors for those experts to consider. The first is that an adapted system must allow for the "speciation" of pharmaceutical innovation. In the historical environment where the CDER evolved, most innovative medicines could be regulated by the same process, and only clinical benefits were considered. In the future, there will be many more – and more different – types of innovative medicine, and the benefits to be considered will be economic as well as clinical. In a world of many kinds of risk/

benefit combinations, the regulatory process may need to speciate far more than it already has.[47] The second is that society, while asking for faster access to better and medicines at less cost, has not reduced its sensitivity to risk. In a world where packets of peanuts must carry a "may contain nuts" warning, regulators will not be able to trade off safety to encourage innovation. Instead, they will need to change, technologically and organizationally, so that faster, cheaper access to improved clinical and economic benefits can become possible without compromising safety. Third, the global nature of pharmaceutical innovation will only increase and, for all its dominance, the US will need to operate within global frameworks and agreements. So, not only will US regulation need to speciate and rebalance risks and benefits, but it will also need to bring the rest of the world along with it.

Like any other adaptation, this will involve the reconsideration of some things that have become norms. Regulatory professionals may need to adjust to the idea that economic and commercial needs become a larger part of their reasoning than before and that provisional approvals and proxy end points may become the new normal. At the same time, innovative companies may need to adjust to a world in which regulatory approval is not a single, relatively standardized hurdle but more of a continuous assessment tailored to the situation, with all the implications for the costs and challenges of product development.

Adopt new R&D technologies and methods

Seeing how much has changed since my time as an R&D chemist in the 1970s and 1980s, I hesitate to criticize the pace of adaptation. But my exploration revealed a gap between what is done and what is possible, a gap that is big enough to make a significant difference to the PIE. And I was struck by how much consensus there is on this point in both the published literature and among my expert informants.

Given the technological complexity, the details of how to modernize and accelerate the pharmaceutical development process are best left to others, some of whom I've cited in this chapter. But, in that complex context, I'm bravely going to suggest three considerations for Chief Science Officers who will have to lead this modernization. First, the speciation in types of innovative medicine suggests that the task won't be to modernize the drug development process, rather to evolve several species of development process, each specific to a technology type. Second, that despite the attractiveness of new technologies, the speciation of development processes will be as much about organization and process as employing shiny new tools. Third, that the connectivity between drug development and regulatory approval is so fundamental that one cannot evolve without the other. Modernizing drug development will be a process that co-evolves with the adaptation of the regulatory process and vice versa.

My perception of those involved in pharmaceutical R&D is that they will not need any encouragement to adapt how drug development is done, either technologically or organizationally. However, to achieve this with urgency might need them to reconsider their role in the affordability of innovative medicines. Modernizing drug development is not simply a way to get more innovative medicines, it is one of the most important things that can be done to ensure a sustainable supply of medicines that are both innovative and affordable.

Improve knowledge sharing in R&D

One of the most striking images painted for me as I explored the innovation habitat was that of a giant data-producing machine made up of thousands, perhaps tens of thousands, of individual research and development efforts. Even more striking was the idea that this equates to expensive duplication of effort and each holding information that could help others. In the context of a world where access to medicines is constrained by cost, the wastefulness of this image was arresting. The existing movement toward pre-competitive collaboration suggested to me that those in the industry were also concerned about that wastefulness. Since the problem exists and is recognized, the opportunity to much improve collaboration within the innovation habitat seems obvious.

As with other ways to improve the innovation habitat, I will leave the mechanics of transforming noncompetitive collaboration to experts in the field and will, again, only offer some considerations they might find useful. The first is that collaboration has benefits of scale, so a radical transformation of noncompetitive collaboration is likely to involve large-scale cooperation of many partners, not simply an extension of current partnerships between a handful of innovators. The second is that collaboration has benefits of scope, so a transformed knowledge sharing system will probably break out of its traditional silos in scientific development and into, for example, health economics, patient behavior, and organizational practices. This implies that a transformational collaboration effort would engage not only with pharmaceutical innovators but also with others who hold information about the use of medicines, including healthcare providers and pharmacy benefit managers. The third is that the foundation of collaboration is trust, and its critics have a point when they say there is no such thing as a truly noncompetitive situation. This implies the need for collaboration brokers who might facilitate trust and sharing. This idea exists already in the sector and could be developed further, perhaps with government or nonprofit involvement.

Getting to a situation where collaboration reduces the unnecessary waste of competition will have technological and organizational challenges, but these will be made easier if society can accept some trade-offs. For example, those who are concerned about antitrust issues may have to accommodate some loosening of those laws, and collaborators will need to be above suspicion regarding anticompetitive practices. Those who wish for a limited role of government in markets may need to consider the value of federal bodies acting as information brokers, given that the market does not seem to have fully addressed this need. Equally, the value of economies of scale and scope means that it may be worth accepting a government role in encouraging commercial entities toward noncompetitive collaboration, much as is already done to achieve common standards in many industries.

Reduce in-market risk for valuable products

As I explored the innovation habitat, the pervasive influence of risk was not surprising. What was less expected was that the capabilities for assessment and mitigation of pre-market risk were so much more developed than for in-market risk. The first is a science, while the second an art. I concluded that, at least in the US, this was due to the historically free-market pricing conditions which, to some extent, mitigate in-market risk. But it was also clear to me that, with the rising power of payers and the threats of price controls, the salience of in-market risk in the US was increasing. This presents an opportunity to nudge the market. If we can reduce in-market risk for socially valuable medicines, we can reduce costs of capital and better align the market to societal needs. Both would improve the capacity of the innovation habitat to support a healthy PIE.

Again, I'll stay above the detail in the hope of providing guidance rather than attempting instruction. There are three things that policy makers might bear in mind here. First, the whole innovation habitat would be helped by a generalized reduction of in-market risk.

This could be achieved if payers, and especially the Health and Human Services (HHS), signaled fewer, clearer priorities to the industry, making clear what there was a market for and what there wasn't. This is further discussed in Chapter 9, about the patient habitat. In-market risk would also be reduced by a broad political consensus over drug pricing policy. This needn't be down to the level of policy detail but an agreement of principles would reduce the compounding effect of political risk on in-market risk. Second, the innovation habitat would be helped by specific reduction of in-market risk in areas of high societal need. A variety of methods could be used to achieve this, from guaranteed volumes or prices to shared development costs. Importantly, these signals of societal need would need to go beyond clinical needs and be used to encourage innovations that reduce systemic costs or have other benefits that are not signaled by free-market pricing. Finally, market signals that pull the innovation habitat away from societal needs, such as legal conditions on formularies, might need to be reconsidered.

"Nudging" the innovation habitat by manipulating in-market risk in this way has huge potential for politicization. It will be made easier and more effective if, as a society, we can agree on some common ground in health policy. Those who are concerned about, for example, society directing the industry might consider that this is exactly what we do, very successfully, in markets such as defense, with which healthcare has some things in common. Those who worry about favoring the industry by guaranteeing markets or sharing development costs might consider that this is what worked to great effect for the COVID vaccines. Even with the political divisions of US public life, it ought to be possible to accept both that the innovation habitat needs freedom to innovate as it sees fit and guidance as to what innovation best meets the terms of the social contract.

Will this be enough?

These five suggestions, limited to broad guidance rather than specific policy recommendations, flow from the issues that seem to constrain the ability of the innovation habitat to meet the requirements of a healthy PIE. If all five were implemented with alacrity, they would take the innovation habitat much of the way toward that goal. They would be especially effective if they were enacted in a coordinated way, because all five issues and suggestions revolve around the mitigation of risk, the pervasive issue of the innovation habitat. There are other remedies that might also be tried but, with the help of the expert informants and researchers who have preceded me, I think I've captured the most important issues in these five recommendations.

The ecosystem perspective reminds us, however, that intervention in any one habitat, however effective, may be necessary but is unlikely to be sufficient. Even a perfectly functioning innovation habitat cannot deliver what that the PIE needs from the other habitats. To achieve that goal, we need to consider and address those other habitats.

Notes

1 Innovation is often conflated with invention and, more recently, ideation. Definitions of all these terms emphasize newness or novelty. Exactly what the semantic differences are is one of those questions academics love to debate like medieval theologians arguing about how many angels might dance on the head of a pin, and I want to avoid that rabbit hole in this chapter. Suffice it to say that, if you listen to enough of these arguments carefully enough, you can discern two points of differentiation between innovation and invention. First, innovation is about creating value in some way and, while some inventions may create value, not all do. Second, innovation is almost always the novel synthesis of multiple ideas, while invention is typically associated with a single new idea. In this, I am especially influenced by the ideas of Peter Drucker, but most researchers in the innovation field converge on the same points.

2 This view illuminates a choice I made in structuring my research. I could have added to this list "Gain market access and customer preference," but I chose to leave that activity to later chapters about value and pricing because it fits better with those activities, even though it happens during the latter stages of the innovation process.

3 The risks and probabilities in the innovation habitat are sometimes divided into pre-market and in-market. The former is the probability that the company will be able to develop the product and get it approved. The industry term for this is PTRS, probability of technical and regulatory success. The latter, in-market risk, is the probability that the product once approved will make the returns on which the investment decision was made. It is composed of factors such the probabilities that the sales volumes, prices, and profit margins will be as expected over the lifetime of the product.

4 Outsourcing of this kind is driven by the efficiencies of scale and scope made possible by specialization. It is also driven by changes in capital markets and the availability of "cheap money." There are those who think that changes in the cost of capital will soon cause a reversal in this trend. See 1. For now, outsourcing of research and development is a remarkable trend in the innovation habitat, but it is a complex picture. Some large contractors offer comprehensive "end to end" service, while many more offer specialized services within the innovation process. At the same time, most pharmaceutical companies also retain significant internal R&D capabilities. Outsourcing represents an organizational rather than scientific change in the innovation habitat. The same work is being done, often by the same people, but in different buildings under different names. For more discussion on this important trend in pharmaceutical innovation, see refs 2 and 3.

5 Open innovation is a much wider topic than this, and again, I've made the choice not to go too far into this subject here. Open innovation is in part driven by risk mitigation. In simple terms, larger pharmaceutical companies may prefer to let smaller biotechs take the higher risks of very early development and "place

their bets" when the probability of success is clearer. An additional argument to this point, often made by biotechs, is that focus and lack of bureaucracy makes them more effective and efficient than their big-pharma equivalents. A very good, recent literature review on this subject can be found here: see ref 4.

6 The surge of venture capital into the innovation habitat is very large. Globally, some $36 billion dollars were invested in 2020, with the US being the leader in this area. See refs 5 and 6. It is an important subtlety to this development, often emphasized by the venture capitalists, that they contribute not only capital but also valuable knowledge to the innovation habitat.

7 In biology, holobionts are assemblies of many species that work as a unit. Coral reefs are holobionts and so, with your microbiome, are you. It's an appropriate term because just as a biological holobionts can't survive as separate species, holobionts in the innovation habitat can't innovate as separate firms. For more on "the holobiont shift" in the pharmaceutical industry, see ref 7.

8 Importantly, the FDA and CDER see their role as not only to ensure drugs are safe and effective but also to encourage pharmaceutical innovation by making the approval process as quick and inexpensive as is consistent with safety. Although the FDA is not, of course, a commercial entity, it is appropriate to think of it as part of the holobiont. This is especially true since the FDA depends on income from the fees companies pay for regulatory approval. For further background on how the role of the FDA in innovation has changed over time, see refs 8 and 9.

9 This is a long-standing and widely recognized issue, of course, one that is well summarized by Attila A. Seyhan. To quote:

> A rift that has opened between basic research (bench) and clinical research and patients (bed) who need their new treatments, diagnostics and prevention, and this rift is widening and getting deeper. The crisis involving the "translation" of basic scientific findings in a laboratory setting into human applications and potential treatments or biomarkers for a disease is widely recognized both in academia and industry. Despite the attempts that have been made both in academic and industry settings to mitigate this problem, the high attrition rates of drug development and the problem with reproducibility and translatability of preclinical findings to human applications remain a fact and the return on the investment has been limited in terms of clinical impact.

See ref 10.

10 This short video is worth watching, both for its content and for the sincere passion and clarity with which Christopher Austin discusses the issue. See https://www.youtube.com/watch?v=Of58MAW34y8.

11 Note that I'm making a deliberate choice here to avoid talking about drug safety. No medicine is absolutely safe and, in practice, all innovative medicines carry some risk. The regulatory process is a decision about whether that risk is outweighed by the benefits. Regulatory approval also includes issues of manufacturing standards and other things, but I'm focusing on this risk/benefit question as it is most pertinent to the innovation habitat.

12 There is an important point here that might not be obvious to a layperson. To a large degree, pharmaceutical innovators "teach to the test." The development work and clinical trials they carry out may not be the most appropriate to demonstrate effectiveness and safety but are designed to gain approval. As one anonymous expert informant said, "There's real science and then there's regulatory science."

13 There is not one, standardized regulatory process for all new drugs. In recent years, it has developed "Fast Track," "Breakthrough Therapy," and "Priority Review" processes to meet the needs of specific innovative medicines. It has also become more flexible regarding the sort of evidence it allows. For example,

regulators increasingly accept "proxy" data, such as biochemical tests that imply clinical outcomes, rather than the outcomes themselves. Accelerated approval processes are, as you might expect, a contentious subject. See ref 11.

14 The challenges for regulators created by advanced therapies are really quite significant. Developments in this area carry all the hallmarks of a system running to catch up with the technological environment. See refs 12 and 13.

15 In fact, some research evidence suggests that the FDA is approving drugs more quickly but is doing so on the basis of weaker evidence. See ref 14.

16 This is the Critical Path Initiative. See https://www.fda.gov/science-research/science-and-research-special-topics/critical-path-initiative.

17 The key organization here is the ICH, The International Council for Harmonisation of Technical Requirements for Pharmaceuticals for Human Use. To quote from its website: "ICH's mission is to achieve greater harmonisation worldwide to ensure that safe, effective and high-quality medicines are developed, and registered and maintained in the most resource efficient manner whilst meeting high standards." This is a laudable goal, but of course it means that significant changes in regulatory practice, which also interact with global trade policies, can't be made unilaterally. See https://www.ich.org/.

18 While it is generally agreed that the costs of drug development and the time taken are increasing, there's a lot of debate about the precise numbers and methodologies. Estimates of cost vary widely depending on methods used, with recent studies varying from $314 million to $2.8 billion. See refs 15 and 16. In all of this debate, what does not seem in question is that the industry's efforts to improve the costs and duration of pharmaceutical innovation have not led to an overall reduction in either. Of course, these efforts may simply be slowing the increases that we might expect to see as we develop more complex drugs, but this is very hard to unravel.

19 See, for example, refs 17 and 18.

20 To quote one paper in this area:

> The drug research and development process includes creating a drug, conducting preclinical and clinical studies, and receiving marketing approval after its regulatory review. This process is associated with an extremely low success rate, ~ 1 in 20,000–30,000. Additionally, the clinical development of a candidate compound, from the start of a clinical trial to marketing approval, has a low success rate (10%–20%) and requires a huge investment that continues increasing year by year, which indicates that the efficiency of this process has been decreasing.

See ref 19.

21 It's obviously beyond the scope of this book to detail the diverse changes in the drug development domain. In any case, these topics have been covered by many researchers. Some examples of the most salient topics in this area are given here. For a review of AI's possibilities, see refs 20–22. For the relevance of computer-aided drug design, see ref 23. For a view on adaptive trials, those that can be modified during execution, see ref 24. For a view on the use of wearable technology, see ref 25. For the influence of big data and precision medicine on clinical trial design, see ref 26.

22 Real-world data (RWD) are the term the industry uses for data collected as patients use the medicine outside of carefully controlled clinical trial conditions. There seems to be great potential for these data to support clinical trials, and the 21st-century Cures Act mandated that the FDA should provide guidance about the circumstances under which manufacturers can use RWD to support the approval of a medicine. See ref 27.

23 Biomarkers are indications of patient's condition other than symptoms. They include things like blood pressure and heart rate, but increasingly, diagnostic

technology can detect molecules in, for example, the bloodstream that give a quantitative indication of a patient's condition or the progression of a disease. Personalized medicine is medicine that is targeted to a single person or sub-group, often based on their genetic profile. It is sometimes also referred to as stratified medicine. Both these developments have significance for how clinical trials are designed. See, for example, ref 28.

24 A 2019 McKinsey report identified ten areas for improvement and calculated that drug development time could be reduced by 500 days and costs by 25%. While skeptical about such generalized claims – they are unlikely to be equally true across all kinds of pharmaceutical development – this supports the general consensus that emerges from the report. See ref 29.

25 As I described in Chapter 2 with reference to "ontological communalities," this is not simply a metaphor. What takes place in the pharmaceutical industry is not *like* Darwinian evolution, it *is* Darwinian evolution.

26 Although the terms data, information, knowledge, and insight are often used in-terchangeably, in the knowledge management field, they have distinct meanings. See ref 30.

27 Studies of collaborative research in clinical research, for example, show that while collaboration has benefits, research organizations vary greatly in their collaborative capabilities. See ref 31.

28 There is an important distinction here between pre-competitive sharing of knowledge and alliances to further competitive capabilities. The latter are obviously constrained more by commercial confidentiality and laws around anticompetitive practices. One interesting study of pharmaceutical research consortia identified no fewer than 141 that involve two or more pharmaceu-tical firms.

29 Models of collaborative research are evolving. In a study of different models, Allarakhia identified several types. To quote:

> It can be suggested that we have moved beyond the use of joint ventures, merg-ers and acquisitions, and outsourcing strategies to the usage of novel models of collaboration including: prediscovery consortia where open source strate-gies prevail; R&D networks spanning disciplines and geographies; centers of excellence focused on key areas of technological and human capital develop-ment; public-private partnerships involving new and unexpected stakeholders; crowd-sourcing where shared, public innovation dominates; and web-based col-laboration platforms that virtually link stakeholders. The opportunity to employ these emerging models of open innovation is not only determined by organiza-tional structure and size, but equivalently by the evolving need for ... knowledge dissemination and shared governance of intellectual assets; access to large scale knowledge based assets such as tools, equipment, and infrastructure; as well as human capital.

See ref 32.

30 In a fascinating study of 141 research consortia between large pharmaceutical companies, researchers found that "firms financially support such consortia, in part, because their value creation activities benefit members without dis-rupting the value capture or other aspects of the incumbent industry struc-ture." See ref 33.

31 To quote from this work:

> the current 'pre-competitive' approach to partnership strategies in pharmaceutical innovation is fundamentally flawed for two reasons. First, it ignores the compet-itive market pressures that both shape what is deemed to be 'pre-competitive' and fuel tensions within partnerships between sharing knowledge and staking out

proprietary rights to gain competitive advantage. Second, it limits partnerships to areas where sharing already occurs instead of concentrating them in areas where greater sharing is badly needed but unlikely to occur.

See ref 34.

32 The pharmaceutical market is relatively unusual in that the visibility of clinical trials and the results for other products under development provides a great deal of information to inform pre-market risk. There are consultancies that specialize in this area, and recently, machine learning has been applied to the question. See ref 35.

33 In-market risk includes the risk that the market may not be as large as anticipated, the risk of competitive response, the risk that payers will not cover the product, the risk that anticipated market price levels won't be achieved, and the risk that the costs of marketing the product will be greater than anticipated. In general, in-market risk is larger for new markets and smaller for well-established markets. In all markets where there is significant capital investment needed and the returns are long term, in-market risk is important, and most industries are quite sophisticated in how they assess and manage it. For a more detailed examination, see ref 36.

34 See for example, https://www.pharmexec.com/view/measuring-probability-pricing-and-access-success. While this sort of approach is typical for the industry, it is quite unsophisticated compared to other sectors.

35 For example, the in-market risk created by price controls such as reference pricing (limiting prices to those charged in other countries) has been observed to influence how soon a product is launched in that market. See https://scholar.harvard.edu/files/lucamaini/files/reference_pricing_as_a_deterrent_to_entry.pdf and https://www.lse.ac.uk/business/consulting/assets/documents/the-impact-of-external-reference-pricing-within-and-across-countries.pdf.

36 This, of course, is what we observe when innovative companies target unmet clinical needs (that is, those where the threat of competitive response is low) and where the market is less sensitive to price (for example, rare diseases and some oncology markets). In my other writing, I've described these as "obligation exploiter" business models that become attractive when small patient numbers and distressing clinical needs make society unusually willing to pay relatively high prices compared to other markets. See ref 7.

37 As previously mentioned, this time value of money factor is incorporated into risk-adjusted net present value calculations that guide investment decisions. Because of the high pre-market and in-market risks involved, the discount rate applied to pharmaceutical innovation investment decisions is very high. Depending on the nature of the investment, it can be as high as 40%. This means that returns made soon after the investment is made, in the early years after launch, are much more valuable than revenue projected many years later. It also means that an investment that might not be attractive can be made attractive, without any change in revenue, if the discount rate can be reduced, for example, by guaranteed prices or revenue. See ref 37.

38 The antibiotic market is the prime example of market failure in this respect. See refs 38 and 39.

39 This is an emerging issue with some advanced therapies, such as some cell and gene therapies. See, for example, Wylie, Craig; Wadman, Rebeka; Unger, Thomas, et al. "Transforming Healthcare—How Curative Therapies Will Disrupt the Market." *Arthur D. Little*. 2019. Web.

40 There is a long history of evidence that investing in preventative medicine would benefit society, but that pharmaceutical innovation in this area is problematic. See refs 40 and 41.

120   The innovation habitat

41 If you're skim reading or dipping into the book here, this distinction between translational science and translational research is very important. See Chapter 3.
42 Evolutionary scientists would see this as an example of a "fitness trough," meaning that to get from a state of low fitness to a state of high fitness, the transition involves going through a state of even lower fitness. When these conditions exist, evolutionary change is hindered.
43 This mantra is often used to abbreviate concerns about the state funding basic research that is then capitalized upon by private enterprise. See ref 42.
44 Pull models are the general term for the sort of patents and profit model that is currently dominant in pharmaceuticals, while push models include subsidies and innovation prizes. Neither is perfect, although their merits and demerits vary in different situations. To quote from a very good review of this topic:

> ... I emphasize three points. First, both push and pull policies have generally promoted pharmaceutical research for diseases with large burdens. Second, imperfections in product and capital markets undermine the efficiency of pull policies. Similarly, the allocation of public funds is not always optimal, which limits the efficacy of push policies. Finally, interactions with other domestic policies and with policies in other countries are often overlooked in both economic studies of pharmaceutical research and development as well as policy choices.

See ref 43.
45 While many sectors have been criticized for tax avoidance, the pharmaceutical sector has been the subject of particular criticisms over its use of transfer pricing. Whether these criticisms are valid or not is not within the scope of this book. But it is reasonable to connect public perceptions of tax avoidance behavior with public funding of basic research that is then exploited by pharmaceutical companies. See https://www.cfr.org/blog/tax-games-big-pharma-versus-big-tech and https://www.pharmaceuticalprocessingworld.com/big-pharma-resists-international-corporate-tax-proposal/.
46 The Haldane principle emerged in the UK just after the First World War. See ref 44.
47 I recognize, of course, that CDER's different pathways are already a step toward this "different approval processes for different medicines," and I am simply proposing that this evolution will need to be extended to perhaps a more radical speciation of approval pathways. One important consideration when doing this is that approval pathways which grant approval on condition of provision of future evidence must follow up to ensure that happens. This is an issue with some accelerated approval pathways. See ref 45.

References

1 McMeekin P, Lendrem DW, Lendrem BC, Pratt AG, Peck R, Isaacs JD et al. Schrödinger's pipeline and the outsourcing of pharmaceutical innovation. *Drug Discovery Today.* 2020;25(3):480–4.
2 DeCorte BL. Evolving outsourcing landscape in pharma R&D: Different collaborative models and factors to consider when choosing a contract research organization. *Journal of Medicinal Chemistry.* 2020;63(20):11362–7.
3 Landhuis E. Outsourcing is in. *Nature (London).* 2018;556(7700):263–5.
4 Yeung AWK, Atanasov AG, Sheridan H, Klager E, Eibensteiner F, Völkl-Kernsock S et al. Open innovation in medical and pharmaceutical research: A literature landscape analysis. *Frontiers in Pharmacology.* 2020;11:587526-.

5 Cancherini LL, Joseph; da Silva, Jorge Santos; Zemp, Alexandra. What's ahead for biotech: Another wave or low tide? McKinsey & Company; 2021. Available from: https://www.mckinsey.com/industries/life-sciences/our-insights/whats-ahead-for-biotech-another-wave-or-low-tide.

6 Lerner J, Nanda R. Venture capital's role in financing innovation: What we know and how much we still need to learn. *Journal of Economic Perspectives.* 2020;34(3):237–61.

7 Smith BD. *Darwin's Medicine: How Business Models in the Life Science Industry are Evolving.* Abingdon: Routledge; 2016.

8 Wang W, Wertheimer AI. History, status, and politicization of the FDA. *Research in Social and Administrative Pharmacy.* May 2022; 18(5):2811–16.

9 Van Norman GA. Update to drugs, devices, and the FDA: How recent legislative changes have impacted approval of new therapies. *JACC: Basic to Translational Science.* 2020;5(8):831–9.

10 Seyhan AA. Lost in translation: The valley of death across preclinical and clinical divide – identification of problems and overcoming obstacles. *Translational Medicine Communications.* 2019;4(1):18.

11 Gyawali B, Ross JS, Kesselheim AS. Fulfilling the mandate of the US food and drug administration's accelerated approval pathway: The need for reforms. *JAMA Internal Medicine.* 2021;181(10):1275–6.

12 Iglesias-Lopez C, Agustí A, Vallano A, Obach M. Current landscape of clinical development and approval of advanced therapies. *Molecular Therapy Methods & Clinical Development.* 2021;23:606–18.

13 Pimenta C, Bettiol V, Alencar-Silva T, Franco OL, Pogue R, Carvalho JL et al. Advanced therapies and regulatory framework in different areas of the globe: Past, present, and future. *Clinical Therapeutics.* 2021;43(5):e103–e38.

14 Darrow JJ, Avorn J, Kesselheim AS. FDA approval and regulation of pharmaceuticals, 1983–2018. *JAMA.* 2020;323(2):164–76.

15 Wouters OJ, McKee M, Luyten J. Estimated research and development investment needed to bring a new medicine to market, 2009–2018. *JAMA.* 2020;323(9):844–53.

16 Schlander M, Hernandez-Villafuerte K, Cheng C-Y, Mestre-Ferrandiz J, Baumann M. How much does it cost to research and develop a new drug? A systematic review and assessment. *PharmacoEconomics.* 2021;39(11):1243–69.

17 Paul SM, Mytelka DS, Dunwiddie CT, Persinger CC, Munos BH, Lindborg SR et al. How to improve R&D productivity: The pharmaceutical industry's grand challenge. *Nature Reviews Drug Discovery.* 2010;9(3):203–14.

18 Munos B. Lessons from 60 years of pharmaceutical innovation. *Nature Reviews Drug Discovery.* 2009;8(12):959–68.

19 Yamaguchi S, Kaneko M, Narukawa M. Approval success rates of drug candidates based on target, action, modality, application, and their combinations. *Clinical and Translational Science.* 2021;14(3):1113–22.

20 Paul D, Sanap G, Shenoy S, Kalyane D, Kalia K, Tekade RK. Artificial intelligence in drug discovery and development. *Drug Discovery Today.* 2021;26(1):80–93.

21 Jayatunga MKP, Xie W, Ruder L, Schulze U, Meier C. AI in small-molecule drug discovery: A coming wave? *Nature Reviews Drug Discovery.* 2022;21(3):175.

22 Spreafico R, Soriaga LB, Grosse J, Virgin HW, Telenti A. Advances in genomics for drug development. *Genes.* 2020;11(8):942–62.

23 Medina-Franco JL. Grand challenges of computer-aided drug design: The road ahead. *Frontiers in Drug Discovery.* 2021;1: 1–4.

24 Mahlich J, Bartol A, Dheban S. Can adaptive clinical trials help to solve the productivity crisis of the pharmaceutical industry? - A scenario analysis. *Health Economics Review.* 2021;11(1):4-.

25 Izmailova ES, Wagner JA, Perakslis ED. Wearable devices in clinical trials: Hype and hypothesis. *Clinical Pharmacology & Therapeutics.* 2018;104(1):42–52.

26 Li A, Bergan RC. Clinical trial design: Past, present, and future in the context of big data and precision medicine. *Cancer.* 2020;126(22):4838–46.

27 Ramagopalan SV, Simpson A, Sammon C. Can real-world data really replace randomised clinical trials? *BMC Medicine.* 2020;18(1):13.

28 Louie AD, Huntington K, Carlsen L, Zhou L, El-Deiry WS. Integrating molecular biomarker inputs into development and use of clinical cancer therapeutics. *Frontiers in Pharmacology.* 2021;12: 1–8.

29 Agrawal G, Harriet K, Prabhakaran M, Michael S. The pursuit of excellence in new-drug development. McKinsey and Company; 2019. Available from: https://www.mckinsey.com/industries/pharmaceuticals-and-medical-products/our-insights/the-pursuit-of-excellence-in-new-drug-development#.

30 Smith BD. *Creating Market Insight.* 1st ed. London: Wiley; 2008.

31 Ippoliti R, Ramello GB, Scherer FM. Partnership and innovation in the pharmaceutical industry: The case of clinical research. *Economics of Innovation and New Technology.* 2021;30(3):317–34.

32 Allarakhia M. Evolving models of collaborative drug discovery: Managing intellectual capital assets. *Expert Opinion on Drug Discovery.* 2018;13(6):473–6.

33 Olk P, West J. The relationship of industry structure to open innovation: Cooperative value creation in pharmaceutical consortia. *R&D Management.* 2020;50(1):116–35.

34 Vertinsky LS. Patents, partnerships, and the pre-competitive collaboration myth in pharmaceutical innovation. *UC Davis Law Review.* 2015;48(4):1509.

35 Vergetis V, Skaltsas D, Gorgoulis VG, Tsirigos A. Assessing drug development risk using big data and machine learning. *Cancer Research.* 2021;81(4):816–9.

36 McDonald MHB, Smith BD, Ward KR. *Marketing Due Diligence: Reconnecting Strategy to Share Price.* Oxford: Elsevier; 2005.

37 Villiger R. *Discount Rates in Biotech.* Biostrat Biotech Consulting; 2021.

38 McKenna M. The antibiotic paradox: Why companies can't afford to create life-saving drugs. *Nature (London).* 2020;584(7821):338–41.

39 Plackett B. Why big pharma has abandoned antibiotics. *Nature.* 2020;586:3.

40 Reynolds T. Investing in prevention: What incentive does the pharmaceutical industry have? *JNCI: Journal of the National Cancer Institute.* 2002;94(23):1736–8.

41 Sherzai D, Sherzai A. Preventing Alzheimer's: Our most urgent health care priority. *American Journal of Lifestyle Medicine.* 2019;13(5):451–61.

42 Mazzucato M. *The Entrepreneurial State: Debunking Public vs. Private Sector Myths.* London: Anthem Press; 2013.

43 Kyle MK. The alignment of innovation policy and social welfare: Evidence from pharmaceuticals. *Innovation Policy and the Economy.* 2020;20:95–123.

44 Masood E. A 100th birthday wish: Uphold academic freedom in dark times. *Nature (London).* 2018;563(7733):621–3.

45 Mahase E. FDA allows drugs without proven clinical benefit to languish for years on accelerated pathway. *British Medicine Journal.* 2021;374:n1898.

5 The coalition habitat

Precis

- The coalition habitat is the part of the pharmaceutical innovation ecosystem where the assets, resources, and capabilities needed to turn scientific discoveries into innovative medicines are assembled.
- The coalition habitat is inhabited by academic scientists, university technology transfer offices, venture capitalists (both private and corporate), and a host of specialized contractors and support service firms.
- The coalition habitat connects the innovation and discovery habitats by creating holobionts, networks of these organizations with the necessary assets, resources, and capabilities.
- A healthy PIE requires that the coalition habitat efficiently and effectively assembles holobionts with a high degree of complementarity and allocates investment capital optimally.
- The coalition habitat's ability to support a healthy PIE is constrained by:
  - its localized, relationship-based "cottage industry" characteristics
  - its neglect of management science relative to biological and medical science
  - its adaptation to a high-risk, high-return market environment
- The coalition habitat would be better able to support a healthy PIE if:
  - it matured to improve its practices, becoming more global and less relationship based
  - it developed and employed its ability to apply management science, especially regarding holobionts
  - it became more diverse in its range of investors

DOI: 10.4324/9781003330271-5

In Chapter 4 (the innovation habitat), I described an important shift in how and where pharmaceutical innovation happens. The historical model in which a large, fully integrated company would pick up a basic scientific discovery, take it through all stages of development and launch it, is now the exception rather than the rule. More common now is for a scientific discovery to be translated into an innovative medicine by a "holobiont," a network of entities centered on a "NewCo." This is usually a firm set up solely to develop that medicine or perhaps several therapies based on the same discovery. A NewCo might take its products all the way to market or it may, at some stage in the development process, license its product, sell itself to a large pharmaceutical company, or exploit the resources of a larger firm in some other way. Although there is an increasing trend for such companies to go to market themselves, these represent only a minority of new product launches.[1] This is because the latter stages of development and launch often require the resources and capabilities of a large pharmaceutical company. When it comes to marketing on a global scale, even large pharmaceutical companies sometimes find it better to work with partners.

The assembly and growth of a holobiont is an important process within the pharmaceutical innovation ecosystem (PIE); its effectiveness and efficiency influences whether the innovative medicine is developed and, if it is, the properties of that innovation, including its cost. As I explored the PIE, I came to realize that the holobiont assembly process happens in its own habitat, closely linked to the discovery and innovation habitats; I've called it the coalition habitat. I chose that term because these assemblies are temporary, expedient, and self-serving associations, ways of achieving a shared goal, much as we see in political contexts. I say that not to denigrate them but to emphasize that, although its outputs are innovative medicines based on new science and technology, pharmaceutical innovation holobionts are an essentially sociological phenomenon.

Just as a natural habitat is shaped by fundamental and exigent factors such as weather and geology (in ecologist's terms, the abiotic environment), the coalition habitat is shaped by fundamental realities of pharmaceutical innovation. Most fundamental of all is the unusual concentration of assets, resources, and capabilities needed to bring an innovative medicine to market, and the high probability that the innovation process may consume those costly inputs without ever making a penny of profit. This has always been true of pharmaceutical innovation, but the coalition habitat is a relatively new way of managing this reality. Until about the turn of the millennium, the best, or at least most common, way to manage this difficult assembly process and to mitigate the risk was the integrated pharmaceutical company. You can think of the late 20th-century "big pharma" model as similar to the early 20th-century shipbuilding or mid-20th-century auto companies who owned their own steel works, paint shops, and everything in between. For many decades, this corporate, bureaucratic way of assembling capabilities and dispersing risk was the best way to do things. We might look askance at that model today, but it worked well for many decades.

Understanding why this integrated model declined relative to the holobiont model is the sort of topic that academics like me love to research and is the subject of many PhD theses.[2] I've described this "holobiont shift" in some detail in my earlier work.[3] I risk the ire of my academic colleagues when I simplify explanations for the holobiont shift into three broad schools of thought, but these are useful ways of understanding what happens in the coalition habitat.

The first explanation – the resource-based school[4] – is that the resources needed to develop innovative medicines have become much more specialized. When all drugs were small molecules that were "built" by organic synthesis, a large drug company could assemble the resources to develop pretty much any drug. But as science has advanced and drugs can be small molecules, proteins, a strip of ribonucleic acid (RNA), or some other entity, that's less true. It's hard and inefficient for a single firm to build and maintain a broad range of very narrow knowledge assets. Instead, it is easier to form a NewCo with some of those assets and then assemble the rest of the holobiont around the NewCo. Perhaps you can see the loose analogy with the way a modern automobile "screwdriver plant" works as a design and assembly hub supported by thousands of suppliers.

The second school of thought is transaction cost economics.[5] This school explains integrated firms by noting that it is costly in time and money to find, assemble, and organize a whole load of different assets, resources, and capabilities and, in the days of letters and faxes, the best way to do this was to have a CEO look at their huge organization chart and issue orders down the corporate hierarchy. This vertically integrated approach was the most efficient because you didn't need to look for a capability; you knew that it could be found in an office three floors below you. But today, the cost and difficulty of assembly has changed. Transaction cost economists argue that it is now easier to do an internet search and email an expert in, say, protein characterization than to maintain a vast R&D department capable of doing this and everything else you might need. In other words, it is often easier to buy-in than it is to develop and maintain an in-house capability. If you've ever ordered some small domestic necessity from Amazon, rather than going to find it somewhere in the depths of your garage, you will perhaps see the analogy.

The third school is the financialization school, which looks at things through the lens of how to optimize shareholder returns.[6] This school argues that, while it may have made financial sense in the past for a large, integrated pharmaceutical company to tie up capital in early-stage development, it no longer does. From the financialization perspective, it's better for shareholders, although not necessarily for other stakeholders, to let venture capitalists (VCs) and others invest in NewCos and, once the risk has attenuated, to either buy the NewCo or license its part-developed innovative medicine. If you've ever bought young but established plants for your garden, rather than growing from seed, you've done something analogous to what the financialization school describes.

Which of the resource-based, transaction cost, or financialization schools is correct? My reading of it is that they all are. As is the way in academic business research, these three schools are looking at different parts of the same animal and reaching different but complementary conclusions, just like in the ancient Asian parable.[7] Each perspective is helpful in understanding how the coalition habitat works. Whatever the explanation, and whether we call it the holobiont shift, disintegration, open innovation or one of the other terms that have been applied to it, this is a real and significant phenomenon in pharmaceutical innovation.[8] There are counterforces and there are researchers who claim to identify sub-types of this phenomenon,[9] but the research is clear that this has been happening since the early years of the 21st century. This means that, were I writing this book in 1990, I'd have written about how big pharma coordinates its internal R&D resources, but since I'm writing in 2022, I need to explore what goes on in the coalition habitat.

What happens in the coalition habitat and who inhabits it?

What happens in the coalition habitat can be thought of as a coalescence process, the agglomeration of resources and capabilities around one or more scientific discoveries which, when patented, are often referred to as the asset. As with everything else in the PIE, it is easy to get lost in the detail of how this coalescence process happens and useful to step back and see the big picture.

Two things are important to understand. First, although the process isn't complete until all the necessary resources, assets, and capabilities are assembled, this doesn't happen in a single step; it's a gradual process.[10] Second, this process is less like assembling building blocks, with fixed components, and more like the way an enzyme changes shape to fit with its substrate. Biologically minded readers will understand that simile to mean that the different parts of the agglomeration aren't fixed, they change shape to allow a better fit with each other. The structuring of the deal between discoverers and investors is an example of this mutual accommodation. So, although no two holobiont building processes are the same, they generally follow a similar, gradual process of reciprocated adjustment. There are three sets of entities that are central to this process.

The first are the founders, often the scientists behind the discovery, and their institutions, usually represented by the technology transfer offices of their universities. These bring to the coalition the explicit, protected, intellectual property, and the tacit know-how acquired while making the discovery. Because so much of the scientific knowledge is tacit, the founders are often the embodiment of the scientific discovery and consequently quite indispensable at this early stage. As they enter the coalition habitat, their goal is to find the resources and capabilities needed to develop their discovery, while giving away as little of its potential future value as possible.

The second major entity set in the coalition habitat is investors. Typically, these are VC firms who specialize in pharmaceuticals, but some are the venture capital funds of established, large pharmaceutical corporations. To give a sense of scale, venture capital funding for biotech in 2020 was about \$36 billion[11] and about 20% of investment rounds involved corporate funds.[12] Increasingly, these investors have tried to differentiate, focusing their activity by therapy area, stage of investment, or both. It's important to remember that most pharmaceutical innovation holobionts involve many investors, usually with a lead investor coordinating a round of investment. The most obvious role for investors is that they bring the financial investment needed. Less obviously, they bring expertise. For example, a significant investment often comes with the appointment of executives whose technical or commercial knowledge is needed by the coalition. In return for providing capital and expertise, investors seek to capture as much of the discovery's potential value as possible, creating an inevitable tension with the founders.

The third major set of entities in the coalition habitat are the providers of specialist services and knowledge. These include contract research organizations that provide scientific services or professional service firms, from lawyers and accountants to human resources and business strategy consultants. Since these service organizations are almost always specialized to pharmaceuticals and often sub-specialized within the industry, they provide many of the specific capabilities required by the coalition.[13] This halo of supporting organizations makes it possible to create a functioning NewCo relatively quickly by building a small core supported by external service suppliers. Primarily, the role of these providers in the coalition habitat is to provide services and to make as much profit as possible doing so. But, since they typically work with many innovative companies, they also form a web of connections through which tacit knowledge and social capital flows.

So, the coalition habitat has the appearance of simplicity – people with discoveries and people with money, each looking to get the most out of each other while giving away as little as possible and employing service providers to help them do that. But specialization and technological fragmentation makes the reality somewhat messier. In an ecosystem where it is not interfirm competition but inter-holobiont competition that matters, it's not enough to build a viable holobiont. The aim is to build the optimal holobiont. So, discoverers need investors who bring not only money but also knowledge and industry contacts relevant to their specific discovery. Likewise, investors need discoveries but they particularly value those discoveries that fit their investment portfolio and to whom their specialized expertise can add value. And even when discoverers and investors are well matched, they can do little until they find the most appropriately specialized service providers whose capabilities are relevant to the discoverer and whose networks can accelerate development. As I read about the coalition process and talked through it with my expert informants, it became clear that it is much more than a mere matchmaking process. When done well, building the optimal holobiont is a delicate process of mutually balancing and complementing capabilities. It is complementarity[14] that is the characteristic feature of a good holobiont, and it was with this concept in mind that I considered what the PIE would require of the coalition habitat.

What does a healthy PIE require of the coalition habitat?

The coalition habitat connects the discovery and innovation habitats by enabling the aggregation of the diverse assets, resources, and capabilities needed to translate scientific discoveries into innovative medicines. A well-functioning coalition habitat, capable of supporting a healthy PIE, takes signals from elsewhere in the PIE, especially the discovery habitat, and creates the appropriate holobionts needed by the innovation habitat. For the PIE to be healthy requires three things of the coalition habitat.

The coalition habitat must assemble holobionts effectively

The coalition habitat brings together discoverers, investors, and service providers. But a healthy PIE requires more than that. It requires the coalition habitat to assemble a highly effective holobiont to progress the development of the discovery, one complete with an optimal degree of complementarity in assets, resources, and capabilities. A coalition habitat that fails to create highly effective holobionts is unlikely to sustain a healthy PIE.

The coalition habitat must assemble holobionts efficiently

A healthy PIE not only requires that the coalition habitat assembles an effective holobiont but also that it does so with minimal direct and indirect costs. These assembly costs include searching for and selection of holobiont members and the maintenance of the intra-holobiont relationships.[15] By contrast, a coalition habitat that consumes a disproportionate amount of time, financial, or other resources to assemble and sustain the holobiont is unlikely to sustain a healthy PIE.

The coalition habitat must allocate investment capital optimally

A healthy PIE not only requires that investment is allocated to discoveries but also that it is allocated at a cost proportionate to the discovery's risk-adjusted rate of return. This includes both providing capital at an appropriate price and providing a level of return appropriate to the risk involved. A coalition habitat that does not allocate sufficient capital, or that does so at a disproportionate cost, or which fails to provide appropriate risk-adjusted returns on investment, is unlikely to sustain a healthy PIE.

So, as summarized in Figure 5.1, a well-functioning PIE requires that the coalition assembles the optimal set of assets, capabilities, and resources, appropriate specifically to each scientific discovery. This includes allocating resources where they can create value and not where they would not. The PIE also requires that resources be allocated quickly, efficiently, and at an appropriate cost of capital. Given the variation and uncertainty around scientific discoveries and the specificity and intricacy of the holobionts needed, this is a difficult task.

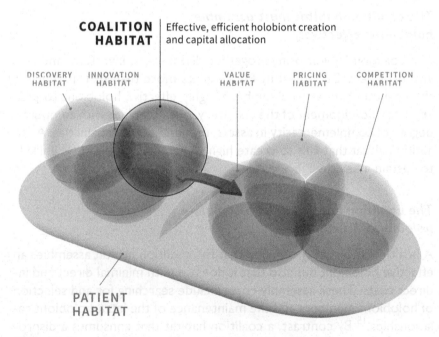

COALITION HABITAT | Effective, efficient holobiont creation and capital allocation

DISCOVERY HABITAT   INNOVATION HABITAT   VALUE HABITAT   PRICING HABITAT   COMPETITION HABITAT

PATIENT HABITAT

Figure 5.1 The coalition habitat's contribution to a healthy PIE

But it is what the PIE needs to deliver the sustained innovation and affordability that we're asking for. As in the other habitats, I wanted to understand whether the coalition habitat was capable of meeting these requirements for a healthy PIE, so that's where my exploration took me next.

Is the coalition habitat capable of supporting a healthy PIE?

Just as many parts of a natural habitat are invisible to a casual observer, the coalition habitat goes unnoticed by most people. Most of those outside of the industry are probably only vaguely aware that the translation of scientific discoveries into innovative medicines has shifted so significantly from integrated pharmaceutical companies to holobionts centered on NewCo biotechs funded largely by venture capital. And yet, just as much as the more visible discovery and innovation habitats, the coalition habitat is essential to the creation of innovative medicines and the working of the PIE. If assets, resources, and capabilities are not assembled effectively and efficiently, and capital is not allocated optimally, it will have a negative effect on the pharmaceutical innovation that emerges from the PIE. It will influence not only how many innovative medicines will emerge but for what conditions, how valuable they are, how much they cost, and the other characteristics of pharmaceutical innovation I listed in Box 1.1 (see Chapter 1).

The importance of the coalition habitat to the PIE makes it reasonable to question how well it meets the needs of a healthy ecosystem. As I did so, the technological and sociological changes in the PIE directed my attention toward three questions.

The first question is raised by the increasing specialization in pharmaceutical innovation. In a world where knowledge is becoming ever deeper and ever narrower, is the habitat able to assemble not just a coalition but a coalition with the optimal and complementary assets, resources, and capabilities?

The second is raised by heterogeneity of the habitat. If this were simply like swiping tinder until a match is eventually made, it might be straightforward. But it is more like assembling a crew of astronauts for a long mission to Mars in time to catch the launch window. With so many financial, scientific, and interpersonal factors at play, is the coalition habitat capable of assembling the optimal holobiont without consuming too much time and money in the process?

The third is raised by the sociology of the habitat. The holobiont shift to external, open innovation replaces one key relationship (between big pharma and academic scientists) with another (between VCs and the technology transfer offices of universities). It would be naïve to expect that changed relationship not to influence the dynamics of capital allocation. With pharmaceutical innovation now being significantly influenced by venture capital, is the habitat capable of allocating capital optimally, at an appropriate cost, and generating appropriate returns? With these thoughts in mind, I scoured the literature and asked my expert informants about the working of the coalition habitat. Again, trying to see the forest for the trees, I uncovered three causes for concern.

The coalition habitat is localized and relationship based

An explorer of the PIE who travels through the PIE's various habitats becomes used to an ecosystem dominated by "big beasts," from the systemically critical Food and Drug Administration (FDA) and National Institutes of Health (NIH) to the concentrated insurers, pharmacy benefit managers (PBMs), and healthcare providers, to the global pharmaceutical companies. Most parts of the PIE seem to fit with what most of us imagine it to look like, an ecosystem dominated by relatively small numbers of very large organizations with worldwide reach and importance. Crossing over the border into the coalition habitat, the difference is palpable. The largest venture capital firms in life sciences, RA Capital and OrbiMed,[16] for example, have employee numbers in the low hundreds, and even the largest VCs represent only a very small amount of the venture capital invested in the PIE.

The same fragmentation is seen in biotech companies. About three quarters of research in this part of the PIE is done by 3000 or so companies who each spend less than $200 million a year on R&D,[17] compared to several billions for a typical large pharmaceutical company. These minnow companies are tightly geographically clustered around nexus of academic research, with the large majority of activity being concentrated in just a handful of centers in the US.[18] It is both a cause and effect of this clustering that biotechs receive most VC funding from geographically close investors[19] and that physical proximity seems to enable access to investors' nonfinancial resources, such as knowledge and networks.[20] Many of those I spoke to described the habitat as a "cottage industry," with many relatively small, interdependent entities tightly sharing a web of personal relationships.

This difference between habitats is striking. To understand why the coalition habitat looked so different from other habitats, I spoke to Killian McCarthy, an academic whose work in this area is well respected.

> *When firms form relationships, geography still matters. There are lots of explanations for this and I think they are all part of the truth. There's a "home bias" effect, borders, culture and language still matter; and there is still what you might call a "Friday Night Beer" effect, meaning that the mechanism for forming business relationships is as much sociological as it is technological.*
>
> *Killian McCarthy*

Other expert informants also stressed this sociological basis of how the coalition habitat works, and it is a common theme in the literature.[21] It is reminiscent of how industries are often born in specific places, such as Wall Street and Detroit. Predictably, given its relatively short history, the coalition habitat seems to have the characteristics of an embryonic industry. It is localized, unconsolidated, and relies heavily on personal networks. This is what we might expect in a habitat that has only really emerged this century, forming to fill the ecological gap left by the retreat of integrated pharmaceutical companies.

This sharp contrast between the coalition habitat and the other, more mature habitats is interesting in itself, but it becomes more significant in light of the way the PIE is changing. Look, for example, at what expert informant Joe Damond told me about the biotech sector.

> *The biotech industry has historically been US focused with other countries playing a minor part. But, whilst the US remains the leader in the sector, it is becoming more global, with European, Chinese and other hubs becoming important. This has important implications for regulatory affairs, ethics, IP protection, market access, data flow across borders and many other issues. Increasingly, the sector needs to overcome cultural and legal barriers and start coordinating activities more globally.*
>
> *Joe Damond*

Other themes both in the literature and among the expert informants also pointed to the current coalition habitat lagging changes in its environment. Consider Joerg Holenz's comments, for example.

> *Building the right organization rests on the idea of complementarity between the science, the finance, the development, and commercial capabilities. It's a complex, multifaceted problem that is easier in good times but harder in an*

environment where good assets are rare, talent is rare and there are different cultural perspectives. The current way we do it works sometimes, doesn't others. Compared to the systematic way we develop a drug, the way we develop the organizations for developing the drugs is a much less formal, less structured process.

Joerg Holenz

Numerous comments from investors and discoverers alike pointed to the imperfections of the coalition building process with, predictably, each side critical of the other. The academic literature confirms this view, revealing how holobiont building is often ineffective, inefficient, or both. One reported example of this is that holobiont partners may work harder at knowledge appropriation than at knowledge creation.[22] Another is that founding entrepreneurs and investors may have very different perceptions of risk.[23] The biotechnology business literature also suggests that neither scientists nor investors find the holobiont building process to work well. Scientists complain of investors' short-term thinking, framed strongly by their earlier experience.[24] They are also critical of the volatility of "tourist" investors.[25] On the other side, investors complain of the difficulty of sorting the "wheat from the chaff" and of intense competition for a small number of attractive assets.[26]

When I'd finished my discussions and reading the research, I looked for a wider explanation of what I'd observed. It seemed clear that I was looking at an example of evolutionary lag in the PIE. The current coalition habitat seems well adapted to a world where only a broad, approximate fit between assets, resources, and capabilities is sufficient, and everything needed can be found within a taxi ride of Kendall Square, Cambridge. It seems less well adapted to a world that demands an optimal holobiont, with a high degree of complementarity, whose components might be spread across two or three continents. This lag makes the coalition habitat less able to support a healthy PIE.

The coalition habitat has an unbalanced knowledge base

My exploration of the coalition habitat was enabled by my own career background. Although it's many years since I stood at the bench, I trained and worked as a research chemist. I've never lost my love of pharmaceutical science, so it was genuinely exciting to hear and read of the scientific discoveries around which holobionts coalesce. At the same time, it was totally absorbing to listen to biotech executives and VCs describe the construction of the holobionts needed to translate those discoveries into innovative medicines.

This aspect of the coalition habitat was especially fascinating to me because I've spent the last two decades as an academic, researching how the life sciences industry works and I now supervise a small research group in this area. So, looking simultaneously at the application of pharmaceutical science and management science was made easier because of my slightly atypical combination of natural- and social-science training. Looking through those combined lenses revealed a marked and fascinating contrast. To put it simply, the coalition habitat seems much more accomplished at pharmaceutical science than management science. Among many who described this to me, I found expert informant Mark Ralph's perspective very helpful.

> *The central challenge is achieving complementarity between, for example, biotechs (who are often VC funded) and big pharma. Each side is good at different things but they have very different perspectives. I think we underestimate the difficulty of achieving this complementarity, especially when so much of it can be a water cooler thing that isn't like a codified science.*
>
> Mark Ralph

Mark Ralph's comment, and others like it, revealed that the inhabitants of the coalition habitat are generally much better versed in pharmaceutical science than in management science. This is not to say that there is little or no management science about how networks of complementary organizations work. Starting from around the turn of the millennium, a stream of academic research explored this issue with a particular focus on the life sciences industry.[27] But, while the coalition habitat's inhabitants seize life sciences discoveries with alacrity, the lack of translation of management science into management practice is striking.

For example, there are significant bodies of academic research about complementariness in pharmaceutical innovation networks,[28] the distribution of value and property rights in biotechnology R&D alliances,[29] the behavioral issues that shape biotechnology alliances,[30] biotechnology alliance management capabilities,[31] and many more directly relevant topics. Yet almost nowhere in my research did I come across executives talking about that management science. This was in stark contrast to the way that their scientific colleagues immerse themselves in the biological and medical literature. I probed hard during my research to find the management equivalent of those scientific institutes that focus on translating academic biological research into innovative medicines. There are academics with a special interest in the pharmaceutical industry, including those I've cited above. They do of course publish, teach, and run executive programs. But what does not exist in anything like the same way are the management science equivalents of, for example, the Scripps Translational Science Institute. This points to a culture in the coalition habitat that values pharmaceutical science over management science when, in practice, both are needed.

What I drew from this part of my research was that the coalition habitat operates on an unbalanced knowledge base. It positively teems with scientists who are at the front of their individual fields. They read the literature and attend conferences. A high proportion of those working in biotechs and other parts of the coalition habitat have PhDs and academic research training in the biological sciences. Consequently, there is fluency in a common language and a high level of professional competence with respect to biology and drug development. The same cannot be said about the habitat's management science knowledge base. While the scientific development of innovative medicines uses the very best knowledge available, the design and management of the holobionts that are needed to execute that development does not. This choice to value one body of knowledge over another isn't conscious; it's an implicit feature of the habitat's culture. But it seems ill-suited to meeting the needs of the PIE.

The coalition habitat is adapted to a high-risk, high-return market

Ecologists refer to some organisms as indicator species, the presence or absence of which reflects something about the environment. For example, algal blooms are a sign that fertilizer run-off from agricultural land has changed the nutrient composition of a lake. The presence of buckthorn plantains reveals, to an ecologist, that the soil is especially salty. The rise of venture capital in the coalition habitat is the same sort of signal. From an ecological perspective, the holobiont shift doesn't just show that one species of investor, the VC, has filled the gap left by another, the integrated pharmaceutical company. It also signifies that there's something about the coalition habitat that makes it more habitable for venture capital than for other species of investor.

VCs, whether private or arms of pharmaceutical companies, are an indicator species because they are found only in one part of the product development environment. For the most part, they are not found funding basic science or in well developed, mature markets. Instead, they tend to concentrate on the early-stage drug development space between those two life cycle stages.[32] Venture capital thrives in that environment for the same reason that the salt-loving plants thrive in the pavement cracks beside salt-treated roads. Those plants have better mechanisms, compared to others, for controlling the salt concentrations inside their cells. Analogously, VCs have a variety of better mechanisms for mitigating the risks of early-stage pharmaceutical development – from how they select investments to how they structure their deals to how they construct their investment portfolios.[33] The details of these mechanisms are beyond the scope of this book, but it's their implications that matter here. VCs, the species that has become so prevalent in the coalition habitat, are an indicator species, and what they indicate is that the early stages of drug development are a high-risk, high-return environment. This point was expressed eloquently by expert informant Harald Stock.

> *VCs are not identical of course, there are variations, but they all follow a similar model that is centered around mitigating risk. Their investors, the Limited Partners, are charged both fees and a proportion of profits, the so called 2 and 20 model. Then, in the deals they cut with biotechs, VCs emphasize the value their knowledge brings, the risks they are taking and the returns required to match those risks. Often, even when dealing with an experienced academic technology transfer office, there is an asymmetry of knowledge and experience that gives VC has the upper hand.*
>
> Harald Stock

This idea that the prevalence of VCs indicates a high-risk, high-return environment has important implications for the present and future functioning of the PIE. First, if VCs are the primary source of capital for early-stage pharmaceutical innovation, then the costs of capital will be higher than if it were funded by other sources, such as stock markets or internal capital from within a large company. This higher cost of capital has obvious implications for the cost of developing innovative medicines.

Second, should the risk profile of pharmaceutical innovation change substantially, VCs may no longer be the best source of capital. So, for example, if advances in translational science significantly de-risked pharmaceutical innovation in the discovery habitat, as discussed in Chapter 3, then VCs may not be the most appropriate source of early-stage capital investment.

Third, VCs add most value in the coalition habitat when their knowledge and experience give them superior risk mitigation capabilities. The practical implication of this is that while knowledgeable, experienced VCs may fit the habitat well, so-called "tourist" VCs, who lack those capabilities but are attracted by high returns, may not help the working of the PIE.

Finally, should the returns available to pharmaceutical innovation become less, or the risks increase, VCs may leave the PIE. This implies that steps that reduce returns (such as price controls) or increase risks (such as changes to exclusivity) might disproportionately discourage venture capital from the coalition habitat.

This being a high-risk, high-reward habitat fits with my observations in the discovery and innovation habitats. Weak translational science creates uncertainty and demands risk mitigation capabilities, and this attracts VCs who can provide them. A high-risk, high-reward habitat is inconsistent with our goal of affordable, innovate medicines. It might be better to aim for a coalition habitat in which risk mitigation and the costs associated with it are less important. In any case, the parallels with natural ecosystems also tell us that indicator species are particularly sensitive to things we might do to change their environment. Venture capital has flooded into the coalition habitat because the environmental conditions suited it. If those conditions change, it will leave just as quickly.

Stepping back to look at the coalition habitat as a whole tells us that, if we want it to support a healthy PIE, we have three issues to address. The first is that its localized, small-scale cottage industry structure may not be right for efficiently and effectively building holobionts of optimal complementarity from specialized assets, resources, and capabilities in a global world. The second is that its culture of neglecting management science, relative to its pharmaceutical science comfort zone, hinders its ability to build and run those holobionts. Finally, the dominant role of VCs makes pharmaceutical innovation both more expensive than it might otherwise be and also particularly dependent on a market in which prices are high. Unless these three issues are addressed, the coalition habitat is unlikely to support a healthy PIE.

How can we improve the coalition habitat?

As is the way with complex, adaptive ecosystems, the weaknesses of the coalition habitat are largely the unintended consequences of the choices we've made. For example, we've chosen to invest a great deal of money and effort into making basic scientific discoveries but made less effort to advance translational science.[34] We've also chosen to leave the funding of most drug development to private, profit-seeking investors rather than burden the taxpayer with it. Finally, we've also chosen, even if implicitly, a financialized economic system that is driven by risk and return on investment.

Those decisions have had consequences. Just as if the apothecary had chosen to scatter seeds, rather than carefully propagate them, we've chosen a high failure rate in the so-called valley of death between discovery and innovation. And, just as if the apothecary had decided to economize by using salty roadside soil in the garden, these conditions have caused one species of investor to withdraw and another to spread. In saying this, I imply no value judgment on the decisions our society has made; it is simply that the coalition habitat we have is the result of our implicit and explicit choices, and its weaknesses are the consequences of those decisions. This means that, in theory, we could cultivate a different coalition habitat, for example, one funded more cheaply by massive federal funding of drug development and not fueled by high-risk, high-return capital. But, in my research, I found no mainstream appetite for completely transforming or abolishing the current coalition habitat in this way. In any case, such a radical approach seems so far away from American values and political sentiment that it is not practical to consider.

That said, there are ways to improve the coalition habitat. Like any diagnosis, the weaknesses suggest remedies. In this section, I'll offer three pragmatic suggestions toward improving the working of the coalition habitat so that it might be better able to meet the requirements of a healthy PIE.

Mature the coalition habitat

We ask a lot of the coalition habitat. We depend on it to allocate investment well under conditions of high uncertainty, to build holobionts of optimal complementarity and to do both of those things efficiently and effectively. In its current localized, relationship-dependent, "cottage industry" form, the coalition habitat isn't well adapted to this task. All the habitat's inhabitants – discoverers, VCs, pharmaceutical companies, and others – complain of the difficulty of assembling the optimal holobiont. Most VCs complain of being inundated with pitches for investment. Most discoverers complain of multiple lengthy and laborious pitches to gain investment. Pharmaceutical companies complain of unrealistic NewCos. All those involved complain of high failure rates attributable not only to scientific factors but also to failure of the process for building and managing holobionts.[35] A healthy PIE needs better than this. It needs a coalition habitat that has matured past its cottage industry stage.

Maturing the coalition habitat is not amenable to Harry Potter's magic wand. It needs to grow and improve its capabilities for assembling and managing holobionts, and that sort of sector maturation isn't achieved by single actions. Rather, it involves the collective action of those who work in the habitat. To those who work in this part of the PIE, I offer three ideas that emerge from my research.

First, industry maturation tends to be driven by keystone species, such as market-leading firms. In this case, that is likely to be some of the leading specialist VCs, some of the technology transfer offices of the leading life science research universities, and the venture arms of some of the leading pharmaceutical companies. These leaders might cooperate to improve holobiont building in the same way that, for example, pharmaceutical companies have cooperated to improve clinical trial practice. This would use their experience, but it should also build on management science (see below).

Second, although all entities in the coalition habitat would claim to have global perspective and involvement, the evidence is that localization is a deeply embedded cultural trait, reinforced by the disproportionate profitability of the US market. This suggests that those leading players will need to deliberately change their habits and aim to work more globally, not just contracting out but taking a less US-centric view of the market.

Third, while the coalition habitat's marked dependence on personal relationships is partly embedded in human psychology, it also indicates a weakness in other channels of information. Firms rely on personal relationships because they perceive there is no other mechanism as good for knowing what science is available, which firms are seeking and offering investment or the capabilities of potential holobiont partners. Some way of making information flow more freely and rendering the habitat more transparent would accelerate the process of maturation. In any case, a coalition habitat in which leading firms drive forward practices, that operates more globally, and depends more on information and less on handshakes would better support the health of the PIE.

Unlike some of the changes I suggest in other chapters for other habitats, a drive to mature the coalition habitat doesn't present political dilemmas or societal choices. Instead, it requires strategic choices by the habitat's leading players. Those choices don't need to be guesses. They can draw on lessons about entrepreneurial funding outside of the pharmaceutical sector, where the growth of global funds, global investors, and the rise of nontraditional VCs are all signs of maturity.[36] The maturation of the coalition habitat ought to be one of the easier challenges facing the PIE, but it does need the habitats' leaders to make it happen.

Develop the coalition habitat's management expertise

The coalition habitat connects the discovery and innovation habitats. The former provides new science, and the latter translates that science into innovative medicines. But this is only possible because the coalition habitat aggregates the necessary assets, resources, and capabilities. While the functioning of the discovery and innovation habitats depends heavily on applying scientific knowledge, the functioning of the coalition habitat depends on the application of knowledge about organizations, management, and, especially, how holobionts work. As I've described above, this knowledge is available but largely ignored. There is a lot of valuable academic research available, but its application to practice is limited. For the coalition habitat to work well, it needs to be as good at harnessing management science as the discovery and innovation habitats are at applying biology and medicine.

In some ways, developing the coalition habitat's management expertise is analogous to the translational science challenge described in Chapter 3 on the discovery habitat. It isn't simply about how to build a given holobiont. It is about understanding how holobionts work in general, and developing that understanding into good practice, so that more holobionts succeed and fewer fail. This knowledge can be found, fragmented, and unevenly distributed, in academic research and current practice. Turning it into transferable best practice will need a determined, deliberate effort of knowledge creation, just like turning new science into new technology. The detail of how this might be done is the subject for another book, but I will offer three lessons that emerge from my research.

The first is that part of the reason this knowledge doesn't already exist is because the inhabitants of the coalition habitat don't perceive a need for it. So, if we want to improve the working of the habitat, we'll need to change those perceptions first. Again, this task probably lies with the habitat's most important leaders, who act as the habitat's thought leaders.

The second is that this sort of applied management science lies in what some call the Pasteur Quadrant and is what academics call Type 2 knowledge,[37] meaning it is basic research but carried out with application in mind. This sort of expertise can only be developed collaboratively between academics and practitioners, as neither has all of the competencies to create this kind of knowledge.

The third idea is that this kind of knowledge production rarely fits well within a purely academic or purely business environment. It may well need the focus provided by a specialized entity. Models for this academia–business co-creation of knowledge exist in some other fields. It might be, for example, that something like a Scripps Holobiont Research Institute is needed.

If we understood how best to build holobionts as well as we understood how to formulate medicines, it would be a significant step toward our goal of sustainable, affordable innovative medicines. That knowledge would increase the effectiveness and efficiency of the coalition habitat and so of the innovation process. Relatively speaking, the cost and effort of creating this understanding would be miniscule, and unlike some other issues facing the PIE, there is no trade-off, dilemma, or political conflict to resolve. All that is needed is a change in mindset among the leading inhabitants of the coalition habitat, a shift toward accepting that organizational and management science is as important as biology and medicine.

Encourage a diversity of investor species into the coalition habitat

As in any habitat, the species that populate the coalition habitat reflect its conditions. There are few fish in the desert. From that ecological perspective, the relatively recent dominance of venture capital, private and corporate, is an indication that the coalition habitat is currently perceived as the sort of a high-risk, high-return environment that favors venture capital. That sort of environment may be necessary when failure rates are as high as they are, but it isn't consistent with affordable medicines. As I have and will discuss in other chapters, one aspect of managing the PIE for sustainable affordability involves reducing both its risks and returns.[38] If this is achieved, the VC will no longer be the only species of investor that can thrive in the coalition habitat. Venture capital will still have its place in pockets of the highest risk, but the coalition habitat will be able to, and should, support a more diverse population of investors and include those adapted to a lower risk, lower return environment.[39]

There are already other species of investor in the PIE's coalition habitat, who might be encouraged by a lower risk environment. Family offices, angel investors, crowdfunding, patient groups, charities, grants, or loans are among the minor species funding early-stage pharmaceutical innovation.[40] The challenge is to match the diversity of pharmaceutical development – which varies widely in risk and returns – with a corresponding diversity of sources of capital at various costs. This matching will become more important if, as discussed above, changes to the other habitats shift the distribution of risk and return to lower levels. Increasing the diversity of life science investors will obviously be a dynamic, market-led, process and I won't attempt to suggest how it might be achieved. But, to those inhabitants of the coalition habitat who will undertake this, I offer three implications of my research.

The first is that improvements in the discovery and innovation habitats will, if successful, reduce the risks associated with pharmaceutical innovation. In that case, not only would some innovative medicines no longer need the risk management capabilities of VCs but, with risk reduced, the high costs of venture capital would become inappropriate. The second is that my suggestions in the value, price, and competition habitats may have the effect of polarizing the risks and returns found in the PIE. In this new environment, venture capital will only be appropriate in some, riskier parts of the PIE. The third is that my suggestions in the patient habitat would also make the risks and returns of the PIE more heterogeneous. This would imply the need for a wider range of investor species.

Diversification of the investor species ought to be a consequence of the decisions made in other habitats. It should present no trade-offs or dilemmas and it should fit well with American free market values. It would require the rethinking of some assumptions about which sources of capital best suit the PIE but that does not necessarily mean excluding any source of capital. Rather, it would mean creating a more healthily diverse coalition habitat.

Will this be enough?

Of all the PIE's habitats I have explored and made suggestions for, the coalition habitat is the one least in need of specific policy recommendations, even if I were making them. My suggestions lie mostly in the hands of the coalition habitat's inhabitants, rather than any policy-making body.

Changes to the coalition habitat are needed, however. The current habitat is well adapted to, and helps to perpetuate, a high-risk, high-return pharmaceutical market. Such a market is at odds with aims of sustainable affordability and innovation. A pharmaceutical market whose discovery and innovation habitats are reshaped as I've suggested in other chapters doesn't fit with a coalition habitat dominated by venture capital. Equally, a pharmaceutical market whose value, price, competition, and patient habitats are reshaped (as I'll suggest in subsequent chapters) needs a more diverse range of investor species.

Alone, changes to the coalition habitat won't help and may even harm our aim. What we have now is adapted to the PIE we have now, and to change it in isolation would deprive the PIE of both capital and expertise. But, if we change the other habitats, the current coalition habitat will have to adapt to those changes. As is the logic of a complex, adaptive ecosystem, changing the coalition habitat will be necessary to a healthy PIE but alone it won't be sufficient.

Notes

1 About a quarter of new launches are now by companies launching a product for the first time. See https://www.mckinsey.com/industries/life-sciences/our-insights/first-time-launchers-in-the-pharmaceutical-industry and https://www.mckinsey.com/industries/life-sciences/our-insights/building-a-global-biotech-taking-a-first-time-launch-into-international-markets.
2 If you're interested in this, look up "make or buy." It is one of the most fundamental topics in management science. We usually trace the roots of this thinking back to Ronald Coase. See ref 1.
3 I've referred to this as the "Holobiont Shift." See ref 2.
4 For a further explanation of this thinking, see ref 3.
5 For a thoughtful explanation of how transaction cost economics addresses the issue of vertical disintegration, see ref 4.
6 For a good discussion of this specific to the pharmaceutical industry, see ref 5. For a rather more critical appreciation of how financialization has impacted medical innovation, see ref 6.

7 See, for example, John Godfrey Saxe's poem "The Blind Man and the Elephant." https://en.wikisource.org/wiki/The_poems_of_John_Godfrey_Saxe/The_Blind_Men_and_the_Elephant.

8 For a comprehensive review of the literature in this area, see ref 7.

9 In this literature, open innovation overlaps into other areas. Schuhmacher, for instance, says, "In recent years, multiple extrinsic and intrinsic factors induced an opening for external sources of innovation and resulted in new models for open innovation, such as open sourcing, crowdsourcing, public–private partnerships, innovation centers, and the virtualization of R&D." See ref 8.

10 As a general guide to the stages of this process, see 9. The funding of NewCos set up to develop innovative medicines usually happens in rounds, for example, pre-seed, seed, Series A, Series B, Series C, as the development progresses. See https://www.investopedia.com/articles/personal-finance/102015/series-b-c-funding-what-it-all-means-and-how-it-works.asp.

11 At the time of writing, venture capital investment in pharmaceutical innovation is booming. See https://www.mckinsey.com/industries/life-sciences/our-insights/whats-ahead-for-biotech-another-wave-or-low-tide?cid=eml-web.

12 The data here are taken from Evaluate. See https://www.evaluate.com/vantage/articles/data-insights/venture-financing/retreat-corporate-venture-funding.

13 The evolution of this part of the habitat seems to have begun with firms to service big pharmaceutical companies and then evolved into a more complex network. See ref 10 and 11.

14 The idea of complementarity of actions, assets, resources, and capabilities is one that underpins much systems thinking and is especially relevant in the PIE. For a general but quite excellent discussion of the subject, see ref 12.

15 From a transaction cost economics point of view, the cost of assembling and running a holobiont is typically seen as falling into these three categories of finding the right partners, reaching agreement, and then maintaining the agreement. Anyone familiar with, for example, the building and running of a biotech holobiont will be familiar with the time and money costs of all three stages.

16 The venture capital market is a dynamic one, so the picture changes constantly. After consulting with various expert informants, I took these data from https://news.crunchbase.com/news/most-active-biotech-investors-in-2021-ra-capital-orbimed/.

17 Again, this is a dynamic picture, but the fragmentation of the smaller biotech sector is one of its characteristics. For more on this, see https://www.iqvia.com/insights/the-iqvia-institute/reports/emerging-biopharmas-contribution-to-innovation.

18 For a fascinating example of this, see 13. For a description of clusters in the US, see https://www.genengnews.com/a-lists/top-10-u-s-biopharma-clusters-8/.

19 Geography seems to be especially important earlier in the development process and wanes a little for larger VC firms and more developed science. See refs 14 and 15.

20 To quote a fascinating study of complementarity between venture capitalists and biotechs:

> We specify three mechanisms that affect the influence of complementary resources. (1) absorptive capacity enhances the ability of the company to grasp and utilize investor knowledge; (2) business similarity helps nurture the technologies of innovative companies, and (3) geographic proximity enables approachability.

See ref 16.

21 See, for example, ref 17. These authors express the relationship-based nature of holobionts as "... a smart innovation ecosystem presents ... a portfolio of

relationships that privileges informal and non-redundant ties within small communities focused on specific themes."

22 In academic jargon, this is known as the balance between knowledge creation and knowledge appropriation. See refs 18 and 19.

23 It seems to be a widespread perception among investors that discoverers are naïve with respect to the risks of developing an innovative medicine. See ref 20.

24 See, for example, https://www.labiotech.eu/in-depth/biotech-startups-alternative-funding/.

25 Tourist investors is a somewhat disparaging term I heard often in the coalition habitat. It refers to investors who are not specialized in the life sciences and usually invest in other sectors but who have been attracted to life sciences by fashion and the prospect of high returns. See https://www.ft.com/content/c90d17c6-6196-4c8a-88c2-e2cef9a692f2 and https://www.evaluate.com/vantage/articles/insights/other-data/bubble-bursts-biotech-stocks.

26 Again, a pervasive issue among investors is that new assets are easy to find, and good assets are hard to find. See, for example, https://www.forbes.com/sites/forbesbusinesscouncil/2021/03/10/all-that-glitters-isnt-gold-questions-to-ask-yourself-before-investing-in-biotech/?sh=2ae47a6f6032.

27 There really is a wealth of good academic research in this area, but like much management research, it seems to have little influence on how the coalition habitat works. See, for example, refs 21, 22, and 23. I also acknowledge here what I've learned in private communication from one of my doctoral candidates at the University of Hertfordshire. Zaki Sellam is very experienced in this part of the PIE and, as I write, is writing up his PhD thesis on exactly this topic.

28 See, for example, refs 24–28.

29 See, for example, refs 29 and 30.

30 See, for example, refs 31.

31 See, for example, refs 32.

32 A good description of this phenomenon can be found here. See ref 33.

33 For a very good overview of how the biotech venture capital market works, see https://www.baybridgebio.com/blog/vc_basics_2.html.

34 To be clear, I'm referring to translational science as distinct from translation research, as defined and differentiated in Chapter 3.

35 A common theme that emerges from the literature is lack of management expertise in both discoverer and investor. For discussion of this, see https://www.labiotech.eu/opinion/mismanaged-projects-biotech-pharma/ and https://www.forbes.com/sites/brucebooth/2019/05/20/biotech-startups-and-the-hard-truth-of-innovation/?sh=7038472c3867.

36 It's important to remember that investors in pharmaceutical innovation, such as venture capitalists, are connected to a wider investment capital ecosystem so that lessons can be imported from outside the PIE. See ref 34.

37 See refs 35 and 36.

38 Here I am referring to the transformation of translational science idea I proposed in Chapter 3.

39 To pre-empt "straw man" objections to this point, I'm not suggesting that pharmaceutical innovation might ever be low risk, only lower than it is at present.

40 For discussions of these non-VC funding methods, see https://www.labiotech.eu/in-depth/biotech-startups-alternative-funding/ and https://www.universitylabpartners.org/blog/unconventional-funding-sources-for-biotech-and-medtech-startups. See ref 37.

References

1 Coase R. The nature of the firm. *Economica.* 1937;4(16):386–405.

2 Smith BD. *Darwin's Medicine: How Business Models in the Life Science Industry are Evolving.* Abingdon: Routledge; 2016.

3 Barney JB. Resource-based theories of competitive advantage: A ten-year retrospective on the resource-based view. *Journal of Management.* 2001;27:643–50.

4 Gilson RJ, Sabel CF, Scott RE. Contracting for innovation: Vertical disintegration and interfirm collaboration. *Columbia Law Review.* 2009;109(3).

5 Gleadle P, Parris S, Shipman A, Simonetti R. Restructuring and innovation in pharmaceuticals and biotechs: The impact of financialisation. *Critical Perspectives on Accounting.* 2014;25(1):67–77.

6 Sell SK. 21st century capitalism and innovation for health. *Global Policy.* 2021;12(S6):12–20.

7 Yeung AWK, Atanasov AG, Sheridan H, Klager E, Eibensteiner F, Völkl-Kernsock S et al. Open innovation in medical and pharmaceutical research: A literature landscape analysis. *Frontiers in Pharmacology.* 2021;11.

8 Schuhmacher A, Gassmann O, McCracken N, Hinder M. Open innovation and external sources of innovation. An opportunity to fuel the R&D pipeline and enhance decision making? *Journal of Translational Medicine.* 2018;16(1):119.

9 Tajonar A. How to start a biotech company. *Molecular Biology of the Cell.* 2014;25(21):3280–3.

10 Landhuis E. Outsourcing is in. *Nature (London).* 2018;556(7700):263–5.

11 Lane RF, Friedman LG, Keith C, Braithwaite SP, Frearson JA, Lowe DA et al. Optimizing the use of CROs by academia and small companies. *Nature Reviews Drug Discovery.* 2013;12(7):487–8.

12 Roberts J. *The Modern Firm.* 1st ed. Oxford: Oxford University Press; 2004.

13 Catini R, Karamshuk D, Penner O, Riccaboni M. Identifying geographic clusters: A network analytic approach. *Research Policy.* 2015;44(9):1749–62.

14 Powell WW. Learning from collaboration: Knowledge and networks in the biotechnology and pharmaceutical industries. *California Management Review.* 1998;40(3):228–40.

15 Powell WW, Koput KW, Bowie JI, Smith-Doerr L. The spatial clustering of science and capital: Accounting for biotech firm-venture capital relationships. *Regional Studies.* 2002;36(3):291–305.

16 Shuwaikh F, Dubocage E. Access to the corporate investors' complementary resources: A leverage for innovation in biotech venture capital-backed companies. *Technological Forecasting and Social Change.* 2022;175:121374.

17 Panetti E, Parmentola A, Ferretti M, Reynolds EB. Exploring the relational dimension in a smart innovation ecosystem: A comprehensive framework to define the network structure and the network portfolio. *The Journal of Technology Transfer.* 2020;45(6):1775–96.

18 Samant S, Kim J. When do firms really share? Common benefits versus private benefits for alliance partners. *Academy of Management Proceedings.* 2019;2019(1):18549.

19 Samant S, Kim J. Determinants of common benefits and private benefits in innovation alliances. *Managerial and Decision Economics.* 2021;42(2):294–307.

20 Ciao B. Business founding in biotech industry: Process and features. *Management Research Review.* 2020;43(10):1183–219.

21 Roijakkers N, Hagedoorn J. Inter-firm R&D partnering in pharmaceutical biotechnology since 1975: trends, patterns, and networks. *Research Policy.* 2006;35(3):431–46.

22 Depret M-H, Hamdouch A. Innovation networks and competitive coalitions in the pharmaceutical industry: The emergence and structures of a new industrial organization. *European Journal of Economic and Social Systems.* 2000;14(3):229–70.

23 Paruchuri S. Intraorganizational networks, interorganizational networks, and the impact of central inventors: A longitudinal study of pharmaceutical firms. *Organization Science*. 2010;21(1):63–80.

24 Sabidussi A, Lokshin B, Duysters G. Complementarity in alliance portfolios and firm innovation. *Industry and Innovation*. 2018;25(7):633–54.

25 Hess AM, Rothaermel FT. When are assets complementary? Star scientists, strategic alliances, and Innovation in the pharmaceutical industry. *Strategic Management Journal*. 2011;32(8):895–909.

26 Mindruta D, Moeen M, Agarwal R. A two-sided matching approach for partner selection and assessing complementarities in partners' attributes in inter-firm alliances. *Strategic Management Journal*. 2016;37(1):206–31.

27 Hagedoorn J. Inter-firm R&D partnerships: An overview of major trends and patterns since 1960. *Research Policy*. 2002;31(4):477.

28 Hagedoorn J, Wang N. Is there complementarity or substitutability between internal and external R&D strategies? *Research Policy*. 2012;41(6):1072–83.

29 Adegbesan JA, Higgins MJ. The intra-alliance division of value created through collaboration. *Strategic Management Journal*. 2011;32(2):187–211.

30 Delerue H. Shadow of joint patents: Intellectual property rights sharing by SMEs in contractual R&D alliances. *Journal of Business Research*. 2018;87:12–23.

31 Kavusan K, Frankort H. A behavioral theory of alliance portfolio reconfiguration: Evidence from pharmaceutical biotechnology. *Strategic Management Journal*. 2019;40(10):1668–702.

32 Cabello-Medina C, Carmona-Lavado A, Cuevas-Rodriguez G. A contingency view of alliance management capabilities for innovation in the biotech industry. *BRQ Business Research Quarterly*. 2019.

33 Zider B. How venture capital works. *Harvard Business Review*. 1998;76(6):131–9.

34 Klonowski D. Transformations in the venture capital ecosystem post COVID-response. In Klonowski D, editor. *Venture Capital Redefined: The Economic, Political, and Social Impact of COVID on the VC Ecosystem*. Cham: Springer International Publishing; 2022. p. 61–92.

35 Gibbons GRL, C, Nowotny H, Schwartman S, Scott P, Trow M. *The New Production of Knowledge: The Dynamics of Science and Research in Contemporary Societies*. London: Sage; 1994.

36 Stokes DE. *The Pasteur Quadrant*. Washington, DC: Brookings Institution Press; 1996.

37 López JC, Suojanen C. Harnessing venture philanthropy to accelerate medical progress. *Nature Reviews Drug Discovery*. 2019;18(11):809–10.

6 The value habitat

Precis

- The value of an innovative medicine is a second-order construct, the relationship between its costs and benefits.
- Value is relative, subjective, context-dependent, and varies over time.
- The value habitat is the part of the pharmaceutical innovation ecosystem (PIE) where the value of innovative medicines is assessed.
- The value habitat is inhabited by pharmaceutical companies, insurance companies and PBMs, healthcare providers, plan sponsors, patients, and health technology assessment bodies.
- The value habitat adjoins and interacts with the pricing and competition habitats.
- A healthy PIE requires that the value habitat uses all appropriate sources of information to make ecologically valid value assessments that are communicated to the market.
- The value habitat's ability to support a healthy PIE is constrained by:
  - its inadequate information infrastructure
  - its incompletely evolved methods for assessing comparative effectiveness
  - its weak capabilities for making valid and legitimate assessments of wider relative value assessments
  - the market imperfections that hinder the value habitat's connection to the PIE
- The value habitat would be better able to support a healthy PIE if:
  - it developed a data infrastructure that made use of large-scale, real-world data
  - it developed ecologically valid value assessments
  - it adopted transparent value assessment practices

DOI: 10.4324/9781003330271-6

So far in my journey through the PIE, I've explored the interconnected discovery, innovation, and coalition habitats that work together to bring innovative medicines to market. In each habitat, I discovered weaknesses in their working that limit their ability to contribute to a healthy PIE, which I've defined as one that can sustainably provide us with medicines that are both innovative and affordable. For each habitat, I offered broad suggestions for how we improve the current situation, giving pointers but necessarily leaving the detail to the experts in each area. In Chapters 3–5, I've explored as far as the innovative medicine reaching the market. I now enter the part of the ecosystem after regulatory approval, when the medicine is available for purchase, prescription, and use.

In my explorations so far, I've said very little about the value of innovative medicines, which is the subject of this chapter. The value of the innovative medicines that emerge from the PIE is analogous to the yield of the apothecary's garden; it's a measure of its output. The concept of value is important for our question of how to maintain a sustainable supply of affordable, innovative medicines, so I wanted to explore it. But, as I did, it soon became clear that I was again running into Voltaire's issue about defining terms. To make sense of this part of the journey, I need to be clear about three things when I talk about the value of innovative medicines.

First is the tricky and contentious issue of value. Generally, but particularly in the context of healthcare, it's one of those terms that means different things to different people.[1] That said, among researchers in this area, there's an identifiable consensus about the nature of value and I used that to craft a working definition of the value of an innovative medicine (see Box 6.1).

Box 6.1 What is the value of an innovative medicine?

Almost all discussions of value agree on five central points:

- Value is a second-order construct, the relationship between costs and benefits.
- Costs can be defined narrowly, as simply the price of the product, or broadly, as the sum of all costs incurred or obviated in the use of the product, or somewhere in between.

- Benefits can be defined narrowly, as those arising directly from the use of the product, or broadly, to include all indirect benefits associated with a product's use, or somewhere in between.
- Value is a relative construct, comparative to that of obtaining the same benefits by other means, via either direct or indirect substitution of the product, including non-use.
- Since costs, benefits, and alternatives might be perceived differently by different people or might vary between contexts and over time, value is a subjective, context-dependent, and dynamic construct.

Building on these uncontentious points, I chose to apply a working definition of the value of an innovative medicine as "the relation between its benefits and costs, as perceived by the person or organization paying for it, in a given context and at a given time." I appreciate that this is an imperfect definition, but I think it's sufficient to guide us in our exploration of the value habitat without getting sucked into its semantic swamps.

Second is the question: what are we valuing? The work that occurs in the innovation habitat turns important but unusable scientific discoveries into innovative medicines that we know how to use, when to use, for whom, and with an understanding of their balance of risks and benefits. It creates, in other words, usable products. But, to use an old marketing maxim, nobody buys products; they buy solutions for their problems. When the problem is an illness, the solution includes not only the product but also the services that allow it to be used effectively and, importantly, the price. This means that, when we talk about the value of an innovative medicine, we need to be clear about whether we mean the value of the product or the value of the solution. In this chapter, I'll talk about the value of the product, the innovative medicine. In later chapters, especially Chapter 7 on pricing, I'll touch on the value of the wider solution. For the moment though, it's important to recognize that the value of an innovative medicine and the value of the solution are related but distinct issues.

Third, it's become commonplace in the discussion of drug pricing to conflate the terms price and value. Some people use "better value" as a synonym for "lower price." Price is a component of value of course, but it's not the same thing. A more expensive, highly effective drug can be better value than a cheaper, ineffective drug, and a slightly less effective drug can be better value than its much more expensive but only marginally more effective alternative. To quote expert informant Peter Neumann:

> *Valuing innovative medicines appropriately doesn't simply mean making them all cheaper: the appropriate price, the price that reflects the value of the medicine, might be higher or lower than the current price. And, even if all innovative medicines were appropriately priced in relation to the value they deliver, we'd still have an issue of affordability for some medicines in some cases. That's an issue of how we pay for healthcare, quite distinct from the value of innovative medicines.*
>
> *Peter Neumann*

The value of an innovative medicine, as defined in Box 6.1, sets one of the boundary conditions of that medicine's price, the upper limit of what the buyer is usually prepared to pay. The other boundary limit is the cost of the innovative medicine, the lower limit of what the seller is usually prepared to accept. The overlapping zone of these two variable, dynamic parameters is the market for that innovative medicine. Whether they overlap, and at what values, determines the availability and price range of the product. All of this means that how we understand the value of innovative medicines is important to how we manage the PIE for sustainable, affordable medicines. In Chapter 7, I'll explore the pricing of innovative medicines. In this chapter, I'll explore the part of the PIE where value is understood, which I'll call the value habitat.

What happens in the value habitat and who inhabits it?

Like the other habitats, the value habitat isn't a clear-cut, well-defined construct. It's simply a way of thinking about how one part of the PIE works, without ever forgetting that all of the habitats function holistically as components of a complex, adaptive system. In the value habitat, information is created, synthesized, and processed with the aim of making a judgment about the value of an innovative medicine. That information includes the costs and benefits of the medicine and those of the alternatives to it, all of which are subjective, dynamic, and context-dependent, as described in Box 6.1. That information sometimes also includes the needs and preferences of those who administer and consume the medicines and of other stakeholders in the system. Once that accumulation of diverse information is processed, it allows a judgment about the value to feed back into the PIE. That judgment influences what medicines are made available, used, and ultimately, which medicines are developed.[2] Although I describe it in simple terms, this is not a straightforward, standardized judgment. It emerges from the complex interaction of everyone involved in the value habitat which, just like any natural habitat, is populated by several species, each playing their necessary, different, and complementary roles.

At the center of the value habitat sit payers, the organizations that give money to the makers of the innovative medicines. In the US, of course, most innovative medicines are paid for by insurance, either private or public,[3] although individuals also contribute via various out-of-pocket means. Since they are the majority payers, it is these public and private insurers who hold the ultimate role in judging the value of an innovative medicine and using that judgment to inform what medicines are made available (in the jargon, deciding coverage). At its very simplest, this "what do we think is worth paying for?" decision is the role payers play in the value habitat. But two other payer-related factors are important to how the habitat works.

First, there are many different payers, each making their value judgments more or less independently. In the private sector, there are over 900 health insurers, both profit and non-profit. To these can be added the various public programs, including Medicare, Medicaid, Veterans Affairs, and the Children's Health Insurance Program.[4] This payer complexity, which makes the US quite unique among developed countries, has an important practical implication for how the value habitat works. It means that it is very unlikely that any one approach to understanding value would be acceptable to all payers.[5]

Second, although most payers put costs and benefits at the core of their process for understanding the value of medicines,[6] they also consider many other factors, ranging from the commercial to the legal to the ethical. This multifactorial nature of coverage decision means that no single source of information, such as a comparative effectiveness assessment between two competing medicines, can satisfy the multiple information needs of a payer making their decisions. Together, the multiplicity of payers and the multifactorial nature of their decisions make the value habitat a very messy place.

Although their role is central, payers are not the only inhabitants of the value habitat. Their role in synthesizing and acting on information about value depends on inputs from four other species of organization, which share the value habitat and interact with payers.

Pharmaceutical companies have a critical role to play in the value habitat. Primarily, they create the information about costs and benefits of their own products. But their other role is to make payers aware of additional, wider benefits they may not have considered or costs that their own product may obviate. Of course, pharmaceutical companies are more likely to adopt this secondary role when it might shift the value judgment in their favor and they are not disinterested parties.[7]

Patient advocacy groups, often working with pharmaceutical companies,[8] also try to shape payers' value judgments. Fearing that the value judgment might be too narrowly focused on clinical benefits and economic costs, patient groups often raise the salience of non-clinical needs such as the patient's experience or patient's direct costs. In doing so, they hope that value judgments will more accurately reflect the needs and wants of the patient rather than those of the payer. Sometimes, physicians will lend their professional support to this patient advocacy effort.

A third important, but less prominent, inhabitant of the value habitat is the plan sponsor, the customer of the payer, who is typically an employer or other organization. Although the responsibility for understanding value and deciding coverage is in the hands of the payer, plan sponsors have an interest, as it affects the cost of the insurance for which they pay. Plan sponsors in competitive labor markets also have an interest in coverage which is attractive to employees, because it either offers a choice or has low costs to the patient, or both. So, while plan sponsors don't always get involved in the details of coverage, they may influence it by their preferences for health plan design. In this, plan sponsors often cooperate[9] and work with specialist advisory companies.

The last of the four most important species in the value habitat is the health technology assessment (HTA) body. HTA bodies are much less significant in the US than they are in Europe, and there is no equivalent to, for example, the UK's NICE or Germany's IQWIG, both of which are agencies of the national government.[10] The nearest equivalent in the US is the Institute for Clinical and Economic Review (ICER), an independent HTA body. ICER's self-proclaimed mission is to conduct evidence-based reviews of health care interventions, including innovative medicines.[11] As such, ICER has a unique role in the value habitat. Although it has no official role and limited resources, it provides the sort of comparative cost-effectiveness information that is a staple of the habitat in Europe but has historically been absent in the US. In doing so, it is becoming increasingly influential in the habitat.[12]

So, as I explored the value habitat and tried to see the forest for the trees, what I saw was hundreds of payers, of different kinds, all trying to make multifactorial judgments about the value of innovative medicines, a construct that is subjective, dynamic, and context-specific. Because this judgment is so multifactorial, payers draw on many kinds of information about cost, benefits, alternatives, and other factors, including non-clinical needs and their own commercial or financial goals. This information flows to them from pharmaceutical companies, patient groups, plan sponsors, and increasingly from ICER. The coverage decisions that are informed by these judgments are central to the working of the PIE. In both its inhabitants and the nature of their interaction, the value habitat in the US is very different from that of other advanced economies. It was with this exceptional and messy picture in my mind that I continued my exploration, asking what the PIE requires of the value habitat.

What does a healthy PIE require of the value habitat?

An apothecary gardener would have watered, fed, and tended her garden.[13] In return, she would have expected a harvest commensurate with her time, effort, and expense. In the same way, today's society enables the PIE with NIH investment, intellectual property protection, and by buying much of its outputs. In return, society expects a proportionate harvest of valuable, innovative medicines. This is the basis of the social contract discussed in Chapter 2. And, just as apothecaries might have examined the yield and quality of their harvests, the value habitat examines the collective and individual value of the PIE's produce. Taking inputs from the innovation habitat and other parts of the ecosystem, it processes them and feeds its judgments back into the PIE. This process is essential to the healthy functioning of the PIE. Without the value habitat effectively assessing the value of innovative medicines and sending that information back into the PIE, the ecosystem might make medicines that society doesn't want or medicines it wants but at prices it isn't willing to pay. To avoid this situation, the PIE requires five things from the value habitat.

The value habitat must make ecologically valid[14] value assessments

A well-functioning value habitat will influence the allocation of limited healthcare resources both between competing medicines and between pharmaceutical and non-pharmaceutical interventions. To do so effectively, a healthy PIE requires that the value habitat provides value assessments that reflect the value of pharmaceutical innovation in a real-world setting. Further, the value habitat must provide assessments that are comparable not only against other pharmaceuticals but also against non-pharmaceutical interventions. A value habitat whose value assessments reflect only artificial conditions or that does not allow meaningful comparison against other possible uses of the same expenditure would not sustain a healthy PIE.

The value habitat must make appropriate use of all relevant forms of cost, benefit, and comparator information

The value of an innovative medicine is multifactorial and context-dependent. To allow for this, a healthy PIE requires that the value habitat provides value assessments based on all relevant information. Where appropriate to the context, information may be quantitative or qualitative and it may relate to the costs, benefits, and alternatives of all stakeholders involved. A value habitat whose value assessments are incomplete or are based on incomplete information, relative to context, would not sustain a healthy PIE.

The value habitat must dynamically adjust its value assessments as costs, benefits, comparators, and other factors change over time

The first-order variables that determine the value of an innovative medicine – costs, benefits, comparators, and other factors – are not fixed. This makes any value assessment only temporarily valid, while a healthy PIE requires value assessments that reflect the current situation. To provide these, the value habitat must be able to identify, acquire, and process any relevant new information, and use it in a timely manner, to change value assessments as appropriate. A value habitat whose value assessments do not reflect changes in costs, benefits, comparators, or other contextually relevant information is unlikely to sustain a healthy PIE.

The value habitat must clearly communicate its value assessments to the market

A healthy value habitat will influence the allocation of limited health-care resources by communicating its value assessments, through either price mechanisms or alternative, non-price mechanisms such as market access permission. To do so effectively, a healthy PIE requires that the value assessments are reflected in price levels or other mechanisms that favor high-value innovations over lesser-value alternatives. A value habitat whose value assessments are not significantly and accurately reflected in price or non-price mechanisms would not sustain a healthy PIE.

The value habitat must be politically legitimate[15]

The outputs of the value habitat have significant real-world implications, which will inevitably have political significance. To be sustainable under these conditions, a healthy PIE requires that the processes and mechanisms of the value habitat are as transparent as reasonably possible. In particular, the decision criteria and information considered must be clear and explained. A value habitat whose workings are not

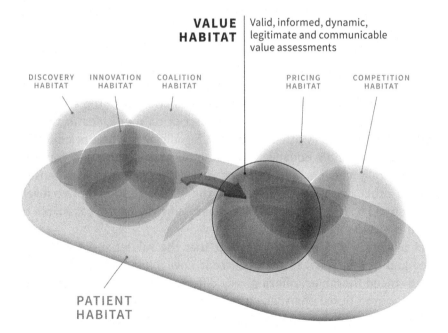

Figure 6.1 The value habitat's contribution to a healthy PIE

transparent enough to allow public examination and maintain legitimacy would be unlikely to maintain the public legitimacy needed to
sustain a healthy PIE.

These five requirements are not easy for any system to meet, and
if you are familiar with the existing value habitat, you may see that it
appears to fall far short of these requirements. But it's hard to see
how we can maintain a healthy PIE without meeting them. So, as in
the other habitats, I wanted to understand what factors, if any, constrained the value habitat from supporting a healthy PIE.

Is the value habitat capable of supporting a healthy PIE?

There are three principal reasons why we might question how well
the value habitat contributes to a healthy PIE. The first, and most
obvious, is that the US stands alone among large, developed economies in not having an explicit, government-supported system of value
assessment along the lines of the UK's NICE or Germany's IQWIG.
There are good arguments for why this is so. Cultural and political differences would make it difficult to copy and paste such a system onto
the US. Equally, it's reasonable to question how a value assessment
system designed for a single payer system like the UK[16] or even one
from a multi-payer system, like Germany, might work in the US, with
its close to 1000 payers. But those points still leave open the question
of whether some elements of other countries' systems might help the
US value habitat meet the needs of the PIE.

A second reason to wonder about the functioning of the value habitat is the relatively high prices of prescription medicines in the US
compared to those in other countries. Significantly, these price differentials do not apply equally across all medicines; unbranded generics
are generally cheaper and branded drugs generally more expensive
than in other countries.[17] Given that the US's exceptional price levels
correspond to its exceptional way of assessing value, it's reasonable to
ask if the two might be linked.

Finally, even if one were to accept that the value habitat functions
well and is well adapted to its current environment, the emergence
of advanced therapies, offering very different costs and benefits compared to traditional pharmaceuticals, makes it reasonable to ask if the
value habitat will still work when advanced therapies become more

common.[18] Based on these three justifications, I explored the value habitat and uncovered four causes for concern.

The value habitat's information infrastructure is inadequate

Value assessment is an information processing exercise, and as I've described above, the information relevant to any given assessment is context-specific.[19] In almost all cases, value assessment requires information about costs and outcomes. This is typically processed by a HTA body such as ICER. The outcome is a comparative cost-effectiveness assessment, which forms part of the overall value assessment. At present, however, the sources of both costs and outcomes of information are inadequate to the task of making an ecologically valid value assessment. Outcomes information is typically derived from clinical trials whose primary purpose was to provide information for regulatory approval, which is concerned with safety, quality, and efficacy but not cost-effectiveness.[20] Sometimes, trials are adapted to provide information that is more useful to value assessment.[21] Sometimes, the so-called real-world evidence is gathered after approval and launch of the product to assess comparative effectiveness[22] but, for the most part, the outcomes of the value assessment are, currently, heavily reliant on the opportunistic use of limited data gathered for purposes entirely different from value assessment,[23] and few comparative effectiveness studies use big data and real-world data.[24] Of course, there are good reasons why pharmaceutical companies don't generally produce lots of effectiveness data before launch; it is very expensive and time-consuming. This leads to an obvious tension between wanting to launch as soon as possible but with the best evidence possible. Expert informant Philip Naughten explained this to me.

> Health economics outcomes research can come in later in the development pathway and carries with it concerns about complicating or delaying regulatory approval. In some cases, due to many factors it is done without a direct comparator or inclusion of endpoints that help differentiate or pull out all value elements at launch. Post launch, the aim is to gather more evidence, from a variety of sources, that supports claims for different kinds of value, such as adherence or the wider impact on the healthcare system.
>
> Philip Naughten

To compound this problem of inadequate effectiveness data, the cost data available for HTA, and so to the value habitat, is also problematic. An innovative medicine may have many different prices, depending on discounts, and these prices are often not publicly available. Since these prices can differ significantly, this obviously makes a significant difference to the outcomes of a HTA.[25]

Although they are often conflated, the quantitative HTA of cost-effectiveness is not identical to the value assessment process, which may be a much wider and more subjective judgment. However, a comparative cost-effectiveness assessment will usually be an essential part of that wider value assessment. Given the PIE's requirements that the value assessment is ecologically valid, reflecting real-world conditions, the current situation of relying on opportunistic use of limited outcomes data and estimated costs means that the information infrastructure available to the value habitat is inadequate to the task. As it stands, it cannot meet the requirements of a healthy PIE.

The value habitat's methodologies have not fully evolved

The inadequacies of the value habitat's information infrastructure are a significant issue on their own. But, even if that issue were solved tomorrow, there would still be methodological challenges around assessing the comparative effectiveness of innovative medicines, challenges that would hinder the ability to make ecologically valid value assessments.

In my exploration of this subject, it wasn't difficult to find criticisms of comparative effectiveness research and, in a US context, most of these are inevitably directed at ICER as the nation's standard bearer for such work. Some criticisms center on the use of meta-analyses, the synthesis of costs, benefits, or cost-effectiveness ratios from multiple different studies. As might be obvious, this creates problems if the combined studies are not designed identically.[26] Others point to the failure to allow for price changes over time, meaning the cost-effectiveness assessment may not reflect current conditions.[27] Other criticisms of cost-effectiveness assessment concern how uncertainty is managed and communicated.[28] But the most passionate criticism of comparative effectiveness research is centered on its use of a unit of measurement called a QALY (quality-adjusted life year) as an indicator of outcomes.[29] This unit is used because it is generalizable and so allows comparison between different medicines and interventions.

But its critics argue that it is not appropriate in certain cases and, particularly, when the patient is old or disabled.[30] Expert informant Sue Peschin, who has a particular interest in the needs of the elderly, expressed it as follows:

> *Yes, we need value-based pricing of pharmaceuticals but QALYs are not the way to do it. They are very poor at allowing for the heterogeneity of a patient population. This causes them to be highly inconsistent in the recommendations they lead to.*
>
> Sue Peschin

For all the criticisms leveled at the QALY, there is no clear consensus on what might replace it. There are alternatives, but they too have their shortcomings.[31] As some have said, QALY is the worst way to measure health, except for all the others.[32] More generally, the same can be said of all current approaches to comparative effectiveness assessments. The many and varied criticisms of them have merit but that doesn't mean the methods have no utility at all. As expert informant Sarah Emond, a passionate advocate of cost-effectiveness assessments, put it:

> *It's very easy to point to the imperfections in ICER's methods but we need to be wary of the perfect being the enemy of the good. Existing comparative effectiveness methods can contribute to understanding the value of alternative therapies and interventions. Some of the criticisms made of current methods are just reluctance to accept their implications, for example in calling out overpriced medicines or inappropriate allocation of healthcare resources, rather than of than the methods themselves.*
>
> Sarah Emond

As I explored this part of the value habitat, what emerged was a polarized discussion in which the truth lay in between the poles. The current state of the art of comparative effectiveness methods is neither fully adequate to the functioning of the habitat, nor is it wholly inadequate. To my eyes, what we're observing in real time is the evolution of comparative cost-effectiveness methods.[33] This evolution will gradually resolve many of their current weaknesses, but it may never satisfy those who are unhappy with the choices that comparative effectiveness studies imply.[34] For the present, however, the value habitat is hindered in its ability to meet the needs of the PIE by comparative cost-effectiveness methods that have not fully evolved.

The value habitat lacks wider value assessment capabilities

As I've argued in the preceding two points, the value habitat isn't fully capable of meeting the requirements of the PIE because both the information available and the methods for processing that information are currently far from adequate. That is not to say that the work of ICER and others who attempt cost-effectiveness analyses is useless. As the saying goes, "in the kingdom of the blind, the one-eyed man is king" and, in the absence of anything better, current HTAs are both helpful and an evolutionary step toward what is needed. So, if you gave me Harry Potter's magic wand today, among the first things I would wish for the value habitat is comprehensive information and robust methods. But, as I continued to explore the value habitat, it became clear that even those ambitious wishes would not be enough.

Although they need the input of other inhabitants of the value habitat, the responsibility for deciding the relative value of an innovative medicine lies with the payer. It is a case, as my Scottish wife reminds me, of "he who pays the piper calls the tune." They have the difficult task of synthesizing comparative effectiveness assessments with many other factors to make a wider assessment of the innovative medicine's relative value. Compared to other developed countries, the US healthcare system has made relatively little use of value assessments, so it would be surprising if these essential value assessment capabilities were currently well developed. And the evidence suggests that they aren't.

Payers are certainly interested in value assessment but developing these capabilities isn't easy and is proving to be problematic for them.[35] As expected, payers value a broad range of information sources and the way they use them varies between payers and between therapeutic areas.[36] A look at payer practices reveals that they are moving toward being competent at value assessment but are far from their destination. As expert informant Edmund Pezalla put it:

> With a few, small, exceptions, nobody has a clinical policy that says we're constructing formularies on cost-effectiveness grounds. A lot of plans look at cost effectiveness and they use it to project what they might want to do if they're signing an outcomes-based contract or if they're actively trying to promote one treatment over another. But most insurers don't have formal policies allowing them to use cost-effectiveness research in decision making.
>
> Edmund Pezalla

In a natural habitat where species coevolve traits together, the rate of coevolution is limited to that of the slowest-evolving species. In the same way, it seems that payers' slow evolution of value assessment capabilities hinders the evolution of complementary capabilities in other inhabitants of the value habitat. In pharmaceutical companies, for example, the need to develop stronger capabilities to support value assessment – what those in the industry call market access capabilities – was explained by expert informant Lisa Morris:

> *Demonstrating and communicating the value of innovative medicines requires the development of new approaches by pharmaceutical companies, working together with insurers, PBMs and others. I envisage a future of 'big data' in health economics outcomes research, where we pool relevant information from many sources and use that to support value claims. But this needs everyone involved in the ecosystem to work together, agreeing standards and methods and being less proprietary about trials and data. The need for that complex cooperation is part of what slows down the evolution of the system.*
> Lisa Morris

The same pressing need for capability development can be discerned in patient groups, who increasingly see patient involvement as important to value assessment,[37] and in employers, who as plan sponsors have become somewhat detached from the value habitat, even though its decisions directly affect them.[38] A well-functioning value habitat would see patient groups feeding patient needs into the value assessment process.[39] Similarly, employers would push to have their needs, and those of their employees, recognized.[40] At present, although there is some limited evidence of both, neither has a significant impact on value assessment processes.

So, as I considered how the value habitat might make use of the perfect information and fully evolved methods I might wish for them, I realized that the habitat currently lacked the capabilities to make use of those gifts. For reasons of the US's exceptional history, payers and the other inhabitants of the value habitat have not needed to coevolve strong capabilities in making wider value assessments. Consequently, the value habitat doesn't currently have the capabilities to combine comparative cost-effectiveness with the other, varied information needed to make an ecologically valid, context-sensitive, and dynamic value assessment. In other words, even with perfect information, the value habitat can't currently meet the needs of the PIE laid out earlier in this chapter.

The value habitat's connection to the PIE is weak

Together, the preceding three points paint a picture of how we'd like the value habitat to be but isn't. In a well-functioning value habitat, payers would use developed capabilities to appropriately combine all relevant information to make ecologically valid value assessments that reflected current conditions. An important, but not the only, element of this would be the application of robust cost-effectiveness analysis methods using accurate, comprehensive, and dynamic information about costs and outcomes. If it did all these things, the value habitat would meet the first three of the PIE's requirements, as described earlier in this chapter. And that would put it in a position to meet the fourth requirement, communicating its value assessment to the market. At this point in my exploration, I found myself in the border territory where the value habitat overlaps with the pricing habitat, so I'm only going to touch on this point briefly here and refer you to Chapter 7.

How the value habitat is supposed to communicate its value assessments to the market was explained to me by expert informant Rena Conti.

> *Value assessments have two main functions in the market. First, they differentiate between relatively valuable medicines, which may then justifiably command higher prices, and undifferentiated medicines, which can only compete on price. Second, by giving the payer information about relative value, they inform the allocation of limited healthcare dollars between valuable medicines and other alternatives. So, although value assessment is sometimes painted as a constraint on free markets, in practice it enables them because markets function best when value information is available. Value assessment is what you, I and everyone else does every time we buy anything.*
>
> Rena Conti

Rena Conti's quotidian comparison made me consider how value assessments might have been communicated to the market in the times of the apothecary's garden. If our apothecary judged that a plant was an especially valuable remedy, meeting the varied needs of her patients exceptionally well, she would charge as high a price as her patients were willing to pay. But if she found that a plant offered only the same benefits as many competing remedies, she would be forced by competition to adjust the price accordingly. Or perhaps she might choose not to grow that plant at all and spend her limited time on growing more valuable plants.

Something like this is supposed to happen for today's innovative medicines. The prices paid by payers for innovative medicines should reflect their value assessments and those prices should be reflected in the prices paid by patients to the payers.[41] As I'll discuss in Chapter 7 on the pricing habitat, the link between price and value seems weak.[42] The most obvious explanation of this is the one implied by the three preceding points. Lacking adequate information, methods, and capabilities, the value habitat is unable to make ecologically valid assessments of innovative medicines. Given how far the value habitat is from meeting the first three requirements of the PIE, that is likely to be a large part of the reason value and price are not closely linked in pharmaceutical markets. But there is another factor to consider. In my metaphor of the apothecary passing value assessments on to the market, I assumed competition; undifferentiated medicines of low relative value would find a market price based partly on what other apothecaries were charging for alternatives. But what if competition were weak? What if, in each town or district, one, two or three apothecaries controlled most of the market for remedies and their patients found it difficult to shop around? In this imaginary case, it is hard to believe that apothecaries would reduce their prices to align with relative value. You will see where I'm heading. This concentrated market situation is not imaginary; it is the US health insurance market, which, along with that for healthcare providers and PBMS has become very concentrated, a topic I expand on in Chapter 7.

So, having found that the value habitat was very unlikely to meet the first three requirements of the PIE, I then found that it was unlikely to meet the fourth. It lacks the data, methods, and capabilities to make wide value assessments based on the appropriate use of ecologically valid cost-effectiveness assessments and other context-relevant information. But, even if this situation was rectified, payers might not choose to communicate value assessments to the market through price mechanisms, if there is little competitive pressure to make them do so.[43]

As should now be obvious, my exploration of the value habitat led me to conclude that it is unable to give the PIE what it needs. There are positive signs, such as the development of comparative effectiveness methods and patient involvement in value assessments. These and other things are steps on an evolutionary path. But, as it stands today, the PIE's health is hindered by the dysfunctions of the value habitat. Its information infrastructure is inadequate; its comparative assessment methods are still evolving; the habitat's inhabitants have, for good historical reasons, not yet developed the capabilities to synthesize eclectic sources into robust assessments of real-world, context-specific value. Finally, even if all these weaknesses are put aside, the highly concentrated payer environment may lack the competitive motivation to communicate such value assessments to the market. Viewed together, these factors make it very unlikely that the value habitat can give the PIE what it needs to provide the sustainable flow of affordable innovative medicines we ask of it. I pass no judgments on those who work in the value habitat. They are trying to address an awesomely difficult problem. Please remember that my observations are of the emergent properties of a complex adaptive system, not of good or bad actors. And having made these observations, I pushed on to the question of how the working of the value habitat might be improved.

How can we improve the value habitat?

A well-functioning value habitat is essential to the health of the PIE. Without one, we have little hope of a sustainable supply of affordable, innovative medicines, and much of the money we spend on medicines will be spent unwisely. Today, the value habitat in the US is a place out of time, like an insular religious community clinging to eighteenth-century lifestyles when surrounded by the modern world. Today's healthcare environment demands that we allocate pharmaceutical spending wisely, but our value habitat is adapted to an earlier world where pharmaceutical spending can rise steadily without concern. There are promising signs of evolution, but these are small, slow steps toward a far-away destination that we need to reach sooner, rather than later. If we want a value habitat, and therefore a PIE, well adapted to the middle decades of the twenty-first century, there's a lot to be done in a short time. In this section, I describe some ways we might accelerate that necessary journey.

Develop a value data infrastructure

In a world where Amazon knows more about my reading interests than my friends do, the value habitat still depends on the opportunistic use of limited data that is inadequate to the task of ecologically valid value assessment. Much of the data about medicine usage – who uses what, at what cost, with what outcome – is recorded electronically, but the proportion of that vast sea of information that is used to assess the value of innovative medicines is tiny. This means that those assessments can't be as ecologically valid, dynamic, and context-sensitive as they need to be. Assessments that don't meet those criteria can't enable the market, and their legitimacy will be constantly challenged by those whose interests they do not serve. What the value habitat needs is an information infrastructure that uses the technological capabilities of the twenty-first century to meet the needs of our time.

How to build and use this information infrastructure would fill another book, but I will suggest three success criteria to help those who might write that book. The first is that any infrastructure will need to combine information that is currently fragmented across the healthcare environment. That means, for example, we may need to combine information from PBMs about usage and real costs and from healthcare providers about outcomes. The second is that it will need to include all information that is relevant, including qualitative information about patient needs, for example. This means we need to find ways of measuring what matters and not just using what we know how to measure. The third is that this information infrastructure will need to somehow avoid the limitations of proprietary information that is protected for commercial purposes. This implies some sort of honest broker for that information, one that is trusted to curate an information source that is a public good rather than a private asset.

Building an infrastructure that allows us to make ecologically valid value assessments is a massive task technologically but, to be possible at all, it would need to be preceded by some political and cultural decisions. We'd need to accept that it is worth making some concessions on privacy and commercial confidentiality in order to create a national information asset that is as important to the healthcare system as, for example, databases of genetic information or records of infectious diseases. We'd also need to accept that innovative medicines, for all their differences from other products, are not immune to the laws of the market and that they merit value assessment as much as in other markets. Neither of these ideas is fully accepted in US society today, which suggests that there is a role for political leadership here.

Develop value assessment capabilities

Like much else about US society in general and its healthcare system in particular, its value habitat is exceptional. Historically, the role that value assessment has played in the US market is very small in comparison to comparator countries. This exceptionality has many complex antecedents and one significant consequence: there do not currently exist within the value habitat all of the capabilities necessary to make value assessments good enough to fully inform the market and to maintain political legitimacy. This capability gap has two principal components. The first is that comparative effectiveness assessment methods have not sufficiently developed to fully meet the needs of a very heterogenous market. The second is that the inhabitants of the habitat, centered around payers, haven't yet developed the capabilities to make wide value assessments, based on all relevant factors, and communicate them to the market. What the value habitat needs is for both capability weaknesses to be corrected.

This task lies with the inhabitants of the value habitat. I won't attempt to tell them how to do their job but I will again offer some guidelines. The first is that because the value is context-dependent, it is likely that value assessment will need to speciate to its sub-environments. This means that even if comparative effectiveness assessments share many common methods, the wider value assessment of which they are part will not be the same in all cases. We may need to develop different assessment approaches for, say, curative therapies for children compared to managing chronic conditions in the elderly. The second guideline is a consequence of the first. If value assessment is a specialized and difficult task that is different in different contexts, then payers may not feel they want to do it all themselves. They may think it better to contract out value assessment in much the same way as they do other specialized tasks and those contractors may well segment according to particular kinds of value assessment. The third guideline is a corollary of the second. If value assessment is to be both valid and legitimate, but executed by a number of different entities, it may need an oversight body whose role is to ensure the effectiveness and validity of their value assessments.

As with harnessing big, real-world data, building the capabilities of the value habitat is such an evolutionary leap from today that it will require shifts in attitudes before any practical changes are possible. One of these is the acceptance that, as Confucius said, "a diamond with a flaw is better than a pebble without one." We may need to resist the temptation to reject, for example, improved methods for comparing effectiveness on the grounds that they have faults. Our criteria for acceptance may need to be an improvement, not perfection.

Another required attitudinal shift will be that the inhabitants of the value habitat, while having different perspectives, will need to accept their shared goal. Rather than pushing narrow agendas, such as patient choice, reduced employer premiums, or higher product margins, everyone in the habitat will need to accept that assessing value effectively is in their own interest.

Adopt transparent value assessment practices

The decisions that flow from value assessments are very unlikely to please all the people, all of the time. Whether they disappoint a patient by refusing access to a medicine that they hope will work but doesn't, or a pharmaceutical company by declining to cover an over-priced drug, or a payer by contradicting a commercially attractive formulary decision, valid value assessments will often displease. And, because medicine is a financially significant, emotionally salient, and politically charged issue, value assessments will often be criticized. When they are opaque or only weakly valid, they are especially open to such challenges. So, what the value habitat needs is to build and maintain the political legitimacy of value assessment, even in the face of those challenges.

As with other aspects of public life, the legitimacy of value assessment will not be built easily and will require constant maintenance. This task will be shared by all those in the value habitat and those in the political arena, too. To them, I offer three suggestions. First, the information infrastructure and capabilities for value assessment discussed above are likely to be "hygiene factors." That is, without them, challenges to value assessment will be justified and impossible to defend against. Second, value assessments that systematically discriminate, even inadvertently, against parts of society cannot sustain legitimacy. This means that they must be designed to accommodate society's diversity, such as the needs of the elderly or disabled. Finally, legitimacy is much easier if processes are transparent and insulated from vested interests.[44] This means that value assessments will be trusted more if they are administered or at least overseen by non-commercial entities, as is the case with regulatory approvals, for example.

Given the potential for criticism, building and maintaining the legitimacy of value assessment will be essential to its success. This will require the reconsideration of certain norms that are well-established in the value habitat. First, it will require payers and others to allow an unprecedented amount of sunlight into their value assessment decisions. Many firms, used to opaque decision-making, will find this uncomfortable. Second, it may mean uncoupling the price of innovative medicines from the service that goes with them. This again will be a major change for payers, who are used to "bundling" their service with medicines. Finally, and perhaps most difficult to achieve, effective value assessment will be enabled by political moderation. Value-driven coverage decisions will provide many opportunities for political point scoring, talk of "death panels" or of profiteering. The value habitat, the PIE, and society will be better served by apolitical pragmatism.

Will this be enough?

I have again limited these three suggestions to broad guidance rather than specific policy recommendations, which are better developed by those with deeper expertise in this area. These suggestions flow from the issues that constrain the working of the value habitat and its ability to meet the requirements for a healthy PIE. To successfully execute all three would be very difficult but would take the habitat much of the way toward good health. This would be especially true if they were executed as an integrated program because they each rely on the others. Further, these changes to the value habitat offer positive synergies with adaptation of the regulatory habitat and changes in the role of PBMs and healthcare providers suggested elsewhere in this book. Even so, these three suggestions would not be enough to restore the health of the value habitat. That would also need the habitat's connection to the market to be strengthened, so that value and price were more closely aligned. That would require a balancing of the market forces between manufacturers, payers, providers, and patients, topics that I cover in the following chapter.

Important as it is to the functioning of the PIE, the value habitat is only one part of this complex adaptive ecosystem. Even a value habitat that met all the PIE's requirements would not guarantee a sustainable supply of affordable, innovative medicines. To achieve that goal, we need to consider and address the other habitats including, in the next chapter, the pricing habitat.

Notes

1 In a good example of academic understatement, Mazorati and Pravettoni said "Nonetheless, a large consensus on the meaning of 'value' is still lacking: patients,

physicians, policy makers, and other health care professionals have different ideas on which component of value may play a prominent role." See ref 1.

As a further example, one interesting survey of what is understood by value in healthcare found:

> There are fundamental differences in how [patients, physicians and employers] define value in health care and to whom they assign responsibility for achieving it. Value, it seems, has become a buzzword; its meaning is often unclear and shifting, depending on who's setting the agenda. As a result, health care stakeholders, who for years thought they were driving toward a shared destination, have actually been part of a fragmented rush toward different points of the compass.

See ref 2.

2 I am using the word judgment carefully here because I don't want to imply that value is always calculated in a systematic way. The process is much too variable and subjective to be described like that. I've also been careful to say that the value judgment influences, rather than determines, what medicines are made available because value is not the only factor in this decision. In particular, commercial factors also influence what medicines are made available, as discussed in later chapters.

3 Some may balk at the categorisation of Medicare, Medicaid and other government programmes, but that's the loose definition I'm giving them.

4 For this information, I relied heavily on the excellent work found in "The US Healthcare Ecosystem: Payers, Providers and Producers" by Robert Lawton Burns. McGraw-Hill 2021.

5 This is important to bear in mind when comparing the US value habitat with other countries, such as the UK, who have "single payer" systems. Even other countries with insurance-based systems, such as Germany, have much less complicated insurance systems than the US. Also pertinent to this is that the US is the only large, rich country that doesn't provide health care to all its citizens, the so-called universal health care, and about 8% of Americans have no health insurance. See https://www.census.gov/library/publications/2021/demo/p60-274.html.

6 For example, the Center for Medicare and Medicare Services, which oversees Medicare, Medicaid and the Children's Health Insurance Programme, has The Medicare Evidence Development & Coverage Advisory Committee (MEDCAC), while private health insurers, operating through Pharmacy Benefit Managers, typically have Pharmacy and Therapy Committees. Both have similar roles to provide expert advice on the makeup of formularies, the list of medicines that are covered by the insurer. See https://www.cms.gov/Regulations-and-Guidance/Guidance/FACA/MEDCAC. See ref 3.

7 Pharmaceutical companies are constrained by the same laws about honesty in business as other businesses and, generally speaking, they have well developed processes to comply with those laws. In addition, the industry has developed an extensive system of voluntary self-regulation. That said, there is considerable concern that pharmaceutical company involvement in the production and dissemination of scientific data may reduce the trustworthiness of some medical knowledge. See ref 4.

8 Pharmaceutical companies and patient groups often share the same goals of ensuring patient access to the company's medicines. This has led to some concern about the ethics of the relationship between them. See refs 5 and 6.

9 See for example the National Coalition on Benefits at https://www.coalitionon-benefits.org/.

10 Health technology agencies are now common in many countries. See https://www.who.int/health-technology-assessment/NationalAgencieHTA.pdf.

11 See https://icer.org/who-we-are/.

12 See https://www.forbes.com/sites/joshuacohen/2019/04/17/icers-growing-impact-on-drug-pricing-and-reimbursement/?sh=364aecc46b53.

13 Although it was rare in earlier centuries for women to run an apothecary business, they were often skilled in making medicinal recipes and other important activities. Widows of apothecaries were also sometimes given the chance to take over their husbands' businesses. See https://www.sciencehistory.org/distillations/womens-business-17th-century-female-pharmacists.

14 In using the term ecological validity, I've displaced a concept from psychology, in which field ecological validity is a measure of how a test predicts behavior in real-world settings. So, in this context, ecological valid value simply means value in a real-world context. See ref 7.

15 This requirement of the value habitat emerged strongly from discussions with expert informants and the literature review. It is an area where the PIE overlaps onto wider issues of how society chooses to provide healthcare to its member and the ethics and legitimacy of healthcare rationing. The value habitat functions in a context of limited healthcare resources that, as in all healthcare systems, implies a form of rationing. See https://www.commonwealthfund.org/blog/2019/does-united-states-ration-health-care. Since this rationing is facilitated by the value habitat, it is only sustainable if its decisions are held to be politically legitimate. In the case of healthcare rationing, Weber's concept of rational-legal legitimacy seems especially relevant. (See https://plato.stanford.edu/entries/legitimacy/.) Such rational-legal legitimacy is typically associated with transparency and perceptions of effectiveness. See refs 8 and 9. From this and related work, I drew the conclusion that the value habitat must be sufficiently transparent to allow public examination and maintain political legitimacy.

16 Although NICE and ICER use similar methodologies, ICER lacks the mandatory power that NICE has, which obviously makes a big difference to its processes and recommendations. That said, many have suggested that some of NICE's experience might be transferable to the US context. See refs 10 and 11.

17 A 2021 RAND Corporation report found that US prescription drug prices were 256% of those of 32 comparison countries, or 190% after adjusting for rebates and discounts. For unbranded generics, US prices were 84% of the comparator countries. See 12. Although this work didn't distinguish between innovative medicines and others, its category of "branded, originator" drugs seems a fairly close proxy for innovative medicines, and if so, then it is those medicines where the price differential between the US and other countries is problematic. Similar international price differentials have been reported in other studies. See ref 13.

18 Advanced therapies, including gene therapies, promise benefits not provided by conventional therapies, including cures for currently incurable conditions but they are also relatively very expensive. This creates new challenges for how their value might be assessed. See, for example, ref 14. This issue of adapting value assessment to the future was well expressed by Stephen Pearson of ICER: "We need to think hard about whether the methods of technology assessment and cost-effectiveness analysis are ready to capture the potential for the broader benefits of these treatments" (ICER press release, November 12, 2019).

19 To illustrate this, first imagine a value assessment for an innovative medicine that is second to market and is very similar to the first to market product, with no significant differences in side effects, ease of use, contraindications etc. In this context, the relevant information might only include the costs and outcomes, gathered in a way to make a valid comparison. Now, imagine a second

case in which a second to market product claims to be a significant improvement because it is a once-a-day treatment and far less significant side effects, compared to the three-a-day for the first in market competitor. In this context, the relevant information would still include costs and outcomes. But it might also include the relative severity of the side effects and their impact on the patient and differences in adherence and the impact of that on outcomes. My point is that the information required to make an ecologically valid value assessment will always include its cost and clinical outcomes but often include other contextually specific factors.

20 In this context, there is an important semantic difference between efficacy and effectiveness. Broadly speaking, efficacy is the performance of a medicine under carefully controlled conditions and effectiveness is performance under real world conditions. There are many reasons why the two may differ. See ref 15.

21 The adaptation of clinical trials to include the so-called HEOR (health economic and outcomes research) is an emerging trend but is not yet fully established. See ref 16.

22 Like adapting clinical trials to provide health economic data, the use of real-world evidence in cost effectiveness is an emerging but not yet fully established trend. To quote from one study of the topic,

> RWE has been commonly used to inform pharmaceutical value assessments conducted by ICER. However, there has been relatively limited use of RWE to inform drug-specific effectiveness, despite calls for greater inclusion of RWE in value assessments for real-world drug effectiveness.

See refs 17 and 18.

23 The lack of adequate data would be an issue for cost-effectiveness studies in any case, but there is concern that this problem is being exacerbated by "permissive" trends in drug approval that produce less data or rely not on outcomes data but proxy data, such as biomarkers. See https://icer.org/wp-content/uploads/2021/04/Strengthening-the-Accelerated-Approval-Pathway-_-ICER-White-Paper-_-April-2021.pdf.

24 To quote from a systematic study of this topic,

> The review shows that RWD has been increasingly applied in conducting the cost-effectiveness analysis. However, few CEA studies are based on big data. In future CEA studies using big data and RWD, it is encouraged to control confounders and to discount in long-term research when decision-analytic models are not used.

Notably, the European Medicines Agency (EMA) is establishing a coordination center to "provide timely and reliable evidence on the use, safety, and effectiveness of medicines for human use, including vaccines, from real-world healthcare databases across the European Union." See https://www.ema.europa.eu/en/about-us/how-we-work/big-data/data-analysis-real-world-interrogation-network-darwin-eu. See ref 19.

25 An interesting exposition of this problem is revealed by a US Department of Veterans Affairs analysis. Effectively, the cost of pharmaceuticals used in cost-effectiveness analysis is usually estimated rather than known. https://www.herc.research.va.gov/include/page.asp?id=pharmaceutical-costs.

26 Even studies designed to examine the costs and benefits of the same medicine are often designed in quite different ways, making them hard to combine. To quote from one study of this issue,

> however, a meta-analysis of incremental cost-effectiveness ratios, costs, or health benefits (including quality-adjusted life years) is fraught with issues largely due to

heterogeneity across study designs and methods and further practical challenges. Therefore, meta-analysis is rarely feasible or robust.

See ref 20.

27 This was one of many criticisms in an especially sharp document that implied ICER was only pseudo-scientific. See ref 21.

28 See ref 22.

29 QALY stands for quality-adjusted life year. To use the definition used by the UK's NICE HTA body, it is

a measure of the state of health of a person or group in which the benefits, in terms of length of life, are adjusted to reflect the quality of life. One quality-adjusted life year (QALY) is equal to 1 year of life in perfect health. QALYs are calculated by estimating the years of life remaining for a patient following a particular treatment or intervention and weighting each year with a quality-of-life score (on a 0 to 1 scale). It is often measured in terms of the person's ability to carry out the activities of daily life, and freedom from pain and mental disturbance.

30 One especially trenchant criticism of QUALYs wrote: "The entire super-structure of the QALY methodology is built upon philosophical sand: subjective value judgments." See https://www.statnews.com/2019/02/22/qaly-drug-effectiveness-reviews/.

31 A study of alternatives to QALY found no fewer than nine alternatives but concluded, "Our work is the first comprehensive evaluation of proposed alternatives to the conventional QALY. We found a robust literature but few options that were feasible to be implemented in current healthcare decision-making processes." See ref 23.

32 This description is gratefully borrowed from Neumann, Cohen, and Ollendorf. See ref 24.

33 The idea that assessment methodologies are evolving but not yet fully evolved was well expressed by Dubois and Westrich.

This analysis found that value assessment frameworks are moving closer to meeting the challenge of accurately measuring value and reliably informing health care decisions, but more progress is needed before widespread adoption and use. While value assessments are potential inputs that can be considered for health care decision making, none of them should be the sole input for these decisions. Considering the limitations, they should, at most, be only one of many tools in the toolbox.

See ref 25.

34 Interestingly, an analysis of changes in ICER's estimates of cost-effectiveness between its draft and revised reports was small, but also noted that criticisms often lacked clarity or failed to offer alternatives. This implies that evolution of comparative effectiveness methodologies depends both on HTA bodies like ICER and on their critics developing their capability to criticise constructively. See ref 26.

35 To quote one study of payers' perspective on value in the use of pharmaceuticals:

Although there is interest in including value assessment frameworks during the decision-making process in the United States, there are significant challenges to operationalizing them. The current environment in the United States restricts payers' ability to make favorable contracts with manufacturers, and changes to the U.S. health system design are needed to facilitate this effort. Adoption of a value assessment framework in Medicare or Medicaid would accelerate adoption of these tools by private payers in the United States.

See ref 27.

36 A study of what information sources payers use and prefer found that

> On a scale from 1 to 5 (not important to very important), interview respondents most valued published peer-reviewed studies, technology assessments, and internal data on drug utilization as sources of information (means = 4.68, 4.22, and 4.14, respectively). Randomized controlled trials (RCTs) and systematic reviews/meta-analyses were the most valued types of evidence (means = 4.40 and 3.66, respectively); economic and observational data studies received low ratings (means = 3.19 and 3.03, respectively). There was substantial variation in the process of evidence review, who and how individuals participated in the process, and outcomes related to formulary tier placement and utilization management.

See ref 28.

37 To quote from Holtorf and Cook,

> Whereas patient-focused drug development may once have been considered a 'nice to have,' it has since moved on to a point where patient involvement and partnership is now an essential and necessary component of the drug development process, in order to successfully meet the demands of regulatory and reimbursement authorities, and indeed deliver new products which meet the expressed needs of patients for which they are intended.

See ref 29.

38 As will be discussed later in the book, the rising role of pharmacy benefit managers has, to a degree, encouraged employers to step back from decisions about coverage and formularies. As described by Kimberley Westrich,

> Many employers are completely reliant on their consultants and PBMs to direct their employee health benefits ... The result is that employers don't always know if their plan design is aligned to their own priorities and goals for their employees.

See https://www.pharmexec.com/view/market-access-employers-barriers-value.

39 For examples of attempts to involve patients in the value assessment process, see the work of PAVE at the University of Maryland. See https://www.pharmacy.umaryland.edu/centers/patient-driven-values-healthcare-evaluation-pave/ and pValue at University of Colorado. See https://pharmacy.cuanschutz.edu/research. For a wider discussion on this topic, see https://www.ispor.org/publications/journals/value-outcomes-spotlight/vos-archives/issue/view/overcoming-vaccine-hesitancy-injecting-trust-in-the-community/value-assessment-that-puts-patients-at-the-forefront.

40 I am using employers as examples of plan sponsors here because of their dominant role in provision of private health insurance but, of course, the discussion refers to all sponsors. Interestingly, this discussion takes place in the context that employers' role health insurance may decline. See ref 30.

41 Of course, the price that payers charge patients for innovative medicines is not a simple matter. They are charged through their insurance premiums but also through out-of-pocket costs such as co-pays, co-insurance, and deductibles. Formulary design also involves an element of manipulating what the patient gets for their money.

42 While this will be discussed further in Chapter 7, it's worth quoting here an article on this topic that expressed this point clearly.

> *For most products, markets set prices, but markets fall short in the context of pre-scription drugs because numerous non-competitive conditions make it difficult for consumers to judge for themselves the value of therapies and challenging for the health system to assign suitable prices.*

See ref 31.

43 Competition authorities the world over associate high market concentration with increases in market power over both suppliers (e.g. healthcare provid-ers and pharmaceutical companies) and customers (e.g. patients), and what evidence exists suggests that health insurers are exercising this power. See refs 32 and 33.

44 As an illustration of the concern felt in this area, shortly before I completed the writing of this book a number of health groups called for an end to redacted clinical trial data in technology assessments. See ref 34.

References

1 Marzorati C, Pravettoni G. Value as the key concept in the health care system: How it has influenced medical practice and clinical decision-making processes. *The Journal of Multidisciplinary Healthcare.* 2017;10:101–6.

2 Pendleton RC. We won't get value-based health care until we agree on what "value" means. *Harvard Business Review.* 2018 February 27.

3 Goldberg RB. Managing the pharmacy benefit: The formulary system. *Journal of Managed Care & Specialty Pharmacy.* 2020;26(4):341–9.

4 Sismondo S. Epistemic corruption, the pharmaceutical industry, and the body of medical science. *Frontiers in Research Metrics and Analytics.* 2021;6.

5 Ehrlich O, Wingate L, Heller C, de Melo-Martin I. When patient advocacy or-ganizations meet industry: A novel approach to dealing with financial conflicts of interest. *BMC Medical Ethics.* 2019;20(1):96.

6 Fabbri A, Parker L, Colombo C, Mosconi P, Barbara G, Frattaruolo MP et al. In-dustry funding of patient and health consumer organisations: Systematic review with meta-analysis. *British Medical Journal.* 2020;368:I6925.

7 Andrade C. Internal, external, and ecological validity in research design, con-duct, and evaluation. *Indian Journal Psychology Medicine.* 2018;40(5):498–9.

8 Etzioni A. Is transparency the best disinfectant? *The Journal of Political Philosophy.* 2010;18(4):389–404.

9 Fung AG, Mary WD. *Full Disclosure: The Perils and Promise of Transparency.* Cam-bridge: Cambridge University Press; 2007.

10 Thokala P, Carlson JJ, Drummond M. HTA'd in the USA: A comparison of ICER in the United States with NICE in England and Wales. *Journal of Managed Care & Specialty Pharmacy.* 2020;26(9):1162–70.

11 Watkins JB. ICER's version of HTA is positioned to guide U.S. health care re-form. *Journal of Managed Care & Specialty Pharmacy.* 2020;26(9):1171-.

12 Mulcahy AW, Whaley CM, Gizaw M, Schwam D, Edenfield N, Becerra-Ornelas AU. *International Prescription Drug Price Comparisons: Current Empirical Estimates and Comparisons with Previous Studies.* Santa Monica, CA: RAND Corporation; 2021.

13 GF KS-YDMSMA. Using external reference pricing in medicare Part D to reduce drug price differentials with other countries. *Health Affairs.* 2019;38(5):804–11.

14 Chapman RH, Kumar VM, Whittington MD, Pearson SD. Does cost-effectiveness analysis overvalue potential cures? Exploring alternative methods for applying a "shared savings" approach to cost offsets. *Value in Health*. 2021;24(6):839–45.

15 Revicki DA, Frank L. Pharmacoeconomic evaluation in the real world. Effectiveness versus efficacy studies. *Pharmacoeconomics*. 1999;15(5):423–34.

16 Flight L, Julious S, Brennan A, Todd S, Hind D. How can health economics be used in the design and analysis of adaptive clinical trials? A qualitative analysis. *Trials*. 2020;21(1):252.

17 Jiao B, Veenstra DL, Lee W, Carlson JJ, Devine B. The use of real-world evidence in ICER's scoping process and clinical evidence assessments. *Journal of Managed Care & Specialty Pharmacy*. 2020;26(12):1590–5.

18 Lee W, Dayer V, Jiao B, Carlson JJ, Devine B, Veenstra DL. Use of real-world evidence in economic assessments of pharmaceuticals in the United States. *Journal of Managed Care & Specialty Pharmacy*. 2021;27(1):5–14.

19 Lu ZK, Xiong X, Lee T, Wu J, Yuan J, Jiang B. Big data and real-world data based cost-effectiveness studies and decision-making models: A systematic review and analysis. *Frontiers in Pharmacology*. 2021;12.

20 Shields GE, Elvidge J. Challenges in synthesising cost-effectiveness estimates. *Systematic Reviews*. 2020;9(1):289.

21 Langley PC. Resolving lingering problems or continued support for pseudoscience? The ICER value assessment update. *Innovations in Pharmacy*. 2017;8(4).

22 Cohen JTO, Natalia ODA, Neumann PJ. The certainty of uncertainty in health technology assessment. *Health Affairs*. 2022 January 26.

23 Carlson JJ, Brouwer ED, Kim E, Wright P, McQueen RB. Alternative approaches to quality-adjusted life-year estimation within standard cost-effectiveness models: Literature review, feasibility assessment, and impact evaluation. Value in health. *The Journal of the International Society for Pharmacoeconomics and Outcomes Research*. 2020;23(12):1523–33.

24 Neumann PJC, Joshua T, Ollendorf DA. *The Right Price: A Value-Based Prescription for Drug Costs*. Oxford: Oxford University Press; 2021.

25 Dubois RW, Westrich K. As value assessment frameworks evolve, are they finally ready for prime time? *Value in Health*. 2019;22(9):977–80.

26 Cohen JS, Madison C; Ollendorf, Daniel A; Neumann, Peter J. Does the institute for clinical and economic review revise its findings in response to industry comments? *Value in Health*. 2019;22(12):6.

27 Brogan AP, Hogue SL, Vekaria RM, Reynolds I, Coukell A. Understanding payer perspectives on value in the use of pharmaceuticals in the United States. *Journal of Managed Care & Specialty Pharmacy*. 2019;25(12):1319–27.

28 Leung MY, Halpern MT, West ND. Pharmaceutical technology assessment: Perspectives from payers. *Journal of Managed Care Pharmacy*. 2012;18(3):256–65.

29 Holtorf A-PC, Nigel. The role of patients in market access. In Kockaya G, Albert, W editor. *Pharmaceutical Market Access in Developed Markets*. SEEd; 2018. pp. 267–88.

30 Geyman J. The future of work in America: Demise of employer-sponsored insurance and what should replace it. *International Journal of Health Services*. 2022;52(1):168–73.

31 Neumann PJ, Cohen JT, Ollendorf DA. Drug-pricing debate redux — should cost-effectiveness analysis be used now to price pharmaceuticals? *The New England Journal of Medicine*. 2021;385(21):1923–4.

32 Dafny LS. Are health insurance markets competitive? *American Economic Review.* 2010;100(4):1399–431.
33 Dafny LS, Ody CJ, Schmitt MA. Undermining value-based purchasing — lessons from the pharmaceutical industry. *The New England Journal of Medicine.* 2016;375(21):2013–5.
34 Mahase E. Health groups call for end to redacted clinical trial data in technology assessments. *British Medical Journal.* 2022;376:o149.

7 The pricing habitat

Precis

- The pricing habitat is the part of the pharmaceutical innovation ecosystem where the prices of innovative medicines are set.
- The role of the pricing habitat is to maintain stability in the PIE, equivalent to homeostasis in biology.
- To achieve stability, the pricing habitat needs to distribute the profit associated with innovative medicines in a sustainable way.
- The pricing habitat is inhabited by pharmaceutical companies, insurance companies and PBMs, healthcare providers, plan sponsors, and patients.
- The pricing habitat adjoins and interacts with the value and competition habitats.
- A healthy PIE requires that the pricing habitat achieves four balance points:

  - the net price balance point between producers (manufacturers) and payers
  - the point of care balance point between payers and patients and their proxies
  - the moral hazard balance points between payers, providers, and patients and their proxies
  - the public trust balance point.

- The pricing habitat's ability to support a healthy PIE is constrained by:

  - its lack of strong connection to ecologically valid value
  - the concentrated market power of intermediaries such as insurers, PBMs, and providers
  - a lack of incentives for intermediaries to innovate

DOI: 10.4324/9781003330271-7

- the existence of payer and provider moral hazard
- the opacity of innovative medicine pricing.

- The pricing habitat would be better able to support a healthy PIE by:

  - establishing value-based net pricing as the norm for innovative medicines
  - redressing imbalances in patients' market power
  - making the pricing of innovative medicines transparent.

In Chapter 6, I found that the value habitat is not currently able to support a healthy PIE, one that can give us a sustainable supply of affordable, innovative medicines. But, when I explored the value habitat, I focused on the value of innovative medicines at the level of the payer. That is the value at the price paid for the medicine by the payer and received by the pharmaceutical company. But this is what you might call an "under the hood" issue. For most Americans, what matters and what affects the social contract is the price they pay for innovative medicines through their plan sponsors, their own insurance premiums, out-of-pocket costs, or through the tax dollars that support Medicare, Medicaid, and other public spending. This chapter is about that price and the part of the PIE that determines it, which I'll call the pricing habitat.

When thinking about the pricing habitat, remember that we don't buy innovative medicines, we buy solutions to our healthcare problems. Of the money that Americans spend on healthcare, only about 14% is spent on medicines.[1] This means that, when we pay for our healthcare, only a small part is for the medicine and the rest is for the solution that it is part of. But, because the price of the medicine and the solution are so intertwined, we must think about them both. That other 86% includes everything needed to get the medicine from a box in the manufacturer's warehouse to coursing its way around your body. It includes physical distribution and pharmacy dispensation. It includes the medical services to diagnose you, get the medicine into you, and any medical care you might need. It also includes the risk-sharing that you buy when you purchase insurance and the administration that goes with that, including the aggregation of demand and negotiation services that payers do on your behalf. Most of this intertwined activity is necessary but makes understanding the pricing habitat horribly complicated. It is with good reason that, in a recent *Fortune* article on the subject, the author paused to say, *Feel free to take a break and apply cold compresses to your forehead.*[2]

The ecosystem paradigm I chose in Chapter 2 lets me look at pricing habitat through the eyes of an ecologist. From that perspective, the pricing habitat does what every ecosystem needs; it maintains homeostasis, the ecologists' term for maintaining a balanced, steady condition.[3] Think of the pharmaceutical market as a very large profit pool, the economists' name for the sum of all the profit available in the market.[4] Everyone involved in getting the innovative medicine into the patient wants to drink as much from that pool as they can[5] but none of them, from insurers to wholesalers to hospitals, can drink from the pool without the help of the others. Everyone is symbiotically dependent on everyone else, just as in natural ecosystems. This means they need some way of sharing the profit between them and keeping the ecosystem stable. That's the function of the pricing habitat in the PIE. It shares the profit pool, with each type of business getting enough to survive but not so much that their partners don't. An unhealthy, malfunctioning pricing habitat would mean some types of businesses not getting enough profit from the profit pool and exiting the market. If, for example, all wholesalers or all hospitals left the market the PIE would become unstable. So, from an ecological perspective, the pricing habitat is equivalent to the feedback mechanisms that keep natural ecosystems in balance. Armed with this idea of the PIE's "homeostasis mechanism," I began to explore the pricing habitat further.

What happens in the pricing habitat and who inhabits it?

Because we buy solutions rather than just medicines, the pricing habitat is populated by a bewildering variety of entities, all of which have some influence on the price that we pay. Pharmaceutical companies, public and private insurers, PBMs, healthcare providers, pharmacies, wholesalers, plan sponsors, and patients all engage in what an ecologist would see as finding the homeostatic balance that allows each of them enough profit to operate, but not so much that others don't, which would cause ecosystem instability. In the US's labyrinthine pharmaceutical market, there are many of these balance points and it's beyond the scope of this book to discuss them all. But, stepping back again to see the forest for the trees, there are four balance points that the pricing habitat must find if the PIE is to remain in balance.

The net price balance point between producers and payers

Producers, that is pharmaceutical manufacturers, are mostly for-profit businesses that are publicly or privately owned. They are tasked by their owners with optimizing risk-adjusted return on investment, remembering that their investment wasn't only in the medicine that reached the market but also the sunk investments in those medicines that didn't. Consequently, their aim is to maximize profits. Notwithstanding calculations about how price influences demand, this equates to charging what they think the market will bear.

Their immediate customers, payers such as insurers and hospitals, are also businesses. Their owners also ask them to maximize their risk-adjusted return on investment, partly by minimizing the price they pay to the pharmaceutical companies. The balance point they find is the net price paid by the payer to the producer. It is called a net because it is the list price net of discounts. Contrary to what many people think, the cost of developing and making an innovative medicine has little role in determining its net price, other than to set the lower limit that the producer will accept. Instead, the balancing price point depends on how much the producer and payer need each other. Where the producer has a unique, valuable drug with no alternatives or competitors (such as Vertex's Trikafta for cystic fibrosis)[6] or the payer is small, so that their business is less consequential to the producer, then the balance point tends toward a higher price, favoring the producer. Under the opposite circumstances, a payer negotiating for a medicine that has strong competitors (such as AbbVie's Mavyret for Hepatitis C)[7] will tend toward a lower-priced balance point, especially if that payer is so large that their business is important to the producer. Additionally, the payers' power is amplified if it is easy to switch between competitors and vice versa. As of May 2022, public payers, such as Medicare and Medicaid, don't currently negotiate directly but their prices are correlated to those negotiated by other payers, so they effectively "piggyback" on those. As we'll come to, the mechanics of how this net price balance point is reached, through purchasing consortia, PBMs and discounts are important details, but they shouldn't distract from the fundamental point – the net price that the producer is paid by the payer is determined by their relative negotiating strengths. This contest is played out in the pricing habitat.

The point of care price balance point between payers and patients and their proxies

As well as trying to minimize what they pay producers, payers also aim to maximize their profits; this equates to charging as much as they can for as little as possible. They have various ways of doing this, from premiums and other fees to "cost sharing" out-of-pocket expenses. They can also, through the design of formularies, limit their customers' choices and push them toward medicines that give the payer better profits. The payers' customers, patients and their proxies such as their plan sponsors, behave like customers in any other market. They try to get as much benefit as possible for as little cost as possible, with as much choice as possible. Payers and patients obviously have opposing goals at this point, and the balance point between them is the price the payer receives from the patients and their proxies, which I'll call the point of care price. It is typically a combination of insurance premiums and out-of-pocket payments, rather than a single, simple figure.

Again, contrary to popular belief, the cost of delivering the payers' services has little role in determining the point of care cost, other than to set the lower limit that the payer can accept. As with the net price, the point of care price is determined by how much payer and patient need each other. When there are few payers, little competition between them and individual patients or relatively small plan sponsors who are individually unimportant to payers, the balance point tends toward a higher price. By contrast, if competition between payers is intense and there are large aggregations of patients, such as in large plans, who are relatively important to the payers, the balance point tends toward a lower price. This is especially so if it is easy to switch between payers. Public insurers don't negotiate with their patients in the same way but also aim to minimize costs. Again, the mechanics of the relationship between payers and patients is complicated, especially with respect to whether the medicine is taken at home or under medical care, but the same fundamental point applies. As with the net price, the balancing price point at the point of care is determined by the relative negotiating strength of the buyer (i.e. the payer) and the seller (i.e. the patient or their plan sponsor), and the contest between them is played out in the pricing habitat.

The moral hazard balance points

The pricing balance points between manufacturers, payers, and patients described above are text-book stuff[8] and not unique to the pharmaceutical market. The same thing is seen when Kellogg's, Walmart and retail shoppers "find" the price points that balance how to share the profits from a box of cornflakes.

What is peculiar to the pharmaceutical market is a third type of balance point that the pricing habitat also has to find. I've called these the moral hazard balance points, for reasons I'll explain. Moral hazard is the economists' concept that, if something is free, or very low cost, you may abuse it. In healthcare, it's most commonly framed as a patient's moral hazard. For example, if visits to your family physician were free, you might visit for every sniffle and headache. But patient moral hazard is only one of three moral hazards found in healthcare.[9] Insurers' moral hazard exists when they can improve their profits, through coverage restrictions, co-pays, and deductibles, for example, with little loss of revenue. Providers' moral hazard exists when they can charge more than necessary, without the cost of lost business. Prescribing an expensive medicine that is profitable for the provider when a less expensive but less profitable medicine would suffice is an example of this.

All three moral hazards create balance points that the pricing habitat must find. The out-of-pocket costs patients pay for medicines must balance affordability against risks of inappropriate use. The terms insurers apply must balance patients' medical needs against the costs of the insurer. The services and fees of providers must balance the needs of the patient, the costs of the provider, and the costs to the insurer. Finding moral hazard balance happens in the pricing habitat, along with net price and point of care price balance. And all three are determined by the negotiating power of those involved. For example, an insurer operating in a cozy, oligopolistic market is more likely to abuse their ability to extract profit from patients than one faced with intense competition for patients who can switch easily.

The public trust balance point

The fourth balance point that the pricing habitat must find is another one peculiar to the conditions of the pharmaceutical market. In Chapter 1, I described how the pricing of medicines was socially and politically salient in a way that is not true for most other goods. This salience creates another balance point between public trust on the one hand and commercial confidentiality on the other. In most markets, commercial confidentiality is seen as more important than the transparency of pricing mechanisms and the public trust it engenders. Nobody cares too much about the deals Kellogg's cuts with Walmart. Consequently, the balance point is set toward commercial confidentiality, and pricing arrangements are opaque. But in some markets, such as public procurement, public trust is more important. In those markets, the balance point is more toward transparency. It is a function of the pricing habitat to find this balance point in the pharmaceutical market. Unlike the other three balance points, public trust is not defined in terms of dollars or contractual terms. It is defined as how transparent pricing is for innovative medicines. In a well-functioning pricing habitat, the balance point allows enough transparency to engender public trust and enough confidentiality to allow commercial activity to operate. Like the other balance points, the public trust balance point is determined by the relative power of the two sides involved. In this case, the information on how prices are arrived at is held mostly by pharmaceutical companies and payers; the need for transparency and trust is felt by the American public.

In discussing these four important functions of the pricing habitat, I've chosen to leave many details for later. For example, I've largely conflated insurers and PBMs into payers, because ownership of the latter by the former makes this a reasonable first approximation. I've not differentiated the roles of PBMs and healthcare providers in pricing, even though they play different roles for retail and specialty medicines. I've not mentioned the roles of pharmacists, wholesalers, and others who are involved in the supply chain and are part of the pricing habitat. Nor have I mentioned the statutory constraints around the functioning of the pricing habitat, such as the 340b Drug Pricing Program. For now, I've chosen to strip away those details so you can see the most fundamental point about how the pricing habitat works. In its role as a "homeostasis mechanism," it doesn't rationally calibrate prices and other balances with the best interests of the habitat in mind. The balance points reached reflect the power of those involved and, as we see when humans exploit natural ecosystems, the result is not necessarily a stable ecosystem. This is the important, realistic point to keep in mind as we consider what the PIE demands of the pricing habitat and how able it is to meet those requirements.

What does a healthy PIE require of the pricing habitat?

In a healthy PIE, profits and returns are distributed in a sustainable way, moral hazards addressed, and public trust is achieved and maintained. This means that the PIE requires four things of the pricing habitat.

The pricing habitat must balance net pricing levels

A well-functioning pricing habitat will provide returns sufficient to in-centivize continuing pharmaceutical innovation, but no more. To do so effectively, a healthy PIE requires that the pricing habitat discovers prices that provide sufficient returns on investment across the innova-tors' portfolio. A pricing habitat that provides returns that are below or above this level would not sustain a healthy PIE.

The pricing habitat must balance price at the point of care

A well-functioning pricing habitat will provide returns sufficient to in-centivize continuing provision of and innovation in the services required for the use of innovative medicines. To do so effectively, a healthy PIE requires that the pricing habitat discovers prices at the point of care that provides sufficient returns on those services and encourages innovation in more valuable services. A pricing habitat that provides returns that are below or above this level would not sustain a healthy PIE.

The pricing habitat must balance the moral hazards of patients, providers, and payers

A well-functioning pricing habitat will avoid moral hazards for patients, providers, and payers whilst enabling the appropriate use of innovative medicines. To do so effectively, a healthy PIE requires that the pricing habitat discourages the patient, provider, and payer from abusing their pricing and contractual terms. A pricing habitat that encourages any of these three forms of moral hazard would not sustain a healthy PIE.

The pricing habitat must balance public trust with necessary commercial confidentiality

A well-functioning pricing habitat will engender public trust in the set-ting of prices for innovative medicines without unduly compromising

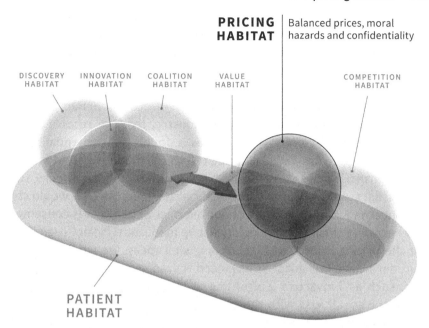

PRICING HABITAT | Balanced prices, moral hazards and confidentiality

DISCOVERY HABITAT   INNOVATION HABITAT   COALITION HABITAT   VALUE HABITAT   COMPETITION HABITAT

PATIENT HABITAT

Figure 7.1 The pricing habitat's contribution to a healthy PIE

normal commercial activity. To do so effectively, a healthy PIE requires that the pricing habitat allows for the maximum feasible degree of transparency in setting the prices of innovative medicines. A pricing habitat whose opacity encourages public distrust or significantly hinders normal commercial activity would not sustain a healthy PIE.

These four requirements (Figure 7.1) are demanding but that's as we might expect. By asking for a sustainable supply of affordable innovative medicines, we're making great demands on the PIE. Metaphorically, the PIE is pushing back, saying that it can only meet our demands if the pricing habitat does these four difficult things. It is hard to see how the PIE can be healthy unless the pricing habitat meets these requirements. This led me to explore how well the pricing habitat is currently able to support a healthy PIE.

Is the pricing habitat capable of supporting a healthy PIE?

Of all the habitats of the PIE, the pricing habitat is the most intimidating in its complexity. The vast profit pool has attracted many different types of businesses to drink from it, and the interrelationships that have evolved between them are tangled and not always obvious. I was especially grateful to my guides, the expert informants, in this part of my exploration. With their help, I saw that the case for questioning the health of the pricing habitat is clear. First, concerns about pricing are the primary cause of the tension in the social contract. Whether those concerns are justified or uninformed, it's important to both sides of that contract, society, and industry, that we resolve them. Second, pricing of innovative medicines is doubly consequential. Most attention is given to "financial toxicity," the provocative term for patients' financial stress and affordability issues.[10] But even were this addressed, as in some countries, by socialized medicine, we would still be concerned about the share of our national wealth that is consumed by a relatively small number of innovative medicines. Finally, even if we felt the pricing habitat was functioning well today, we would want to consider how it will adapt as advanced therapies with very large price tags, such as Novartis's Zolgensma at $2.1 million,[11] become more commonplace. It was with these points, and the four "balance point" requirements of the pricing habitat, in mind I explored how capable the pricing habitat is of supporting a healthy PIE. Cutting through the detail and tangled complexity, I uncovered five issues of concern.

The pricing habitat is untethered from ecologically valid value

The pricing habitat adjoins the value habitat, yet the connection between them is weak. To find the net price balance point that incentivizes valuable innovation without allowing returns in excess of that, the pricing habitat needs to know the ecologically valid value of an innovative medicine. Without that, the net price balance point will be based on the relative market power of the pharmaceutical company and the payer and that price might be far above or below what is needed to incentivize future innovation. I remember expert informant Mark Trusheim guiding me through this.

> Today, pricing is only sometimes based on value evidence and, even then, that evidence is often imperfect. More often, the price of an innovative medicine is based on the negotiating power of the two sides. This may sometimes be acceptable as a starting point but not as a permanent basis for setting prices.
>
> *Mark Trusheim*

There are some promising examples of value assessments influencing the negotiation between pharmaceutical companies and payers, such as CVS Caremark's use of ICER reports,[12] but this is not yet routine practice. Even if it were, the value habitat is not yet fully capable of guiding those negotiations with ecologically valid, dynamic, and context-sensitive value assessments. The reasons for this are described in Chapter 6, so I won't reiterate them here; but I will re-emphasize two important points made in that chapter. First, the comparative assessment methods that currently exist, such as those used by ICER, are far from perfect. They are steps on an evolutionary road toward effective value assessment, and we shouldn't allow the perfect to be the enemy of the good, but they are far from fully developed. Second, effective value assessment is not simply a technical issue of improving methods and the information infrastructure that supports those methods. It is also an organizational issue of the capabilities of the payers, pharmaceutical companies, and others who inhabit the value habitat. As value assessments become more ecologically valid, and as they become more influential in the price negotiations between pharmaceutical companies and payers, the pricing habitat will become more capable of finding appropriate, well-balanced net price levels. Until then, the pricing habitat is not fully capable of meeting the requirements of the PIE.

The pricing habitat has concentrated market power in intermediaries

A fundamental feature of all markets is that distribution of the profit pool is influenced by market power. For the producers (pharmaceutical companies), market power usually flows from having a differentiated and valuable product that faces little competition. For patients or their proxies, market power comes from being able to switch easily between many competing suppliers. For intermediaries who sit between producers and patients, such as insurance companies and healthcare providers, market power flows mostly from the size and scope of their business. An intermediary who strongly influences the channel to market can negotiate strongly with a pharmaceutical company for lower net prices. An intermediary who faces limited competition for patients can charge higher prices than if they were in a highly competitive market. These fundamentals of market power are important when thinking about how innovative medicines get to patients.

Stepping back to see the forest for the trees, there are two main channels to market innovative medicines. Some medicines go from manufacturers through wholesalers and pharmacies to patients. These "retail" medicines are generally pills and potions, swallowed and applied in the home. The majority of retail medicines, by volume, are cheap generics but some are relatively expensive branded drugs, like the novel anticoagulants Xarelto and Eliquis.[13] This channel to market is largely controlled by PBMs and insurers. Other medicines go from the manufacturer through wholesalers to healthcare providers and specialty pharmacies. These "specialty" medicines are generally infusions or injections given under medical supervision. Increasingly, innovative medicines go through this specialty channel.[14] Importantly, the shift in drug spending away from retail and toward specialty means that the latter market is increasingly important and increasingly concentrated on a small number of costly, innovative medicines. For example, just 10 medicines constitute 43% of Medicare Plan B's medicines.[15] This specialty channel to market is largely controlled by healthcare providers and the payers who agree on what they can use. Of course, I've simplified this picture for clarity but, even if time and space allowed a full description, my basic point would stand. To reach their patients, the manufacturers of an innovative medicine must go through two powerful intermediaries: the insurers and PBMs for retail medicines, and the insurers and providers for specialty medicines. Any exploration of the pricing habitat must look at the fundamentals of market power in those two channels to market.

Both retail and specialty channels have undergone what business school professors call consolidation and integration. The first means fewer companies having a greater share of their market, growing the scale of their businesses. The second means spreading their activities wider, growing the scope of their businesses. A wave of acquisition has led to 95% of prescriptions being handled by only six PBMs and the three largest processing 77% of prescriptions. In addition, five of the six largest PBMs are part of large vertically integrated organizations that combine insurers, PBMs, specialty pharmacies, and healthcare providers.[16] Half of physicians and three-quarters of hospitals are now part of health systems.[17] Health insurance markets in three-quarters of metropolitan districts are now classified as highly concentrated.[18] By contrast, pharmaceutical manufacturers are much less concentrated, with the even the largest companies holding around 5% market share.[19] At the other end of the market, plan sponsors are small in comparison to the health insurers with whom they must negotiate, making their negotiating capabilities relatively weak.[20] And of course, individuals have almost no negotiating power. In short, consolidation and integration have led to market intermediaries with the size and scope that is almost always associated with market power. That is not to say producers are powerless, especially those with unique and patent-protected products or with wide portfolios of products. Nor is it to say that large plan sponsors cannot negotiate more strongly than small sponsors. But market concentration like this usually has implications for the way a market works.

In trying to understand what the consolidation and concentration of payers and providers meant for the affordability of innovative medicines, I turned to my expert informants. Many of them, including those who worked for intermediaries, helped me to see patterns in the detail. Larry Abrams, in particular, engaged in a detailed email and video exchange with me to help me make sense of it, as summarized here.

> In essence, the situation is straightforward. We choose to give pharmaceutical manufacturers a form of monopoly power to incentivize innovation. To prevent monopoly manufacturers making profits in excess of what is needed to incentivize them to innovate, that monopoly power needs a countervailing power.[21] In the current market, that is provided by the large insurers, PBMs and providers, whose market power allows them to demand discounts. But there are agency factors here. Like any commercial organization, insurers, PBMs and providers act in their own interest, not those of their customers. To make the market work and pass those discounts on to the patient and plan sponsors, we need to countervail the countervailers.
>
> Larry Abrams

Although this view was very common among the expert informants, being the skeptical scientist that I am, I looked for evidence to support this in the pricing of innovative medicines, both at net price and the price at the point of care. Like everything else in the pricing habitat, information in this area is fragmented, opaque, and every point seems to be disputed, but two points seem incontestable.

First, intermediaries have been able to use their market power to take more of the profit pool from patients and their proxies. Here, it's difficult to separate the costs of innovative medicines from other medicines and healthcare generally but there are myriad indications of intermediaries using their market power to shift the price at the point of care in their favor. The cost of an employer-sponsored family policy increased by 47% between 2011 and 2021. As a proportion of median income, premiums and other costs have increased to over 11% over the same period.[22] At the same time as these direct prices to patients have increased, other costs to patients and plan sponsors have also risen, particularly for those with private insurance.[23] Among many examples, a recent study concerning Hepatitis B treatment Entecavir showed increased out-of-pocket spending in exactly the situation where that would not be expected unless intermediaries were capturing value, namely when there is strong generic competition.[24] Insurers and PBMs are not alone in using their market power; hospitals and other providers also do so. For example, areas with the highest levels of hospital market concentration have annual premiums that are 5% higher than those in the least concentrated areas.[25] Providers' market power is also seen in the way they can extract profits from the administration of high-priced innovative medicines.[26]

Second, intermediaries have used their market power to extract larger profits from producers, although the contest between these two strong market players has played out in an unusual way. Typically, one would expect to see a strong buyer, such as a PBM, force down the net prices offered by producers. Instead, the two sides seem to have colluded in the "gross to net bubble,"[27] allowing net prices to rise but list prices to rise even faster. In a recent study, these increases were 60% and 159% respectively between 2008 and 2016, representing a large increase in the difference between list and net prices.[28] This has the effect of allowing both payer and provider to drink more from the profit pool. The losers in this arrangement are patients whose out-of-pocket costs are related to list prices. Interestingly, more recent evidence of list and net prices suggests that net prices have leveled off whilst list prices have continued to increase.[29] If true, this suggests that the increasing consolidation of the payers is allowing them to shift the net price balance point even more in their favor. Further evidence of this shift of power to the intermediaries is seen in payers' more deliberate use of formulary design to both pressure producers and improve their own margins.[30] Whether and where a payer places a product in a formulary is important to the success of an innovative medicine and one of the key points of negotiation between producer and PBM/payer.[31]

For all its detailed complexity, what we see here is exactly what the textbooks in competitive strategy tell us to expect. The intermediaries that sit between producer and patients have expanded their scope and scale. This has given a few larger intermediaries the power to control the routes to market and increased their market power relative to both producers and patients. Producers, especially those with innovative medicines, have been able to push back somewhat, producing the bubble that allows a win–win for them and payers. Patients and their proxies, with less market power, have consequently endured rising costs. This is the wholly unsurprising outcome of intermediary consolidation and integration. Market power pulls prices in favor of the intermediaries. This makes it less likely that the pricing habitat will be able to find the balance points at both net price and point of care price, that a stable, sustainable PIE needs.

The pricing habitat does not encourage service innovation

The concentration of market power into intermediaries is perhaps the most salient factor in the pricing habitat, hindering its ability to find stable balance points. But this is not the only negative implication of the consolidation and integration that has occurred in the channels between producer and patient. Those channels are meant to innovate, in Peter Drucker's sense of making resources and knowledge more valuable. Yet there is little sign of innovative value creation by payers and providers, even though there are three significant unmet needs that the channels to market could and should address.

The first is the need for information infrastructure, described in Chapter 6, the value habitat. Much of the real-world information required to make ecologically valid value assessments resides with the intermediaries. Between them, insurers, PBMs, pharmacies, and healthcare providers know which patients use which medicines at what prices and to what effect. For the most part, this information isn't available to health technology assessors, pharmaceutical companies, or plan sponsors. Intermediaries are essential to any future information infrastructure. As expert informant Kim Caldwell put it:

> Although it is fraught with technological, legal, and organizational difficulties, there is an enormous opportunity to create value from managing data, information, and knowledge in the healthcare system. Realizing this opportunity is less about collecting more data and more about connecting what we already have. We might need to start small, for example with the most expensive medicines, and we might need to learn lessons from other areas, such as drug safety surveillance. But the payers and providers are sitting on a gold mine of

information and not realizing the value, partly because it is less complicated
for them to run the business their traditional ways.

Kim Caldwell

Although the use of "big data" in health economics is beginning to emerge, it is still in its infancy.[32] It is an example of a failure to innovate in the services that form part of the innovative medicine solution, something that seems to have its origins in the failure of the pricing habitat to incentivize service innovation.

A second example is the cost of administration in the US healthcare system, which is estimated to be between 15 and 25% of national health expenditures.[33] The administration around medicines is a significant part of this. To quote from that research:

> *The prescription drug market provides a microcosm of the issue. Patents for*
> *new drugs are granted to allow innovative firms to charge high prices and thus*
> *encourage innovation. However, when patents are combined with insurance,*
> *the resulting prices can be exorbitant. Insurers, in an effort to counteract*
> *the market power of manufacturers, develop institutions to offset some of*
> *the manufacturer market power. These institutions (e.g., pharmacy benefit*
> *managers, which have market power to possibly command high fees) generate*
> *administrative costs related to formulary development, utilization manage-*
> *ment, and the bewildering system of rebates and related efforts to avoid plan*
> *cost-sharing provisions.*

The issue of poor use of data goes wider than its costs. Expert inform-ant Surya Singh expanded on this issue for me.

> *It not just that the administrative complexity adds costs, which it does, it also*
> *reduces transparency and trust and creates opportunities for arbitrage from*
> *the chaos. A less complex system would enable both patients and plans to*
> *make more informed choices. It would also help healthcare to move away*
> *from purely transactional relationships, a step in the direction of integrated*
> *delivery networks and value-based care.*

Surya Singh

Together with waste in the healthcare system, failures, over- and under-treatment, fraud and abuse, administrative costs are estimated to be between $760 and $935 billion a year.[34] Most of the opportunity to address this lies with intermediaries. Their failure to do so is another example of the lack of innovation in the services associated with medicines. Again, it suggests that the pricing habitat discourages or at least does not incentivize service innovation.

A third example of latent opportunities for service innovation around innovative medicines lies in the design of payment models. Advanced therapies and small-volume markets such as rare diseases create particular issues for current pricing models, which have their evolutionary roots in small-molecules and large markets.[35] As expert informant, John LaMattina explained to me:

> *However efficient we become, and even if pharmaceutical companies made very modest profits, we're still going to have the issue that pharmaceutical innovation is going to bring us ever more amazing therapies. Even if they are worth every penny, they will be expensive. Complaining against the cost of these innovations misses the point. We want them and they are expensive. We need innovation in how we pay for them to match the innovation that made them.*
>
> *John LaMattina*

There are already promising signs that the pricing habitat is developing alternative pricing models, but these are far from fully developed[36] and there remains an underexploited opportunity for innovation in pricing models, which lies with producers, payers, and patients and their proxies.[37] This unmet need again suggests that the pricing habitat discourages or at least does not incentivize service innovation.

Taken together, these three examples suggest a lack of innovation by payers, providers, and other intermediaries. Administration and waste, information infrastructure, and pricing models are all unmet needs that could make the PIE and the wider healthcare system more productive. The hopeful early signs of innovation in each area show that these needs are recognized. That those initiatives are not more fully developed suggests that the pricing habitat is failing to incentivize the shared effort that would need. Expert informant Michael Rothrock suggested that this might be the case.

> *I think many insurers and PBMs appreciate that their business models will need to evolve to fit a more value-oriented market. Many are moving in that direction. But progress is hindered when everybody points fingers at everyone else. To improve things will need producers (drug manufacturers), payers, providers, and others to jointly develop value-based business models. It's the difficulty of co-evolving that's the challenge, not the recognition of the issues.*
>
> *Michael Rothrock*

The pricing habitat fails to balance moral hazard

Moral hazard is an old insurance industry term with its roots in seventeenth-century England, but its modern use can be traced to the 1960s Nobel Laureate Ken Arrow.[38] In essence, it describes when a firm or individual takes a course of action because they can benefit and the costs or risks lie with someone else. The degree of moral hazard is increased when the potential gain is higher and the risk or cost falls more on the other party. As I described earlier, most people think first of patients' moral hazards (as in, "I'll misuse health services because my insurance covers the costs."), but there are also payer moral hazards (such as, "I'll reduce patients' choice and increase their costs because it increases my profit and the risks and costs fall on the patient.") and provider moral hazards (e.g., "I'll prescribe more tests and the most expensive medicine because it increases profits and the risks and costs fall on the insurer, patient, and plan provider.") All three of these connected moral hazards exist in the US healthcare system and it is one of the roles of the pricing habitat to find the point of balance for each of them. Although the term is rarely used, the phenomenon is well understood by those in the field, as indicated by an expert informant, Sue Peschin.

> At every level of the market, there are perverse incentives. Payers, PBMs, providers all have strong incentives to maximize their returns but relatively little incentive to reduce the costs to the patient.
>
> Sue Peschin

There is extensive research literature on patient moral hazard.[39] It is usually used to justify cost-sharing on the basis that this makes health insurance markets more efficient and premiums lower. Others argue the opposite: that cost-sharing makes necessary care unaffordable, which makes health insurance less efficient, and that incentivizing efficient use of healthcare is better than deterring inefficient use.[40] Somewhere in the middle of this debate is the centrist view that a good balance of patient moral hazard is when unnecessary use of healthcare is deterred without making necessary care unaffordable. The evidence is that, at present, the pricing habitat fails to find that balance point. For example, in a study of cancer patients, half suffered some and a third suffered severe financial consequences, and predictably, this issue was concentrated in particular socio-economic groups.[41] Amongst adult diabetics, 16% do not adhere to their medications for cost reasons.[42]

Across disease types, cost-related nonadherence was associated with 15–22% higher mortality.[43] Many other studies show similar findings. There seems little doubt that the balance of moral hazard is set too far in favor of insurers and, consequently, too far against patients.

Moral hazard for providers takes the form of overprescribing or prescribing behavior influenced by financial or other non-clinical considerations. This form of moral hazard occurs because medical treatment is a credence good, meaning only the physician knows if it is necessary or effective.[44] The pricing habitat is meant to find the balance point between too much and too little prescribing or treatment. Again, the evidence is that the current pricing habitat fails to find the correct balance. Out of 36 studies of physician prescribing, 30 revealed an association between financial payments and prescribing.[45] In a study of the effect of medical insurance on physicians, insurance was associated with overtreatment.[46] A review of 33 studies of prescribing behavior found that it was "not only geared for patient benefit, but also towards personal interest."[47] There seems little doubt that the balance of provider moral hazard is set too far in favor of providers and, consequently, too far against insurers, and patients and their proxies.

In a market based on credence products and risk sharing, moral hazard is an important consideration; but this is wider than a patient moral hazard. Patient, provider, and payer moral hazards interact and a functioning pricing habitat keeps them in balance. But a malfunctioning pricing habitat can lead to unbalanced hazards, inefficient use of resources, and exploitation of patients and insurers, making the PIE unsustainable. So, ensuring balance is one of the important but less obvious functions of the pricing habitat. At present, the evidence is that it is not performing this function well and so cannot meet the requirements of a healthy PIE.

The pricing habitat's opacity reduces public trust

Although the pricing habitat, the PIE, and the US healthcare system are integral parts of the US's free-market, capitalist economy, they are different from almost all other parts of that economy in their reliance on the social contract, as discussed in Chapter 1. To a much greater extent than other parts of the economy, healthcare, pharmaceuticals and, especially, innovative medicines depend on the legal, political, and social environment that society has created to favor them.

Without NIH, patent protection, tax relief for health insurance, and public health spending, pharmaceutical innovation in the US would be a shadow of its current self. The corollary of this dependence of pharmaceutical innovation on the social contract is that, much more than in any other market sector, public trust matters. As discussed in Chapter 1, if American society loses trust in how the PIE works, if they think the system is being played to their disadvantage, they can tear up the social contract. And the danger is that, in their anger, they do so in a way which irrevocably damages the pharmaceutical innovation. Professor James C Robinson of the University of California, Berkeley put it well.

> The U.S. pharmaceutical system needs a new social contract binding manufacturers, payers, and policymakers. Manufacturers need to reduce their prices in line with evidence-based benchmarks developed by independent third parties. Payers need to relieve physicians and patients of onerous utilization management and cost sharing. Policymakers need to expand non-price incentives for R&D, including research grants, tax credits, and innovation prizes. Physicians and patients will need to support this new social contract by selecting the most cost-effective options within the range of clinically effective treatments for their conditions. Without such a realignment, the pharmaceutical will remain locked in the contemporary war of all against all.[48]
>
> Professor James C Robinson

During my exploration of the PIE, it became clear that the pricing of innovative medicines played a central part in how Americans view their social contract with the pharmaceutical industry.[49] First and foremost, this is a matter of pricing and value. Net pricing that reflects ecologically valid value is important; but point-of-care pricing that is affordable even more so, as discussed earlier in this chapter. But it is also clear that, whilst value and affordability are the visible issues of the social contract, the things that are talked about are not necessarily the most fundamental issues. Beneath them lies the deeper issue of public trust. In other words, the maintenance of the social contract requires not only that the PIE delivers value and affordability but also that it is seen to do so. This is evidenced in the attempts by society, through its politicians, to make drug pricing transparent. The Prescription Drug Sunshine, Transparency, Accountability and Reporting (STAR) Act[50] and California's SB-17 drug transparency bill are examples of this, as are the 35 laws passed in 22 states that include a transparency component.[51] Internationally, these sentiments are echoed in the World Health Assembly resolution to share net prices.[52] Ranged against this public desire for pricing transparency are arguments for commercial confidentiality. Opponents of pricing transparency in the pharmaceutical supply chain argue that it would hinder price differentiation based on willingness to pay, it might risk collusion between suppliers, and cause prices to level upward, not downward.[53] As with everything else in the pricing habitat, there is a balance point to be found, and finding that balance between trust-enabling transparency and necessary commercial confidentiality is one of the functions of the pricing habitat.[54]

The current situation in the US is one of opacity in both prices and how those prices are arrived at.[55] As expert informant Jim Kenney explained it to me:

> *Although list prices are reasonably transparent, after that, pricing is opaque. Partly, this is deliberate, with many contracts stipulating that price must be confidential. Partly, it's just complexity, with so many different prices. And it's not just the prices that are opaque, the pricing processes are too. PBMs, for example, often make their decisions about formulary tiers based on rebates. This leads to those decision processes being confidential. Even if PBMs and insurers were making their coverage decisions in the patients' best interests, this secrecy would create the impression that they were not.*
>
> Jim Kenney

All contracts depend on trust, but implicit social contracts especially so. Maintaining public trust in the social contract around pharmaceutical innovation is obviously important. That trust is built by valuable, affordable medicines but eroded by lack of transparency of drug prices and pricing processes. The pricing of relatively expensive innovative medicines, which is often amplified by the services they are bundled with, is especially susceptible to this erosion of trust. There are commercial arguments against total transparency but the current state of disrepair of the social contract tells us that the pricing habitat has not found the balance between these two perspectives. Until it does, it cannot meet the requirements of a healthy PIE.

At the end of my exploration of the pricing habitat I concluded, as I had for other habitats that, in its current state, it could not support a healthy PIE. It has many serious weaknesses, any one of which might compromise a sustainable supply of affordable and innovative medicines. Its disconnection from the value habitat would be an issue even if that habitat were working well. The concentration of market power into intermediaries is enough to distort any market, and it seems to do so here. Not only does it distract those intermediaries from realizing the value they could, from information and service, but it also creates payer and provider moral hazard. This is ironic, given the current pricing system claims to counter patient moral hazard. Finally, more subtly but more perniciously, the current pricing habitat erodes trust and corrodes the social contract on which the entire PIE depends. Acting holistically, as is the way of a complex adaptive system, these factors make it unlikely that the pricing habitat can or will give the PIE what it needs to provide affordable, innovative medicines. Having made that assessment, I pushed on to the question of how the functioning of the pricing habitat might be improved.

How can we improve the pricing habitat?

The pricing habitat has a central role in supporting the health of the PIE. A malfunctioning pricing habitat would fail to find the balance points for allocating returns amongst its many inhabitants, rendering the PIE as unstable as any organism that couldn't achieve homeostasis. It would also create various moral hazards and, most destructively of all in the long term, undermine trust in the social contract on which the PIE depends. Today, the pricing habitat shows signs of all those failings. Concentration of market power has shifted both net price and point of care balance points to unsustainable positions. It has also led to payer- and provider moral hazard. And, although Americans may understandably struggle to grasp the detail of how the pricing habitat is malfunctioning, they can feel that it is. Their reaction to those feelings is perhaps the biggest threat to the PIE. If we want a pricing habitat that repairs the social contract and sustains the PIE, significant changes are required. In this section, I suggest what they might be.

Establish value-based net pricing

The foundation of a healthy pricing habitat is that the net prices that a pharmaceutical company receives for its innovative medicines must reflect their ecologically valid value. Without that, the pricing habitat is untethered from the rest of its ecosystem and pharmaceutical innovation is not properly incentivized. Value-based net pricing also has another, no less important, impact on the pricing habitat. To the extent that the net price is then reflected in the point of care price (see market power, below), a clear connection between price and value engenders public trust in the way that innovative medicines are priced and so strengthens the social contract. Establishing value-based net pricing as the norm for innovative medicines would be an important step toward a pricing habitat that enabled a healthy PIE.

In practice, this means payers incorporating ecologically valid value assessment into their price negotiations with producers in a substantive, meaningful way. The current pricing habitat is only showing the earliest signs of doing this, so creating this new norm would require significant change. For those who must make this change, I suggest three guiding principles for this evolution of the pricing habitat. First, it would need to be accompanied by comprehensive, connected changes in the value habitat, as suggested in Chapter 6. But I would suggest that we should not wait for the never-arriving day when the value habitat is functioning perfectly. Value-based net pricing will need to coevolve incrementally with ecologically valid value assessment. Second, value-based pricing should apply to both the specialty and retail channels to market. Although smaller in volume, the former is the most important for innovative medicines, so both PBMs and insurers as well as the purchasing organizations through which providers purchase medicines should build value-assessment into their purchasing processes and into their formulary design decisions. Third, I suggest that these changes would require a significant reconsideration of the role of payers' Pharmacy and Therapeutic committees. These scientific bodies, who guide the decisions about how formularies are constructed, seem maladapted to an environment where value is as important as efficacy. They may need to evolve into pharmacy, therapeutic, and value committees and add health economics to their capabilities.

I am not naïve about the scale of change this requires, especially for payers and providers. Value-based decisions about what price to pay and what to cover may be inconsistent with parts of their current business models. For example, value-based decisions might run counter to how they monetize their use of market power and their control over channels to market, for example, through formulary tiering. However, this change would accelerate the necessary evolution of payers and providers in three ways. First, it allows them to "walk the talk" of their missions, which emphasize patient needs. Second, it aligns with the goal of improving healthcare outcomes, which is surely their ethical responsibility. Finally, it removes the misaligned incentives to seek rent from their market position. This encourages a focus on value creation in services such as reducing administrative waste, real-world effectiveness information and innovative pricing models.

Redress imbalances in patients' market power

Connecting net prices to value is only a first step toward a functioning pricing habitat. An effective pricing habitat will also find a balanced point of care prices that incentivize payers and providers to innovate and improve services, without extracting any more from the profit pool than is necessary. Either side of this balance point destabilizes the PIE. Too far toward patients damages the channels to market, and exploiting patients and their proxies weakens the social contract. Today, a high market concentration of payers and providers has led to relatively low competition between them. Inevitably, this has led to point-of-care prices – which include premiums, out-of-pocket costs, and providers' charges – being set too far away from a stable point. It also creates the moral hazard to give patients poor value. Value-based net prices are a necessary starting point but don't address the market power imbalance between highly concentrated payers and providers on the one hand and, on the other, patients and plan sponsors who are inevitably much more fragmented and relatively smaller. Redressing this imbalance of market power is the second necessary step toward a pricing habitat that allows a healthy PIE.

In theory, this rebalancing of market power could be achieved in two ways: by reducing that of intermediaries or by amplifying the countervailing market power of patients, plan sponsors, and other proxies. In practice, some of both are likely to be needed. Those tasked with doing this might consider three guiding ideas. First, whilst anti-trust legislation is always an option in highly concentrated markets, there are economies of scale and scope among both payers and providers that are valuable to society. For example, reducing intermediaries' power reduces their ability to countervail producers' market power. Second, there seems to be significant, unrealized potential for aggregating patient and plan sponsor buying to create a countervailing market force.[56] Third, there is potential for federal or state government to counter intermediaries' market power, both by providing some form of public option health insurance and by allowing CMS (the Centers for Medicare and Medicaid Services) to aggregate and use its pharmaceutical purchasing power.

As with the suggestion to embed value-based net pricing, these suggestions for rebalancing the point of care price are ambitious and I don't for a moment underestimate the difficulty. Nor do I ignore the secondary and tertiary issues involved. For example, if plan sponsors' market power was amplified by aggregation, it would also amplify the challenge of balance between plan sponsors and patients. If state or federal market power was enabled, it might create a significant monopsony issue. In any case, amplifying state and federal power, however it is done, illuminates the political choices Americans need to make about public involvement in healthcare markets.[57] Against these difficulties, the CMS taking a role as genuine negotiator may obviate many of the market complexities created to substitute for those, such as 340b and regulations around Medicaid and Medicare best price mandates, all of which have had unintended consequences.[58]

Make the pricing of innovative medicines transparent

In a pricing habitat where prices are connected to value and balanced well between equally powerful producers, payers, providers, and patients, we might reasonably expect most of its issues to be resolved. Returns would be distributed appropriately, and the moral hazards poised against each other. This would address the first three requirements the PIE has of the pricing habitat, and to use my earlier metaphor, we might hope for homeostasis. But to meet the fourth requirement, for those prices to engender public trust in the pricing habitat, both those prices and the process of setting them need to be transparently fair. In today's pricing habitat, neither of those things is true. A deeply embedded culture of commercial confidentiality, combined with labyrinthine complexity, hides prices and shrouds their processes in mystery. And providers' practices of bundling services with the prices of innovative medicines, so that the price of the medicine includes a service element, magnify this problem. To regain the balance between confidentiality and trust, the pricing habitat would need to both disentangle the pricing of innovative medicines from the pricing of services and make those isolated prices visible and comparable.

Responsibility for doing this lies mostly with the payers and providers and, whilst it sounds a very easy thing to do, there would be large practical challenges. To those responsible for overcoming them, I offer four suggestions. First, pricing secrecy is a deeply embedded cultural practice. It is not reasonable to expect payers and providers to adopt new practice without encouragement, which suggests a role for legislation. Second, if the aim is to balance public trust against commercially necessary confidentiality, then the demands for transparency should not to go too far. Price transparency is not the same as total transparency of costs and profits. Third, experiences from markets such as financial services tell us that visibility of prices doesn't always equate to comparability. It may be necessary to complement price visibility with comparison facilities, just as we see in many other markets. Fourth, experience of price transparency elsewhere in the world suggests that it is a poor cost control mechanism on its own because it encourages levelling up of prices. Price transparency is probably best used as a complement to, not a replacement for, value-based pricing and the balancing of market power.

As with my other two suggestions for improving the functioning of the pricing habitat, I am not discounting the difficult choices involved and the many corollary issues of price transparency. It will illuminate the costs of both innovative medicines and associated services, so demanding their justification. It will bring into focus those prescribing decisions that are both clinical and economic, which is an issue we are sometimes reluctant to face. But against these, it will also encourage payers and providers to innovate so that the value of their services reflects their costs.

Will this be enough?

In this chapter, I've maintained my approach of limiting myself to broad guidance rather than specific policy recommendations. The latter are beyond the scope of this book. My guidance reflects the issues that constrain the pricing habitat's ability to meet the requirements of a healthy PIE. They would, if acted on fully and in an integrated way, greatly improve the functioning of the habitat and so of the PIE. They would also complement the suggestions I make for other habitats in the ecosystem, such as encouraging competition after patent expiration. Even so, these four suggestions would leave some issues of pricing unaddressed. Two in particular are problematic. The first is the pricing of expensive drugs for small patient populations, such as rare diseases. Even if good value, these would still be unaffordable in many cases. The second is the pricing of very valuable drugs, such as curative therapies that replace a lifetime of illness and costs with good health. The value-based net price for these innovative medicines may be in excess of the price necessary to incentivize innovation. Both issues overlap onto the social and political issues that I'll cover in the next two chapters.

Notes

1 Headline figures like this can hide important detail. Almost 90% of the prescriptions dispensed in the US are generics, which are relatively cheap. The remaining 10% or so of prescriptions are branded drugs. But that 10% consumes about 80% of drug spending because branded drugs are much more expensive than generics. In round numbers, about two-thirds of spending on medicines goes through retail pharmacies and about one-third paid for as part of an associated health care service. In some therapy areas, the proportion of the healthcare cost that is the medicine can be much higher or lower than the average of 14%. See 1.
2 Predictably, the healthcare provider industry and the pharmaceutical industry each claim the other is responsible for drug prices. See 2.
3 To quote from the Encyclopaedia of Ecology,

> Homeostasis is the ability of ecological systems to maintain stable system properties despite perturbations. Properties of systems reflect the system as a whole and are not solely determined by the identity of the species in the system. Homeostasis is a common trait of complex systems.

See ref 3.
4 The profit pool in a market is the sum of all the profits made by everyone along the value chain. So, in our case is it all the profit to be made from treating a patient with an innovative medicine. See 4. In the concept of the profit pool, patients, plan sponsors, and taxpayers don't extract from the pool but they desire to contribute to it as little as possible, which amounts to the same thing.
5 Many entities in the healthcare system call themselves non-profits. Although they may differ in where they allocate any profits they make, they still extract money from the system, just as a for-profit does. From an ecological perspective, there is no practical difference between for-profits and non-profits.
6 Trikafta is breakthrough treatment for Cystic Fibrosis. See https://www.statnews.com/2019/10/23/we-conquered-a-disease-how-vertex-delivered-a-transformative-medicine-for-cystic-fibrosis/ However, even it has been challenged that its price exceeds its value. See https://icer.org/wp-content/uploads/2020/08/ICER_CF_Final_Report_092320.pdf.
7 Since the launch of Sovaldi created the market in 2013, competition has reduced the net cost per unit from about $1000 to about $200. See https://www.pcmanet.org/wp-content/uploads/2021/06/hcvdrugs_Infographic.pdf.
8 Readers with a business education will quickly recognize that this is the work of Michael Porter. See ref 5.
9 Interestingly, the idea that payers and providers have moral hazard as well as patients was often raised by expert informants during the research for this book but never using the term. My research observations were crystalized by the work of Donald W Light. See https://www.ias.edu/ideas/three-moral-hazards-health-insurance.

10 The term financial toxicity is used loosely to encompass many issues associated with economic access to medicines. See https://www.cancer.gov/publications/dictionaries/cancer-terms/def/financial-toxicity and See ref 6. See also 7 and 8.

11 Zolgensma is gene therapy for children with spinal muscular atrophy but, at a $2.1 million per patient cost, Zolgensma is inaccessible to some patients even where it has been approved. It is illustrative of wider issues around advanced therapies in general and gene therapies in particular. See ref 9 and https://fortune.com/2020/02/07/zolgensma-high-drug-prices/.

12 In August 2018, CVS Caremark announced that it would use comparative effectiveness studies as part of an approach to making drugs more affordable, see https://cvshealth.com/sites/default/files/cvs-health-current-and-new-approaches-to-making-drugs-more-affordable.pdf.

13 One of the important points of detail in this picture is that, whilst the many of the most expensive innovative medicines tend to be biologics, like Humira, that are administered under medical supervision, many innovative medicines are small molecules that can go through retail channels, like Xarelto and Eliquis. See https://themedicinemaker.com/manufacture/why-small-molecules-are-still-a-big-deal.

14 This division between retail and specialty drugs is not unique to the US, but the division is more pronounced in the US than elsewhere. See ref 10.

15 Medicare Plan B covers these physician-administered medicines so, although this doesn't necessarily mean that 43% of all such medicines are accounted for by ten drugs, it's likely that this figure is similar for private insurance. See https://www.kff.org/medicare/issue-brief/relatively-few-drugs-account-for-a-large-share-of-medicare-prescription-drug-spending/.

16 These data are taken from the Drug Channels Institute. See https://www.drugchannels.net/2021/04/the-top-pharmacy-benefit-managers-pbms.html.

17 The trend toward consolidation amongst providers seems to be accelerating. See ref 11.

18 The consolidation amongst health insurers is amplified by their local concentration. See https://www.ama-assn.org/press-center/press-releases/ama-publishes-new-study-monitoring-competition-us-health-insurance.

19 This figure, however, is an average across the market. In any given therapy area or disease market, market shares are generally more concentrated than this. See https://www.statista.com/statistics/309425/prescription-drugs-market-shares-by-top-companies-globally/.

20 To quote one article on this topic, "Even after decades of being health care purchasers, companies ranging from small shops to Fortune 500 companies may not fully understand the health coverage they're buying and often pay more as a result." The Commonwealth Fund's view is consistent with this, stating,

> Some of the biggest U.S. employers have tried and failed to rein in the prices they pay for their employees' health insurance benefits. Part of the reason is that large and small firms alike often lack the critical mass of employees needed to drive changes in a local market. Some also lack the expertise needed to negotiate better contracts with their providers or are loathe to ask their workers to change how they get their care. As a result, employees' own costs keep rising, as employers shift more of the cost burden onto their workers.

See https://www.commonwealthfund.org/publications/2022/apr/tackling-high-health-care-prices-look-four-purchaser-led-efforts Also see https://www.axios.com/employers-health-benefits-consultants-hr-rebates-67b458a1-2c7e-4801-b3fe-51a328a81bba.html.

21 Here, Larry Abrams is drawing on JK Galbraith. See ref 12.

22 See https://files.kff.org/attachment/Summary-of-Findings-Employer-Health-Benefits-2021.pdf.
23 The picture here is complicated by the Affordable Care Act reducing the risk of very high out of pocket expenses for most Americans but leaving middle-income earners at risk. See https://www.commonwealthfund.org/publications/issue-briefs/2020/apr/catastrophic-out-of-pocket-costs-problem-middle-income. In general, out-of-pocket expense has risen faster than inflation, representing further evidence that insurers are using their market power. See https://www.statista.com/statistics/484568/us-total-out-of-pocket-health-care-payments-since-1960/.
24 To quote from this work,

> Entecavir, a generic drug that is one of the first-line agents used for treatment of CHB, has had a steep decline in the average price that pharmacies pay for the drug (i.e., national average drug acquisition cost [NADAC]) because of manufacturer competition. Yet, the list price—which correlates with out-of-pocket spending—has remained high.

See ref 13.
25 To a greater extent than insurers and PBMs, geographical concentration of providers seems to influence market power. See ref 14. Interestingly, this research also reported, "Additionally, while an increased number of insurers was independently associated with lower premiums, that was not sufficient to offset the effects of increased hospital concentration on premium costs."
26 This is again a very complicated picture but hospitals' fees for administering innovative medicines are related to their price. This encourages them to prescribe higher priced medicines and makes those medicines still more expensive. A very good explanation of how this "Buy and Bill" system works can be found at https://www.drugchannels.net/2021/10/follow-vial-buy-and-bill-system-for.html and further discussion in See ref 15.
27 I acknowledge Adam Fein, of Drug Channels, for this term.
28 To quote from a study of this work, "In this analysis of branded drugs in the US from 2007 to 2018, mean increases in list and net prices were substantial, although discounts offset an estimated 62% of list price increases with substantial variation across classes." See ref 16.
29 This is seen amongst six of the largest manufacturers, rather than across the market as a whole. See https://www.drugchannels.net/2021/04/gross-to-net-bubble-update-net-prices.html.
30 The exclusion of some medicines from the list of medicines available to patients ("formulary exclusions") is one way for intermediaries to negotiate with producers and increase their margins. See https://www.drugchannels.net/2021/01/the-big-three-pbms-ramp-up-specialty.html.
31 When there is clinical equivalence, PBMs will generally award better formulary positions to the product that makes the most profit to them. See https://www.commonwealthfund.org/publications/explainer/2019/apr/pharmacy-benefit-managers-and-their-role-drug-spending Payers' may then adapt those formulary recommendations, which determines their patients' access to medicine. Whilst this may achieve the payers' goals of reducing spending on medicines, it may increase other, non-drug, medical costs. To quote from one study of this, "Formulary coverage decisions may have unintended consequences on patient and payer outcomes despite lower drug utilization and pharmacy cost savings; therefore, careful evaluation of restrictions before policy implementation and continued re-evaluation after implementation is warranted."

32 Interestingly, this possibility for better knowledge management in healthcare doesn't seem to be contentious in the least. There seems to be a strong consensus in the PIE that the better use of data could yield enormous savings in US healthcare generally and on the use of medicines in particular. See refs 17–19.

33 These administrative costs are highly concentrated in a few areas. To quote from this research, "...administrative spending was $950 billion in 2019, of which 94% was in 5 functional focus areas: financial transactions ecosystem, industry-agnostic corporate functions, industry-specific operational functions, customer and patient services, and administrative clinical support functions." See ref 20.

34 To quote from this research,

> In this review based on 6 previously identified domains of health care waste, the estimated cost of waste in the US health care system ranged from $760 billion to $935 billion, accounting for approximately 25% of total health care spending, and the projected potential savings from interventions that reduce waste, excluding savings from administrative complexity, ranged from $191 billion to $286 billion, representing a potential 25% reduction in the total cost of waste. Implementation of effective measures to eliminate waste represents an opportunity reduce the continued increases in US health care expenditures.

See ref 21.

35 The authors of one paper summarized the situation well.

> Payers are adopting a wait-and-see stance towards ATMPs (Advanced Therapy Medicinal Products) rather than implementing large-scale changes to current funding and reimbursement models. The imperative for biopharmaceutical manufacturers is to work with payers ahead of launch to understand the potential impact of an individual ATMP, and lead on designing a market access model that seeks to mitigate risk.

See ref 22.

36 The idea of value-based pharmaceutical contracts is evolving along analogous contracts for purchasing healthcare, and obviously, the two are interconnected. There seems to be much work to be done to make such contracts work well. See https://www.forbes.com/sites/joshuacohen/2020/05/01/use-of-value-based-contracting-for-pharmaceuticals-is-underwhelming/?sh=4ea15042366d and see ref 23.

37 A central issue here is that value-based contracts often depend on risk-sharing which, itself, implies information-sharing. As one thoughtful paper expressed it,

> It is concluded that there is not yet a gold standard methodology in relation to the type of agreements to be practiced. Moreover, its opportunity cost, including the cost of implementation, remains to be scrutinized. However, regardless of the type of agreement, the advantages of adopting these agreements are well known, inevitably related with challenges of implementation. The need for an infrastructure to support information sharing is undisputed and urgent. The future of therapeutic innovation and increased pressure on health budgets will require alternative, more flexible models, personalized reimbursement models that allow alignment of medicines prices with the value they deliver in treating the several diseases.

See ref 24.

38 If you're not familiar with the concept of moral hazard, the history of the term and its interpretation is both fascinating and relevant to its discussion in the context of the PIE. See ref 25.

39 A comprehensive and useful review of the topic can be found at see ref 26.

40 This argument is well made here. See ref 27. To quote from this paper, "I find cost-sharing never to be an optimal solution as it produces two novel inefficiencies by limiting access. An alternative design, relying on bonuses, has no such side effects and achieves the same incentivization."

41 This data taken from See ref 28.

42 This data taken from See ref 29.

43 This data taken from https://www.cdc.gov/pcd/issues/2020/20_0244.htm.

44 For more on this important feature of innovative medicines. See ref 30.

45 To quote from this paper, "The association between industry payments and physician prescribing was consistent across all studies that have evaluated this association. Findings regarding a temporal association and dose-response suggest a causal relationship." See ref 31.

46 Interestingly, this work also showed that competition moderated overtreatment. See ref 32.

47 I qualify this reference with the observation that this effect is seen not just in the US but elsewhere. See refs 33 and 34.

48 This quote taken from https://www.statnews.com/2020/03/13/mending-broken-social-contract-pharmaceutical-pricing-innovation/.

49 As I wrote this chapter, a new survey from the Kaiser Fund Foundation reported that limiting drug prices was a top priority for 61% of respondents and important for another 30%. See https://www.kff.org/health-costs/poll-finding/kff-health-tracking-poll-march-2022/.

50 At time of writing, this Act has not yet passed.

51 See ref 35. Notably, this work concluded that no state legislation provided effective transparency across the entire supply chain.

52 Internationally, the issue of price transparency has subtle implications. To quote from this work,

> We argue that while it is possible that stakeholders may benefit to some extent from greater transparency on prices, several important policy and economic issues need to be carefully considered. Such transparency, combined with widespread use of international reference pricing, might undermine companies' differential pricing strategies, which are important in fostering wider access to medicines in low- and middle-income countries in particular, noting that access to medicines issues can occur in high-income countries as well. Moreover, there is a further risk that these types of proposals will lead to price fixing, less competition and higher prices than might otherwise be the case.

See ref 36.

53 This point is made here: See ref 37 and https://www.weforum.org/agenda/2019/10/transparency-drug-pricing/.

54 The pros and cons of price transparency are a complex issue, but they have been studied. The fullest, most balanced review of this topic concluded that, from a global point of view, it was a mixed blessing. It reduces corruption and improves competition. But, for innovative medicines, transparency in pricing forces a leveling up of prices rather than leveling down. From a US-only perspective, these issues do not seem important. See https://www.ohe.org/news/price-transparency-good-or-bad-what-does-literature-and-theory-tell-us.

55 To quote one recent review of the topic,

> Prescription drug prices in the United States are opaque. Manufacturers set list prices, which are publicly disclosed, but then negotiate confidential rebates with insurers and pharmacy benefit managers (PBMs), often to secure

preferred formulary placement. Because of warped incentives in the drug supply chain, rebates and other discounts have grown in recent years, driving 'net' prices substantially below list prices for many brand-name drugs. The secrecy of negotiations means that patients and policymakers have no way of knowing the actual prices paid for prescription drugs.

See ref 38.

56 The birth and death of Haven, the venture formed by Amazon, Berkshire Hathaway, and JPMorgan Chase is a salutary story that illustrates both the need for a rebalancing of market forces in healthcare and the difficulty of doing so. See https://hbr.org/2021/01/why-haven-healthcare-failed.

57 This debate overlaps onto that around whether the US might adopt a single payer or other system of financing healthcare. This is beyond the scope of this book, but the debate is very well summarized here: See ref 39.

58 The 340B Drug Pricing Program is a US federal government program created in 1992, which requires drug manufacturers to provide outpatient drugs to eligible health care organizations and covered entities at significantly reduced prices. Many have argued that the program is open to abuse and needs reform. See ref 40. The Medicaid best price policy requires drug manufacturers to give Medicaid programs the best price among nearly all purchasers. For a discussion on how the Medicaid best price has had unintended consequences, see https://www.forbes.com/sites/joshuacohen/2020/08/09/cms-proposes-changes-to-medicaid-best-price-rule-a-potential-boost-to-value-based-contracting/?sh=3cee8dbb1e8f. For a discussion on how it might hinder innovative, value-based pricing models. See ref 41.

References

1 Conti RM, Turner A, Hughes-Cromwick P. Projections of US prescription drug spending and key policy implications. *JAMA Health Forum.* 2021;2(1):e201613–e.
2 Colvin G. Big Hospitals vs. Big Pharma: Which industry is most to blame for soaring health care costs? *Fortune.* 2021 April 8.
3 Ernest SKM. Homeostasis. In: Jorgensen EF, Brian D editor. *Encyclopedia of Ecology.* Oxford: Elsevier; 2008.
4 Gadiesh O, Gilbert JL. Profit pools: A fresh look at strategy. *Harvest Business Review.* 1998;76(3):139–47.
5 Porter ME. *Competitive Strategy.* 1st ed. New York: Free Press; 1980.
6 Mols F, Tomalin B, Pearce A, Kaambwa B, Koczwara B. Financial toxicity and employment status in cancer survivors: A systematic literature review. *Supportive Care in Cancer.* 2020;28(12):5693–708.
7 Wang SY, Valero-Elizondo J, Ali H-J, Pandey A, Cainzos-Achirica M, Krumholz HM et al. Out-of-pocket annual health expenditures and financial toxicity from healthcare costs in patients with heart failure in the United States. *Journal of the American Heart Association.* 2021;10(14):e022164–e.
8 Desai A, Gyawali B. Financial toxicity of cancer treatment: Moving the discussion from acknowledgement of the problem to identifying solutions. *EClinicalMedicine.* 2020;20:100269-.
9 Hampson G, Towse A, Pearson SD, Dreitlein WB, Henshall C. Gene therapy: Evidence, value and affordability in the US health care system. *Journal of Comparative Effectiveness Research.* 2018;7(1):15–28.

10 Naci H, Kesselheim AS. Specialty drugs — a distinctly American phenomenon. *New England Journal of Medicine.* 2020;382(23):2179–81.

11 Furukawa MF, Kimmey L, Jones DJ, Machta, RM, Guo J, Rich EC. Consolidation of providers into health systems increased substantially, 2016–18. *Health Affairs.* 2020;39(8):1321–5.

12 Galbraith JK. *American Capitalism: The Concept of Countervailing Power.* London: H. Hamilton; 1952.

13 Alpern JD, Joo H, Link B, Ciaccia A, Stauffer WM, Bahr NC et al. Trends in pricing and out-of-pocket spending on entecavir among commercially insured patients, 2014–2018. *JAMA Network Open.* 2022;5(1):e2144521–e.

14 Boozary AS, Feyman Y, Reinhardt UE, Jha AK. The association between hospital concentration and insurance premiums in ACA marketplaces. *Health Aff (Millwood).* 2019;38(4):668–74.

15 Werble C. Medicare Part B. *Health Affairs Health Policy Brief.* August 10, 2017.

16 Hernandez I, San-Juan-Rodriguez A, Good CB, Gellad WF. Changes in list prices, net prices, and discounts for branded drugs in the US, 2007–2018. *JAMA: The Journal of the American Medical Association.* 2020;323(9):854–62.

17 Agrawal R, Prabakaran S. Big data in digital healthcare: Lessons learnt and recommendations for general practice. *Heredity.* 2020;124(4):525–34.

18 Dash S, Shakyawar SK, Sharma M, Kaushik S. Big data in healthcare: Management, analysis and future prospects. *Journal of Big Data.* 2019;6(1):54.

19 Iacocca K, Vallen B. Using analytics to gain insights on U.S. prescription drug prices: An inductive analysis. *Journal of Public Policy & Marketing.* 2021;40(4):538–57.

20 Chernew M, Mintz H. Administrative expenses in the US health care system: Why so high? *JAMA.* 2021;326(17):1679–80.

21 Shrank WH, Rogstad TL, Parekh N. Waste in the US health care system: Estimated costs and potential for savings. *JAMA.* 2019;322(15):1501–9.

22 Del Carlo A, Paglia R, Carter EA, Schwartz J, Dyson S, Areteou T et al. The growing number of high-cost advanced therapy medicinal products (ATMPS) pose unprecedented pricing and funding challenges to current models of healthcare. *Value in Health.* 2018;21:S40–S1.

23 Kannarkat JT, Good CB, Parekh N. Value-based pharmaceutical contracts: Value for whom? *Value in Health.* 2020;23(2):154–6.

24 Gonçalves FR, Santos S, Silva C, Sousa G. Risk-sharing agreements, present and future. *Ecancermedicalscience.* 2018;12:823-.

25 Rowell D, Connelly L. A history of the term 'moral hazard'. *Journal of Risk & Insurance.* 2012;79(4):1051–79.

26 Zweifel PM, WG. Moral hazard and consumer incentives in health care. In Culyer AJN, JP editor. *Handbook of Health Economics.* Vol. 1A. Amsterdam: Elsevier; 2000. p. 409–59.

27 Fels M. Incentivizing efficient utilization without reducing access: The case against cost-sharing in insurance. *Health Economics.* 2020;29(7):827–40.

28 Esselen KM, Gompers A, Hacker MR, Bouberhan S, Shea M, Summerlin SS et al. Evaluating meaningful levels of financial toxicity in gynecologic cancers. *International Journal of Gynecologic Cancer.* 2021;31(6):801–6.

29 Kang H, Lobo JM, Kim S, Sohn M-W. Cost-related medication non-adherence among U.S. adults with diabetes. *Diabetes Research Clinical Practical.* 2018; 143:24–33.

30 Dranove D. Information asymmetry: Consumers and producers. In Pauly MVM, Thomas GB, Pedro P, editor. *Handbook of Health Economics*. Oxford: Elsevier; 2011.

31 Mitchell APT, Niti U, Gennarelli L, Tabatabai SM, Goldberg JD, Luis A, Korenstein D. Are financial payments from the pharmaceutical industry associated with physician prescribing? *Annals of Internal Medicine*. 2021;174(3):353–61.

32 Huck S, Lünser G, Spitzer F, Tyran J-R. Medical insurance and free choice of physician shape patient overtreatment: a laboratory experiment. *Journal of Economic Behavior & Organization*. 2016;131:78–105.

33 Davari M, Khorasani E, Tigabu BM. Factors influencing prescribing decisions of physicians: A review. *Ethiop Journal Health Science*. 2018;28(6):795–804.

34 Price SM, O'Donoghue AC, Rizzo L, Sapru S, Aikin KJ. What influences healthcare providers' prescribing decisions? Results from a national survey. *Research in Social and Administrative Pharmacy*. 2021;17(10):1770–9.

35 Ryan MS, Sood N. Analysis of state-level drug pricing transparency laws in the United States. *JAMA Network Open*. 2019;2(9):e1912104–e.

36 Shaw B, Mestre-Ferrandiz J. Talkin' about a resolution: Issues in the push for greater transparency of medicine prices. *Pharmacoeconomics*. 2020;38(2):125–34.

37 Ostby JT, Solli O. Good reasons for confidential drug prices. *Tidsskriffet: Den Norske Legeforening*. 2019 March 11.

38 Feldman WB, Rome BN, Avorn J, Kesselheim AS. The future of drug-pricing transparency. *The New England Journal of Medicine*. 2021;384(6):489–91.

39 Donnelly PD, Erwin PC, Fox DM, Grogan C. Single-payer, multiple-payer, and state-based financing of health care: Introduction to the special section. *American Journal of Public Health*. 2019;109(11):1482–3.

40 Desai S, McWilliams JM. Consequences of the 340B drug pricing program. *The New England Journal of Medicine*. 2018;378(6):539–48.

41 Sachs R, Bagley N, Lakdawalla DN. Innovative contracting for pharmaceuticals and medicaid's best-price rule. *Journal of Health Politics, Policy and Law*. 2018;43(1):5–18.

8 The competition habitat

Precis

- The competition habitat is the part of the pharmaceutical innovation ecosystem where forces for limiting competition and for enabling imitation interact.
- The role of the competition habitat is to achieve a balance between incentivizing valuable innovation and encouraging valuable imitation.
- The pricing habitat is inhabited by pharmaceutical innovators, imitators such as generics and biosimilars manufacturers, and legislators and their agencies, such as the FDA, USPTO, and FTC.
- The competition habitat adjoins and interacts with the value and pricing habitats.
- A healthy PIE requires that the competition habitat meets three requirements:
  - It must incentivize valuable innovation.
  - It must encourage valuable imitation.
  - It must create a predictable competitive environment.
- The competition habitat's ability to support a healthy PIE is constrained by:
  - the patent system's inability to discriminate between incremental and radical innovation
  - the regulatory exclusivity system's insensitivity to different kinds of pharmaceutical innovation
  - the lack of predictability of the competitive habitat
  - the role of know-how and trade secrets in pharmaceutical innovation
  - market forces and inertia that hinder the adoption of imitators, especially biosimilars

DOI: 10.4324/9781003330271-8

- The pricing habitat would be better able to support a healthy PIE by:
  - improving the application of patent law to enhance its discriminatory power
  - aligning regulatory exclusivity incentives more closely to societal needs
  - improving the predictability of loss of exclusivity
  - enabling market forces to pull through lower cost, imitative products
  - providing alternative imitation mechanisms for hard-to-imitate products

So far in my explorations of the PIE, competition has been assumed but not discussed explicitly or in any detail. It's now time to pay attention to competition, an important issue that pervades the ecosystem. In a healthy PIE, innovative medicines result from investment, investment is incentivized by returns, returns are a function of price, price depends on value, and value is relative to competitors. So, if we want to manage the PIE for a sustainable supply of innovative, affordable medicines, we must consider the role played by competition. That's the purpose of this chapter.

Like any ecosystem, the PIE is a fiercely competitive place, with innovative companies and their medicines competing to optimize the returns on their risky investments. But the PIE is far from an economist's definition of a perfect market in which anybody can sell anything to anyone in unrestrained rivalry. Instead, the PIE is run through with a pervasive web of economic and legal limitations, which shape competition in the PIE so that it is very different from, for example, a consumer goods market. Limitations begin with economic barriers to entry, such as the relatively high investment needed to enter and compete at scale with large, established competitors. The economic barriers are complemented by regulatory hurdles that, by requiring specialized processes and capabilities, create further impediments to new entrants. Together, these factors make the pharmaceutical market, especially the more innovative part of it, hard to enter, particularly for firms lacking experience in the market. For evidence of this, look at any list of the largest pharmaceutical companies. You will find it dominated by companies such as Roche, Johnson and Johnson, Bayer, Merck, Lilly, Pfizer, and other "big pharma" firms that have histories stretching back into the 19th century. By contrast, new entrants into the PIE are relatively rare, except as smaller, special-ized biotech firms, which are often acquired by or work through the established players.[1]

Even when these barriers to entering the market are overcome, or when an existing player wishes to compete, competitors face a raft of intellectual property and quasi-intellectual property laws, whose intent is to constrain competition within the market for innovative medicines (see Box 8.1).

Box 8.1 Limits on competition in innovative medicines

If you wanted to compete in the innovative pharmaceuticals mar-ket in the USA, you would need to think about three principal and separate constraints on your ability to compete:

- Patents, the intellectual property rights granted by the US Patent and Trademark Office (USPTO). Patents are granted on the basis that the invention is useful, novel, non-obvious and hasn't been previously disclosed. They can be granted not only for the pharmaceutical itself but also for the pro-cesses involved in making it. A patent lasts for 20 years from the date of filing but can be extended for five years to com-pensate for regulatory approval time.
- Regulatory exclusivity, the delays and prohibitions on ap-proval of competitor drugs. Exclusivity, which is effectively an exclusive marketing right, is granted by the FDA and lasts five years for a new drug, seven years for a drug covered by the Orphan Drug Act, and 12 years for a biological drug.[2]
- Trademarks and copyrights, which apply to pharmaceuticals as much as other sectors. These laws limit what a pharma-ceutical product can be called and how it can be presented. Pharmaceuticals can also be protected by "trade dress," such as the physical appearance of a pill, if the look of the product is strongly associated with its source.

In reality, the intellectual property and regulatory exclusivity con-straints on competition are much more complicated than this but their details are beyond the scope of this book. The lesson to draw here is that patents and exclusivity create significant constraints on competition in addition to the economic and regulatory barriers to entry. These are, however, only the statutory constraints on competition. As I'll discuss later, there are also commercial factors that make it difficult for new drugs to compete after they have entered the market and when patents and exclusivity are not an issue.

At first, it might seem surprising that the United States, with its strong free-market traditions, should constrain market forces in this way but, looked at from an ecological perspective, it's another example of the PIE trying to achieve homeostasis or balance between competing pressures. On one side is the desire to maximize competition, with the aim of encouraging value-adding activity that improves products and reduces costs. On the other is the need to limit competition so that the market is profitable enough to justify investment in innovation. These two countervailing considerations apply to all markets, and most countries have intellectual property laws aimed at achieving the right balance between encouraging innovation and enabling imitation. So fundamental is this innovation/imitation balancing act that it was included in the US constitution.[3] There are skeptics, who believe that patent law hinders innovation; but even they acknowledge that pharmaceuticals are a special case where the benefits outweigh the costs.[4]

As in other parts of the PIE, there are some specific characteristics of the pharmaceutical market that make finding the balance between innovation and imitation especially important. These include the relatively high costs of innovation (around $1.3 billion) compared to the relatively low costs of imitation (in the millions or low hundreds of millions)[5] and the relatively high risks that a pharmaceutical innovation might fail. Both these factors discourage investors in innovation and imply the need to compensate by limiting competition. At the same time, the USA's unusually unregulated pricing and the social implications of high medicine costs both favor encouraging competition with the aim of limiting prices. We can add to these factors political goals to support an economically important industry and to encourage innovation toward specific areas, such as rare diseases. The aggregated result of these forces is the unusually constrained nature of competition in innovative pharmaceuticals, as described in Box 8.1. I've chosen to call the part of the PIE where these forces interact and find their balance point the competition habitat. In this chapter, I'll explore how it works and how it both helps and hinders the healthy functioning of the PIE.

What happens in the competition habitat and who inhabits it?

Although competition is inextricably bound up with the rest of the PIE, thinking of the competition habitat as a distinct part of the overall PIE is a useful way of understanding how it works and how it interacts with the other habitats. In essence, the competition habitat tries to optimize both innovation and imitation by balancing innovation-incentivizing constraints on competition and competition-enabling free markets against each other. Its outputs are laws, like Waxman-Hatch and the Orphan Drug Act, that take the competitive environment further away from totally unconstrained competition (see Box 8.1). Since the instruments of competition constraint are statutory, the competition habitat has two primary mechanisms: influencing legislators to shift the balance and fighting legal battles to establish the effect of that legislation. This means that there are three principal inhabitants of the competition habitat: the innovators, the imitators, and the legislators and their agencies.

The interests of pharmaceutical innovators lie in making patent, exclusivity, and trademark laws as protective of innovation as possible, pulling the balance point toward limiting competition. They do this through their internal resources such as Government Affairs Departments, their trade organizations (e.g. PhRMA and BIO), and an extended array of lobbying firms, specialized lawyers and industry-sponsored Political Action Committees. This is a very large-scale effort. In 2020, the pharmaceuticals and health products industry spent twice as much on lobbying ($306 million) as any other industry.[6] Between 1999 and 2018, the industry spent $4.7 billion on lobbying and campaign contributions.[7] Prior to the 2020 presidential election, more than two-thirds of Congress received some funding from pharmaceutical companies.[8] Not all of this was spent by pharmaceutical innovators and not all of this effort was directed at shifting the balance in the competitive environment, some were also aimed at influencing drug pricing regulation and other aspects of the commercial environment, such as the negotiating power of Medicare.[9] However, the bulk of lobbying effort can be attributed to the research-intensive part of the industry. In 2021, for example, PhRMA spent approximately $30 million on lobbying while the Biotechnology Innovation Association, its biotech counterpart, spent around $13 million.[10]

On the other side of the equation are those seeking to limit constraints on competition and enable imitation. These are represented by alliances such as CAPA (the Campaign Against Patent Abuse), the AAM (Association for Accessible Medicines), and the Biosimilars Forum. In contrast to the pharmaceutical innovators, these counterbalancing entities in the competition habitat are a relatively heterogenous coalition, whose interests overlap in places, rather than a homogeneous and focused industry grouping whose interests align closely. They include those who wish to compete with the innovative companies with generics and biosimilars and those who might benefit from lower medicine costs, such as healthcare providers, insurers, and patient groups. The scale of this counterbalancing effort is also considerably less than that of the innovative medicine companies. The AAM, for example, spent $2.8 million on lobbying in 2021, about one-tenth of what PhRMA spends, an amount that places AAM about 30th in the table of the pharmaceutical healthcare lobbying effort.[11] Salient among those on this side of the debate are the Arnold Foundation that has spent over $100 million since 2010 in support of lower drug prices.[12]

It's worth noting that both of these lobbying efforts are perfectly legal and in many ways positive. Well-informed legislators are better than ill-informed legislators, and lobbyists are one source of legislators' information. There is evidence that firms' innovation performance is associated with political connections.[13] Equally, however, there is evidence that lobbying does shape the legislative environment[14] in favor of innovators.

Between these two forces lie legislators and the agencies through which they act, such as the FDA and USPTO. Compared to many other issues, there is significant bipartisan consensus on the need to find the right balance both in the law and in its enactment.[15] That said, my exploration of the competition habitat found a great deal of concern over the effective balance of patent law and its application.[16] Some of this concern arises from the significant overlap between government bodies and the pharmaceutical industry lobbying network, with close to 60% of lobbyists being former government employees.[17] In any case, reform of patent law and other legislation relating to the competition habitat is a long-standing issue, and there has been little significant progress in recent years.[18]

Compared to other habitats, the competitive habitat appears relatively simple: two sides, fighting to influence the legislative environment that sets the balance between rewarding innovation and enabling competitive imitation. The costs and risks that are characteristic of pharmaceutical innovation make this balancing act especially difficult but, at the same time, the social and economic importance of pharmaceutical innovation make it especially important. It was with this difficulty and importance in mind that I set out to understand what a healthy PIE requires of the competition habitat.

What does a healthy PIE require of the competition habitat?

A healthy PIE requires that the competition habitat achieves a balance between encouraging valuable innovation and enabling price-reducing imitation. The history of the habitat, with repeated adjustments, shows how difficult this is in practice, while the continuing debate and ongoing criticism of the current patent and regulatory exclusivity systems suggest that even those adjustments might not have achieved the right balance. To do so, a healthy PIE needs three things of the competition habitat.

The competition habitat must incentivize valuable innovation

A well-functioning competition habitat will allow risk-adjusted rates of return sufficient to incentivize continuing investment in pharmaceutical innovation but no more than that. To do so effectively, a healthy PIE requires that the competition habitat reduces the risk of direct imitators for sufficient time that, at a price based on ecologically valid value, the innovator can achieve a risk-adjusted rate of return that justifies their investment. A competition habitat that does not limit direct competition well enough or long enough or that limits competition beyond what is needed to incentivize valuable innovation, would not sustain a healthy PIE.

The competition habitat must enable valuable imitation

A well-functioning competition habitat will enable direct imitators to enter the market as quickly, easily, and inexpensively as possible after the period of limited competition needed to incentivize innovation, but not before that. To do so effectively, a healthy PIE requires that the competition habitat minimizes the possibility that the period of limited competition can be ended before or be extended beyond that needed to incentivize innovation. A competition habitat that can be subverted to allow premature direct imitation or can be manipulated to delay that direct imitation would not sustain a healthy PIE.

The competition habitat must maximize the predictability of the competitive environment

A well-functioning competition habitat will enable all innovators, imitators, and other stakeholders to confidently predict both the extent and the period of limited competition. To do so effectively, a healthy PIE requires that the competition habitat minimizes ambiguity about the parameters of competition and their time periods. A competition habitat that allows significant unpredictability of protection from direct competition would not sustain a healthy PIE.

These three requirements flow directly from the purpose of the competition habitat, which is to balance the incentivization of innovation with the enablement of imitation, while recognizing the complementary purposes of other habitats, especially the value and pricing habitats. The first requirement recognizes that the incentive to invest in valuable

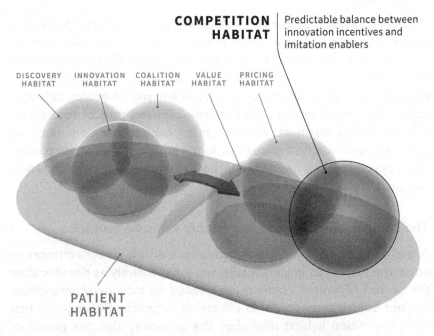

COMPETITION HABITAT   Predictable balance between innovation incentives and imitation enablers

DISCOVERY HABITAT   INNOVATION HABITAT   COALITION HABITAT   VALUE HABITAT   PRICING HABITAT

PATIENT HABITAT

Figure 8.1 The competition habitat's contribution to a healthy PIE

innovation is created by the returns possible and that this is a function of both the period of exclusivity and the value-based price, which is an output of healthy value and price habitats. The second requirement recognizes that valuable imitation is enabled not just by the returns possible but by the ease of realizing those returns. The ease and therefore cost of imitator-entry becomes especially significant when profits are relatively low, as they are likely to be once competitive restraints are ended. The third requirement recognizes that both innovation and imitation are influenced not only by returns but also by the probability of achieving those returns. This is partly a function of the predictability of the limits on competition, since a competition constraint (such as a period of patent protection) that may be lengthened, shortened, or removed is a business risk that influences the decision to innovate or imitate.

It's important to note too what these requirements don't include. They don't recognize any need for the competitive habitat to influence the direction of innovation and imitation toward particular diseases or technologies. This is a significant point of departure from the current competition habitat that, via the Orphan Drug Act and other means, tries to differentially incentivize some therapies. In a market where price is strongly tethered to value, this role for the competition habitat would be obviated by value-based pricing, as described in Chapter 7 (the pricing habitat) and, in some cases, by recommendations included in Chapter 9 (the patient habitat). This doesn't mean that the competition habitat has no role to play in directing research; it still has a role in complementing a value-based pricing system and perhaps correcting the limitations of a market system. But the primary role of the competition habitat is to encourage valuable innovation and to enable valuable imitation.

So, it was with these three requirements in mind that I examined, with the help of my expert informants and an extensive prior literature, how well the competition habitat was currently able to support a healthy PIE.

Is the competition habitat capable of supporting a healthy PIE?

No exploration of the PIE would be complete without considering the role of the competition habitat. As I did, my expert informants talked to me about three different but important reasons to worry about its ability to support a healthy PIE.

The first is the competition habitat's role as a positive feedback loop. A malfunctioning competition habitat, one that gets the balance between unrestricted and constrained competition wrong, would inappropriately hinder either innovation or imitation. The former is obviously detrimental for the provision of innovative medicines but so too is the latter. Imitation, for example via generic or biosimilar competition, creates competition that drives down the prices of older products. This enables healthcare spending to shift from those older products toward newer, innovative medicines. In this indirect way, imitation enables further innovations. The two are linked in a virtuous circle, the sort of positive feedback loop that is found in all ecosystems.

The second is the risk of regulatory capture. In any market, unequal distribution of lobbying resources is a warning sign that one interest group might have undue influence over the government agencies involved. So too is evidence of "revolving doors" between industries and their regulators.[19] In the case of pharmaceutical innovation, there is a large imbalance in both the scale and coordination of political activity and, for decades, authors have expressed concern that the competition habitat is out of balance.[20]

The third is that history may have given us a sub-optimal competition habitat. The laws around competition show all the signs of evolutionary adaptation. From the Orphan Drug Act of 1983, the Waxman-Hatch of 1984, the FDA Modernization Act of 1997, the Best Pharmaceuticals for Children Act of 2002, the Biologics Price Competition and Innovation Act of 2009 to the 21st Century Cures Act of 2016, along with other legislation, we can follow attempts to adapt a simple system to evolve in the face of selection pressures from a complex environment. But evolution is not teleological; it does not have an end goal. It is a messy, incremental process that focuses on immediate problems. This leads to evolutionary kludges, clumsy solutions you would never choose to design that way.[21] Given the history of the competition habitat, we ought to expect to see these, and for them to hinder the working of the habitat and the health of the PIE.

To be clear, I'm *not* saying that these three issues – the feedback loop, regulatory capture and evolutionary kludges – are proven problems in the competition habitat. But they are all issues that make it reasonable to consider the working of this habitat. With these in mind and using the PIE's requirements of the competition habitat as my indicators of proper functioning, I explored the competition habitat and distilled my findings to five principal issues.

The patent system discriminates against difficult and radical innovation

The purpose of the patent system is to indirectly incentivize innovation by temporarily limiting direct imitation. As such, patents have become very important to the PIE because they act as a signal of future profitability, which attracts investment. But the patent system, at least as it is currently applied to pharmaceuticals, is largely indiscriminate regarding the difficulty of the innovation. Expert informant Thomas Dorazio explained this to me.

> Without a good patent, it's very hard to get investment. And it has become increasingly binary; you either have a patent and get investment or you don't and you don't. But the patent system doesn't really discriminate well between small, relatively easy innovations and large, difficult innovations. Inevitably, this influences R&D strategy.
>
> Thomas Dorazio

This lack of discriminatory power is significant because incremental innovation is generally easier, cheaper, and faster than radical innovation, so the same fixed-term patent award may encourage quick and easy innovation over slow and difficult innovation. The current system recognizes this and tries to compensate in a limited way by allowing patent extensions for up to five years to allow for delays in regulatory approval. But the time taken to develop an innovative medicine is a function of many things, including the therapeutic class, the molecule type, and other factors, such as whether the therapy manages, cures, or prevents a disease.[22] As a result, the effective patent life for a small, quick innovation, may be much longer, even with a patent extension, than for a more impactful innovation with a lengthier development time. If so, the implication is that the fixed-term patent system discriminates against innovation with longer development times. To the extent that these are typically more radical and clinically valuable, this must shape the nature of the pharmaceutical innovation to emerge from the PIE.

The evidence seems to support this implicit discrimination by the current patent system. One extensive study of the subject found that "the U.S. legal system may be systematically skewing drug research incentives away from the harder problems."[23] Researchers who looked more specifically at investment in cancer clinical trials found that firms invest less in drugs that take a long time to bring to market.[24] Another study found that 78% of drugs associated with new patents were existing products rather than new ones.[25] This focus on incremental innovations seems to translate into some new products not being substantially better than existing products. For example, other work found that 41% of drugs that were approved through the FDA's non-expedited channels offered either no or negative improvement on existing treatments.[26] This is consistent with the results of a study of 147 new drugs authorized by the European Medicines Agency, which found that less than half of them were valuable by the standards of German health technology assessments.[27]

Taken as a whole, it seems clear that the patent element of the competitive habitat is a blunt tool with respect to encouraging innovation. Even with patent extensions to allow for longer development times, it does not fully compensate for the greater time, cost, and difficulty of "harder" more radical innovations compared to incremental innovations. The evidence would suggest that this nudges the focus of innovation away from the former and toward the latter. This is not, of course, to impugn the value of incremental innovations, which are sometimes valuable in both their economic and health impact.[28] But both the nature of scientific research and the risk-adjusted rate of return drivers of pharmaceutical innovation inherently favor incrementalism over radical innovation, and the patent element of the competition habitat does not fully compensate for that. This hinders its ability to meet the first requirement of a healthy PIE, that of encouraging valuable innovation.

Regulatory exclusivity directs innovation crudely

Like the patent system, the FDA regulatory exclusivity system aims to incentivize innovation by limiting competition. But it differs from the patent system in that it offers different periods of exclusivity – and therefore different incentives – to different kinds of pharmaceutical innovation. By offering, for example, five years of exclusivity to a small molecule drug, seven years to an orphan drug, and 12 years to a biologic, it makes a judgment and sends a signal about what innovations might merit investment more than others. And, unlike patents, since these terms begin at registration, they don't run into the same issue of variable effective length. One informant, an expert in regulatory exclusivity who chose to remain anonymous, described its effect to me.

*The various differences in exclusivity period are intended to encourage inno-
vation and, in the case of biologics for example, they seem to have done this.
But, as with patents, the exclusivity system for small molecules has its issues,
most notably in the case of 505 b(2) applications, where the product relies on
another product's safety studies and a narrow approval can be interpreted to
block subsequent applications for those additional differentiated products for
a disease, especially those that have the same active moiety.*

Anonymous

In effect, the regulatory exclusivity system tries to do what the patent
system doesn't – segment pharmaceutical innovations and encourage
innovation toward certain types of products. The seven-year period
for orphan drugs, for example, is intended to compensate for the
small market size of these products, which might otherwise deter investment. The 12-year period for biologics is aimed at compensating
for the greater cost and duration of those products' development,
which are very different from traditional, small-molecule drugs. And,
although other factors are also at play, these attempts at steering
pharmaceutical innovation seem to have had a marked effect. In 2019,
44% of FDA approvals went to orphan drugs.[29] As of 2020, biologic
drugs were about one in four of all new drug approvals.[30] So, at first
sight, this segmentation of exclusivity incentives approach would seem
to be working. But, as I learned time and time again in my exploration
of the PIE, the picture is almost always more complicated than it first
appears. So, I explored further, and three issues emerged.

The first is that using disease categories and molecule types is a
very crude way to segment pharmaceutical innovation. For example,
while some drugs take longer than others to develop, the biologic/
small-molecule categorization is a poor proxy for that, and there is
some evidence that biologics are less likely to fail during development
and approval.[31] At the same time, while the orphan drugs category
includes both orphan and ultra-orphan drugs, their exclusivity period
takes little account of these drugs differing from each other in development time.[32] Targeting exclusivity by these simple categories seems
clumsy, somewhat like targeting consumers by age or gender, an approach that marketers found ineffective decades ago.

The second is that this incentivization approach is open to abuse,
particularly in the case of orphan drugs.[33] The US Government Accountability Office found that the FDA's application of the Orphan
Drug Act wasn't meeting the intent of the law. Other studies have

identified a range of tactics to take advantage of orphan drug status. These tactics include "salami slicing" a common disease into smaller indications, repurposing mass-market drugs and repurposing an adult drug for children. Perhaps the most questionable use of orphan drug status has been its application to Remdesivir to treat Covid-19 on the basis that, in March 2020, there were sufficiently few confirmed cases that it met the criteria for an orphan drug.[34] Again, targeting exclusivity by simple categories seems open to abuse, much like some forms of targeting social benefits has been found to be.

The third but arguably least considered weakness in the targeting of regulatory exclusivity lies in its intent and echoes back to my observations in Chapter 3 (the discovery habitat), regarding the cultural orientation of the PIE toward clinical rather than social sciences. The current framing of incentives via regulatory exclusivity focuses on innovative medicines with better clinical outcomes but, while these are obviously important, they are not the only dimension of what society expects of the social contract. Health economic outcome or "bang for bucks" is also important. It's arguable that innovative medicines that provide the same outcomes for much lower healthcare costs are as important as those that improve outcomes but at higher overall healthcare costs.[35] And, like generics or biosimilars, "better bang for bucks" therapies would allow a shift in healthcare spend toward more innovative medicines and treatments. Yet the current exclusivity system, based on disease and molecule categories, seems to make no attempt at incentivizing better health economic outcomes except those that coincide with better clinical outcomes. Recently, some researchers have proposed linking regulatory exclusivity to health impact and its proposed price[36] but, at present, targeting incentives by regulatory exclusivity largely neglects the health economic needs of society.

Looked at in the round, the regulatory exclusivity system seems in poor shape. It directs innovation clumsily, is open to abuse, and doesn't consider innovation that might provide better value without better clinical outcomes. As with the patent system, this part of the competition habitat doesn't seem fully capable of supporting a healthy PIE.

The competition habitat hinders predictability

Being able to predict how much protection from competition an innovative medicine has and when imitation will occur is valuable for many stakeholders in the PIE. For payers, patients, and plan sponsors, it influences their choices and allows prediction of future costs. For innovators, it allows a more accurate calculation of overall returns, which influences the quality of investment and pricing decisions. For imitators, predictability informs judgments about what to imitate. Predictability also strengthens the social contract since it reassures all parties about the terms of the contract and reduces fears of contract abuse. There is a secondary effect from predictability too. In any economic system, uncertainty and risk are compensated for by higher capital costs. A well-functioning competition habitat, that protects innovation with certainty and enables imitation with confidence, ought to reduce capital costs and help affordability. Certainty and confidence about the limitations on competition are essential properties of a well-functioning competition habitat, as the third requirement, above, implies.

Any explorer of the competition habitat can't help but notice that it is a very noisy place. There are vociferous arguments that the competition habitat works well and equally voluble contentions that it is hindering both innovation and affordability. As I explored, I had to listen carefully to separate the subjective from the objective. Among my expert informants, the common ground was that the competition habitat did not provide the predictability the PIE needs. The views of Scott Lassman and John Glasspool were typical.

> *The whole innovation system depends on a cycle of innovation followed by loss of exclusivity and imitation. But this cycle can be and is damaged when the mechanisms of copying are hindered. We see this happening in the intellectual property tactics of some firms and it creates a perverse incentive for firms to compete with their patent lawyers rather than via genuine scientific innovation.*
>
> *John Glasspool*

> *The FDA's leeway in the interpretation of the exclusivity system creates uncertainty and legal risk. This is compounded by limited resources at the FDA and some regulations, on the review of orphan drugs for example, that need review. The system would work better if it were simplified.*
>
> *Scott Lassman*

To test this view that the habitat doesn't provide the required amount of predictability, I examined the research literature on the topic. It's complicated but, when I stepped back from the detail, four clear points came into view.

First, efforts by innovators to delay and diminish competition from imitators is a well-documented phenomenon[37] and a Congressional Budget Office report identified four main methods.[38]

- **Evergreening**: prolonging of effective patent protection by adding new patents as old ones expire
- **Product Hopping**: switching patients from an expiring brand to a newer version with later-expiring patents
- **Patent thickets**: amassing a large number of patents relating to a single product, sometimes with multiple parties
- **Pay for delay**: paying imitators to delay their market entry

Often, these methods are used in combination to extend the period of limited competition from generics or biosimilars. For balance, it's appropriate to note that many of these tactics can be justified in one way or another. For example, most pharmaceutical innovations can be improved on after initial patenting and those improvements may deserve some protection. But, overall, the picture is one of a determined effort by pharmaceutical innovators to slow down or prevent imitation as much as legally possible. This, inevitably, increases unpredictability in the competition habitat.

Second, the way the innovation to imitation cycle works looks very different depending on if you are looking at small molecule drugs or biologics. In the former, the US leads the world in substituting brand-name drugs with imitative generics. By volume, around 90% of drugs are generic. This is a higher rate than Europe, Canada, or other developed countries, and only India, at 97%, has higher generic substitution. But the picture looks very different for biologic drugs and their imitators, the biosimilars. At the time of writing, only 31 biosimilars have been approved in the US, compared to 70 in Europe. Only two have been given interchangeability status which means they can be used in place of a branded product in the same way as a generic small molecule drug.[39] As of 2020, biosimilars had only about 16% share of the biologics market and only about 30% of the markets for which they are approved, a significant lag compared to Europe.[40] It seems that, for many and varied reasons, the "biosimilarization" of biologic innovative drugs is not simply an echo of the "genericization" of small molecule drugs. Again, this increases the unpredictability of the competition habitat.

Third, the period that an innovative medicine is protected from competition varies in both predictable and unpredictable ways. For example, although this period has stayed fairly constant, at about 14 years after registration for small molecules, it varies according to how large the market is.[41] For many leading drugs, the period of protection varies widely between disease areas but independently of the degree of innovativeness.[42] And, predictably, the period of protection is significantly longer for biologics than for small molecules, at 21 vs 14 years.[43] As an illustration of the complexity of the variation, even a quite sophisticated model for predicting generic entry, developed by researchers at Harvard Medical School, was only able to achieve "reasonable" accuracy for some medicines and substantially overestimated others.[44] But the most obvious feature of this part of the debate is that the complexity of protection from competition has favored some skillful firms. By carefully navigating the system, some firms have been especially effective at extending their periods of protection from competition. One study of the 12 best-selling drugs in the US found that, on average, each drug has 125 patent applications, 71 patents issued, and 38 years of potential exclusivity.[45] The tactics used to extend protection from competition are detailed and arcane, but a dominant theme is the use of secondary patents filed after approval.[46] Even if such effective use of the system has little impact on average figures, such as the median period of protection from competition, it has a disproportionate impact on confidence in the social contract. Taken as a whole, the complexity of the patent and exclusivity systems clearly hinders the predictability of innovation and imitation and the ability of the competition habitat to meet that requirement of the PIE.

Finally, it's not clear that patent law always provides the strong protection it intends, since patents are only as strong as the holders' ability to defend them. Several expert informants pointed out that defending a patent was sometimes an impractical proposition for small organizations. In this, they were echoing a stream in the literature about the unpredictability of patent law and its effect on pharmaceutical innovation.[47] It seems reasonable to imply that protection from competition is not only a function of the pharmaceutical innovation but may vary with the competence of a firm's lawyers.

With all the sound and fury about patents, regulatory exclusivity and other aspects of the competition habitat, it's not always easy to pick out the signals from the noise but, taking these four points together, a clear message does emerge. It is one of variability and unpredicta-bility. The complexity of the competition habitat offers extensive op-portunities both to challenge and to extend protection, and some firms have adapted to work in this environment more effectively than others. This results in unpredictability for both innovators and imita-tors, both of whom have to navigate a maze of protections that vary with interpretation and the details of the context. And, in the case of biologics, the unpredictability of the patent and regulatory systems is amplified by the complications of the approval and interchangeability systems. Whatever other merits the competition habitat has, provid-ing predictability is not one of them.

As a scientist and not a lawyer, this unpredictability perplexed me. Thankfully, I was able to call on the expertise of Graham Dutfield, an expert informant who has recently written the definitive text on the history of the pharmaceutical industry with an emphasis on the role of intellectual property.[48] He explained to me that these traits of the competition habitat were artifacts of the system's history.

> We have a system that wasn't designed but evolved. It's useful to recall that the patent system developed for relatively simple inventions, things like chemi-cals, and that it covers products and processes. In that respect, small molecule drugs, with their simple structures and synthetic pathways, are not too far away from what the authors of patent law had in mind. By contrast, modern drugs, especially biologics, are more like a web of product and process inven-tions. When innovator companies execute intellectual property strategies that include evergreening, patent thickets and so on they're not doing anything illegal. They're just taking advantage of a system that wasn't really designed to cope with complex products.
>
> Graham Dutfield

This historical explanation clarifies the issue but doesn't resolve it. It seems clear that the current patent and regulatory exclusivity system doesn't provide predictability regarding how much protection from competition an innovative medicine has or when imitation will occur. As such, it seems unable to meet the needs of a healthy PIE.

Know-how and trade secrets limit imitation of advanced therapies

Given the preceding three points, it's useful to remind ourselves that incentivizing innovation, mostly by limiting competition, is not the only function of the competition habitat. Its other role is to enable imitation. Historically, patents have fulfilled that role by requiring the innovator to make public information that would help imitators to imitate once the protection expired.[49] One expert informant, who asked me not to identify him or his firm, made this point strongly

> Some critics of the pharmaceutical patent system pay too little attention to the benefits of the disclosure. It makes public information that helps generics and biosimilars to compete with the originator company. If patents didn't exist, or we changed the system so that pharmaceutical companies didn't think patents were worth applying for, that would push this useful information back into the trade secrets of the companies and hinder the innovation-imitation cycle.
>
> *Anonymous*

This informant's important point is supported in the research literature, which generally shows how patent disclosure shapes firms' research trajectory and encourages competition, but with a complex picture of mixed and unintended consequences.[50] Other expert informants also echoed this benefit of patents but, as they did so, another theme emerged. Increasingly, this information value of patents is being eroded as innovative medicines become more complicated. Another expert informant who chose to contribute anonymously summarized this well.

> It was true, and may still be true, that for simple, small molecule drugs made by traditional synthesis methods the patent and exclusivity systems were both the main source of protection from competition and enabled competition after loss of market exclusivity. But that's becoming less true for biologics and the other advanced therapies that are emerging now. Firstly, those advanced products often involve a lot of know-how, trade secrets and tacit knowledge, not only in development but also in manufacturing. Secondly, some new therapies are personalized, an individual product for each patient or for a small sub-group of patients. Together, these two things make it much harder to copy a product in the way that generics copy small molecule drugs because the information disclosed in its patent doesn't – and maybe can't – include this sort of knowledge. One consequence of this may be that, in future, patents may become less valuable to imitators and some products may be uncopiable.
>
> *Anonymous*

These points, which represent common views among the expert informants, combine to create a very important threat to the working of the competition habitat. Trade secrets are a legal category of information quite separate from patents, protected by law from theft but not from independent invention. Increasingly, the sophistication of innovative medicines and the processes for making them means that innovative companies develop large amounts of trade secret information that is not shared in patent disclosures. Combined with an international legal trend toward broadening what is classed as a trade secret, this means that the value of information disclosed in patents is in relative decline.[51] The research literature in this area suggests that this prediction of uncopiable products and less-valuable future patents might already be coming true. Some research already points to trade secrets in biologics manufacturing as being a key reason for the relatively slow penetration of biosimilars.[52] Others point to a complementary trend toward "stealth innovation" in drug development, the withholding of information that might previously have been disclosed.[53] Still others argue that, unlike small molecule drugs, advanced therapies such as biologic drugs are so dependent on the specifics of their manufacturing process and the uniqueness of their structure that they are "natural monopolies" that can't be copied and require different approaches to making the innovation-imitation cycle work.[54]

On balance, it seems likely that the disclosure requirements of patents will continue to be valuable enablers of imitation, especially for small molecule drugs. But for biologic drugs and other advanced therapies, we may be approaching a situation where the non-disclosed trade secret information makes it impossible to imitate some innovative therapies even after the loss of patent or regulatory exclusivity.[55] To the extent that imitation becomes impossible, the competition habitat will have fundamentally changed and, unless it adapts in some way, it won't be able to meet the requirements for a healthy PIE.

The adoption of approved imitative products is hindered by market forces and inertia

Compared to that for other goods and services, the competition habitat for innovative medicines is heavily shaped and influenced by patent laws and regulatory exclusivity. That's why I felt it appropriate, in the preceding four points, to focus on those legal and regulatory aspects of the habitat that protects innovations and then makes imitation possible.

There is of course more to the competitive habitat than whether imitation is legally allowed. There is also the question of whether imitators are able to displace the incumbent innovators. This is true for both small molecules and for advanced therapies, such as biologics, although, as the different market share figures show, the competitive dynamics between those two areas are very different. By and large, genericization of small molecule markets has been much more extensive than the equivalent biosimilarization of the markets for biologics. This is important because of the relatively high cost of the latter.

The economic benefits of replacing biologic drugs with biosimilar imitators are undisputed and were summarized by expert informant Sean McGowan.

> *The US is at the "tweener" stage of biosimilar adoption and significantly behind Europe. Such adoption as there is has mostly been for drugs administered in hospitals and doctors' offices but it will come for drugs taken at home. When it does happen, switching to biosimilars pushes down average selling prices, which in some cases also reduces the fees charged for administering the drug and both those factors become more important when insurers push more costs onto patients. There are other benefits too. Biosimilars extend choice and of course they push innovative companies to innovate further.*
>
> *Sean McGowan*

Sean McGowan's main point here, that biosimilars would reduce costs, is supported by quantitative analysis. A scenario analysis by the RAND corporation estimated savings of between \$38 billion and \$124 billion, depending on how quickly biosimilars were taken up and how much price competition they provoked.[56] Other, narrower studies in specific contexts point in the same general direction.[57] What these studies show, in addition to the cost-saving potential, is the sensitivity of their estimates to how well the market mechanism works. If, as in a perfect market, lower cost biosimilars rapidly and fully replace branded reference products wherever medically appropriate, the savings will be substantial. If not, then the innovation-imitation cycle will not be working the way it is intended, hindering the flow of healthcare spending toward new innovative medicines.

The mechanisms of biosimilar price competition with branded reference products lie in the border territory between the competition habitat, the pricing habitat and the value habitat. As I described in Chapters 6 and 7, neither the pricing nor the value habitat meets the requirements of a healthy PIE, so it would be surprising if the competition habitat behaved like an economist's perfect market and enabled full and rapid biosimilar penetration. My discussions with expert informants in this area didn't provide any such surprises, but they did reveal a wealth of detail about how imperfect the competition habitat was with respect to biosimilars. Both the simplicity and the nuances of the situation were described by Juliana Reed and Sonia Oskouei.

> *Biosimilars have to unlock a number of doors to get to the market. First, there's getting past the legal challenges of the originators, then there's getting onto formulary listings, then there's overcoming prescribers' inertia, then there's empowering patients and plan sponsors to demand biosimilars. Each of these steps slows down the cost savings possible from biosimilars.*
>
> Juliana Reed

> *It's important to understand the granularity of the biologics and biosimilar market. Each has a different context and driving uptake is an individual challenge rather than an overall issue. Physician concerns and treatment guidelines, payers and PBM's deals with originators, patients' clinical issues and concerns about equivalence. All of this adds up to a "context thicket" that slows down uptake and requires work to drive adoption.*
>
> Sonia Oskouei

As with other aspects of the competition habitat, it's easy to get sucked into the detail of how imperfect the biosimilar market is but, stepping back, there are really four significant issues.

The first is related to the market power imbalances I described in Chapter 7. Because highly concentrated payers (such as insurance companies) and providers (such as hospitals) have relatively more market power than patients and plan sponsors, they are able to act in their own economic interests rather than those of their customers. For payers, this self-interested behavior includes cutting rebate deals with pharmaceutical companies across a range of products. If the economics of that bundled deal outweighs that of an individual, cheaper biosimilar, then they do what any profit-driven entity does and cut the best deal they can. This tactic used by large originators is known as the rebate wall[58] and has been extensively investigated by the Federal Trade Commission.[59]

The second market imperfection is seen in the prescribing behavior of physicians, who have shown significant inertia in the uptake of biosimilars.[60] The reasons behind this are complex, involving both natural conservatism, lack of knowledge and, in some cases, financial incentives to prescribe more expensive drugs.[61] The third, which connects strongly to the second, is the lack of interchangeability status for most biosimilars.[62] This feeds into physicians' concerns about the substitutability of biologics and, in some cases, makes the switch administratively more cumbersome. Finally, some of the inertia of the market may be attributable to the purchasing mechanisms themselves, as expert informant Ian Henshaw explained.

> *When I look at biosimilar adoption in the U.S. compared to the EU, it's clear that contracting still needs to evolve. Europe has evolved a sophisticated tendering and contracting process. Biosimilars are much more expensive to develop and to make than generics and have a very different risk profile for all parties. In some cases, biosimilar manufacturers have been forced to exit markets because of these unrealistic expectations. The situation is changing daily and the systems in the U.S. seem to be on a steep learning curve.*
>
> *Ian Henshaw*

These various market imperfections combine to produce the relatively slow uptake, to date, of biosimilars in the US.[63] They exist independently of the issues to do with patents and regulatory exclusivity. As I write, there are promising signs that biosimilar uptake is accelerating. Many large biologics are about to lose exclusivity and biosimilars are beginning to spread out of the specialty channel and into the retail channel.[64] If this trend continues, it will mean that this post-approval part of the competition habitat is better able to support a healthy PIE. Until it does, or if it does not, then it won't meet that need.

I was very lucky, as a researcher, to have the help of my expert informants as I explored the competition habitat. I was lucky, too, that many earlier researchers had previously explored parts of this territory and published very good work. Not only did this make my job easier, but it also gave me confidence to stand back, look at the bigger picture, and have confidence in my conclusions. Those conclusions are disappointing. The legal and regulatory elements of the habitat are meant to incentivize innovation and to direct it, but they are poorly designed for either task. Insensitive to degrees of innovation and to the dimensional variations within pharmaceutical innovation, the system shows its history and past political manipulation.

In addition, the patent and regulatory exclusivity systems also fail in their task of providing predictability. Their susceptibility to manipulation, especially for complex and advanced products, introduces uncertainty that weakens the whole system. The future is worrisome too. We may be heading to an era where imitation of the most advanced products is limited by trade secrets and tacit knowledge, which would weaken the innovation-imitation cycle that drives the competition habitat. Even if this were true only for a minority of innovations, this would have serious consequences for the PIE.

Finally, even if by some wave of my magic wand I could make the patent and exclusivity systems work perfectly, I would still be faced with a market that, despite promising signs, is currently made imperfect by vested interests, conservatism, and a misplaced belief that biosimilarization is genericization 2.0. These observations may sound overly pessimistic, especially from the perspective of those for whom the current competition habitat is comfortable. But I'm an optimist and, armed with the knowledge of the habitat's imperfections, I pushed on to how it might be if not perfected then improved.

How can we improve the competition habitat?

A well-functioning competition habitat is essential to a healthy PIE. A competition habitat that doesn't protect innovation and enable imitation, each with a high degree of predictability, would render the PIE incapable of delivering the sustainable stream of affordable, innovative medicines we desire. Equally, a competition habitat that doesn't support the value and pricing habitats in directing the PIE toward valuable innovation would leave important needs unmet and waste innovative resources. An unpredictable competition habitat that makes protection from competition uncertain and susceptible to manipulation would both hinder the PIE and weaken the social contract. And a competition habitat that prevented the shifting of healthcare spend from old products to new would slow the innovation-imitation cycle. As I described above, I ended my exploration of this habitat concluding that it is currently far from where it needs to be. If we want a competition habitat that balances innovation and imitation, sustains the PIE, and supports the social contract, there is much work to be done. In this section, I suggest what the main themes of that work might be.

Improve the discriminatory power of the patent law

A healthy competition habitat must not only incentivize innovation but also recognize that the market, driven by risk-adjusted return on investment, naturally favors lower cost, lower risk incremental innovation and compensate for that. Without that compensation, usually in the form of a higher reward, incremental innovation is favored over radical innovation by default. The patent system, at least as it is currently applied, has evolved so that it doesn't discriminate well between different levels of innovation. Consequently, by omission rather than commission, it nudges pharmaceutical innovation toward incrementalism. Changing the effect of patent law, so that it differentiated more effectively between incremental and radical innovation, would enable the competition habitat to better meet the requirements of the PIE.

In practice, this means finding a way to award more, or the same, protection from competition to radical innovations and less, or none, to incremental innovations. This is obviously a task for highly skilled experts in the field but, to them, I offer three considerations to guide their work. First, US patent law is inextricably connected, via the WTO TRIPS arrangements, to international trade.[65] Even if it were a sub-optimal solution, better application of existing US patent law achieved quickly, might arguably be better than a best-solution change to US patent law, which could take many years to achieve.

Second, the application of current patentability criteria already offers potential for greater discrimination. Some have suggested a more probing application of the "novelty" criterion.[66] Others have focused on the "useful" criterion.[67] Still others think the "non-obvious" criterion has the most potential to improve the discriminatory power of the patent system.[68] Together, these perspectives suggest that changes to the application of patent laws, rather than changes in those laws, might be the most pragmatic way of improving its discriminatory power.

Third, some have argued that the answer to improving the discriminatory power of patents lies in not in their granting, but in what happens after granting of the patent.[69] This means that the discriminatory power of patent law might be improved both pre-and post- granting of the patent.

The complexity of patent law, amplified by its entanglement with international agreements, implies a pragmatic, rather than an extreme approach to improving the discriminatory power of the competition habitat. But even a pragmatic approach ought to result in protection from competition that compensates for the market's inbuilt preference for incrementalism. This means that, in one way or another, incremental innovations would be less protected by patents, compared to radical innovations. Seeing this, an ecologist would warn us to expect innovators to compensate for this in some way. This might take the form of falling back on other forms of protection, such as trade secrets, trademarks, or copyrights. A realist approach to improving the competition habitat should anticipate that and aim to avoid any unintended consequences, such as reduced disclosure in patents. In any case, whether changes are to patent law or only to their application, those changes should aim to incentivize radical innovation as a compensatory mechanism for a market that will always prefer incrementalism.

Align regulatory exclusivity incentives more closely to societal needs

The patent system part of the competition habitat struggles to discern between incremental and radical innovation, let alone heterogeneity in pharmaceutical innovation along other dimensions. Even with the improvements discussed above, it would not be able to direct pharmaceutical innovation toward particular goals. Currently, the regulatory exclusivity system, in alignment with the value and pricing habitats and the accelerated approval pathways in the innovation habitat, attempts to guide the PIE toward the most valuable innovations. But the present system does this only very crudely. It is open to abuse and considers only clinical needs, not economic needs, or wider social impact. By using simple categories – such as orphan drugs and biologics – as crude proxies for types of innovative medicines, it does not address the full heterogeneity of pharmaceutical innovation. An improved regulatory exclusivity system, one that guided pharmaceutical innovation more effectively towards the most valuable innovation, would enable a healthy PIE and strengthen the social contract.

To be effective, an improved approach to regulatory exclusivity would need to achieve two things:

- Group together varied pharmaceutical innovations on the basis of similarity in both their need for incentivization and their social value, independent of the other characteristics such as technology type or patient characteristics.
- Differentially incentivize those groups according to their social value and their need for incentivization beyond that provided by the market.

In other words, an effective regulatory exclusivity system would adopt a portfolio approach to incentivizing pharmaceutical innovation, one in which homogenous and distinct innovation segments were incentivized to different degrees and in different ways. A simplified illustration of this idea is shown in Figure 8.2.

To those tasked with implementing this portfolio approach, I offer four suggestions regarding execution. First, the need for incentivization is very likely to be multifactorial, including market factors, such as the size of the patient population, and technological factors, such as therapy type and intended outcomes. Second, social value is likely to be multifactorial, including clinical factors such as improvement of clinical outcomes, health economic factors such as the scale and scope of economic impact, and socio-political goals such as health equity. Third, those pharmaceutical innovations that have either a low need for incentivization or low social value, but not both, might best

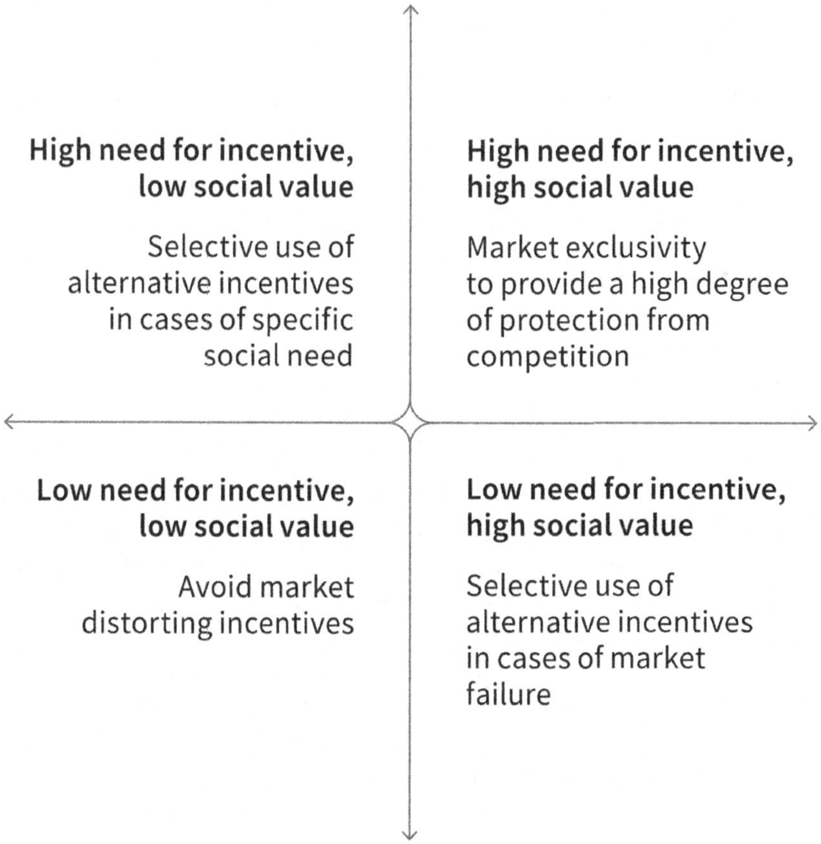

High need for incentive,
low social value

Selective use of
alternative incentives
in cases of specific
social need

High need for incentive,
high social value

Market exclusivity
to provide a high degree
of protection from
competition

Low need for incentive,
low social value

Avoid market
distorting incentives

Low need for incentive,
high social value

Selective use of
alternative incentives
in cases of market
failure

Figure 8.2 A portfolio approach to regulatory exclusivity

be incentivized in a specific and selective manner, using some combination of limited regulatory exclusivity and other incentives, such as direct subsidies or prizes.[70] Finally, use of regulatory exclusivity or other incentives to pharmaceutical innovation should avoid distorting the market by incentivizing innovation that isn't socially valuable and is already incentivized by the market.

I appreciate of course that this suggestion is radical. It might involve scrapping existing approaches, such as the Orphan Drug Act, and setting up a new system of regulatory exclusivity based on informed judgments about the need for incentives and social value. This should not be beyond the capabilities of the FDA, but it does require two societal choices that, ultimately, would have to be politically supported. The first is to accept a role for the FDA – probably working with other parts of the HHS – in making judgments about what is valuable to society. The second is to grant the FDA a degree of autonomy and insulation from political interference in executing this system. A regulatory exclusivity system of this type will invite manipulation, from which it must be protected. Both of these choices relate to the government's role in the healthcare system and as such require political discussion.

Improve the predictability of loss or exclusivity

Provision of predictability and minimization of manipulation are essential characteristics of a well-functioning competition habitat. This is true for both the patent and regulatory exclusivity parts of the habitat and for their joint effect. If it lacks those characteristics, the competition habitat hinders the working of the PIE and encourages competition between innovative lawyers rather than innovative scientists. The current competition habitat performs poorly in this respect, especially regarding more advanced products, mostly because of its complexity and potential for ambiguity. A competition habitat that provided more predictability and offered less potential for manipulation would improve the functioning of the PIE.

In practice, the two preceding suggestions would contribute to improved predictability and reduce manipulation. A more discriminatory patent system and regulatory exclusivity system based on homogenous, distinct innovation segments both offer opportunities to reduce ambiguity and gaming of the habitat. Beyond those two suggestions, there are other opportunities to improve the predictability of protection from competition. To those tasked with making the competition habitat more predictable, I offer three things to think about. First, it might be possible to offer to innovators simplified forms of protection. For example, the so-called "one and done" approach that combines both patent and regulatory exclusivities into a single period with a defined termination date.[71] Executed well, this could both improve the certainty of protection and reduce the possibilities to extend it. Second, improvement in predictability might be achieved by increasing the resources available and effort applied to both patent and regulatory assessments. This would have the merit of being achievable without any change in laws or regulations. Third, improved cooperation between the several government agencies involved in the competition habitat – the PTO, the FDA, and the FTC – might help reduce manipulative or even illegal competitive activity. Again, this would be possible without any legal changes and would not place any added burden on innovative or imitative companies.[72]

On the face of it, this third recommendation appears simpler and easier than the preceding two. A voluntary alternative to the current patent/regulatory system, improved resources for assessment, and cooperation between government agencies all seem to be, in comparison to raising patent standards or rebuilding the regulatory exclusivity system, very simple options. But the apparent simplicity belies the choice for American society implied by these suggestions. This choice would be to accept that the competition habitat is designed not only to incentivize innovation but also to enable imitation. This runs counter to traditionally held views, as implied in the constitution, that its function is only the former. If Americans choose to accept these twin roles, then the above suggestions should be eminently actionable. If not, then ideas like "one and done," more resources for assessment and inter-agency cooperation could very easily be opposed politically and prevented effectually.

Enable market forces to pull through lower cost, imitative products

The PIE needs more than for the patent and regulatory exclusivity systems to incentivize innovation and enable imitation, both with a high degree of predictability. It also requires that lower-cost, imitative products are pulled through to the market by customer demand, allowing healthcare spending to flow from older medicines to newer, innovative medicines. Without that, older, yet still expensive, medicines will absorb the healthcare dollars that ought to reward and incentivize innovation. Metaphorically, this would apply the brakes to the innovation-imitation cycle. In the current competition habitat, the delayed penetration of biosimilars, and sometimes of generic small molecules, suggests that these brakes are at least partly applied. Releasing them, by enabling market forces to pull through lower cost, innovative products would help the competition habitat to support a healthy PIE.

In practice, this means addressing the multiple mechanisms that hinder market forces. The suggestions in Chapter 7 (the pricing habitat) are intended to address some of these, such as the perverse incentives of intermediaries to prefer more expensive medicines. But other issues would remain even if patients and plan sponsors created pull-through for lower-cost medicines. To those who would need to address these remaining issues, I offer three practical considerations. First, the regulatory position on interchangeability will likely hinder biosimilar penetration until it is changed. This makes extending the range of interchangeable biosimilars a priority.[73] Second, the prescribing behavior of physicians is notorious for its conservatism. It is amplified by patients' understandable reluctance to switch from what works. This means that a concerted effort by clinical educators, payers, and providers is probably necessary to both "push" and "pull" the use of lower-cost biosimilars. Third, the economics of biosimilars, both in development and manufacture, are very different from those of generic small molecule drugs. In addition, some clinical issues make switching less straightforward and more costly. Together, these mean that both manufacturers and purchasers of biosimilars will need to co-develop new, mutually acceptable, procurement processes. These are likely to be more sophisticated than those for generics.

It is important not to be naïve about the consequences of and barriers to an enabled market, especially for biologics. Despite their relatively small share of the market by volume, these high-priced products provide much of the pharmaceutical industry's profit stream. Its sudden decline would be difficult for the industry to adapt to and might destabilize the PIE. It might also create issues around security of supply if, as has happened in generics, a small number of companies come to dominate biosimilar production. The first issue is likely to be ameliorated by the inertia of the market, resulting in slower than possible change. In time, reduction in profits from biologic drugs late in their life cycle ought to be compensated for by the suggestions made in Chapters 3 and 4 (the discovery habitat and innovation habitat), which aim to reduce both the costs and risks of innovation. The second issue of supply security can only be addressed by the development of strategic procurement behavior by payers, that is diversifying procurement to support a healthy degree of competition.

Provide alternative imitation mechanisms for hard-to-imitate products

The competition habitat is predicated on a fundamental assumption: once patent and regulatory exclusivity has ended, any product can be imitated and, if the market is attractive, it will be. Should this assumption fail for any reason, patent and regulatory protection from competition becomes irrelevant and the innovation-imitation cycle is broken. In the absence of competitors, inimitable products could maintain high prices and the healthcare dollars they consume could not be diverted toward newer innovative medicines. This would be the case when imitation is constrained or made impossible by trade secrets or personalization. If this happened to a significant degree, either for a large volume of treatments or a smaller number of very expensive treatments, this would have a negative impact on the PIE. A competition habitat that was able to counter this issue would better support a healthy PIE.

In reality, this issue is somewhat speculative. It is based on assumptions about rival firms' inability to duplicate or work around trade secrets and other non-disclosed knowledge. Given the ingenuity of the industry, especially when incentivized by large markets and high-priced incumbents, there are reasons to doubt this assumption. The difficulty of keeping trade secrets in an incestuous industry also weakens the core assumption. That said, it's not impossible to imagine a situation where the difficulty of imitation, limited market size, and a strong incumbent combine to make imitation, if not impossible, then unfeasible or commercially non-viable. In these (currently hypothetical) circumstances, the only solution that has been proposed is price setting by regulation. Those who propose this approach suggest a "cost plus acceptable profit" approach, a sort of compulsory purchasing of the kind normally associated with wartime procurement.[74]

Should this approach prove necessary, it would raise both practical and political difficulties. Practically, the calculation of valid costs is difficult, especially without intrusion into the manufacturers' commercially sensitive information. So too is estimating "acceptable profit," even under the auspices of an independent body. Should it not be possible to reach an agreement, then that would raise the question of

244   *The competition habitat*

whether it is possible to force a manufacturer to allocate resources in a way it doesn't choose to. Putting these objections aside, there are models for this sort of solution both in Medicare's procurement processes for inpatient services and in single-source public procurement, for example in the defense sector. But I have little doubt that this would be very controversial and would become politicized.

Will this be enough?

In this chapter, I characterized the competition habitat and then defined what a healthy PIE requires of it. I then explored the ability of the habitat to meet those requirements. As with other chapters, I found the habitat to be in poor shape and currently unable to support a healthy PIE. In the immediately preceding section, I suggested broad ideas for remedying that situation, again restricting myself to guidance and suggestions. In every habitat, detailed solutions are without question the domain of experts in each field and sub-field.

The five suggestions in this chapter would go much of the way to improving the competition habitat. The interconnected nature of the habitat means that the effectiveness of these measures would be multiplicative: they would work much better as a coordinated program than as stand-alone measures. Equally, the connections between the habitats within the PIE mean that this chapter's recommendations would only achieve their potential if the recommendations regarding the value and pricing habitat (discussed in Chapters 6 and 7), were also acted on fully. Even then, issues in the patient habitat would also need to be addressed. It's that habitat that I turn to next.

Notes

1 It is true, however, that small biotechs are increasingly attempting to launch directly onto the market without the help of big pharma. These are the exceptions that prove the rule, in that it is made possible by assembling a holobiont of resources, as discussed in Chapter 5, the innovation habitat. See https://www.mckinsey.com/industries/life-sciences/our-insights/first-time-launchers-in-the-pharmaceutical-industry.

2 The legislation that creates regulatory exclusivity began with The Drug Price Competition and Patent Term Restoration Act of 1984, commonly known as the Hatch-Waxman Act, which was designed to balance innovation and imitation by creating periods of regulatory exclusivity whilst enabling generic competition (that is, imitation) once patent and regulatory exclusivity has expired. But, since then, there have been various updates and amendments including:

Orphan Drug Act of 1983 (ODA)
Food and Drug Administration Modernization Act of 1997 (FDAMA)
Best Pharmaceuticals for Children Act of 2002 (BCPA)

Medicare Prescription Drug Improvement and Modernization Act of 2003 (MMA)

Biologics Price Competition and Innovation Act of 2009 (BPCIA)

Patient Protection and Affordable Care Act of 2010 (PPACA; informally known as Obamacare)

Food and Drug Administration Safety and Innovation Act of 2012 (FDASIA)

21st Century Cures Act of 2016

This history reflects the shaping of the competitive habitat by legislators in an attempt to find the right balance between incentivizing innovation and enabling competition.

3 Article I, Section 8, Clause 8, of the United States Constitution grants Congress the enumerated power "To promote the progress of science and useful arts, by securing for limited times to authors and inventors the exclusive right to their respective writings and discoveries."

4 In their critique of the patent system, James Bessen and Michael J. Meurer argue that, in most sectors, patent law fails to provide predictable property rights. However, they single out pharmaceuticals as a sector where patent law is closest to achieving the right innovation/imitation balance. See ref 1.

5 The cost of bringing a new drug to market is a much-disputed figure and estimates are very sensitive to the method used. It also varies greatly between type of drug and disease. The figure of $1.3 billion is taken from See ref 2. However, estimates range from $161 million to $4.54 billion. See ref 3. Equivalent figures for bringing a generic small-molecule drug and a biosimilar are less well researched but are in the region of $2-3 million and $100-300 million respectively. See https://www.nature.com/articles/d42473-021-00542-4 Whatever the precise figures, the differential between them is very large. This reflects the lesser amount of research and development work required by the imitator compared to the innovator.

6 These figures taken from https://www.statista.com/statistics/257364/top-lobbying-industries-in-the-us/.

7 This represents a sustained, large-scale lobbying effort and the detail of this spending suggests specific goals. To quote from one study, "In years in which key state referenda on reforms in drug pricing and regulation were being voted on, there were large spikes in contributions to groups that opposed or supported the reforms." See ref 4.

8 https://www.statnews.com/feature/prescription-politics/federal-full-data-set/.

9 See for example https://www.washingtonpost.com/business/2021/11/05/pharmaceutical-industry-drug-price-lobbying/.

10 This data taken from https://www.opensecrets.org/federal-lobbying/industries/summary?id=H04.

11 This data taken from https://www.opensecrets.org/federal-lobbying/industries/summary?id=H04.

12 Gathering data in this area is messy and prone to double counting, since some of the money spent by lobbying groups is provided by the Arnold Foundation. Figures here taken from https://www.arnoldventures.org/grants-search?topics=Drug+Prices and https://prospect.org/health/billionaire-behind-the-fight-for-lower-drug-prices-john-arnold/.

The major efforts of the Arnold Foundation appear directed at supporting research.

13 See for example 5.

14 See for example 6.

15 As an example of bi-partisan concern on this issue, at time of writing the Affordable Prescriptions for Patients Act was before the Senate. See https://www.congress.gov/bill/117th-congress/senate-bill/1435/all-info Notwithstanding this bipartisan interest, about three quarters of pharmaceutical industry funding

towards political parties goes to Republican recipients. See https://www.open-secrets.org/federal-lobbying/industries/summary?id=H04.

16 For examples of these concerns, see https://www.statnews.com/2019/07/16/pharma-still-winning/ https://www.citizensforethics.org/reports-investigations/crew-reports/a-bitter-pill-how-big-pharma-lobbies-to-keep-prescription-drug-prices-high/ and https://newrepublic.com/article/149438/big-pharma-captured-one-percent The history of how intellectual property rights have been influenced by the pharmaceutical industry is described extensively in See 7.

17 See https://www.opensecrets.org/federal-lobbying/industries/summary?id=H04.

18 For a fascinating telling of this story, see https://www.healthaffairs.org/do/10.1377/forefront.20211029.33540/full/.

19 In an across industry study of the USPTO, evidence suggested just this issue. To quote,

> We find that patent examiners grant significantly more patents to the firms that later hire them and that much of this leniency extends to prospective employers. These effects are strongest in years when firms are actively hiring, and these relationships hold for the intensive margin of intellectual property protection. Ultimately, this leads the agency to issue lower quality patents, which we measure in citations. Together with other supporting evidence, we argue these results are suggestive of regulatory capture.

See 8. Other work, in a Canadian context, suggested that the mechanism for this was "Cultural Capture," an affinity of patent assessors with their past and potential employers. See ref 9.

20 See for example refs 10 and 11.

21 In evolutionary biology, my favorite example of "unintelligent design" is the recurrent laryngeal nerve, which carries messages from the brain to the larynx but must loop around major blood vessels on the way. In humans, this is minor detour. In giraffes, it means the nerve is up to 5 meters long. Biologists call this sort of post-hoc work-around an evolutionary kludge, the term for solution that is inelegant and inefficient.

22 The development times of drugs varies with therapeutic class and molecule type but is also influenced by the FDA's various channels for expedited drug approval. See ref 12. One area where there seems to be a particular issue is the time it takes to prove a preventative treatment works. See for example ref 13.

23 To quote this work more fully,

> Longer clinical programs lead to shorter effective patent life, even after PTO has granted patent term restoration. The results are strongly statistically significant and contribute to a growing body of literature raising the alarm that the U.S. legal system may be systematically skewing drug research incentives away from the harder problems — such as a cure for Alzheimer's Disease and interventions at the early stages of cancers.

See ref 14.

24 See refs 15 and 16.

25 To quote from this particularly critical examination of pharmaceutical patenting,

> The results show a startling departure from the classic conceptualization of intellectual property protection for pharmaceuticals. Rather than creating new medicines, pharmaceutical companies are largely recycling and repurposing old ones. Specifically, 78% of the drugs associated with new patents were not new drugs, but existing ones, and extending protection is particularly pronounced among blockbuster drugs. Once companies start down the road of extending protection, they show a tendency to return to the well, with the majority adding

more than one extension and 50% becoming serial offenders. The problem is growing across time.

See ref 17.

26 There's a sampling issue here of course. This study showed, as one would expect, that drugs accepted into the FDA's accelerated approval pathways had greater benefits than those that followed the non-accelerated pathways. Still, that such a high proportion of drugs in the latter, non-accelerated category showed no or negative improvement over existing products indicates that one of the characteristics of pharmaceutical innovation emerging from the PIE is that a significant amount of it offers little or no clinical value. See ref 18.

27 The point of this work was mostly to illustrate that new doesn't always mean better by the standards of Health Technology Assessment used in this study. See ref 19.

28 Incremental innovation makes various contributions to economic and health outcomes that are less obvious than those of new, radical innovations. To quote one report on the topic,

> The advantages of incremental improvements on already existing drugs are paramount to overall increases in the quality of health care. As the pharmaceutical industry has developed, classes of drugs have expanded to provide physicians with the tools they need to treat diverse patient groups. While critics claim that there are too many similar drugs, drugs based on incremental improvements often represent advances in safety and efficacy, along with providing new formulations and dosing options that significantly increase patient compliance. From an economic standpoint, expanding drug classes represent the possibility of lower drug prices as competition between manufacturers is increased. Additionally, pharmaceutical companies depend on incremental innovations to provide the revenue that will support the development of more risky 'block-buster' drugs.

See ref 20.

29 The Orphan Drug Act also provided substantial tax incentives to invest in orphan drugs. There are an estimated 7000 orphan diseases and about 1 in 10 Americans live with a rare condition. Orphan drugs are expected to make up 18% of pharmaceutical sales by 2024. See 21–23. The growth of orphan drugs has been an industry phenomenon. To quote from a recent paper,

> Between 1983 and 2019, a total of 5099 drugs and biologics received orphan drug designation. Designations more than doubled between the 1980s and 1990s, almost doubled between the 1990s and 2000s, and almost tripled in number between the 2000s and 2010s.

See ref 24.

30 It's important to remember that, even though biologics are a quarter of approvals, because they are generally much more expensive than small molecule drugs, this represents a bigger impact on the market than the number of approvals suggests. See ref 25.

31 This seems to run counter to the assumptions underpinning the longer period of exclusivity for biologics. To quote from this paper,

> Our study reviewed pre-market times for all new drugs approved by CDER over the past decade. Although new laws are being considered by policymakers around the world to further expand market exclusivities for biologics, we found no evidence that developing biologic drugs was more time-intensive than developing traditional small-molecule drugs. In addition, biologic drugs appear to be associated with

higher probabilities of success during clinical testing and regulatory approval than small-molecule drugs. Policymakers should prioritize eliminating barriers to biosimilar competition and continue to monitor the potential impact of varying exclusivity protections on biologic versus small-molecule drug development.

See ref 26.

32 Orphan drug development takes 15.1 years to go from first patent filing to product launch, 18% longer than the average time required for all new drugs, according to the Tufts Center for the Study of Drug Development. And development time for drugs to treat ultra-orphan diseases—which affect only a few hundred patients in the U.S.—is even longer: 17.2 years. See https://www.centerwatch.com/articles/12603-tufts-facing-many-challenges-orphan-drugs-take-18-longer-to-develop.

33 The information from this paragraph is taken from the following sources: https://sourceonhealthcare.org/orphan-drug-act-fostering-innovation-or-abuse/.
https://khn.org/news/government-investigation-finds-flaws-in-the-fdas-orphan-drug-program/.
https://khn.org/news/drugmakers-manipulate-orphan-drug-rules-to-create-prized-monopolies/.
https://www.gao.gov/products/gao-19-83.
To be clear, all these tactics are legal but appear to subvert the intent of the Orphan Drug Act.

34 This case is interesting because it reveals a loophole that might be used by other drugs. See ref 27.

35 Please note that I'm referring to overall healthcare costs here. So "better bang for bucks" might mean a significantly cheaper medicine or it could mean a medicine with much lower associated treatment costs or a preventative or curative medicine that obviates long term treatment costs.

36 See ref 28 and 29.

37 These tactics have included legal challenges, paying imitators to delay entry and a tactic known as product hopping, in which users of an old product are switched to a modified version that remains protected by patent. There is a very extensive literature in this area. See refs 30–36. A good recent discussion of this topic can be found at https://papers.ssrn.com/sol3/papers.cfm?abstract_id=3964099.

38 See https://sgp.fas.org/crs/misc/R46679.pdf.

39 When biosimilars are approved, it means they can be used in place of the original biological product, which is known as the reference product, but only on the authority of a health care professional. A biosimilar that meets further regulatory requirements may be classed as interchangeable, which means it can be used in place of the reference product on the authority of the pharmacist. Interchangeability is a valuable status because it makes substitution easier. At the time of writing, the FDA has only given two biosimilars interchangeable status: Cyltezo, which references Humira, and Semglee, which references Lantus.

40 To be clear, the substitution of originator biologic drugs by biosimilars is related mostly to both the approval pathways and intellectual property protection. This picture is changing quickly but the point remains that replacement of biologic medicines, which are relatively expensive, by cheaper biosimilars, is much slower and much less than either generic substitution of small molecule drugs or biosimilar substitution in Europe. See 37. See also https://biosimilarsrr.com/2020/04/23/an-interesting-comparison-the-latest-data-on-us-and-eu-biosimilar-uptake/.

41 See ref 38.

42 See ref 39.

43 See ref 40.

44 See ref 41.

45 See http://www.i-mak.org/wp-content/uploads/2018/08/I-MAK-Overpatented-Overpriced-Report.pdf.
46 To quote from one paper in this area,

> Our investigation reveals that secondary patents filed a median of more than a decade after approval and for which one-fifth lack equivalent patents were predominantly involved in the litigation affecting the market entry of biosimilars for nine key biologic drugs.

See ref 42.
47 See refs 43 and 44.
48 See ref 45.
49 To facilitate this imitative part of the innovation cycle, the FDA publishes lists of drugs that have no patent or exclusivity protection but for which there are no generic equivalents.
50 For a flavor of this debate, some argue that

> patent disclosure induces R&D competition and shapes firms' technological trajectories. In fact, we show that under conditions of uncertainty, patent disclosure can contribute to generate knowledge spillovers, promoting multiple parallel research efforts on plausible targets and stimulating private investment and competition.

See ref 46. Others point to mixed effects: "Our results show that the number of a firm's lagged patents encourages the firm's entry with new products, while rivals' initial stock of patents discourages entry, but more recent patents promote entry by opening new technological opportunities." See 47. Whilst still others express concern that changes to patent law, namely the Leahy-Smith America Invents act of 2011, have "a negative impact on corporate disclosure and information asymmetry." See 48. Despite this diversity of views, it's fair to say that the consensus of the literature is that patent disclosure is a positive feature of the system that should be preserved.
51 To quote from an interesting recent paper in this area, "...we describe how trade secrecy protection comes into conflict with access to medicines—for example, by preventing researchers from accessing clinical trial data, undermining the scale-up of manufacturing in pandemics, and deterring whistleblowers from reporting industry misconduct." See ref 49.
52 See ref 50.
53 For a discussion of "stealth evolution". See ref 51.
54 See ref 52–54.
55 There is, as with everything in the PIE, much debate over how and if advanced therapies will genericize as small molecules have. See https://www.risingtidebio.com/biosimilar-cell-gene-therapy/ and https://medium.com/the-biotech-social-contract/kolchinsky-tbsc-2-45841e4ad095.
56 See ref 55.
57 See for example: 56–58.
58 The rebate wall phenomenon has been well described by Josh Cohen in Forbes magazine. See https://www.forbes.com/sites/joshuacohen/2021/03/01/rebate-walls-stifle-prescription-drug-competition/ For a more academic treatment of the topic. See ref 59.
59 The FTC concluded that the legality of the rebate wall, with respect to antitrust laws, depends on the particular circumstances. See https://www.ftc.gov/system/files/documents/reports/federal-trade-commission-report-rebate-walls/federal_trade_commission_report_on_rebate_walls_.pdf.
60 See ref 60.
61 For recent empirical evidence of this. See ref 61.

62 See   https://www.fda.gov/consumers/consumer-updates/biosimilar-and-interchangeable-biologics-more-treatment-choices.

63 At the time of writing, however, this is a dynamic picture. See ref 62–64.

64 For discussion of recent trends in biosimilar penetration. See ref 65 and https://www.mckinsey.com/industries/life-sciences/our-insights/an-inflection-point-for-biosimilars   and   https://www.zs.com/insights/pharmacy-benefit-is-a-whole-new-ball-game-for-biosimilars.

65 TRIPS is an acronym for Trade-Related Aspects of Intellectual Property Rights. This is a multilateral agreement on intellectual property under the rules of the World Trade Organization. The agreement tries to balance "facilitating trade in knowledge and creativity, in resolving trade disputes over IP, and in assuring WTO members the latitude to achieve their domestic policy objectives." This inevitably means that changes to US patent law can't be considered in isolation from international trade considerations and make changes to patent law more complicated and difficult. See https://www.wto.org/english/tratop_e/trips_e/trips_e.htm.

66 Seymore suggests

> ... *a new framework for evaluating novelty in new-use patent claims. It proposes a probing novelty inquiry that would require inventors to elucidate and disclose mechanistic information to prove that a claimed new use is truly novel. Providing mechanistic information would promote patent law's disclosure function and improve patent (examination) quality.*

See ref 66.

67 Feldman suggests "One avenue for reform might be to enforce a more rigorous utility requirement for pharmaceutical patents, demanding that they actually improve social welfare relative to the prior art." See ref 67.

68 I quote the entire abstract here to give a fuller flavor of this view.

> *The Hatch-Waxman Act is not working. The Patent & Trademark Office (PTO) fails to adequately siphon out obvious patent applications. The PTO's pattern and practice of approving ever-greened pharmaceutical patents drains consumer welfare, stunts productive research, unreasonably extracts from innovators, and compromises generic market entry. As a solution, this note argues that the threshold non obviousness inquiry for follow-on pharmaceutical patents should include a prior art analysis of business practices, within the relevant pharmaceutical sector, to ascertain whether a claimed follow-on invention is truly innovative or simply anticompetitive.*

See ref 68.

69 To quote these authors,

> *Rather than proposing radical changes that categorically exclude potentially valuable improvements from patent protection, reasonable sustainable solutions can in our view therefore be achieved only if reforms in patent law and procedure, which are coherent with the rationales underlying the patent system and absolutely indispensable for a well-functioning innovation system, are complemented by well-balanced changes at the post-grant level. This requires taking into consideration a more predictable interpretation of the research and the so-called 'Bolar' exemptions, competition law, procedural changes in patent litigation, and the multiple instruments provided by pharmaceutical regulatory law, as well as more elaborated guidelines on new models of cooperation, such as Public Private Partnerships, patent pools, standard setting, clearinghouses, or other user-generated ordering and licensing solutions.*

See ref 43.

70 For a discussion of alternative, non-patent, non-regulatory exclusivity mechanisms of incentivizing pharmaceutical innovation. See ref 69 and 70.
71 The one and done idea is proposed by Professor Robin Feldman. For her exposition of this, see https://www.statnews.com/2019/02/11/drug-patent-protection-one-done/.
72 A useful discussion of this topic can be found at https://www.arnoldporter.com/en/perspectives/publications/2021/09/fda-seeks-to-deepen-engagement-with-uspto.
73 At the time of writing, only two interchangeable biosimilars were available in the US. See https://www.centerforbiosimilars.com/view/an-interchangeable-biosimilars-vs-authorized-biologics-battle-may-be-looming.
74 This has been proposed in some detail by Mark Trusheim and his colleagues. See ref 53.

References

1 Bessen J, Meurer MJ. *Patent Failure: How Judges, Bureaucrats, and Lawyers Put Innovators at Risk*. Princeton: Princeton University Press; 2008.
2 Wouters OJ, McKee M, Luyten J. Estimated research and development investment needed to bring a new medicine to market, 2009–2018. *JAMA*. 2020;323(9):844–53.
3 Schlander M, Hernandez-Villafuerte K, Cheng C-Y, Mestre-Ferrandiz J, Baumann M. How much does it cost to research and develop a new drug? A systematic review and assessment. *PharmacoEconomics*. 2021;39(11):1243–69.
4 Wouters OJ. Lobbying expenditures and campaign contributions by the pharmaceutical and health product industry in the United States, 1999–2018. *JAMA Internal Medicine*. 2020;180(5):688–97.
5 Unsal O. Two faces of corporate lobbying: Evidence from the pharmaceutical industry. *The North American Journal of Economics and Finance*. 2020;51: 100858.
6 Chu AC. Special interest politics and intellectual property rights: An economic analysis of strengthening patent protection in the pharmaceutical industry. *Economics & Politics*. 2008;20(2):185–215.
7 Zaitchick A. *Owning the Sun: A People's History of Monopoly Medicine from Aspirin to COVID-19 Counterpoint LLC*; Berkeley: Counterpoint. 2022.
8 Tabakovic HW, Thomas G. *From Revolving Doors to Regulatory Capture? Evidence from Patent Examiners*. National Bureau of Economic Research Working Paper Series. 2018;24638.
9 Yates S, Cardin-Trudeau É. Lobbying "from within": A new perspective on the revolving door and regulatory capture. *Canadian Public Administration*. 2021;64(2):301–19.
10 Mintzberg H. Patent nonsense: Evidence tells of an industry out of social control. *Canadian Medical Association Journal*. 2006;175(4):374-.
11 Morgan JM, Duffy D. The cost of capture: How the pharmaceutical industry has corrupted policymakers and harmed patients. *The Roosevelt Institute*; 2019 May.
12 Brown DG, Wobst HJ, Kapoor A, Kenna LA, Southall N. Clinical development times for innovative drugs. *Nature Reviews Drug Discovery*. November 2021.
13 Colditz GA, Taylor PR. Prevention trials: Their place in how we understand the value of prevention strategies. *Annual Review Public Health*. 2010;31:105–20.
14 Lietzan E, Lybecker KMLA. Distorted drug patents. *Washington Law Review*. 2020;95(3):1317–82.

15 Budish E, Roin BN, Williams H. Do firms underinvest in long-term research? Evidence from cancer clinical trials. *The American Economic Review.* 2015;105(7):2044–85.

16 Budish E, Roin BN, Williams H. Patents and research investments: Assessing the empirical evidence. *The American Economic Review.* 2016;106(5):183–7.

17 Feldman R. May your drug price be evergreen. *Journal of Law and the Biosciences.* 2018;5(3):590–647.

18 Chambers JD, Thorat T, Wilkinson CL, Neumann PJ. Drugs cleared through the FDA'S expedited review offer greater gains than drugs approved by conventional process. *Health Affairs.* 2017;36(8):1408–15.

19 Stiller I, van Witteloostuijn A, Cambré B. Do current radical innovation measures actually measure radical drug innovation? *Scientometrics.* 2021;126(2):1049–78.

20 Wertheimer AIS, Thomas M. Pharmacoevolution: The advantages of incremental innovation. *International Policy Network*; 2005.

21 Pomeranz K, Siriwardna K, Davies F. Orphan drug report 2020. Evaluate Pharma; 2020.

22 Caetano R, Cordeiro Dias Villela Correa M, Villardi P, Almeida Rodrigues PH, Garcia Serpa Osorio-de-Castro C. Dynamics of patents, orphan drug designation, licensing, and revenues from drugs for rare diseases: The market expansion of eculizumab. *PloS One.* 2021;16(3):e0247853.

23 Kwon D. how orphan drugs became a highly profitable industry 2018. Available from: https://www.the-scientist.com/features/how-orphan-drugs-became-a-highly-profitable-industry-64278.

24 Miller KL, Fermaglich LJ, Maynard J. Using four decades of FDA orphan drug designations to describe trends in rare disease drug development: Substantial growth seen in development of drugs for rare oncologic, neurologic, and pediatric-onset diseases. *Orphanet Journal of Rare Diseases.* 2021;16(1):265-.

25 Mullard A. 2021 FDA approvals. *Nature Reviews Drug Discovery.* 2022;21(2):83–8.

26 Beall RF, Hwang TJ, Kesselheim AS. Pre-market development times for biologic versus small-molecule drugs. *Nature Biotechnology.* 2019;37(7):708–11.

27 Chua K-P, Conti RM. Policy Implications of the orphan drug designation for remdesivir to treat COVID-19. *JAMA Internal Medicine.* 2020;180(10):1273–4.

28 Beall RF, Hollis A, Kesselheim AS, Spackman E. Reimagining pharmaceutical market exclusivities: Should the duration of guaranteed monopoly periods be value based? *Value in Health.* 2021;24(9):1328–34.

29 Christie AF, Dent C, Studdert DM. Evidence of "evergreening" in secondary patenting of blockbuster drugs. *Melbourne University Law Review.* 2020;44(2):537–64.

30 Peelish N. Antitrust and authorized generics: A new predation analysis. *Stanford Law Review.* 2020;72(3):791–839.

31 Wouters OJ, Kanavos PG, McKee M. Comparing generic drug markets in Europe and the United States: prices, volumes, and spending. *The Milbank Quarterly.* 2017;95(3):554–601.

32 Anning M. "Pay for delay" legitimate conduct to defend valid patent rights or anticompetitive behaviour? *Law Review (Wellington).* 2018;49(2):25.

33 Gurgula O. Strategic patenting by pharmaceutical companies – should competition law intervene? *IIC - International Review of Intellectual Property and Competition Law.* 2020;51(9):1062–85.

34 Gowda V, Beall RF, Kesselheim AS, Sarpatwari A. Identifying potential prescription drug product hopping. *Nature Biotechnology.* 2021;39(4):414–7.

35 Vokinger KN, Kesselheim AS, Avorn J, Sarpatwari A. Strategies that delay market entry of generic drugs. *JAMA Internet Medicine.* 2017;177(11):1665–9.

36 Jones GH, Carrier MA, Silver RT, Kantarjian H. Strategies that delay or prevent the timely availability of affordable generic drugs in the United States. *Blood.* 2016;127(11):1398–402.

37 The U.S. Generic & Biosimilar Medicines Savings Report. 2021 October 2021.

38 Grabowski H, Long G, Mortimer R, Bilginsoy M. Continuing trends in U.S. brand-name and generic drug competition. *Journal of Medical Economics.* 2021;24(1):908–17.

39 Wang B, Liu J, Kesselheim AS. Variations in time of market exclusivity among top-selling prescription drugs in the United States. *JAMA Internal Medicine.* 2015;175(4):635–7.

40 Rome BN, Lee CC, Kesselheim AS. Market exclusivity length for drugs with new generic or biosimilar competition, 2012–2018. *Clinical Pharmacology & Therapeutics.* 2021;109(2):367–71.

41 Beall RF, Darrow JJ, Kesselheim AS. A method for approximating future entry of generic drugs. *Value in Health.* 2018;21(12):1382–9.

42 Van de Wiele VL, Beall RF, Kesselheim AS, Sarpatwari A. The characteristics of patents impacting availability of biosimilars. *Nature Biotechnology.* 2022;40(1):22–5.

43 Holman CM, Minssen T, Solovy, EM. Patentability standards for follow-on pharmaceutical innovation. *Biotechnology Law Report.* 2018;37(3):131–61.

44 Holman CM. Unpredictability in patent law and its effect on pharmaceutical innovation. *Missouri Law Review.* 2011;76(3).

45 Dutfield G. *That Highest Design of Pure Gold.* London: World Scientific Publishing Co; 2020.

46 Magazzini L, Pammolli F, Riccaboni M, Rossi MA. Patent disclosure and R&D competition in pharmaceuticals. *Economics of Innovation & New Technology.* 2009;18(5/6):467–86.

47 Di Iorio F, Giorgetti ML. Launch of a product and patents: Evidence from the US cardiovascular pharmaceutical sector. *Industry and Innovation.* 2020;27(7):789–803.

48 Huang R, Li L, Lu LY, Wu H. The impact of the Leahy-Smith America invents act on firms' R&D disclosure. *European Accounting Review.* 2021;30(5):1067–104.

49 Durkin A, Sta Maria PA, Willmore B, Kapczynski A. Addressing the risks that trade secret protections pose for health and rights. *Health Human Rights.* 2021;23(1):129–44.

50 Price WN, Rai AK. Are trade secrets delaying biosimilars? *Science.* 2015;348(6231):188–9.

51 Mastellos DC, Blom AM, Connolly ES, Daha MR, Geisbrecht BV, Ghebrehiwet B et al. 'Stealth' corporate innovation: An emerging threat for therapeutic drug development. *Nature Immunology.* 2019;20(11):1409–13.

52 Atteberry P, Bach P, Ohn, JA; Trusheim M. Biologics are natural monopolies (part 1): Why biosimilars do not create effective competition. *Health Affairs Blog.* 2019.

53 Trusheim MR, Atteberry P; Ohn JA; Bach PB. Biologics are natural monopolies (part 2): A proposal for post- exclusivity price regulation of biologics. *Health Affairs Blog.* 2019.

54 Brill AIB. Biologics are not natural monopolies. *Health Affairs Blog.* 2019.

55 Mulcahy AW, Hlavka JP, Case SR. Biosimilar cost savings in the United States: Initial experience and future potential. *Rand Health Q.* 2018;7(4):3-.

56 Baker JF, Leonard CE, Lo Re V, Weisman MH, George MD, Kay J. Biosimilar uptake in academic and veterans health administration settings: Influence of institutional incentives. *Arthritis & Rheumatology (Hoboken, NJ).* 2020;72(7):1067–71.

57 McBride A, Wang W, Campbell K, Balu S, MacDonald K, Abraham I. Economic modeling for the US of the cost-efficiency and associated expanded treatment access of conversion to biosimilar pegfilgrastim-bmez from reference pegfilgrastim. *Journal of Medical Economics.* 2020;23(8):856–63.

58 Morris GA, McNicol M, Boyle B, Donegan A, Dotson J, Michel HK et al. Increasing biosimilar utilization at a pediatric inflammatory bowel disease center and associated cost savings: Show me the money. *Inflammatory Bowel Diseases.* 2022;28(4):531.

59 Zhai MZ, Sarpatwari A, Kesselheim AS. Why are biosimilars not living up to their promise in the US? *AMA Journal of Ethics.* 2019;21(8):E668–78.

60 Maltz RM, McNicol M, Wingate L, Buchanan S, Sandell A, Kim SC et al. There is no substitute for effective education about biosimilars. *Crohn's & Colitis.* 2021;3(4):360.

61 Duarte-García A, Crowson CS, McCoy RG, Herrin J, Lam V, Putman MS et al. Association between payments by pharmaceutical manufacturers and prescribing behavior in rheumatology. *Mayo Clinical Proceedings.* 2022;97(2):250–60.

62 Yazdany J. Failure to launch: Biosimilar sales continue to fall flat in the United States. *Arthritis & Rheumatology (Hoboken, NJ).* 2020;72(6):870–3.

63 Frank RG, Shahzad M, Kesselheim AS, Feldman W. Biosimilar competition: Early learning. *Health Economics.* 2022;31(4):647–63.

64 Bana A, Mehta PJ. *Recognizing Barriers to Entry of Biosimilars in the United States Market and Highlighting the Solutions.* London, England: SAGE Publications; 2021. p. 122–9.

65 Socal MP, Ezebilo I, Bai G, Anderson GF. Biosimilar formulary placement in medicare Part D prescription drug plans: A case study of infliximab. *American Journal of Health-System Pharmacy: AJHP: Official Journal of the American Society of Health-System Pharmacists.* 2021;78(3):216–21.

66 Seymore SB. Patenting new uses for old inventions. *Vanderbilt Law Review.* 2020;73(2):479–534.

67 Feldman RC, Hyman DA, Price WN, Ratain MJ. Negative innovation: When patents are bad for patients. *Nature Biotechnology.* 2021;39(8):914–6.

68 Stoia C. *Redefining Obviousness: How the PTO's Failure to Reject Obvious Patents Impacts Hatch- Waxman Act Policy Objectives.* University of Connecticut; 2021.

69 Grootendorst P. How should we support pharmaceutical innovation? *Expert Review of Pharmacoeconomics & Outcomes Research.* 2009;9(4):313–20.

70 Lee Mendoza R. Incentives and disincentives to drug innovation: Evidence from recent literature. *Journal of Medical Economics.* 2019;22(8):713–21.

9 The patient habitat

Precis

- The patient habitat is the part of the pharmaceutical innovation ecosystem that identifies society's needs and signals them to the rest of the PIE.
- The patient habitat is inhabited by:
  - patients and their proxies, such as plan sponsors and patient groups
  - government agencies, such as those under the HHS
  - pharmaceutical innovators, including academic researchers, pharmaceutical companies, and investors
  - those who deliver innovative medicines as part of their service, such as insurers and healthcare providers
- The patient habitat interacts with all the other habitats by funding basic research, providing tax incentives, shaping patent law and regulatory exclusivity and creating a market by favoring public and private health insurance.
- A healthy PIE requires that the patient habitat meets three requirements.
  - It must enable pharmaceutical innovation that meets society's most important unmet needs.
  - It must incentivize pharmaceutical innovation that meets society's most important unmet needs.
  - It must align enabling and incentivizing signals.
- The patient habitat's ability to support a healthy PIE is constrained by:
  - its reliance on market signals that are disconnected from value
  - its incoherent communication of clinical needs

DOI: 10.4324/9781003330271-9

- its failure to communicate health economic needs
- its lack of knowledge management capabilities
- its failure to communicate society's cultural values
- The patient habitat would be made better able to support a healthy PIE by:
  - building a knowledge management system to identify societal needs
  - establishing clear clinical and health economic priorities
  - aligning societal signals to those priorities
  - agreeing a code of shared cultural values and behaviors

In Chapter 1, I fretted that the social contract between the wider pharmaceutical industry and American society was under great strain. This is worrisome because the industry and society have benefitted greatly from it, both medically and economically, and no one wants to put those benefits at risk. In Chapter 2, I criticized mechanistic ways of thinking about pharmaceutical innovation and made the case for a paradigm shift toward looking at this problem as an issue of ecosystem management. In Chapters 3–8, I recounted my exploration of the pharmaceutical innovation ecosystem, the PIE, concluding that the strains on the social contract could be blamed on malfunctions and weaknesses in its various habitats. In Chapter 3, I wrote about how the fundamental science of pharmaceutical innovation was both breathtakingly brilliant and unnecessarily uncertain. In Chapters 4 and 5, I wrote about how scientific discoveries with potential but unrealized utility are taken up by coalitions of complementary capabilities and translated into innovative medicines that improve, extend, and save lives, but not in the most efficient ways. In Chapters 6–8, I wrote about how America's uniquely free and exceptionally complicated healthcare market delivers those medicines at prices ranging from a few dollars to millions, but again in ways that were imperfect and often inequitable. In those chapters, I also made broad suggestions for the direction of improvement, while leaving the detail to others. Observant readers will notice that in these preceding chapters, I've paid only glancing attention to patients, such as when I mentioned their multifaceted clinical and non-clinical needs and their relative powerlessness in the market. Now, in my last stage of exploration before I reach my conclusions, I will look at what I call the patient habitat.

Please don't infer from my structuring choices that I regard patients as less important than the other inhabitants of the PIE. The opposite is true. I've chosen this structure because patients are the "raison d'être" of the PIE; and everything described in Chapters 3–8 is caused by and for patients. I'm far from the first to say this, although the idea has recently been given a new label of "patient-centricity." The primacy of the patient has long been the public mantra of many who work in the industry and versions of it can be found in the mission statements of many pharmaceutical companies. So the patient as the driver and the mission of the PIE is an uncontroversial reason to place this chapter at the end of my exploration. But it's also a clichéd position and, to be useful, it needs a single paragraph of qualification.

It's trite to say that pharmaceutical innovation is caused by and for patients. To understand it as more than just a platitude, we need to remember three other truths about pharmaceutical innovation that become self-evident with only a little thought. First, because we choose to live in a capitalist system, if we want medicines to be innovative, then pharmaceutical innovation must be attractive to investors. To be sustainable, pharmaceutical innovation must generate a risk-appropriate return on investment. Second, because we live in a complex society, in which everyone's health is intertwined with everyone else's wealth, pharmaceutical innovation isn't only about the individual patient's health needs, it's about the patients' collective health and economic needs, with a very deliberately shifted apostrophe. In other words, to be sustainable, pharmaceutical innovation must meet the health and economic needs of America and not just the health needs of some Americans. Third, because the scientific and commercial risks of pharmaceutical innovation and the financial risks of ill-health are so great, the PIE must rely heavily on risk-sharing, which happens through both public and private institutions. This means that pharmaceutical innovation can't rely purely on unfettered market forces and must involve institutions. Only when we remember these three additional truths does "medicine is for the patient" become more than a virtue-signaling platitude and become useful to understanding the PIE. I suspect this is what George Merck meant in 1950, in his famous speech at the Medical College of Virginia,[1] although it's often truncated to suggest that he meant the patient, singular. George Merck and other founders of the industry knew implicitly that, because the industry is based on a social contract, pharmaceutical innovation is caused by and for patients but with these three important qualifications.

So, to put this chapter in context, Chapters 3–8 described how the supply side of the PIE tries to meet the terms of its social contract in the real-world, three-truths context described above. This chapter is about the patient habitat, the part of the PIE where patients, mostly through institutions acting as their proxies, set out their side of the social contract. This includes both what they want from pharmaceutical innovation and what they're willing to do to support it. Those terms feed into the PIE and influence the properties of the pharmaceutical innovation that emerge from it, such as what medicines are developed and what they cost. In this chapter, I'll explore the patient habitat and how it might be managed to meet the needs of a healthy PIE.

What happens in the patient habitat and who inhabits it?

In essence, the patient habitat is where the PIE receives its information from the wider world, interprets it, and signals its conclusions into the rest of the PIE. The outputs of the patient habitat are societal signals that the rest of the PIE acts on, and that influence the properties of pharmaceutical innovation that emerges from it. Like the other habitats, the patient habitat doesn't lend itself to simple organization charts, but I find it useful to think of it having four types of inhabitants, two of whom send signals and two of whom receive them.

Patients are what ecologists would call the foundation species of the PIE because they have a fundamental role in the ecosystem. More so than in other markets, there is no real distinction between patients and the citizenry in general. Many citizens are patients, many are relatives of patients and those few that are neither, know that they will become so eventually.[2] And because patients and citizens are essentially the same, they engage with the PIE in many different ways. As patients, they create demand, either as plan members, beneficiaries of Medicare and other public insurance, or as out-of-pocket customers. As voters, they shape the political environment that cascades down to laws and regulations. As activists, some patients engage with the

PIE via about 8,000 patient organizations,[3] communicating and amplifying the needs of specific patient groups and, in some cases, funding research.

As well as foundation species, ecologists also define keystone species that hold the ecosystem together. The patient habitat's keystone species are government agencies, who nominally act as proxies for patients' and citizens' interests. The most obvious of these come under the HHS, such as the CDC, FDA, CMS and NIH, which either channel public resources or frame the regulations by which the PIE operates.[4] But, equally important, are agencies that are not specific to healthcare, such as the USPTO and FTC, who enforce further regulations that shape the PIE. In effect, these keystone species act as information nodes, channeling signals from society toward the PIE.

The third type of inhabitants of the patient habitat is the discoverers and innovators who use the signals from the foundational and keystone species to decide where to allocate the PIE's research and development resources. These include the academic researchers who decide what to research, the biotech and pharmaceutical companies that decide what to develop, and the venture capitalists and other investors that decide what to fund.

Finally, there are those who act on the patient habitat's signals when providing the solution that wraps around innovative medicines. These include insurers and PBMs, providers, wholesalers, pharmacies, and others described in Chapter 7 (the pricing habitat). How they interpret the habitat's signals influences the accessibility and costs of innovative medicines which, of course, feeds back to patients, innovators, and government.

Although I've described these four groups of inhabitants as if they were discrete and distinct, it's important to recognize that they aren't. Legislators and agencies are patients too, patient groups and pharmaceutical companies cooperate to shape the market and everybody tries to influence government, whether at the voting booth or via lobbying and political donations. Biotechs and pharmaceutical companies interact with academic researchers to understand what future scientific possibilities may exist. Governments set priorities, such as the CDC's national health initiatives, that influence researchers and investors. More than even some of the other habitats, the patient habitat is a tangled, messy part of the PIE. Out of this messiness emerges its indispensable role in influencing how well the PIE works and how well it fulfills the social contract. I had this role uppermost in my mind as I explored what a healthy, social contract-meeting PIE requires of the patient habitat.

What does a healthy PIE require of the patient habitat?

If the patient habitat is where society sets out its side of the social contract, a healthy PIE requires that it does so clearly, both enabling and encouraging what it sees as valuable. In practice, this means using both enabling "push" signals, such as what research is publicly funded and what R&D activity is given tax breaks, and incentivizing "pull" signals, such as what pharmaceutical innovations are protected from competition and what medicines are prioritized for accelerated approval. To work effectively, these signals must be both individually strong and collectively coherent. To be clear, this isn't the same as a government directing specific solutions to particular problems, like a Soviet government directing a five-year plan for tractor production. It is making what society regards as valuable unambiguous (for example, through market and other signals) and then leaving the solution to emerge from the PIE. Society already tries to do this when, for example, it incentivizes health insurance, orphan drugs, or, more recently, new antibiotics.[5] An extreme form of societal signaling was at the heart of Operation Warp Speed to develop vaccines for Covid 19.[6] In the three-truths context described above, the need for clarity and coherence of societal signaling means that the PIE requires three things from the patient habitat.

The patient habitat must enable pharmaceutical innovation that meets society's most important unmet needs

A well-functioning patient habitat will enable the market to meet its important unmet clinical and economic needs. To do so effectively, the patient habitat will establish its clinical and economic priorities, identify the constraints on meeting them and create the conditions to overcome those constraints, such as the creation of new knowledge in relevant fields. A patient habitat that does not clearly prioritize society's needs, does so only with respect to clinical or economic factors but not both, or that fails to create the conditions to meet those unmet needs would not sustain a healthy PIE.

The patient habitat must incentivize pharmaceutical innovation that meets society's most important unmet needs

It is not sufficient that the patient habitat enables the PIE, it must also incentivize it to meet its important unmet clinical and economic needs. To do so effectively, the patient habitat will establish its clinical and economic priorities, identify where the market does not provide sufficient incentive, and act to shape the market, by methods such as reducing the risk or improving returns. A patient habitat that does not clearly prioritize society's needs, does so only with respect to clinical or economic factors but not both or does not identify and correct market weaknesses or failures would not sustain a healthy PIE.

The patient habitat must align enabling and incentivizing signals

A well-functioning patient habitat will unambiguously communicate its important unmet clinical and health economic needs to the PIE. To do so effectively, the patient habitat must align enabling and incentivizing actions so that they reinforce each other. A patient habitat that does not align its various actions or allows them to contradict or conflict with each other would not sustain a healthy PIE.

In these three demands (Figure 9.1), the PIE is asking a lot of the patient habitat because we're asking a lot of the PIE. If we want the PIE to deliver on the social contract with a sustainable supply of innovative, affordable medicines, the PIE needs society to be clear about the needs pharmaceutical innovation must meet to qualify as valuable. It's necessary but not sufficient to signal to the PIE what important unmet *clinical* needs exist, such as a cure for Alzheimer's disease. It's necessary but not sufficient to signal to the PIE what important unmet *health economic* needs exist, such as for pharmaceutical innovations that prevent chronic disease or can be administered cheaply at home. In some cases, it would not be sufficient to only *enable or incentivize* those pharmaceutical innovations. Where necessary, the patient habitat must do *both* in a coherent way, so that enablers and incentives are aligned to the same ends.

As with other habitats, it's hard to see how the PIE can be healthy unless the patient habitat meets these requirements. If the habitat doesn't enable or incentivize as needed, or if it signals only clinical or

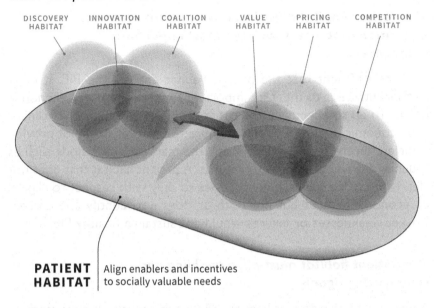

DISCOVERY   INNOVATION   COALITION   VALUE   PRICING   COMPETITION
HABITAT   HABITAT   HABITAT   HABITAT   HABITAT   HABITAT

PATIENT | Align enablers and incentives
HABITAT | to socially valuable needs

Figure 9.1 The patient habitat's contribution to a healthy PIE

health economic needs but not both, or if it sends mixed messages, the pharmaceutical innovation that will emerge from the PIE is unlikely to meet society's needs well enough to sustain the social contract. It was with these three requirements in mind that I set out, with the help of my expert informants and building on the work of earlier researchers, to assess how well the patient habitat currently supports the health of the PIE.

Is the patient habitat capable of supporting a healthy PIE?

The importance of the patient habitat to the working of the PIE is justification enough to question how well it works but, as I explored this part of the PIE, my attention was drawn to three particular points.

The first is the horribly difficult nature of the task that the patient habitat has to perform. To guide the rest of the PIE, it must accurately convey all the information needed for researchers, innovators, investors, and others to make good resource allocation decisions. This information includes the probability of the basic science being translatable into approved drugs, the size of the market for that drug, and the likely share, sales, and profit that might result. To enable a healthy PIE, the patient habitat must provide the information to estimate all of that not just at one moment in time but some years into the future. The difficulty of that task alone makes it worth asking if the habitat is up to the job.

Expert informant Dan Brennan summed up the difficulty of the patient habitat's task well.

> *The decisions involved in investing in pharmaceutical innovation involve estimating multiple risks, each of which is multifactorial and much less understood that we'd like it to be. We're faced with the task of estimating scientific, regulatory, competitive, reimbursement and even political risk with imperfect information, technological change (including obsolescence), and considerable uncertainty from other sources, including financial market or inflationary risks over a long period. That's why investors expect good returns on the few drugs that reach the market. The more that we can increase clarity, reduce uncertainty, and manage those risks, the better the pharmaceutical innovation ecosystem will work.*
>
> Dan Brennan

The second reason to be concerned about how well the patient habitat works is the way that society's needs are evolving. I've already described how the pharmaceutical industry's environment is in the midst of six great shifts, driven by fundamental changes in its sociological and technological environments. One of these is the shift away from defining the value of an innovative medicine only in terms of clinical outcomes, and toward defining value as its health economic value. When a market's definition of value is changing in such an important and fundamental way, it's reasonable to ask if the patient habitat is capable of signaling those new and different needs.

The third and perhaps most immediate cause for concern is the tension in the social contract, already touched on in Chapter 1. When, as they do, polls indicate that over 80% of US adults think drug pricing is unreasonable, they reveal a perception that the PIE is not meeting society's expectations.[7] Whether those perceptions are objectively accurate is beside the point. They indicate a social contract under strain and possibly a patient habitat not working as it should.

With these three concerns in mind and using the three requirements of the patient habitat as my indicators of good health, I explored the habitat and reduced my findings to five principal issues.

The patient habitat relies on market forces that are disconnected from value

In most free and functioning markets, prices are the primary channel through which the demand side communicates with the supply side. The market for innovative medicines is no different from other markets in this respect, as expert informant Cyrus Arman explained to me.

> *Although the possibilities for innovation are framed by the basic science, the direction of innovation – which diseases, which indications and so on – are driven by the economics. The investors that fund pharmaceutical innovation, whether that's venture capital or stock market investors, are free to invest anywhere, inside or outside the life sciences business. The inevitable consequence of this is that investment into pharmaceutical innovation follows wherever the return on investment is thought to be.*
>
> Cyrus Arman

In practice, "following the money" means pharmaceutical innovators listen most closely to those signals that carry information about price and volume. In most markets, these two variables are largely driven by customers' perceptions of value relative to competitors but the pharmaceutical market isn't like most markets. In the market for innovative medicines, the links between price, volume, and value don't work in quite the same way they do for ordinary consumer products.

I won't repeat here findings from the chapters that dealt with these market imperfections (see Chapters 6–8). I'll simply restate that, for the most part, the prices charged for innovative medicines during their periods of limited competition, before imitative generics or biosimilars compete, are not closely related to the value of the medicine. Value is hard to assess, competition is constrained, and pricing is distorted by the market strength of intermediaries such as PBMs, insurers, and providers. Pharmaceutical companies, with their fiduciary duty to shareholders, set prices to maximize their returns, and are limited only by the countervailing market power of intermediaries. The price paid at the point of care is determined by the relative market power of very large, concentrated intermediaries and their relatively smaller, fragmented customers, such as plan providers. The net result is a disconnect between price and value so that, unlike in most other markets, the demand side of the market – patients and their proxies such as public and private insurers – can't fully communicate its perception of value to the makers of innovative medicines.

In addition to the points I covered in earlier chapters, there is other evidence that the patient habitat relies on signals from a dysfunctional market. For example, a systematic review of competition and price among brand name drugs, which included ten empirical studies across multiple disease areas, found that competition had little impact on list prices.[8] Other research has even suggested that imminent competition drives up prices.[9] Other work has found that pharmaceuticals are "price inelastic" meaning that demand doesn't change much as price changes.[10] The reasons that the market for innovative medicines behaves this way are complex, situation-specific, and beyond the scope of this discussion. But the lesson we can draw from it is that, for innovative medicines, price and demand don't communicate value in the same as in other markets.

So, like most other markets, innovation in pharmaceuticals is driven by returns and, consequently, investors use price and demand as signals to direct their decisions. But, unlike other markets, the price of innovative medicines isn't strongly connected to the perceived value and, when competition is constrained, the relationship between price and demand is weak. This implies that a patient habitat that relies heavily on market signals may not be able to communicate what it values in the way that a healthy PIE needs it to.

The patient habitat's communication of clinical needs is incoherent

Since the market is disconnected from value and can't accurately communicate society's need to the PIE, I focused my attention on the complementary, non-price mechanisms that are used to signal what society wants. One expert informant, who asked not to be identified, eloquently summarized this issue for me.

> *Pharmaceutical innovation occurs when three conditions are met. First, there is scientific potential. Second, there is a medical need. Third, there is potential for return on investment. In theory, science policy aligns the first two, but in practice it does so imperfectly. Equally, the markets should align the second two but again they only do so imperfectly. In both cases, there is always significant uncertainty around all three. The system we have works well in some cases, such as rare diseases, and less well in some others, such as new antibiotics. To improve the situation, we must "first do no harm," as the Hippocratic oath goes, but then look at the push and pull mechanisms that enable and incentivize pharmaceutical innovation.*
>
> *Anonymous expert informant*

I've addressed both push mechanisms, such as NIH funding, and pull mechanisms, such as patent protection and regulatory exclusivity, in Chapters 3 and 8, respectively. I won't repeat that discussion here, but it is important to look at how they connect to the patient habitat.

The competition habitat is all about signals. It explicitly signals both that we value innovation and that we preferentially value some kinds of innovation over others. As I described in Chapter 8, the PIE has responded strongly to those signals, with prolific patenting activity and rapid growth in, for example, orphan drugs.

The competition habitat has its weaknesses, such as susceptibility to abuse, but the PIE listens and responds to what it hears. But what is it hearing? Neither patents nor regulatory exclusivity reflects the nation's health priorities very accurately. For example, the leading burdens of disease in the US, which are heart disease, lung cancer, low back pain, and chronic obstructive pulmonary disease,[11] are not specifically incentivized. There is a degree of incentive for some innovative medicines in the FDA's accelerated approval processes but the alignment to the nation's health burden is weak.

In theory, the nation's health priorities are set and communicated by agencies of the Department of Health and Human Services (HHS), including the Office of Disease Prevention and Health Promotion (ODPHP) and the Centers for Disease Control and Prevention (CDC), but their objectives are very wide and poorly focused. ODPHP, for example, has no fewer than 355 core objectives, in addition to its developmental and research objectives.[12] The CDC rolls together its objectives as "National Health Initiatives, Strategies and Action Plans" from which you can infer another diffuse set of priorities. Under that heading, it lists over 50 areas of activity, ranging from hepatitis to bicycle safety.[13] In an unintended confession that health policy is poorly coordinated at the national level, the CDC site adds "This list is not exhaustive, so if you are aware of a national public health initiative or plan that is not included here, let us know." The HHS, CDC, and ODPHP are essential and well-respected bodies who do important work. But it's quite clear that there is very little alignment between how the USPTO, FDA, and other instruments of government use their "pull" and how the HHS sees America's health priorities.

On the push side of the equation, NIH funding is a loud and clear signal that society values pharmaceutical innovation. In Chapter 3, I suggested that the NIH might nudge basic researchers toward what society values. Its strategic plans are the best indicator of how it currently does that. Each of the 21 NIH institutes has its own strategic plan, each with a bewildering array of cross-cutting themes, scientific objectives, and broad research directions.[14] Each has its own set of research priorities. The National Heart, Lung and Blood Institute, for example, has 132[15] and, collectively, NIH research priorities are too many to count. Yet, despite the number of words used to communicate what it is focusing on, it is very hard to find any reference to what research has been *deprioritized*. Nor is it easy to discern any deliberate link between the nation's health priorities, the priorities of the CDC and ODPHP and the research priorities of the NIH. There is overlap in the diseases they talk about, but very little sign of coordination. Again, it's quite clear that there is very little alignment between how the NIH uses its "push" mechanism of research funding and how its sister agencies see what is ailing America.

I'm personally reluctant to criticize those who work so hard to improve the health of Americans, but there is a clear weakness in the patient habitat. Not only is the market poorly equipped to communicate to the PIE what society values, so too are its complementary institutional channels. The powerful push and pull mechanisms for enabling and incentivizing valuable innovation are not working together. As a result, society is sending many signals to the PIE about what it needs, but those signals are neither clear nor coherent, they are more like white noise. This strongly compromises the ability of the patient habitat to meet the requirements of a healthy PIE.

The patient habitat does not signal its needs for health economic innovation

An effective patient habitat would enable and incentivize not only society's clinical priorities but also its most important health economic needs. In the same way as it has signaled, through the Orphan Drug Act, that "a cure for acromegaly would be valuable,"[16] it might also signal, for example, that "orally administered biologics for rheumatoid arthritis would be valuable."[17] The difference between the two signals would be that the first communicated an unmet clinical need, the second would communicate that while current therapy meets clinical needs, a health economic need is unmet. The patient habitat does already signal some unmet health economic needs in the legislation that enables accelerated approvals of small-molecule generics and biosimilars. As I described in Chapter 8, this imitation-led approach to signaling "society values the same outcomes at lower cost" has had contrasting results. It has enabled and encouraged generic imitation of small molecules much more successfully than it has for biosimilar imitation of biologic medicines.

But what I found remarkable as I explored the patient habitat was that, while it strongly signals that imitation is valuable, it does little to signal that it values innovation that meets health economic needs. There are three main ways that innovation, rather than imitation, might produce the same or better outcomes. The first includes innovations that allow the same therapy to be delivered less expensively, such as the oral biologic example I gave above.[18] A second category includes innovations that prevent rather than treat disease and so obviate expensive treatments, much as we do already with statins for hyperlipidemia and ACE inhibitors for hypertension. Increasingly, advances in genomics will allow "precision prevention" medicines that could impact significantly on healthcare costs.[19] The third category is curative therapies. I've already mentioned the impact of curative therapies in Hepatitis C, but advances in cell and gene therapy in particular mean that therapies that fix, rather than just manage a condition will become more possible. For example, the sickle-cell disease may soon be curable by gene therapy.[20] Each of these three categories is a way to innovate to meet society's health economic need to get better "bang for bucks," but this approach is neglected by the patient habitat, in contrast to its signals that enable and incentivize cost saving by imitation.

This weakness to signal the need for cost-saving innovation is especially problematic because other aspects of the PIE constrain innovation aimed at meeting health economic needs. For example, providers have an incentive to favor specialty medicines administered by professionals, rather than at home. Preventative therapies are hindered by the higher costs of demonstrating the effectiveness of prevention, compared to demonstrating immediate symptom remission. Personalized curative cell and gene therapies are often very expensive to develop and make and, since they destroy their own market, those costs have to be recovered in the short term. Further, switching patients between insurance plans gives insurers a disincentive to pay for curative therapies. In these and other ways, the market makes it hard for cost-reducing innovation, which implies an even greater need for the patient habitat to signal that it values them.

During this part of my research, I was especially struck by expert informant Michael Hodin, whose long experience and wisdom gave him a historical perspective. When I asked him about how the patient habitat influenced the PIE, he put it clearly.

> *We have a 1960s system trying to work in the 2020s, when science, technology, behaviors, and expectations have all changed. This leads to structural problems in affordability, regulatory access, and a tendency to paternalistic, centralized thinking. We need to shift attitudes to see healthcare spending as an investment, not a cost, and to see patients, especially older patients, as an asset not a liability.*
>
> Michael Hodin

Michael Hodin was taking a broad view, but one particular aspect of what he describes is that, even though health economic needs have become salient in the 2020s, the patient habitat does not currently signal that to the PIE. Until it does, that weakness will compromise the health of the PIE.

The patient habitat lacks knowledge management capabilities

For the patient habitat to identify, prioritize and signal both its clinical and health economic needs, it needs to know how well current therapies are meeting those needs. And, because those signals will be economically and socially consequential, that knowledge needs to be of good quality. Yet, in my exploration of the patient habitat, I was struck by little we know about the effectiveness of existing therapies, clinically but especially economically. To be clear, there many sources of information. Academic researchers study the clinical outcomes of new therapies. A few of these are studies of cost-effectiveness. Manufacturers produce efficacy data to support regulation and for post-launch marketing purposes. Insurers and PBMs catalogue who gets what medicines and at what cost. Healthcare providers record treatments, health outcomes, and other relevant variables about the patient. Increasingly, patients are generating their own data too, on smartwatches and other wearables. Market research companies like IQVIA produce very good information, mostly to support pharmaceutical companies' planning. Companies like Datavant connect and analyze health data for providers. As a society, our ability to generate haystacks of data has become remarkable. The same cannot be said of our ability to find the needles of knowledge about our clinical and health economic needs.

This needle and haystack problem has two components. The first is the ability to gather and organize data. Healthcare lags other sectors in data analytics because of data fragmentation, confidentiality, and other issues.[21] The second is the ability to translate that data into useful knowledge. Data analytics and knowledge management are complementary but different capabilities that would allow the patient habitat to identify and communicate what it needs to the PIE.[22] At present, those capabilities don't seem to exist in the US, at least not in one or more center of excellence equivalent to, for example, the FDA CDER's expertise in drug regulation or the CDC's expertise in epidemiology. The net result of this is that we have only a poor, fragmented idea of what unmet clinical and health economic needs we would like the PIE to address.

If these issues of immature capabilities and no center of excellence sound familiar, that's because they are similar to those described in Chapter 6 about how to make value assessments. At this point in my exploration, I've wandered into the borderlands between the patient and value habitats and I'm seeing the same landscape from another perspective. So, I won't repeat what I discussed in that chapter, except to put it into the context of this habitat.

As I described in Chapter 6, without high-quality knowledge about the costs and outcomes of using an innovative medicine, it's impossible to assess the value of that particular medicine. On a larger scale, without high-quality knowledge about what medicines are being used at what cost and with what outcome, it's impossible for the patient habitat to identify and prioritize the needs it should signal to the PIE. The same opportunities exist in both cases, in that there are lots of haystacks of data and islands of expertise. The same challenges hinder the effectiveness of the two habitats, including data fragmentation, interoperability, patient and commercial confidentiality, and a political reluctance for government to play a part. But, while the value habitat has at least a prototype center of excellence in ICER, the patient habitat's expertise in data analytics and knowledge management is scattered across every part of the habitat. Even if the first three issues, above, were addressed and all of the right data were available, no one is asking how well current therapies are meeting society's needs and what unmet needs should be signaled to the PIE. Until the patient habitat develops both data analytic and knowledge management capabilities, it will not be fully able to support a healthy PIE.

The patient habitat communicates cultural values only indirectly

My preceding four points revolve around the most obvious function of the patient habitat, the identification, prioritization, and signaling of society's clinical and health economic needs to the PIE. But there was one other point that emerged that was crystallized for me by expert informant Phyllis Barkman Ferrell.

> *The pharma industry, and especially its leading research-based companies, is seeing a shift in its environment. Both investors and society more generally are beginning to judge us not only according to the financial value we add but also by the social impact we have. This has many different aspects, from environmental impact, diversity in clinical trials, access to medicines and many other things. These things are often shorthanded to the term ESG criteria, Environmental, Social and Governance, and companies like ours, with a large stake and a long heritage in American society, are increasingly sensitive to this.*
> Phyllis Barkman Ferrell

This point was raised by several informants. It's also a salient topic in both the academic literature and industry media.[23] This shows that society values not only innovative and affordable medicines but also alignment with core cultural values, such as fairness and honesty. There is, of course, no agency or body that communicates these values to the PIE. That is left to a disparate collection of activist investors using ESG criteria and to public opinion and patient advocacy groups. This leaves the channel dominated by passionate, well-meaning activists who may not accurately represent society's views. It takes only a brief exposure to this part of Twitter to see how vociferous these constituencies are, and how little constructive discussion is involved. This low-fidelity, high volume channel for communicating societal expectations to the PIE is a significant weakness in the patient habitat's ability to support a healthy PIE.

Overall, my assessment of the health of the patient habitat was a negative one. It relies on market mechanisms to direct investment in pharmaceutical innovation, even though that market is disconnected from value. Its push and pull mechanisms are blunt and poorly aligned with the nation's clinical and health economic priorities. Further, they take an imitation-led view of how to meet health-economic needs. This view neither enables nor incentivizes innovation to improve "bang for bucks," even though that kind of innovation particularly needs support. Even if better signaling mechanisms were available, society doesn't have good capabilities for knowing what clinical and health economic needs it should prioritize. Finally, its less tangible but strongly felt needs for fairness and honesty have no conduit other than those whose passion hinders balance. Taken together, these weaknesses mean that the patient habitat, as it is today, cannot provide the PIE with what it needs to be healthy.

How can we improve the health of the patient habitat?

A sustainable supply of affordable, innovative medicines is a lot to ask of the PIE. It is only possible if each of the habitats plays its part and provides what is required of it. The patient habitat has the particular responsibility of signaling to the PIE, through a variety of pull and push mechanisms, what society values. Without those signals, innovative medicines will still emerge, but their costs and benefits may not convince American society that the social contract is worth preserving. Opinion polls suggest we're closer to the tearing up of that contract than is comfortable. Today, the patient habitat is maladapted to an environment where society defines value economically as well as clinically. Frustratingly, many of the components of a fully functioning patient habitat, from huge haystacks of data to capable bodies of experts, are scattered around the PIE, but do not work together to signal society's needs. Consequently, society isn't telling the PIE what it wants in a coherent way. If we want a patient habitat that supports a healthy PIE and preserves the social contract, I suggest there are four things we need to do.

Build a knowledge management capability for societal needs

Any signals that the patient habitat sends to the PIE will be both socially impactful and politically sensitive. To be politically legitimate, they must be based on the best possible knowledge about how current medicines are meeting society's needs, both clinically and economically. This implies the need for a knowledge management capability that gathers and organizes data and analyzes it to create new, useful knowledge about what society needs the PIE to deliver. This might be analogous to the way American society already identifies its defense, transport, and other infrastructure needs.

The design and execution of such a knowledge management capability are beyond the scope of this book, but I will suggest three things for its builders to consider. First, since it will need to connect the relevant usage, costs, and outcomes data that is currently scattered across many parts of the healthcare system, this overlaps with the first task identified in Chapter 6, regarding value assessment, although it has broader goals. Second, it is unlikely that this system could be built in one step. It might be pragmatic to begin this huge task with those innovative medicines that have the highest economic and clinical importance and then build on that. Third, although the knowledge management part of this task – the asking and answering of difficult questions – fits well with the competencies of the HHS, the breadth of the task does not. Creating knowledge about society's clinical and economic needs might need an agency that combines health expertise with economic competencies.

As with any other important change, building this knowledge management capability would face American society with political choices. Culturally, the US has been most comfortable with a highly fragmented healthcare system that relies on market signals. A centralized knowledge management capability of this kind wouldn't replace the market but, in requiring private organizations to pool information for the national good, it represents a small step toward collectivism. Even though this step has some precedents, such as the pooling of data for economic statistics, even this small and valuable augmentation of market forces will doubtless disturb some.

Establish clear clinical and economic priorities

If the knowledge management capabilities described above are developed as suggested, they will reveal how well current medicines meet society's needs and what needs remain to be met by innovation. This will inevitably throw light on two issues. First, American society's clinical and economic demands on the PIE are many and varied. Second, the relative priority of those many needs will be subjective and politically sensitive. Inevitably, advocacy groups representing every patient population will see their needs as worthy of prioritization. Equally, payers and plan sponsors will look at their "big ticket" diseases and make calls to prioritize "bang for bucks" innovation in those areas. All parties will make cogent cases, empowered by evidence and emotion, and some will cooperate with pharmaceutical companies who aim to construct their own profitable ecological niche.[24] This inevitable and predictable behavior threatens to create the sort of "everything is important" situation that makes it impossible for the patient habitat to prioritize its signals to the PIE. If society's push and pull signaling is to be coherent, somebody, somewhere will need to prioritize the societal economic and clinical needs that come out of the knowledge management system.

These prioritizations will inevitably be political, as is appropriate when trying to reconcile conflicting perspectives in our society. As Aristotle observed, one of the purposes of politics is to reconcile differing views.[25] Those politicians involved in that process face an onerous task and I won't attempt to advise how they do it in any detail. But I will suggest four considerations that emerged from my research and that might guide their thinking. First, the variety of society's needs doesn't lend itself to simple prioritization on a linear scale of importance; they vary along multiple dimensions and are hard to compare directly. Second, the criteria for prioritizing society's needs will need to be sophisticated enough to avoid the tyranny of the masses. By that, I mean prioritizing purely in quantitative terms, which would disfavor small patient populations with severe needs. This implies a prioritization approach that combines quantitative and qualitative factors. Third, a more explicit prioritization process will focus the attention of lobbyists from every part of the PIE. The process will need to balance listening with insulating itself from lobbying power. If not, decisions will follow lobbying budgets instead of societal needs. Finally, the PIE is part of the wider health ecosystem that itself is part of a wider social ecosystem. It abuts areas like education and social welfare policies and they mutually influence each other. It would be better if clinical and health economic priorities were set recognizing that wider context rather than framed narrowly as a purely pharmaceutical or healthcare issue.[26]

Setting priorities for pharmaceutical innovation is a difficult task but it is not a new one. It is already embedded in the patient habitat, as we see in basic research investment, patent laws, and regulatory exclusivity. The choice facing American society is not whether to set priorities but how to do so. A deliberate, knowledgeable set of choices will be better than the current piecemeal approach based on weak knowledge. And explicit, transparent decisions will be better than those that are opaque and unquestioned. But thoughtful, explicit decisions will be politically much harder than the current, muddling approach. Choosing to make harder, smart decisions rather than easier, less-informed decisions will be the dilemma our politicians will face if we are to have a fully functioning patient habitat. It is a task for our political leaders.

Align societal signals to clinical and economic priorities

It will be difficult enough to identify and prioritize what American society needs from the PIE. But that effort will be wasted unless those choices are translated into a coherent set of signals that are aligned to reinforce each other and not conflict. This alignment will be made more difficult because it is between very different kinds of signals – "push" enablers and "pull" incentives – and because the signals will emanate from different, currently disconnected parts of the patient habitat, such as the USPTO, the FDA, and the NIH. But an aligned set of signals, that push and pull in the same direction, will be powerfully synergistic, as we've seen with orphan drugs and with Covid vaccines.

The design of signals that clearly communicate America's clinical and economic needs of the PIE will be difficult. The detail is beyond the scope of this book. It would obviously overlap a great deal with my suggestions for the other habitats. But I offer three thoughts for those signal designers to contemplate. First, the expertise involved in targeting different signals, from research investment to patents to regulatory, requires specialist expertise, while their coordination goes across specialisms.[27] This implies a strongly whole-government approach above even the level of government departments like HHS or the Department of Commerce. Second, transitioning from the current incoherent set of signals to an aligned set would face what evolutionary scientists would call a fitness trough. The gradual change in signaling would create more conflicting signals, so things would get worse before they got better. This implies that, unlike most institutional changes, a "big bang" of radical change might be necessary, including a bonfire of current well-meaning but blunt and incoherent signals to the PIE. Third, designing a coherent set of signals might need more than changing the current main signals of research funding and competition restriction. It might involve adding lesser-used push and pull mechanisms such as the risk-underwriting that enabled Covid vaccine development[28] or the innovation prizes or clinical trial funding that have been proposed to promote socially beneficial R&D.[29]

I've no illusions about the difficulty of executing societal priorities through a combination of push and pull. As with other changes to the patient habitat, it involves a political choice to steer the market by a country where government involvement in markets is disdained. But, as with my second suggestion, above, of setting clear clinical and economic priorities, this is not a case of deciding whether or not to direct the PIE. Legislators have done that for many years in successive legislative acts. The choice facing policymakers is whether to do so in an aligned, coherent way or to continue to send our current noisy, disjointed set of signals.

Agree a code of shared cultural values and behaviors

My first three suggestions, above, are steps toward the same goal: signaling clearly to the PIE exactly what clinical and economic needs society thinks is most important. This is necessary to support a healthy PIE. But perhaps my most worrying conclusion from my exploration of the patient habitat is that even if I had waved my magic wand and made those needs clear, the habitat would still not have completed its task. That's because these first three steps concern society's clinical and health economic needs but does nothing to address its cultural values that are relevant to the social contract.

No one who looks closely at the PIE can avoid the unhappy conclusion that, at present, American society doesn't think that pharmaceutical companies, behave honestly, fairly and in the best interests of patients and society. Opinion polls, cited earlier in this chapter and in Chapter 1, show this. If more evidence is needed, take a moment to search for books about the pharmaceutical industry on Amazon. Your search will be dominated by titles like "Sick Money: The Truth About the Global Pharmaceutical Industry," "The Price of Health: The Modern Pharmaceutical Enterprise and the Betrayal of a History of Care," and "Drugs, Money, and Secret Handshakes: The Unstoppable Growth of Prescription Drug Prices." One of the most widely read books about the industry is called simply "Bad Pharma." These, and many other books, articles, and media channels recount practices by the pharmaceutical industry that are perceived as common and typical, including price hiking, withholding trial data, manipulating patents, and other anti-competitive practices. Whether those practices are typical or outliers, as the industry would maintain, is less important than that they are perceived to be the norm. It is this perception that threatens the social contract and, by extension, the future of pharmaceutical innovation.

Like any good contract, the social contract needs to be about more than meeting functional, transactional needs. To sustain the social contract, the patient habitat needs a way of signaling society's behavioral expectations to the rest of the PIE and for the PIE to signal back that it is meeting those expectations. Communicating such intangible needs is difficult and requires long-term effort from both sides. To those two sides, I suggest the following. First, they might jointly develop a set of shared, explicit values. This could build on the values already espoused by leading companies,[30] but with additions that reflect society's modern concern for fairness and equity of access. Second, this set of values might be codified into an industry code of conduct that prescribes acceptable and proscribes unacceptable behavior. Models for this already exist in, for example, codes of conduct for how pharmaceutical companies interact with healthcare professionals,[31] but this code would need to be much wider, to include all issues that concern American society about the pharmaceutical industry, including pricing. Third, this industry code might be enforced by a combination of social and commercial policing. All companies might be expected to sign up to the code, and non-adherence might be adjudicated by a body that represents both the industry and elements of society. Companies judged to have broken the code would suffer reputational damage, investor reaction, and commercial disadvantage. This approach might build on the B corporation movement, which encourages high standards of environmental, social, and governance behavior.[32]

In practical terms, the challenge to this recommendation lies not in agreeing on shared values but in implementing them so that they do not become a meaningless list of platitudes, the pharmaceutical values equivalent of "greenwashing." But, if executed well, a code of conduct would benefit both society and the PIE by being a channel to communicate and agree cultural values. It would present pharmaceutical companies with the choice to align to those values or to ignore them in a very visible way. It would also offer society a channel to communicate what it requires of the PIE in a higher-fidelity, more effective way than social media, polemic books, and activism.

Will this be enough?

As in other chapters, I have again limited my suggestions to broad guidance and avoided making specific policy recommendations. There are many people more qualified than me to execute the detailed mechanics of my suggestions. But the patient habitat has an important role in the PIE and, at present, it is not fulfilling that role. To imitate Henry Kissinger, when the PIE wants to speak to American society, who does it call?

Until the patient habitat meets the requirements laid out earlier in this chapter, the PIE can't deliver what we're asking of it and the social contract is at risk. As with the suggestions I've made in other chapters, my suggestions for the patient habitat would only work fully if they were executed together. And, even more than for other habitats, my suggestions for the patient habitat overlap a great deal with those for other habitats.

Even if all my suggestions were executed fully at once, they would still leave some of society's needs out of reach of the PIE because they are the remit of other social ecosystems, such as the wider healthcare and social welfare ecosystems. The PIE can't solve all of the problems of poverty and unhealthy lifestyle, for example. But, with the addition of these four suggestions to the suggestions from Chapters 3–8, I complete my exploration of the PIE. What remains is not about exploration but about execution and that is the subject of my last chapter.

Notes

1 George W Merck is famously quoted as saying that medicine is for the patient. To quote him more fully,

> We try to remember that medicine is for the patient. We try never to forget that medicine is for the people. It is not for the profits. The profits follow and, if we have remembered that, they have never failed to appear. The better we have remembered it, the larger they have been.

2 To put this in perspective, about 66% of all adults in the United States use prescription drugs. This usage pattern is very age dependent, with over 90% of Americans over 80 using prescription drugs. It also varies by other demographic factors, such as gender, race, ethnicity, income and, predictably, health status. About 64 million Americans are covered by Medicare, about 76 million by Medicaid and CHIP and 9 million by the Veteran's Health Administration. About half of all Americans are covered by employer health insurance. This data assembled

from various sources, see https://hpi.georgetown.edu/; https://www.medicar-eresources.org/; https://www.medicaid.gov; https://www.va.gov/; https://www.kff.org/.

3 Patient Advocacy Organisations are generally non-profit organisations. As of 2017, there were 7835 such organisations in the US, of which 67% received industry funding. See ref 1.

4 The HHS has 11 operating divisions, including the NIH, CDC and FDA, and 15 Offices of the Secretary. See https://www.hhs.gov/about/agencies/orgchart/index.html.

5 The free market has been unsuccessful at incentivizing the development of new antibiotics, which are needed because of the rise of antimicrobial resistance. Various governments around the world are attempting to incentivize the market to do so. See ref 2 and 3. In the US, this has included the Generating Antibiotic Incentives Now Act (GAIN Act) of 2012, which has so far had disappointing results. See ref 4.

6 For a good review of this exceptional example of pharmaceutical innovation. See ref 5.

7 This headline figure conceals findings that are still more indicative of strain on the social contract. Dissatisfaction with drug prices is evenly spread across political allegiances, two thirds of Americans are unconvinced by arguments made by pharmaceutical companies against cost control measures. See https://www.kff.org/health-costs/poll-finding/public-weighs-in-on-medicare-drug-negotiations/.

8 To quote from this paper, "Our findings suggest that policies to promote brand–brand competition in the US pharmaceutical market, such as accelerating approval of non-first-in-class drugs, will likely not result in lower drug list prices absent additional structural reforms." See ref 6.

9 See ref 7.

10 See ref 8.

11 The burden of disease is typically measured in terms of disability adjusted life years or years of life lost. Some diseases stand out as both highly prevalent and highly consequential. Significantly, disease burdens vary markedly with socio-demographic indicators and geographically within the US. See ref 9.

12 See https://health.gov/healthypeople.

13 https://www.cdc.gov/publichealthgateway/strategy/index.html.

14 See for example that of the National Institute of Arthritis and Musculoskeletal and Skin Diseases https://www.niams.nih.gov/sites/default/files/pdf/NIAMS-StrategicPlan-2020-2024-v1.pdf.

15 https://www.nhlbi.nih.gov/about/strategic-vision/research-priorities.

16 Acromegaly is a rare hormonal disorder that develops when the pituitary gland produces too much growth hormone during adulthood. Currently, there are five medications approved by the FDA for this condition as orphan drugs. See https://rarediseases.info.nih.gov/diseases/fda-orphan-drugs.

17 Biologic drugs, such as Humira for rheumatoid arthritis, can't be taken orally as they are broken down in the stomach. They are generally infused or injected under medical supervision, which adds direct and indirect costs. Consequently, orally administered biologics would have significant economic advantages over existing therapies. At the time of writing, few oral biologics are available but the science is looking promising. See ref 10.

18 As a practical example of this, Intract and Celltrion are jointly developing an oral infliximab for irritable bowel disease. It is one of several technologies under development for oral delivery of biologics. See https://www.centerforbiosimi-lars.com/view/chasing-the-holy-grail-of-oral-biologics.

19 The possibilities for "precision prevention" look very exciting See ref 12.

20 See ref 13.
21 There is an extensive literature on data analytics in healthcare that is itself, ironically, fragmented. To quote the Brookings Institute: "Despite the immense promise of health analytics, the industry lags behind other major sectors in taking advantage of cutting-edge tools." See https://www.brookings.edu/research/the-opportunities-and-challenges-of-data-analytics-in-health-care/. See also: refs 14–16.
 Data analytics to understand the clinical and economic effectiveness of innovative medicines is a subset of this literature, and the general theme of that literature is that this field is full of promise but it is its infancy. See refs 17 and 18.
22 See for example refs 19–21.
23 See refs 22 and 23.
24 Niche construction is a term used by ecologists to describe when an organism alters its local environment. Earthworms modifying soil and beavers building dams are examples of this. In some industries, firms create niches by having regulations and technical standards written in their favor. See ref 24.
25 See https://plato.stanford.edu/entries/aristotle-politics/#PolSci.
26 For a good discussion of this topic. See ref 25.
27 Organizational scientists call this the congruency hypothesis. We need each group of specialists to be macrocongruent – aligned to – with their field. We also need them to be microcongruent – aligned to – each other. But, as specialists become more macrocongruent, it becomes harder to be micrcongruent. It is the challenge of specialization vs integration first written about by Adam Smith in 1776. See ref 26.
28 One way of incentivizing innovation is to mitigate the risk involved. For an interesting discussion of this and ideas about how to improve on existing approaches. See ref 27.
29 See ref 28.
30 For perhaps the archetypal example of this, see Johnson and Johnson's credo https://www.jnj.com/credo/.
31 See https://phrma.org/resource-center/Topics/STEM/Code-on-Interactions-with-Health-Care-Professionals.
32 See https://www.bcorporation.net/en-us/certification.

References

1 Rose SL, Highland J, Karafa MT, Joffe S. Patient advocacy organizations, industry funding, and conflicts of interest. *JAMA Internet Medicine.* 2017;177(3):344–50.
2 Dutescu IA, Hillier SA. Encouraging the development of new antibiotics: Are financial incentives the right way forward? A systematic review and case study. *Infection Drug Resistance.* 2021;14:415–34.
3 Morel CM, Lindahl O, Harbarth S, de Kraker MEA, Edwards S, Hollis A. Industry incentives and antibiotic resistance: An introduction to the antibiotic susceptibility bonus. *The Journal of Antibiotics.* 2020;73(7):421–8.
4 Darrow JJ, Kesselheim AS. Incentivizing antibiotic development: Why isn't the generating antibiotic incentives now (GAIN) act working? *Open Forum Infectious Diseases.* 2020;7(1).
5 Mango P. *Warp Speed: Inside the Operation That Beat COVID, the Critics, and the Odds.* New York: Republic; 2022.

6 Sarpatwari AD, Jonathan ZM, Najafzadeh KA. Competition and price among brand-name drugs in the same class: A systematic review of the evidence. *PLOS Medicine.* 2019;16(7).

7 Ellyson AM, Basu A. Do pharmaceutical prices rise anticipating branded competition? *Health Economics.* 2021;30(5):1070–81.

8 Yeung K, Basu A, Hansen RN, Sullivan SD. Price elasticities of pharmaceuticals in a value based-formulary setting. *Health Economics.* 2018;27(11):1788–804.

9 Mokdad AH, Ballestros K, Echko M, Glenn S, Olsen HE, Mullany E et al. The state of US health, 1990–2016: burden of diseases, injuries, and risk factors among US states. *Jama.* 2018;319(14):1444–72.

10 New R. Oral delivery of biologics via the intestine. *Pharmaceutics.* 2020;13(1):18.

11 Mullard A. FDA approves oral version of diabetes biologic. *Nature Reviews Drug Discovery.* 2019;18(11):814–.

12 Bíró K, Dombrádi V, Jani A, Boruzs K, Gray M. Creating a common language: Defining individualized, personalized and precision prevention in public health. *Journal of Public Health (Oxford, England).* 2018;40(4):e552–e9.

13 Eisenstein M. Gene therapies close in on a cure for sickle-cell disease. *Nature (London).* 2021;596(7873):S2–S4.

14 Olaronke I, Oluwaseun O, editors. Big data in healthcare: Prospects, challenges and resolutions. *Future Technologies Conference (FTC).* 2016;6–7Dec: 2016.

15 Mehta N, Pandit A. Concurrence of big data analytics and healthcare: A systematic review. *International Journal of Medical Informatics.* 2018;114:57–65.

16 Khanra S, Dhir A, Islam AKMN, Mäntymäki M. Big data analytics in healthcare: A systematic literature review. *Enterprise Information Systems.* 2020;14(7):878–912.

17 Lu ZK, Xiong X, Lee T, Wu J, Yuan J, Jiang B. Big data and real-world data based cost-effectiveness studies and decision-making models: A systematic review and analysis. *Frontiers in Pharmacology.* 2021;12.

18 Bowrin K, Briere JB, Levy P, Millier A, Clay E, Toumi M. Cost-effectiveness analyses using real-world data: An overview of the literature. *Journal Medicine Economy.* 2019;22(6):545–53.

19 Ferraris A, Mazzoleni A, Devalle A, Couturier J. Big data analytics capabilities and knowledge management: Impact on firm performance. *Management Decision.* 2019;57(8):1923–36.

20 Schaefer C, Makatsaria A. framework of data analytics and integrating knowledge management. *International Journal of Intelligent Networks.* 2021;2:156–65.

21 Shabbir MQ, Gardezi SBW. Application of big data analytics and organizational performance: The mediating role of knowledge management practices. *Journal of Big Data.* 2020;7(1):1–17.

22 López-Toro AA, Sánchez-Teba EM, Benítez-Márquez MD, Rodríguez-Fernández M. Influence of ESGC indicators on financial performance of listed pharmaceutical companies. *International Journal of Environmental Research and Public Health.* 2021;18(9):4556.

23 Paolone F, Cucari N, Wu J, Tiscini R. How do ESG pillars impact firms' marketing performance? A configurational analysis in the pharmaceutical sector. *Journal of Business & Industrial Marketing.* 2021;ahead-of-print(ahead-of-print).

24 Luksha P. Niche construction: The process of opportunity creation in the environment. *Strategic Entrepreneurship Journal.* 2008;2(4):269–83.

25 Kyle MK. The alignment of innovation policy and social welfare: Evidence from pharmaceuticals. *Innovation Policy and the Economy*. 2020;20:95–123.
26 Burrell G, Morgan G. *Sociological Paradigms and Organizational Analysis*. 1st ed. Beverley Hills, CA: Sage; 1979.
27 Manheim D, Foster D. Option-based guarantees to accelerate urgent, high-risk vaccines: A new market-shaping approach. *F1000Res*. 2020;9:1154–.
28 Stiglitz JE, Jayadev A. Medicine for tomorrow: Some alternative proposals to promote socially beneficial research and development in pharmaceuticals. *Journal of Generic Medicines*. 2010;7(3):217–26.

10 Breaking ground, raising the debate

Precis

- There is a strong societal consensus that pharmaceutical innovation is economically and socially valuable.
- There is disagreement about how to ensure that pharmaceutical innovation is both economically sustainable and affordable.
- An ecological perspective suggests that many complementary measures are needed to achieve this aim.
- These measures are interconnected in feedback loops, are synergistic, and involve multiple entities, making them impossible to prioritize in any simple way.
- Their implementation would best be achieved through three projects that recognize this interconnectedness:
  - the valuable innovation project, which would aim to make innovation more efficient and effective
  - the valid value pricing project, which would aim to enable the market via value-based pricing
  - the managed competition project, which would aim to enable the market through balancing innovation and imitation
- Any constructive approach to achieving sustainable, affordable, pharmaceutical innovation must begin by raising the debate to one about how we achieve both sustained innovation and affordability.

You may have read this book assiduously, scribbling notes, underlining sentences, and marking sections with Post-it notes. Or you may have simply skimmed, reading the precis boxes and looking at the figures. Whichever type of reader you are, I hope you've absorbed the four central messages of this book.

DOI: 10.4324/9781003330271-10

- Pharmaceutical innovation is vital to our society. It's important we get it right and just as important we don't mess it up.
- Pharmaceutical innovation is an emergent property of a complex, adaptive ecosystem. This ecosystem perspective helps our understanding and can guide our actions.
- The current pharmaceutical innovation ecosystem (PIE) is unhealthy. If we want affordable, innovative medicines, we must manage it with care.
- There are many things we must do to improve the health of the PIE. There is not a single, simple solution.

In this final, short chapter, I'll begin by very quickly summarizing those points. I'll then suggest how we might begin to manage the PIE. I'll close with a final thought to bear in mind as we engage in this important, difficult, and continuous management task.

Where are we now?

Despite the often vitriolic debate about the affordability of innovative medicines, a remarkable consensus emerged as I researched this book. In reading hundreds of papers and books and interviewing dozens of expert informants, I found a wide agreement that pharmaceutical innovation has been and will be very important to our society – clinically, economically, and in other ways. There is also agreement on, though not satisfaction with, the central pillars of pharmaceutical innovation: publicly funded basic research, private investment in development, regulatory controls, and limited competition. Further, everyone involved in the debate shares the same goal. That is, an economically sustainable supply of new medicines that are both innovative and affordable. It is worth remembering that this sort of consensus is not found for all sectors of our economy. For example, there are those who think that much of the financial sector is not socially useful.[1] Other sectors, such as luxury goods[2] and long-haul tourism,[3] face substantial challenges regarding their societal value and environmental impact. Some argue that the fossil fuel industry must transform into something entirely different.[4] By comparison, nowhere in my extensive research did I find serious thinkers who proposed that pharmaceutical innovation is a bad thing or that it should be done in a fundamentally different way.[5] Instead, both apologists for and critics of the pharmaceutical industry share the same goal of optimizing pharmaceutical innovation, making it as valuable and as accessible as possible. They differ only in how they think that should be done.

In Chapter 1, I presented what I hope is a balanced view of both sides' perspectives on pharmaceutical innovation, which revealed deep disagreements about how to manage the affordability of innovative medicines. I argued that, to resolve these important differences, we needed a better approach to both understanding the issues and achieving our unusually shared goal. I also expressed the fear that, if we didn't find a better way of understanding and managing pharmaceutical innovation, we risked the breakdown of the social contract upon which it depends.

In Chapter 2, I proposed that thinking of pharmaceutical innovation as a mechanistic, x causes y, process was the wrong way to frame the debate. Although few with deep knowledge of innovative medicines really think in such simple terms, this flawed framing shapes the argument that divides American society. On one side of that dialectic are those that call for legislative price controls, through mechanisms such as referencing pricing, and think that simply pulling that lever will improve affordability and access without any unintended consequences. On the other side, are those who argue for the existing (and internationally exceptional) free-pricing model and think that this a gas pedal for innovation without any side effects. I argue that each perspective contains elements of truth, but both are simplistic. Can we expect the removal of a significant amount of the pharmaceutical industry's cash flow to not influence investment in innovation? Can we expect high levels of public distrust and anger about pharmaceutical pricing not to have political consequences? It is naive to hold either position, and that naivety arises from thinking about pharmaceutical innovation as the output of a complicated innovation machine. It is not. As I argue in Chapter 2, pharmaceutical innovation – its quantity, qualities, and costs – is an emergent property of a complex adaptive ecosystem. Complex is not the same thing as complicated, and we need to think of pharmaceutical innovation as if we were gardeners, not mechanics. When we do so, we begin to understand what is going on and what needs to be done. As I researched this book, I found the idea of the pharmaceutical innovation ecosystem (PIE) to be well accepted but misunderstood. The word "ecosystem" is used freely but almost always as a very loose and ill-considered figure of speech and rarely in any precise, scientific sense. To be necessarily clear about a central premise of this book, when I use the term "pharmaceutical innovation ecosystem," I am not speaking metaphorically. I am treating the pharmaceutical environment and biological environments as having "ontological communalities."[6] In plain English, pharmaceutical innovation is not *like* an ecosystem, it *is* an ecosystem.

In Chapters 3–9, I used the ecological paradigm to explore how we might achieve a sustainable supply of innovative, affordable medicines. Dividing the PIE into seven habitats was, I found, a useful device for better understanding it. I hope I reiterated myself often enough to communicate that the habitats are intellectual constructs and shouldn't be considered as discrete entities with defined boundaries. As my use of the term "habitat" was meant to convey, they are intertwined and interconnected aspects of the whole PIE. Semantic and definitional arguments about where their boundaries lie and who their inhabitants are miss the point. Using this device allowed me to untangle what the PIE needs from each habitat if it is to deliver the sustainable supply of affordable, innovative medicines we want. The habitats device also allowed me to better understand what is ailing the PIE and how we might better manage it for sustainable affordability and innovation. As I wrote in those chapters, the constraints on the functioning of the PIE are many, varied, and, as is the way of an ecosystem, connected. The PIE is not in good health and looks unlikely to yield what we ask of it. Many of the people I spoke to agreed with this conclusion. Others did not or thought I had overstated the case. In defense of my conclusion, I point to the huge numbers of diseases not yet cured, the serious issues of affordability, the low reputation in which the industry is held, and the challenge of paying for expensive, advanced therapies in the future. And I make that defense while simultaneously applauding the miraculous yield of the PIE in past years, from rendering HIV a chronic disease to transforming cancer care, to the COVID vaccines to – in Peter Kolchinsky's words – the creation of a huge armamentarium of cheap, effective generics. My conclusion is that we need to manage the PIE for the future just as much as we need to avoid damaging what led to its past successes. This baby and bathwater challenge is the hallmark of any successful evolutionary adaptation to a changing world. Readers with an evolutionary science background will recognize the Darwinian mechanism of variation, selection, and retention/replication implicit in my conclusion.

Breaking ground on a PIE for the future

In each of Chapters 3–9, I identified several steps toward improving the various habitats' ability to support a healthy PIE. I argued that

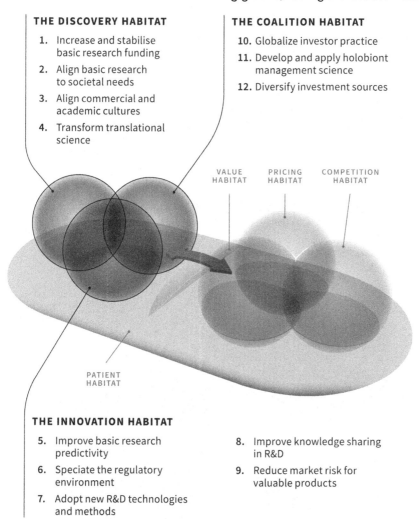

THE DISCOVERY HABITAT

1. Increase and stabilise basic research funding
2. Align basic research to societal needs
3. Align commercial and academic cultures
4. Transform translational science

THE COALITION HABITAT

10. Globalize investor practice
11. Develop and apply holobiont management science
12. Diversify investment sources

VALUE HABITAT

PRICING HABITAT

COMPETITION HABITAT

PATIENT HABITAT

THE INNOVATION HABITAT

5. Improve basic research predictivity
6. Speciate the regulatory environment
7. Adopt new R&D technologies and methods

8. Improve knowledge sharing in R&D
9. Reduce market risk for valuable products

Figure 10.1 Improving the health of the PIE 1

taking these steps would increase the probability of achieving our goal of affordable, innovative medicines in the long run. This number of suggestions (27 in total, see Figures 10.1 and 10.2) is an indication that in a complex, adaptive ecosystem, there are rarely any "magic bullets." It is the nature of ecosystems that they are best managed by many different and complementary interventions. Any ecologist or gardener or farmer knows this. I would argue that those who think the PIE can be "fixed" with just one or two interventions are still thinking mechanistically, and they have failed to make the paradigm shift to complex, adaptive ecosystem thinking.

For the pragmatically minded, the obvious question raised by this list of PIE-modifying suggestions is where to start. Again, I'm reminded of finding myself facing a large garden with many problems. It's important not to think mechanistically and to frame the issue as what order to pull each of these 27 levers. An ecological perspective suggests

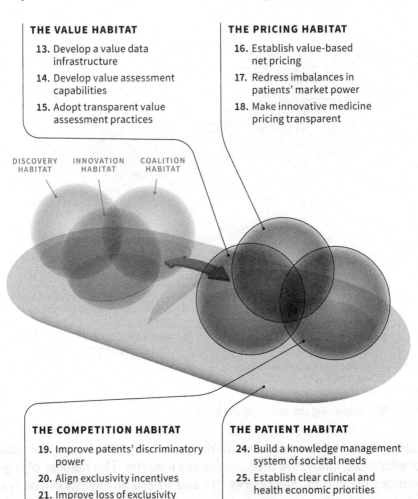

THE VALUE HABITAT

13. Develop a value data infrastructure
14. Develop value assessment capabilities
15. Adopt transparent value assessment practices

THE PRICING HABITAT

16. Establish value-based net pricing
17. Redress imbalances in patients' market power
18. Make innovative medicine pricing transparent

DISCOVERY HABITAT   INNOVATION HABITAT   COALITION HABITAT

THE COMPETITION HABITAT

19. Improve patents' discriminatory power
20. Align exclusivity incentives
21. Improve loss of exclusivity predictability
22. Enable market forces
23. Provide alternative imitation mechanisms

THE PATIENT HABITAT

24. Build a knowledge management system of societal needs
25. Establish clear clinical and health economic priorities
26. Align societal signals to societal priorities
27. Agree a code of shared cultural values

Figure 10.2 Improving the health of the PIE 2

four factors to consider in how we execute these suggestions. First, the interrelatedness of these 27 suggestions implies that a simple prioritization in order of importance would not work. Every suggestion relies on and is relied on by other suggestions. For example, establishing value-based net pricing depends on value assessment capabilities. Second, the feedback loops in the ecosystem are not straightforward. Most involve more than one activity as, for example, in Figure 10.3.

Third, the synergistic mechanisms between activities can be both internal and external.[7] For example, developing a data infrastructure (in the value habitat) and managing knowledge of societal needs (in the patient habitat) would have internal synergy. That is, they would jointly exploit some common assets. Other improvements would have external synergies. That is, they would not share assets, but they would reinforce each other's impact on the ecosystem. For example, advancing translational science (in the discovery habitat), reducing market risk (in the innovation habitat), and diversifying investor types (in the coalition habitat) would have this sort of synergy. Finally, the ecological perspective reminds us that many of these improvements involve the interactions between more than one entity within the

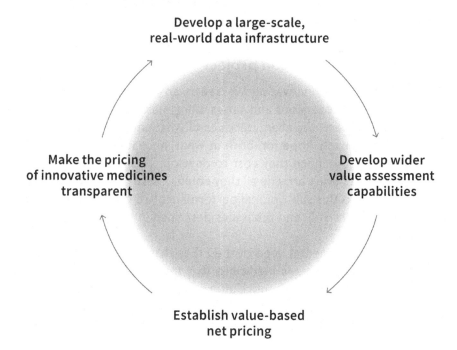

Figure 10.3 The value assessment feedback loop

PIE. Changes in the competition habitat, for example, will require an increase in coordination between United States Patent and Trademark Office (USPTO), Federal Trade Commission (FTC), and Food and Drug Administration (FDA) and perhaps others. Changes in the discovery habitat will require coordination between and within the many sub-units of Health and Human Services (HHS), including the National Institutes of Health (NIH) and Centers for Disease Control and Prevention (CDC). Some changes might require new entities, such as the suggested institute for holobiont research or broker entities to allow knowledge sharing. Taken together, these four factors, which are all consequences of the PIE's complex (as opposed to complicated) nature, imply that improving the PIE should be addressed as a number of major projects, each of which groups together some of the 27 suggestions according to their interrelatedness, synergistic mechanisms, and the entities they have in common. In other words, treating the PIE is akin to system medicine, in which the unit of interest is higher than individual organs but beneath the whole-organism level. Again, the detailed nature of these system-based projects is best left to those more expert in each area of the PIE, but I can suggest three prototype projects for discussion. These do not constitute policy recommendations but are starting points for policy discussions.

The valuable innovation project

The pharmaceutical innovation we see is an emergent property of the PIE. It is heterogeneous and varies along multiple dimensions (see Box 1.1). At present, the characteristics of what emerges are less than we could reasonably hope for, both in what innovative medicines are delivered and how much they cost to develop. This is so because the relevant habitats don't provide all they could. These constraints and issues that lead to this sub-optimal performance are described in more detail in Chapters 3–5, and the issues described in Chapter 9 are also relevant.

Our most fundamental need of the PIE is that it yields more valuable medicines. This means medicines that meet our most important clinical and economic needs more affordably. More highly effective, innovative medicines for important conditions, developed at lower cost, would reduce the strain on and then strengthen the social contract on which the PIE is built.

To influence the characteristics of pharmaceutical innovation that emerge from the PIE, we must make changes in the patient, discovery, coalition, and innovation habitats. These would begin in the patient habitat with the HHS and other government agencies making their priorities, both medical and health economic, clear. While the HHS could start with its already extensive knowledge, these priorities could be improved and made more politically legitimate by a transparent system for managing our knowledge about what society needs. Along with other existing considerations, such as the current state of scientific fields, these needs would then influence NIH research agendas and grant awards. In the discovery habitat, research more aligned to societal needs would be complemented by efforts to transform translational science, as distinct from translational research. Both would be amplified by significantly increased and stable funding. The intended result would not only be more inputs into the innovation habitat but also inputs that had more chance of leading to medicines that were important to society. In the innovation habitat, these more and better discoveries would be translated more efficiently into innovative medicines by the application of new R&D technologies, changes in R&D processes, and much improved knowledge sharing. The patient habitat's clearer priorities would amplify this improved effectiveness via a regulatory system that speciates to better fit different technologies and reflect society's health economic needs. Those needs would also be reflected in lower market risk levels, for example, by market guarantees, as used for COVID vaccines and antibiotics. The working of the innovation habitat would further be enhanced by a maturation of the coalition habitat that included more global, more diverse investors who use management science to create effective, efficient holobionts.

To summarize the valid value innovation project is not to minimize it. These changes would be difficult and require extensive and sustained effort. They would also be open to "straw man" criticisms. To be clear, what I do not envisage is "death lists" of ignored diseases, Stalinist direction of basic research, the abrogation of commercial confidentiality, or a regulatory system that ignores risk for economic purposes. Nor do I suggest that legislation has the dominant role in these changes. An ecosystem paradigm would imagine this project as many small changes by different entities in different parts of the system, designed to combine and interact and so improve the quantity, qualities, and costs of pharmaceutical innovation.

The valid value pricing project

Just as with the other characteristics of pharmaceutical innovation, the prices of innovative medicines are another emergent property of the PIE. Prices are influenced by the costs and risks of development (see above), but they are heavily influenced by the rest of the pharmaceutical value chain, including not only pharmaceutical manufacturers and patients but also those entities in between, such as insurers (commercial and government), pharmacy benefit managers (PBMs), plan sponsors, and others. To a significant degree, the affordability of innovative medicines is currently somewhat less than we could reasonably hope for. Further, the pricing that emerges does not achieve sustainable balance points in the PIE for net prices, point of care prices, moral hazard, and public trust. This is largely because the habitats that contribute to pricing don't contribute to the PIE as they should, as described in detail in Chapters 6–8 in particular.

It would be a significant contribution to the health of the PIE if the pricing of innovative medicines fully reflected their ecologically valid value and achieved these four balance points. Innovative medicines whose pricing rewards innovation, optimizes affordability, allows returns that incentivize investment, and distributes those returns appropriately are necessary to sustain the social contract.

To influence the pricing of the pharmaceutical innovation that emerges from the PIE requires changes, principally in the value, pricing, and competition habitats. These changes would begin in the value habitat with the building of payers' capabilities to make wide and ecologically valid value assessments. Although this might begin with the limited data currently available, these capabilities would be supported by improved methods of comparative effectiveness assessments. In turn, these improved methods would use the outputs of a comprehensive, real-world data infrastructure, which would have many synergies with the patient habitat's knowledge management system for societal needs, suggested above. The legitimacy of payers' value assessment would be enhanced by both good quality data and transparent processes. These valid and legitimate value assessments would then feed into the pricing habitat, enabling the pricing of innovative medicines to reflect value. To allow this, changes in the pricing habitat would need to redress imbalances in market power between manufacturers, intermediaries, and patients. A significant component of this would be enabling the market power of patients and their proxies, such as plan sponsors and Centers for Medicare and Medicaid Services (CMS). This might require changing public procurement policy and correcting the opacity of some current pharmaceutical pricing practices. It might also require steps to limit monopsony issues.

This summary of the valid value pricing project should not disguise its difficulty. These changes represent significant differences from current practice and fundamental changes in the culture of pricing in the PIE. Their positive implications for genuinely valuable innovative medicines would be balanced by negative implications for medicines that offer little incremental value. This will obviously generate "straw man" criticisms, so let me be clear about what I don't suggest. I am not proposing price dictation by a centralized Health Technology Assessment body (HTA) akin to some European practices. Nor am I suggesting legislative price controls or a cost-plus pricing regime. An ecosystem paradigm would imagine this project as the enabling of the market rather than controlling it, resulting in the value-based variation in the prices of innovative medicines rather than prices primarily influenced by the market power of different entities in the value chain.

The managed competition project

The characteristics of the pharmaceutical innovations that emerge from the PIE are influenced by the competition habitat, albeit in concert with the value, pricing, and patient habitats. In particular, the quantity, qualities, and prices of innovative medicines are influenced by the balance between incentives for innovation and enablers of imitation, the predictability of loss of exclusivity, and differential incentives for some types of innovation. At present, the influence of all three of these factors is less positive than we could reasonably hope for. This is the result of constraints and imperfections in the functioning of the value, pricing, and competition habitats, and to some extent the patient habitat, as described in Chapters 6–9.

It would be a significant contribution to the health of the PIE if an appropriate balance between incentivizing innovation and encouraging imitation could be achieved and sustained, if loss of exclusivity were more predictable, and if innovation was aligned more closely with society's clinical and health economic needs. A PIE that both strongly incentivized valuable innovation and enabled the rapid, predictable flow of spending from old to new medicines would help sustain the social contract.

To balance innovation and imitation, improve predictability in loss of exclusivity, and align innovation to societal needs requires changes, principally in the competition habitat. The starting point for this would be a coherent revision of how patent law and regulatory exclusivity work together to incentivize and enable innovation. This may require changes in only the application, rather than the substance, of patent laws, making international alignment easier. It would require a substantive revision of regulatory exclusivity, to align innovation incentives to society's clinical and health economic priorities. This should be designed to be coherent with the speciation of regulatory approval suggested for the innovation habitat, above. Changes to patent application and regulatory exclusivity should also attempt to improve the predictability of loss of exclusivity. To be effective and politically legitimate, these changes would also need to align with societal priorities, informed by a knowledge management system, as discussed above. They would also need to be complemented by the freeing of market forces, such as improving interchangeability of biosimilars and the enabling of patients' market power, discussed above. In some cases, competition might need to be enabled by alternative imitation mechanisms, such as contractual genericization. Finally, but very importantly, the working of the competition habitat should be supported by the development, adoption, and enforcement of an industry code of shared values and competitive behavior.

As with the other two projects, this short summary of the managed competition project belies its difficulty and significance. These improvements to the competition and related habitats represent significant discontinuities with current practice and some changes in the cultural assumptions underlying competitive behavior. They will positively support valuable innovation but discriminate against less valuable developments. This will again generate "straw man" criticisms, so let me be clear about what I don't suggest. I am not proposing wholesale change in patent law, only that its application to pharmaceutical innovation be reconsidered. Nor am I suggesting a "tyranny of the masses" that encourages pharmaceutical innovations on the basis of patient population size alone, only that society's priorities guide innovation incentives. I am not suggesting exclusivity be significantly shortened or reduced, only that it should more predictably allow the returns needed to incentivize innovation and the rapid shift of healthcare spending from older to newer medicines. Finally, I am not suggesting legislative regulation of competitive practice. An ecological perspective would see a commonly agreed behavior code as more effective.

Each of these three suggested projects would improve the health of the PIE and support the social contract. As is the nature of ecosystems, their implementation and their effect would be greater if they were executed together, with consideration for how they interact.

Raising the debate

When I began to research this book, I was somewhat intimidated by the complexity of pharmaceutical innovation in a US context. Even after 40 years of working in and researching the industry, a directly relevant PhD, seven previous books, and hundreds of articles and papers, I was still aware of the gaps in my knowledge and the weaknesses in my understanding. As ever, I took reassurance from the guidance of my kind and wise PhD supervisor, Professor Malcolm McDonald, who many years ago advised me that the secret of good research was to focus on understanding rather than proving a hypothesis.

With this advice in mind, I addressed the question with an open mind. I have not tried to prove any preformed belief. I've simply tried to understand how we might get innovative medicines at affordable prices in the long run.

It is in my nature, and I suspect that of every other researcher and author, that I am never fully satisfied with what I research and write. But I've worked hard and I'm happy to offer my ideas to this important debate. I can summarize them in eight points.

1 Pharmaceutical innovation is a heterogeneous phenomenon that is an emergent property of a complex, adaptive ecosystem that I've called the PIE.
2 The PIE can be understood as seven interconnected habitats.
3 The ability of the PIE to provide a sustainable flow of innovative and affordable medicines depends on each of these habitats functioning well enough to provide the PIE with specific inputs.
4 Each of the seven habitats is significantly flawed in its working, with the result that the PIE is not able to deliver what we would like it to.

5 The failure of the PIE to deliver a sustainable supply of innovative, affordable medicines puts at risk the social contract on which pharmaceutical innovation depends.

6 There are steps we can take to improve the functioning of the habitats, and so the health of the PIE, and so the strength of the social contract.

7 These steps can be understood as 27 improvements spread across all seven habitats.

8 The connectedness and synergies of the 27 improvements mean that they would best be implemented as three complementary projects.

This captures, as succinctly as I can, the answer to my research question: How might we achieve a sustainable supply of affordable and innovative medicines?

There is, however, one other finding, implicit in these eight, that I want to share as my closing thought. As often in research of this kind, I find myself looking at the findings and wondering why they have not already been reported and acted upon. The problem is well recognized, the US has a preponderance of very clever people, and the pharmaceutical and healthcare arenas have more than their fair share of America's brightest. If these findings have not already been addressed, then it can't be a shortage of motivation or intellectual power. Something else must be getting in the way.

I think that "something else" is how American society has chosen to frame the debate. A pervasive theme that emerged during my research was that the debate about drug pricing was polarized, framed as a contest between two opposing forces. Such framing is understandable but erroneous. And this error is exceptionally consequential because the pharmaceutical market is exceptional. Other markets may be important to the economy, but no other market touches the lives of so many of us, in such important ways, at such vulnerable times of our lives. Because of this, the public debate about the pricing of innovative medicines should not be a contest. It should be a dialectic about how to achieve innovation *and* affordability in the long term. It is time to raise the debate, and this book is my contribution.

Notes

1 For a useful discussion of this point, see https://www.theatlantic.com/business/archive/2015/02/does-finance-benefit-society/385176/.
2 In luxury goods, the idea of "minimalist luxury" is emerging. See https://knowledge.wharton.upenn.edu/article/less-is-more-redefining-the-luxury-goods-market/.
3 The environmental ethics of long-haul tourism is one challenge to this industry. See ref 1.
4 For an interesting discussion of the future of the fossil fuel industry, see https://news.climate.columbia.edu/2021/06/01/the-future-of-the-fossil-fuel-business/.
5 The nearest to this sort of fundamental opposition might be Mariana Mazzucato, referenced earlier, but even her far-reaching proposals do not, I argue, constitute a fundamental challenge to the industry's existence or structure.
6 I always hesitate to use this term from fear of appearing academically pretentious, but I can't exclude such a fundamentally important point. See Chapter 2 and my reference to Geoff Hodgson's and Thorbjorn Knudsen's "Darwin's Conjecture."
7 Synergy between entities in an ecosystem requires a mechanism. My thinking here is guided by Goold and Campbell. See ref 2.

References

1 Holden A. Environmental ethics for tourism- the state of the art. *Tourism Review (Association internationale d'experts scientifiques du tourisme)*. 2019;74(3):694–703.
2 Goold M, Campbell A. Desperately seeking synergy. *Harvard Business Review*. 1998;76(5):131–44.

Index

Note: *Italic* page numbers refer to figures and page numbers followed by "n" denote endnotes.

21st Century Cures Act 222
340b Drug Pricing Program 185, 203, 210n58

abiotic environment 36, 38, 66, 67–9, 124
Abrams, Larry 191
adaptive trial design 104
advanced therapies 172n18
Advanced Therapy Medicinal Products (ATMPs) 208n35
affordability of innovative medicines 11–12, 18n23, 24, 284; ecosystem perspective implying for 39; mechanistic paradigm 32–3; radical views 26–8; self-imposed dilemma 25–6, 41–2; translation efficiency influence of 74–5; "wicked problem" 29–30, 43–4; world-imposed dilemma 25–6, 41–2; see also innovative medicines
Affordable Care Act 207n23
anecdotal evidence 47n23
antibiotic market 119n38
anticoagulants 190
applied research 54, 55–6, 84n9; biologics development pathway 59; to develop innovative medicines 56; observations of expert informants 57; small molecule development pathway 58
approved imitative products adoption 232–6
Arman, Cyrus 264
ARPA-H 78, 91n71
Arrow, Ken 196
asset 127
Association for Accessible Medicines (AAM) 218
Austin, Christopher P. 62, 75, 82, 83n1, 86n27, 90n64, 102

balance points of pricing habitat 179; moral hazard 184; net price balance point between producers and payers 182; point of care price 183; public trust 184–5; requirements 188, 199
"bang for bucks" approach 226, 268, 272, 274
basic research in pharmaceutical innovation 54–6, 83n5, 84n6, 84n9; aligning to societal needs 79–80; biologics development pathway 59; increasing and stabilizing research fund 77–9; NIH funding for 68; observations of expert informants 57; predictivity of 106, 109–10; probability of investment in 60; small molecule development pathway 58
Bayh-Dole Act 79, 80, 88n50, 88n53, 90n66
Bessen, James 245n4
Best Pharmaceuticals for Children Act 222
"big data" in health economics 194
"big, hairy, audacious goal" ("BHAG") 50n54
"big pharma" model 125
biological ecosystems 85n17
biologic drugs 225
biologic/small-molecule categorization 225
Biologics Price Competition and Innovation Act 222
biology-specific technologies 67
biomarkers 117–18n23
"biosimilarization" of biologic innovative drugs 228
biosimilars: economics of 242; penetration 242; price competition mechanisms 233–4; substitution of originator biologic drugs by 248n40
Biotechnology Innovation Association 217
biotic environment 36, 70, 89n56
"boiling frog story" 10–11, 18n22
'Bolar' exemptions 250n69

Bourla, Albert 18n28
Brennan, Dan 263
Bush, Vannevar 83n2

"cakeism" 16n2
Caldwell, Kim 193–4
Campaign Against Patent Abuse (CAPA) 218
Cejas, Pedro 67
Center for Drug Evaluation and Research
    (CDER) 98, 116n8
Centers for Disease Control and Prevention
    (CDC) 87n42, 266–7, 289
Centers for Medicare and Medicaid Services
    (CMS) 171n6, 202–3, 292
Chandra, Amitabh 78
Chinese/China: pharmaceutical innovation 9;
    two-strand approach of 18n18
Cilliers, Paul 37, 49n42
co-evolution: of discovery habitat 70–3; of
    entities 81
coalition habitat 63, 123, 124–5; ability
    to support healthy PIE 123–4, 131–1;
    adapted to high-risk, high-return market
    136–8; allocating investment capital 130–1;
    appearance of simplicity 128; assembling
    holobionts 129; coalescence process 127;
    contribution to healthy PIE 130; "cottage
    industry" form of 132, 139–40; development
    strategies 139; encouraging diversity of
    investor species 142–4; entity sets of 127–8;
    holobiont shift 125–6, 132; localized and
    relationship-based nature of holobionts
    132–4; management expertise development
    141–2; maturation of 139–41; optimal
    holobiont 128–9; unbalanced knowledge base
    134–6
Cohen, Daniel 56, 57
collaborative research: fragmentation of 106;
    models of 106, 118n29
Collins, Francis 87n37, 91n71
"common good" principle 10, 11, 18n20
Commonwealth Fund 45n5
competition habitat 213, 266; ability to
    support healthy PIE 213–15, 221; adoption
    of approved imitative products 232–6;
    aligning regulatory exclusivity incentives
    238–40; balance between innovation and
    imitation 216; contribution to healthy PIE
    220; development strategies 236; enabling
    market forces 241–3; enabling valuable
    imitation 219–20; functioning of 217;
    hindering predictability 226–30; improving
    discriminatory power of patent law 236–8;

improving predictability of loss or exclusivity
    240–1; incentivizing valuable innovation 219;
    intellectual property 215–16; interests of
    pharmaceutical innovators 217; know-how
    and trade secrets limit imitation of advanced
    therapies 230–2; limits on competition
    in innovative medicines 215; maximizing
    predictability of competitive environment
    220, 221; patent system discriminates against
    innovation 223–4; providing alternative
    imitation mechanisms 243–4; regulatory
    exclusivity constraints 215–16; regulatory
    exclusivity directs innovation 224–6;
    requirements 213; risk of regulatory capture
    222; role as positive feedback loop 222; sub-
    optimal 222
complex adaptive systems 36–8, 87n40
congruency hypothesis 280n27
Conti, Rena 164
contract research organizations 128
Cook 175
Cordeiro Dias Villela Correa, M. 50n56
cost-effectiveness assessment 160–1
"cost sharing" out-of-pocket expenses 183
"cottage industry" form of coalition habitat 132,
    139–40
COVID-19 pandemic 49n45, 101
cultural values 271–2
Cummings, Elijah E. 48n28
"curiosity driven vs. solution oriented"
    distinction 56

Damond, Joe 133
Darwin, Charles 32
data analytics in healthcare 280n21
Datavant 269
Delphi methodology 51n57
demographic shifts 68
de Tocqueville, Alex 27, 46n7
DiMaggio 84n8
discoverers 134, 140, 259
discovery habitat 53, 57–60, 86n25, 96; abiotic
    environment 66, 68; aligning basic research
    to societal needs 79–80; aligning commercial
    and academic cultures 80–1; capability to
    support healthy PIE 64–6; co-evolution
    of 70–3; contribution to healthy PIE 65;
    development strategies 77; increasing and
    stabilizing basic research funding 77–9;
    investment in basic research 60; neglect of
    translational science commons 73–7; NIH
    role in 61–2; requirement for healthy PIE
    62–5; and sociological environment 68–70;

support to PIE 53–4; and technological environment 65–8; translational science transformation 81–2
Dorazio, Thomas 223
Drucker, Peter 193
drug development time 118n24
drug effectiveness 20n33
Drug Price Competition and Patent Term Restoration Act *see* Hatch-Waxman Act
drug pricing of innovative medicines 24–5, 151–2; characteristics of pharmaceutical market 31; drug affordability 30; ecosystem paradigm 34–6; of expensive drugs 204; free-pricing mechanism 33; issues of 11, 19n28, 19n30; mechanistic paradigm 32–3; paradigm shifts 32; secrecy 204; sterility of 30–1; transparency of innovative medicines 203–4; of valuable drugs 205; "wicked problem" 29–30, 43–4
drug repurposing 12, 20n37
Dubois, R. W. 174n33
Dutfield, Graham 230

ecosystems: biological 85n17; concept of balance in 50n50; paradigm 34–5, 291; unsustainable 50n49; Willis' definition of 49n38
Emond, Sarah 161
Entecavir 192, 207n24
entity sets of coalition habitat: founders 127; investors 127–8; providers of specialist services and knowledge 128
entrepreneurial state 26
epidemiological transitions 69, 88n43
epistemological crisis 30–1
European Medicines Agency (EMA) 173n24, 224
evergreening' method 228
external innovation 71, 88n50
"extremophiles" 85n14

Fauci, Anthony 20n40
FDA Modernization Act 222
Federal Trade Commission (FTC) 249n59, 289
Feldman, R. 250n67
Ferrell, Phyllis Barkman 271
financialization school 126
financial toxicity 188, 206n10
"first do no harm" principle 8–10
"first in class" therapies 12
first iteration syntheses 44
Food and Drug Administration (FDA) 98, 116n8, 132, 218, 289; approvals new innovative medicines 14; "breakthrough" category 12; routes to expedite drug approval 20n34

formulary exclusions 207n30
free-pricing mechanism 33, 285
free market 279n5
"free riding on American innovation" 11
"Friday Night Beer" effect 133

genericization: genericization 2.0 236; of small molecule drugs 228
generic medicines 5, 15, 16n5, 205n1
gene sequencing technology 86n33
Gibbons, G. R. L. 90n66
Glasspool, John 227
Great Value Shift 69, 70, 80

Haldane principle 110, 120n46
Hardin, Garrett 90n67
Hatch-Waxman Act 38, 49n44, 244, 250n68
Health and Human Services (HHS) 70, 88n46, 114, 266, 279n4, 289
health economic and outcomes research (HEOR) 173n21
health economic outcome 226
health technology assessment body (HTA body) 154–5, 162, 292
Henshaw, Ian 235
Hill, Raymond 104
Hodgson, G. M. 35, 48n37
Hodin, Michael 269
Holenz, Joerg 133–4
holobiont(s) 95, 98, 116n7, 124, 142; assembly and growth of 124; building processes 127; coalition habitat assembling 129; cost of assembling and running 145n15; optimal 128–9; relationship-based nature of 132–4, 145–6n21; shift 125–6, 132, 136
Holtorf, A-PC 175
"home bias" effect 133
homeostasis mechanism 181, 185, 205n3
H.R.3 *see* Lower Drug Costs Now Act
Humira 206n13, 279n17

ideation 115n1
imaging technologies 87n34
imitation-led approach 267–8
immunotherapy 13, 14, 20n41
incentivization approach 225–6, 239
incremental innovations of medicines 12, 236–7, 247n28
in-market risk 106, 107–8, 119n33, 119n37; created by price controls 119n35; reduction for valuable products 113–14
innovation 115n1; open 115–16n5, 132, 145n9; patent system discriminates against 223–4;

radical drug 19n32; stealth 232; see *also* pharmaceutical innovation

innovation habitat 54, 60, 62–3, 95–6, 290, 291; adopting new R&D technologies and methods 111–12; capability to support healthy PIE 101; constrained by evolutionary lag in regulation 102–3; contribution to healthy PIE *100*; dependence on discovery habitat 102; development strategies 108–9; functioning of 98; improving knowledge sharing in R&D 112–13; improving predictivity of basic research 109–10; principal activities 97–8; providing economic sustainability 100; providing innovative medicines 99–100; reducing in-market risk for valuable products 113–14; risks and probabilities in 115n3; sensitive to market uncertainty 106–8; speciating regulatory environment 110–11; unrealized potential for sharing knowledge 105–6; unrealized potential for technological and organizational improvement 104–5

innovation-imitation cycle 236, 243

innovative medicines 3, 5–6, 229, 272, 291; cost of 90n63; development 7, 223; investment into 8; limits on competition in 215; transparency in pricing of 203–4; value assessment for 172n19; value of 150–2, 180; see *also* affordability of innovative medicines

Institute for Clinical and Economic Review (ICER) 154–5, 162, 172, 189

insurance-based systems 171n5

insurers 192, 195, 201, 207n25, 269

interchangeability status, lack of 234–5

International Council for Harmonisation (ICH) 117n17

investment capital 130–1

investors 127–8, 134

"Issue Salience" 30, 47n17

Jackson, Michael 57, 73

Kelly, L. M. 50n56

Kenney, Jim 199

Kettering, Charles 31

Kissinger, Henry 278

know-how role in competition habitat 230–2

knowledge hiding behavior 72

knowledge management capabilities: of patient habitat for societal needs 272–3; patient habitat lacking 269–71

knowledge sharing in R&D 112–13

Knudsen, T. 35, 48n37

Kolchinsky, Peter 50n52, 286

Kuhn, Thomas 32, 47n26

LaMattina, John 195

Lassman, Scott 227

Lauer, Michael 87n39

legislators 259

Liberti, Larry 105

life cycle management 12–13

Li, Henry Lishi 45n2

Lloyd, William Foster 90n67

Lower Drug Costs Now Act 48n28

managed competition project 293–5

management science 135

"market access": issues 16n6; model 208n35

market forces 241–3

market imperfection 234, 235

market power: imbalances 234; into intermediaries 189–93, 199–200; pricing habitat redressing imbalances in patients' 202–3

market uncertainty, innovation habitat sensitive to 106–8

Marzorati, C. 170–1n1

Mavyret 182

Mazzucato, Mariana 26, 45n2, 297n5

McCarthy, Killian 133

McDonald, Malcolm 50n55, 295

McGowan, Sean 233

McMahon, Matthew 61

mechanistic paradigm 32–3, 48n30

Medicaid 171n3, 180, 203, 210n58

Medicare 180, 203, 206n15, 258

Medicare Evidence Development & Coverage Advisory Committee (MEDCAC) 171n6

"Medicare for All" approach 45n4

Mencken, H. L. 4, 25, 28

Merck, George, W. 258, 278n1

Meurer, Michael J. 245n4

"minimalist luxury" 297n2

Moore, James F. 35, 36, 49n39, 49n40

moral hazard 208n38; balance points 184; of payers and providers 205n9; pricing habitat balancing 186, 196–7

Morgan, S. 19n33, 20n34

Morris, Lisa 163

Mukherjee, Siddhartha 86n24

National Cancer Institute 61

National Center for the Advancement of Translational Science (NCATS) 76, 90n64

National Center for Translational Science 61

National Heart, Lung and Blood Institute 267
National Institutes of Health (NIH) 13, 109, 132, 289
natural habitat 124
Neilsen, Anders 105, 107
net pricing 198; balance point 182, 188; pricing habitat balancing net pricing levels 186; value-based 200–2
Neumann, Peter 152
NewCo 124–6, 128, 131, 140, 145n10
niche construction 280n24
"non-obvious" criterion 237
non-price mechanisms 265
Novak, Alan 83n4
"novelty" criterion 237

Obama, Barack 30
Office of Disease Prevention and Health Promotion (ODPHP) 266–7
"one and done" approach 241
ontological communality 35, 39, 48n37
open innovation 115–16n5, 132, 145n9
organizational culture 57, 81, 84n10
Orphan Drug Act (ODA) 27n29, 217, 221, 222, 225–6, 240, 267
Orphan Drug Designation 20n46
orphan drug development 248n32
Oskouei, Sonia 234
Oslerian tradition 86n29
Osler, William 86n29
Ostrom, Elinor 90n67
outsourcing of research and development 115n4

paradigm shifts 32
partisan polarization issue 47n19
Pasteur Quadrant 142
Patent & Trademark Office (PTO) 250n68
patent law, discriminatory power improvement of 236–8
patent system 223–4, 235, 237
'patent thickets' method 228
Patient Advocacy Organisations 154, 279n3
patient-centricity 257
patient habitat 255, 290; ability to support healthy PIE 256; agreeing code of shared cultural values and behaviors 276–8; align enabling and incentivizing signals 261–2; aligning societal signals to clinical and economic priorities 275–6; building knowledge management capability for societal needs 272–3; contribution to healthy PIE 262; enabling pharmaceutical innovation 260; establishing clinical and economic

priorities 273–5; incentivizing pharmaceutical innovation 261; incoherent communication of clinical needs 265–7; indirect communication of cultural values 271–2; keystone species 259; lacking knowledge management capabilities 269–71; relies on market forces that disconnected from value 264–5; requirements for healthy PIE 255–6, 260, 262–3; social contract 277; tension in social contract 263; types of inhabitants 258–9; unsignaling needs for health economic innovation 267–9
payers 182; incorporating ecologically valid value assessment 201; moral hazard of 205n9
'pay for delay' method 228
Pearson, Stephen 172n18
Perfetto, Eleanor 54–5
period of exclusivity 221
Peschin, Sue 161, 196
Pezalla, Edmund 162
pharmaceutical innovation 1–3, 26, 54, 96, 106, 257, 283–4, 285, 295; affordability of innovative medicines 11–12; "bang for bucks" approach 13–14; basic research in 54–6, 83n5, 84n6; "boiling frog story" 10–11; China's two-strand approach to acquiring expertise in 18n18; "common good" principle 10, 11; conditions 265; demand for 28; driven by returns 265; ecosystem paradigm 34–6; emerges from PIE 39; exploration of 5–6, 10; "first do no harm" principle 8–10; idea of public good 13; incremental innovations 12–13; individual 2, 3; influenced by venture capital 132; interactions between organizations in 38; investments in 60; as mechanistic metaphor 33–4; pillars of 284; pre-competitive' approach to partnership strategies in 118–19n31; setting priorities for 274–5; social contract 15–16, 46n11, 180, 198; US pharmaceutical market 6, 6–7
pharmaceutical innovation ecosystem (PIE) 24, 34, 36, 54, 86n25, 96, 284, 285–6; ability of pricing habitat to support 179–80, 187, 199–200; assembly and growth of holobiont 124; breaking ground for future 286–9; capability of discovery habitat to support 64–77; capability of innovation habitat to support 101–8; characteristics of pharmaceutical market 216; coalition habitat's contribution to *130*; competition habitat's ability to support 213–15; competition habitat's contribution to healthy PIE *220*; complex adaptive systems 36–8; component habitats

of *44*; contribution of innovation habitat to *100*; discovery habitat requirement for 62–5; homeostasis mechanism 181; implying for affordability debate 39; improving health of *287, 288*; patient-centricity 257; pharmaceutical innovation emerges from 39; rely on risk-sharing 257; requirement of pricing habitat 186–7; research on "wicked problem" 43–4; resolving self-imposed or world-imposed dilemma 41–2; sustainability of 40; systematic management 40–1

pharmaceutical investment 84n11

pharmaceutical manufacturers see producers of medicines

pharmaceutical market 119n32, 181

pharmaceutical science 135

pharmacy benefit managers (PBMs) 11, 19n30, 132, 167, 170, 185, 190, 192, 195, 201, 207n25, 207n31, 269

PhRMA 27, 46n9, 217

"Physic Garden" of plants 3–4, 14

plan sponsor 154

point-of-care prices 202; balance point 183; pricing habitat balancing price at 186

Powell, W. W. 84n8

pragmatism 50n56

Pravettoni, G. 170–1n1

"precision prevention" medicines 268

predictivity: of basic research 106, 109–10; of discovery habitat 63–4

pre-market risk 106, 107–8, 119n37

prescribing behavior of physicians 242

Prescription Drug Sunshine, Transparency, Accountability and Reporting Act (STAR Act) 198

"price inelastic" 265

price transparency 209n52, 209n54

pricing habitat 179, 292; ability to support healthy PIE 179–80, 187, 188; balance points 179; balancing moral hazards of patients, providers, and payers 186; balancing net pricing levels 186; balancing public trust with commercial confidentiality 186–7; concentrating market power in intermediaries 189–93; contribution to healthy PIE *187*; developmental strategies 200; ecosystem paradigm 181; establishment of value-based net pricing 200–2; fails to balance moral hazard 196–7; functioning of 181; moral hazard balance points 184; net price balance point between producers

and payers 182; not encouraging service innovation 193–5; opacity reduces public trust 197–200; physical distribution and pharmacy dispensation 180–1; point of care price balance point 183, 186; public trust balance point 184–5; redressing imbalances in patients' market power 202–3; transparency in pricing of innovative medicines 203–4; untethering from ecologically valid value 188–9

probability of technical and regulatory success (PTRS) 115n3

producers of medicines 182

'product hopping' method 228

providers: market power 192; moral hazard for 184, 197, 205n9

public good, idea of 13

public insurers 183

public payers 182

public trust: balance point 184–5; pricing habitat balancing with commercial confidentiality 186–7; pricing habitat's opacity reducing 197–200

pull mechanisms for valuable innovation 266, 267

pull models 120n44

quality-adjusted life year (QALY) 160, 161, 174n29, 174n31

radical drug innovation 19n32

Ralph, Mark 135

randomized controlled trials (RCTs) 175n36

rational-legal legitimacy 172n15

real-world data (RWD) 117n22, 173n24

real-world evidence (RWE) 173n22

Reed, Juliana 234

reference product 248n39

regulatory environment, speciation of 110–11

regulatory exclusivity system 241, 244n2; alignment of incentives 238–40; of competition habitat 224–6, 229–30, 235; portfolio approach to *239*

regulatory process 103, 106, 111, 116n11, 116n13

Remdesivir 226

research and development (R&D): adopting new technologies and methods of 111–12; changes in R&D processes 290; improving knowledge sharing in 112–13; outsourcing of 115n4

resource-based school 125

ribonucleic acid (RNA) 125
Rittel, Horst W. J. 29–30
Robinson, James C. 198
Rothrock, Michael 195

"salami slicing" 226
Schön, Donald 39, 49–50n47
Schuhmacher, A. 145n9
"Science-The Endless Frontier" report 83n2
scientific peer-review 64
scientific research 72
scientific research, globalization of 89n56
Scripps Holobiont Research Institute 142
Scripps Translational Science Institute 136
self-imposed dilemma 25–6, 41–2
Sellam, Zaki 146n27
service innovation, opportunities for 193–5
Seyhan, Attila A. 90n68, 116n9
Seymore, S. B. 250n66
shared cultural values and behaviors, code of 276–8
Singh, Surya 194
"single payer" systems 171n5
Snow, C. P. 84n7
social determinants of health 69
social sciences and organizational research 54
social value 239, 240
sociological environment, discovery habitat of 68–70
Sofia, Michael 20n39
soil management 86n26
Sovaldi 13, 205n7
specialist services and knowledge, providers of 128
"specialty" medicines 190
stealth innovation 232
Stewart, Potter 83n4
Stoch, Aubrey 76
Stock, Harald 137
Stover, Doug 72
systems biology 66–7, 86n29

tacit knowledge 128, 235
technological environment, discovery habitat of 65–8
technological improvement, unrealized potential of innovation habitat for 104–5
thalidomide tragedy 38, 49n43
tourist investors 134, 146n25
Trade-Related Aspects of Intellectual Property Rights (TRIPS) 250n65
trade secrets 230–2, 236

"tragedy of the commons" 76, 90n67
"tragedy of the translational commons" 76
transaction cost economics 86n28, 125–6
translational research 75–6, 85n21
translational science 75–6; neglect of 73–7; transformation 81–2
Trikafta 182, 205n6
Trimox 5
"Triple Helix" model of education 89n54
Trusheim, Mark 188
TruthinRX 31, 47n22
type 2 knowledge 142

"unintelligent design" 246n21
United States Patent and Trademark Office (USPTO) 218, 246n19, 289
US Government Accountability Office 225

valuable imitation 219–20
valuable innovation project 219, 290–1
value: data infrastructure development 166–7; meaning of 170–1n1; valid value pricing project 291–2; value-based net pricing 200–2, 203, 205; value-based pharmaceutical contracts 208n36; value-based price 221
value assessments 164; capabilities development 167–9; feedback loop 293; for innovative medicine 172n19; legitimacy of 169; practices adaptation 169–70
value habitat 149, 193; ability to support healthy PIE 149–50, 158–9; adopting transparent value assessment practices 169–70; contribution to healthy PIE 157; development strategies 166; functioning of 152–3; HTA body 154–5; information infrastructure 158–60; lacking value assessment capabilities 162–3; lack of evolution in methodologies 160–1; making ecologically valid value assessments 156–8; plan sponsor role in 154; role of payers in 153–4, 155; role of pharmaceutical companies 154; value assessment capabilities development 167–9; value data infrastructure development 166–7; value of innovative medicines 150–2; weak connection to PIE 164–6
Varmus, Harold 87n36
venture capital/capitalists (VCs) 98, 107, 126, 132, 135, 136, 140; market 145n16; nontraditional 141; prevalence in coalition habitat 137; role in pharmaceutical innovation 137, 139; "tourist" 138

Wallace, Alfred 32
Waxman-Hatch Act 217, 222
Webber, Melvin M. 29–30
Westrich, K. 174n33
Westrich, Kimberley 175n38
"wicked problem" of drug pricing 29–30, 43–4
Woodcock, Janet 18n16

Woollett, Gillian 103
world-imposed dilemma 25–6, 41–2
World Health Assembly resolution 198–9
World Trade Organization (WTO) 250n65

Zieff, Gabriel 27, 45n3
Zolgensma (Novartis) 19n31, 188n 206n11

Printed in the United States
by Baker & Taylor Publisher Services